CW00551229

THE EUROPEAN INSOLVENCY REGULATION:
LAW AND PRACTICE

The European Insolvency Regulation: Law and Practice

by

MIGUEL VIRGÓS

*Professor, School of Law, Universidad
Autónoma de Madrid, Spain*

and

FRANCISCO GARCIMARTÍN

*Professor, School of Law, Universidad de
Castilla-La Mancha, Spain*

A C.I.P. catalogue record for this book is available from the Library of Congress.

ISBN 90-411-2089-0

Published by:
Kluwer Law International
P.O. Box 85889
2508 CN The Hague
The Netherlands

Sold and distributed in North, Central and South America by:
Aspen Publishers, Inc.
7201 McKinney Circle
Frederick, MD 21704 USA

Sold and distributed in all other countries by:
Extenza-Turpin Distribution Services
Stratton Business Park
Pegasus Drive
Biggleswade
Bedfordshire SG18 8QB
United Kingdom

Printed on acid-free paper

Printed in The Netherlands

Preface

From its inception, the objective of this work has been to provide an impartial explanation and integral interpretation of the Regulation on Insolvency Proceedings (EC 1346/2000), including its most significant legal aspects and characteristics.

Hence our approach to the Regulation from a "neutral" viewpoint, a necessary prerequisite to provide a uniform commentary that distances (yet does not detach) itself from the different legal systems of the Member States. This explains why many valuable works that centre on the impact of the Insolvency Regulation on a given national system have not been expressly cited as references although, naturally, they have been taken into account.

Central to this approach has been the interpretation of Community law as a legal system. Thus, we have studied the Insolvency Regulation not as an isolated piece of legislation, but as part of Community law, viewed in relation with other rules, such as the Directives on the restructuring and winding-up of credit institutions or insurance undertakings. As a result, arguments flow from one rule to another, as elements of a coherent system.

Key to the understanding and interpretation of the Insolvency Regulation has been the Virgós/Schmit report on the 1995 Brussels Convention on Insolvency Proceedings, a treaty whose implementation was initially frustrated by Community policies (it was one of the many victims of the so-called "mad cows" crisis), but which was later set in motion, once it had been transcribed as Community Regulation, by these same policies. The weight of the genetic argument in the book is easily justified, at least in the first stages of application of the Insolvency Regulation by the courts, as that report provides valuable information on the teleology of its rules.

With a view to mitigating the somewhat abstract nature of the Regulations' rules, we have tried to relate them to the different stages of insolvency proceedings, thereby providing an answer to the most recurrent problems posed by trans-border insolvencies.

Designed to be accessible for judges and practitioners alike, the commentary has not been ordered sequentially, article by article, but rather thematically, to accommodate the Regulation to a judge's or practitioner's view of an insolvency proceeding and its different phases.

Works on the interpretation and application of the Regulation on Insolvency Proceedings in different Members States must rely heavily on information from private sources. With a view to improving the information provided here in any subsequent editions of the work, should these be printed, we would be very pleased to receive comments and papers on the subjects covered by this work and, in particular, on the national application of the Regulation. Materials can be sent to M.Virgós, Facultad de Derecho, Universidad Autónoma, Cantoblanco, 28049 Madrid, Spain.

We are grateful to a number of people who have facilitated in various ways the preparation and publications of this edition, in particular to Prof. Bob Wessels. The present members of the Department of International Law at the UAM and UCLM were most supportive and tolerant of the time which had to be devoted to the preparation of this work. At home, our debt to our wives and children for their patience can only be expressed by the token of dedicating this book to them. Finally, we would like to thank the reader for having chosen this book and can only hope to meet his expectations.

Miguel Virgós Soriano
Francisco Garcimartín Alférez

Summary Table of Contents

Table of Contents

About the Authors

Miguel Virgós is professor at the School of Law of the Universidad Autónoma de Madrid, member of the Spanish Law Commission and Of-Counsel at Uría & Menéndez, Madrid. He is coauthor of the Virgós/Schmit Report on the 1995 Convention on insolvency proceedings from which the Insolvency Regulation stems and has participated in the drafting of the new Spanish Insolvency Law. *Francisco Garcimartín* is professor at the School of Law of the Universidad de Castilla-La Mancha and Spanish delegate for the negotiation and drafting of the Convention on the Law Applicable to Certain Rights in respect of Securities held with an Intermediary, drawn up by the Hague Conference on private international law. Both authors have ample experience providing legal advice in regard to international business transactions and litigation.

Any comment on this book will be welcome at either <miguel.virgos@uam.es> or <francisco.garcimartin@uclm.es>

Abbreviations

A.B.L.J.	American Bankruptcy Law Journal
A.E.D.I.P.	Anuario Español de Derecho Internacional Privado
BOE	Boletín Oficial del Estado
CML Rev.	Common Market Law Review
Dir.Fall.	Diritto Fallimentare
EC	European Community
ECB	European Central Bank
ECJ	European Court of Justice
E.L.F.	European Legal Forum
EuZW	Europäische Zeitschrift für Wirtschaftsrecht
Int. Insolv. Rev.	Internacional Insolvency Review
IPRax	Praxis des Internationalen Privat-und Verfahrensrecht
JIBFL	Journal of International Banking and Finance Law
KTS	Zeitschrift für Insolvenzrecht
L.Q.R.	Law Quarterly Review
Mich.L.Rev.	Michigan Law Review
NJW	Neue Juristische Wochenschrift
O.J.E.C.	Official Journal of the European Community
R.C.D.I.P.	Revue Critique de Droit Internacional Privé
R.D.M.	Revista de Derecho Mercantil
R.E.D.I.	Revista Española de Derecho Internacional
Riv.Dir.Internat.Pr. e Proc.	Revista di Diritto Internationale Privato e Processuale
Riv.Dir.Proc.	Rivista di Diritto Processuale
Riv.trim.dr.pr. e proc.	Rivista trimestrale di diritto privato e processuale
Uniform L.Rev.	Uniform Law Review
Yale L.J.	Yale Law Journal
ZfVR	Zeitschrift für Rechtsvergleichung
ZIP	Zeitschrift für Wirtschaftsrecht
ZZP	Zeitschrift für Zivilprozeβrecht

Part I

General Issues

Chapter 1

The European Community Regulation on Insolvency Proceedings: The Rule and its Context

1. LEGAL BASIS

1. Cross-border insolvency has been the object of considerable attention during the past years. This attention goes hand in hand with the fact that companies have become increasingly international in both their physical presence and market activities. This process has taken place at a faster pace within the European Community. For this reason, the need to coordinate national insolvency proceedings is also more acute at the European level. Council Regulation (EC) No. 1346/2000 on Insolvency Proceedings[1] (hereafter, the *Insolvency Regulation*) aims precisely at establishing a common framework for cross-border insolvency among the Member States. Its general goal is to promote the proper functioning of the internal market, by enabling insolvency proceedings to operate efficiently and effectively throughout the Community.

The Insolvency Regulation was adopted by the European Council under Articles 61c and 67(1) in relation with Article 65 of the European Community Treaty, as amended by the Treaty of Amsterdam[2] with effect from 1 May 1999. These articles form part of a new Title IV of the EC Treaty, which is concerned with the progressive establishment of an area of *"freedom, security and justice"*. This Title provides the purposive framework within which the Insolvency Regulation has to be interpreted and prescribes the role that the European Court of Justice plays in the interpretation of this Regulation.[3]

NB. The powers conferred on the European Community by this Title in the area of judicial cooperation in civil matters with cross-border implications have already given rise to other Community legal instruments in the sector of Private International Law.[4] From the point of view of judicial cooperation, the Insolvency Regulation "supplements" Council Regulation (EC) No. 44/2001 on Jurisdiction and the Recognition and Enforcement of Judgements in Civil and Commercial Matters, which does not cover insolvency proceedings. This is an

---

[1] Council Regulation (EC) No. 1346/2000 of 29 May 2000, Official Journal of the European Communities (hereafter, *OJ*) L 160, 30.06.2000, p. 1; as from 1 February 2003 this Journal is known as the Official Journal of the European Union.

[2] Treaty of Amsterdam amending the Treaty on European Union, the Treaties establishing the European Communities and related Acts, *OJ* C 340, 10 November 1997. See further amendments by the Treaty of Nice, *OJ* C 80, 10 March 2001.

[3] FLETCHER in MOSS/FLETCHER/ISAACS, pp. 16–17.

[4] See, with further references, KHOLER, *passim*; BORRAS, *passim*; BASEDOW; *passim*.

important factor for the interpretation of some of the Insolvency Regulation solutions, as we will explain later on.

2. The Insolvency Regulation has, according to Article 249 II of the European Community Treaty, "*general application*", is "*binding in its entirety*" and is "*directly applicable*" in all Member States. Thus, the Insolvency Regulation takes effect automatically and simultaneously in the legal order of all Member States. It establishes a set of *uniform rules* for all Member States, without these needing to be transposed into the national legislation.

Pursuant to Article 69 of the EC Treaty, the position of the *United Kingdom* and *Ireland*, on the one hand, and *Denmark*, on the other, with regard to the new *Title IV* of the EC Treaty is subject to special rules.[5] Without wishing to go into too much detail, it is sufficient for our purposes to state that the United Kingdom and Ireland expressed their wish to participate in the adoption by the Council of the Insolvency Regulation (see Recital 32) and are therefore bound by it. Denmark, on the other hand, has not participated in the adoption of the Regulation; consequently, unless it revises its position, the Insolvency Regulation is not applicable to this country (Recital 33).[6] For the time being, then, and for the purposes of the Insolvency Regulation, Denmark must be considered by the other Member States as if it were a non-Member State.

Article 299 of the EC Treaty governs other aspects of the territorial scope of application of the Insolvency Regulation, such as the status of European territories subject to special arrangements (e.g the Channel Islands and the Isle of Mann, to which the Regulation does not apply[7]), European territories for whose external relations a Member State is responsible (e.g. Gibraltar, to which the Regulation applies[8]) and non-European territories.

2. INTERPRETATION

3. As a result of this legal basis, the *Court of Justice of the European Communities* (hereafter, the *ECJ*) has jurisdiction to give preliminary rulings concerning the validity or interpretation of the Insolvency Regulation; specifically, to resolve any questions

---

[5] See Article 3 of the Protocol on the Position of the United Kingdom and Ireland, and Articles 1 and 2 of the Protocol on the Position of Denmark, annexed to the EC Treaty.

[6] See Re: Arena Corporation Limited, 12 December 2003, [2003] EWHC 2032 (Ch.); in this case an Isle of Man company had its centre of main interest in Denmark and the proceedings were not subjected to the regulation. On the possible solutions presented by the "Danish problem", HEß, pp. 28, 30; LEIBLE/STAUDINGER (2000), p. 537 (suggesting the possibility of a parallel agreement based on Article 293 of the EC Treaty or a bilateral convention between the EU and Denmark).

[7] ISAACS/BRENT, in MOSS/FLETCHER/ISAACS, p. 16.

[8] However, the procedure set forth in the Agreement between the United Kingdom and Spain of 19 April 2000 (Council document 7998/00) has to be taken into account. Decisions of the Gibraltar courts will need to be certified by the United Kingdom/Gibraltar Liaison Unit for EU Affairs of the Foreign and Commonwealth Office based in London. See the United Kingdom statement on Council Regulation (EC) No. 44/2001 of 22 December 2000 on jurisdiction and the recognition and enforcement of judgments in civil and commercial matters (Official Journal C 013, 2001). On the part of Spain, see the *Resolución* of 20 February 2001 (*BOE* 8 March 2001). The same arrangement is applicable in the case of the Insolvency Regulation.

concerning the interpretation of the regulation, which might arise in a case pending before a national Court. According to Article 68 of the EC Treaty, when an interpretative question is raised in a case pending before a national court or tribunal against whose decisions there is no judicial remedy under national law,[9] that court or tribunal shall, if it considers that a decision on the question is *necessary* to enable it to give judgement, request the Court of Justice to rule on the issue. In addition to this, Article 68.3 of the EC Treaty endows the Council, the Commission or a Member State with the power to make a reference to the European Court of Justice on questions of interpretation (but not on questions of validity). The ruling given by the Court of Justice in response to such a request shall not apply to the judgments of courts or tribunals of the Member States which have become *res judicata*.

Problem: the mandatory and suspensive nature of the preliminary ruling.[10] The Insolvency Regulation establishes a set of uniform rules on insolvency proceedings. In order to remain common and to properly fulfil their functions, uniform rules also require uniform interpretation by the national courts. The possibility of seeking a preliminary ruling from the ECJ provides an institutional guarantee of this uniformity. Nevertheless, the process before the ECJ entails a delay in the insolvency proceedings. This delay can jeopardise the effectiveness of the insolvency proceedings themselves. This conflict between uniformity on the one hand and effectiveness on the other manifests itself with special intensity in two aspects of the request for a preliminary ruling: its *mandatory* or facultative nature and its *suspensive* effect.

In the system established by the *1995 Convention on Insolvency Proceedings*, the recourse to the ECJ for a preliminary ruling moved away from the general model (i.e. from that of Article 234 EC Treaty). On the one hand, it was *facultative* for the national court and, on the other hand, the possible *suspensive effect* of the filing of the request *on the national proceedings* was to be determined by the law of each State. The main reason for this difference was to prevent excessive delays. In insolvency proceedings the time factor is fundamental: "These proceedings are opened as a consequence of a financial crisis. Promptness of action is imperative to avoid a depreciation of existing assets".[11] The imposition of a mandatory and suspensive model of preliminary rulings could jeopardise these objectives, and this is why a facultative system was preferred and why it was also decided to refer the suspensive effect of the request to the procedural law of each State.[12]

The conversion of the original Convention into a Regulation might present difficulties on this point, as the request for a preliminary ruling is now governed by Article 68 of the EC Treaty. This provision establishes a request for a preliminary ruling which, in principle, is *mandatory* for those national courts of last instance and, furthermore, has *suspensive* effects (see Articles 68 and 234 of the EC Treaty; Article 242 does not apply to this case). As we have just indicated, the risks of delay which this arrangement might entail for the effective administration of insolvency proceedings may well be substantial.

Nevertheless, these risks are reduced if we take various factors into account: (a) the fact that, according to Article 68, the request *only* corresponds to the national court which is dealing with the matter in the last instance. Neither the courts of opening of first instance, nor the court of appeal (save where there is no judicial remedy under national law) may have recourse to the ECJ. (b) The national court must consider that a decision on a point of

---

[9] Critics of the limitation of this possibility to the courts of opening of last instance, i.a. BASEDOW, p. 695; JAYME/KOHLER, p. 458; FUMAGALLI, pp. 706–707.

[10] On this point, see also STAUDINGER, p. 104; EIDENMÜLLER (2001a), pp. 7–8; LEIBLE/STAUDINGER (2000), p. 572.

[11] VIRGOS/SCHMIT Report, Margin Nos 289–292.

[12] *Ibid.*

Community law is *necessary* before it can give judgement. The obligation to refer to the ECJ is limited to those cases in which the hermeneutic doubt determines the resolution of the issue in question. The criteria set forth by the ECJ in the interpretation of (today) Article 234 EC Treaty are also applicable. Therefore, the request *is not* necessary when: (i) the correct application of Community law is so obvious as to leave no scope for any reasonable doubt as to the manner in which the question raised is to be resolved (*acte clair*); or (ii) the issue in question is substantially the same as another already decided on by the ECJ (*acte éclairé*).[13] (c) The procedures of the European Court of Justice are governed by its own Statute and Rules of Procedure. The latest revision of these rules make it possible for a national court to request the European Court to apply an *accelerated procedure*.[14]

Alongside these elements, we must also bear in mind the existence of teleological reasons that may persuade the European Court of Justice to adapt the *general regime* of Article 68 and 234 to the peculiarities of insolvency proceedings. The Insolvency Regulation is both community law and private law. From the point of view of its interpretation, *two logics* may be taken into account: the "logic of integration" and the "logic of insolvency law". In this respect, the motives behind the special solution adopted in the 1995 Insolvency Convention (a facultative regime whereby the suspensive effect is determined by national law) remain valid after its conversion into a Regulation. The need for speed in insolvency proceedings does not disappear simply because it has been transformed into EC law; the risk of a rapid devaluation of the worth of the enterprise or its assets remain (i.e. the logic of integration should not override the logic of insolvency law). Therefore: (a) The suspensive effect should not be taken further than is strictly necessary, so that a partial problem should, as far as possible, be dealt with as an incident or separate item; the aim is to prevent incidental problems from altering the main course of the insolvency proceedings.[15] (b) Furthermore, national courts could exclude the suspensive effect when the effectiveness of the insolvency proceedings is at stake, as they are in a better position to appreciate and control that risk. The most important case may be that in which the point under discussion is the international jurisdiction, according to Article 3.1 IR, of the court of the opening of insolvency proceedings. To impose the interruption of the insolvency proceedings may jeopardise the economic and legal functions of the insolvency proceedings themselves. If such is the case, the insolvency proceedings should continue. However, the insolvency court cannot avoid the fact that the interpretative ruling by the ECJ may entail the rejection of its international jurisdiction and must provide for the appropriate safeguards.

4. Leaving aside the general principles of interpretation that apply to it as a matter of Community law,[16] the history of the Insolvency Regulation is of particular interest for its interpretation.

In fact, the adoption of the Insolvency Regulation is the result of a long process of negotiations among Member States in which successive attempts to achieve an agreement ended in failure.[17] The immediate background to the Insolvency Regulation lies in the Convention on Insolvency Proceedings signed in Brussels on 23 November 1995 (hereafter, the *1995 Convention on Insolvency Proceedings*). This text was adopted by way of application of former Article 220 (now Article 293)

---

[13] See VIRGOS/SCHMIT Report, Margin No. 287; LEIBLE/STAUDINGER (2000), p. 573.

[14] See Articles 104.3 and 104 bis, Rules of Procedure of the ECJ, Official Journal L 122, 24 May 2000.

[15] VIRGOS/SCHMIT Report, Margin No. 291.3 *in fine*.

[16] See FLETCHER, in MOSS/FLETCHER/ISAACS, pp. 23–28.

[17] See a complete historical overview in FLETCHER, MOSS/FLETCHER/ISAACS, p. 1 *et seq.*; see also, TORREMANS, pp. 133–136; REINHART (2003), pp. 703–706; WIMMER, (2002), pp. 2498–2501.

of the EC Treaty then in force, when the new Title IV, concerned with the progressive establishment of an area of freedom, security and justice, did not exist. The Convention was signed by all Member States with the exception of the United Kingdom, apparently for motives unrelated to the convention itself. For this reason, it never actually came into force. On the basis of Article 67 of the 1997 revised version of the EC Treaty, and on the initiative of the Federal Republic of Germany and Finland, the decision was taken to transform the convention into an EC Regulation.[18] The text nevertheless remained practically unchanged. This explains why, for the purposes of interpreting the Insolvency Regulation, regard may legitimately be had to the *Explanatory Report* which accompanied the 1995 Convention on Insolvency Proceedings. As with other conventions based on Article 220 of the EC Treaty (now Article 293), the 1995 Convention on Insolvency Proceedings was accompanied by an *Explanatory Report*: the so-called *VIRGOS/SCHMIT Report*.[19] This report was negotiated by all of the (then) contracting States and explains the origin and teleology of each of its Articles. Notwithstanding the fact that the expert delegates of the Working Party agreed upon its terms, the report itself was not approved by the European Council, nor officially published in the Official Journal, because the United Kingdom did not sign the 1995 Insolvency Convention. That is why, with regard to the *Insolvency Regulation* itself, the explanatory report only has persuasive authority. The report provides an essential reference for understanding the meaning of legal terms as intended by the historical legislator and the aims pursued by its rules. Nevertheless, it is also clear that the nature of the interpretations contained therein is not binding and does not therefore prevent other canons of interpretation from coming into play.

3. CONTENT

5. The Insolvency Regulation has three basic goals: (1) to provide for legal certainty in cross-border insolvency; (2) to promote the efficiency of insolvency proceedings, by favouring those solutions which facilitate their administration and improve the *ex ante* planning of transactions; (3) to eliminate inequalities among Community-based creditors with regard to access and participation in such proceedings. In order to achieve these goals, the Insolvency Regulation does not seek to establish a uniform code of insolvency law in the European Community. The Regulation is based rather on the principle of respect for substantive diversity; each Member State retains its own insolvency law. What the Regulation seeks to establish is a uniform set of *Private International Law rules* on insolvency. Namely, rules regarding *international jurisdiction, applicable law, recognition of insolvency*

---

[18] On the relationship between the Insolvency Regulation and the 1995 Insolvency Convention see also LEIBLE/STAUDINGER (2000), pp. 535–537, or EIDENMÜLLER (2001a), p. 2. Many of the doctrinal references included as footnotes were intended for the text of the Convention; nevertheless, we shall use them as if they had been made with reference to the Regulation where they are still substantively valid.

[19] The VIRGOS/SCHMIT report, as finalized by the Legal Linguistic experts' working party, has the EU Council reference 6500/1/96, Rev 1, DRS 8 (CFC), bearing the date 8 July 1996.

proceedings, and coordination of parallel proceedings which are common to all Member States.[20] These rules of Private International Law are accompanied by certain uniform procedural and substantive rules of an auxiliary nature whose main aim is to ensure the effective functioning of the system, but national insolvency law remains in force beyond this sphere.

6. The *legal reasons* for this restriction should be sought in the interaction of the *principles of subsidiarity* and *proportionality* (Recital 6). The smooth functioning of any integrated market requires cross-border insolvency proceedings to be conducted efficiently and effectively. This involves the need to remove incentives for the parties to behave opportunistically by transferring assets or judicial proceedings from one Member State to another to obtain a more favourable legal position in their own interests and to the detriment of third parties (Recitals 2 and 4).[21] This risk is greater in integrated markets such as the European Community, because freedom of establishment and of the movement of goods, capital and persons facilitate opportunistic behaviour. However, substantive uniformity which would have displaced the laws of the States was not considered necessary in order to achieve these objectives and prevent these risks. Therefore, each State can retain its insolvency law. The intervention of the EC legislator has been limited to standardising the rules of Private International Law insofar as this sufficiently enables the objectives of the Regulation to be achieved and, at the same time, avoids the costs associated with substantive standardisation. What the Regulation does is to provide operators with certainty as to which European courts have jurisdiction to open insolvency proceedings, and which state's laws they are going to apply, in addition to ensuring the cross-border effectiveness (within Europe) of the decisions handed down by those courts.

Development. The Regulation *does not completely eliminate* the risk of opportunistic behaviour on the part of the operators because, under certain circumstances, they can move assets from one State to another and thereby seek a more favourable forum to the detriment of the other parties involved. However, it does *relatively* reduce these possibilities, as it establishes connection criteria which are difficult for any of the parties to manipulate. And it also reduces the possibilities of opportunistic behaviour on the part of the States themselves by removing the possibility of their taking advantage of the national rules of Private International Law for the purposes of benefiting national parties at the expense of others.

4. The Insolvency Regulation as Part of a European Insolvency System

7. The Insolvency Regulation is not the only instrument adopted by the European institutions in the sphere of insolvency. Together with the Insolvency Regulation, we

---

[20] We shall use the expression Private International Law in a broad sense, i.e. to include problems of international jurisdiction, applicable law and the recognition and execution of decisions issued by foreign courts.

[21] For a more detailed treatment, see Virgos, pp. 1–4; Leible/Staudinger (2000), pp. 537–538; Beltran Sanchez, pp. 33–34; Torremans, pp. 138–139.

should be aware of other pieces of European legislation which are more specific in scope. This legislation can be divided into two groups of instruments.

On the one hand, those legal instruments whose object is to regulate the insolvency of institutions excluded from the sphere of application of the Insolvency Regulation: credit institutions, insurance undertakings and investment undertakings (see Recital 9 and Article 1.2 of the Insolvency Regulation). The reason for this exclusion is that these institutions are normally subject to special schemes of prudential supervision by the national authorities, which are granted wide-ranging powers of intervention in cases of financial difficulties. Two directives have been approved to date: *Directive 2001/17/EC, of March 19, regarding the reorganisation and winding-up of insurance undertakings*; and *Directive 2001/24/EC, of 4 April 2001, regarding the reorganisation and winding-up of credit institutions*. At the time of writing, no Directive regarding investment undertakings which provide services involving the holding of funds or securities for third parties or collective investment undertakings has been approved. The legal basis of these Directives is different from that of the Insolvency Regulation (see Articles 47.2, 55, and 251 EC Treaty). For this reason, Denmark, which is excluded from the Insolvency Regulation, is nevertheless bound by these Directives. Furthermore, the extension of these legal instruments to the *Economic European Area* countries must be taken into account.

On the other hand, there are specific rules on insolvency to be found in EC texts whose main objective is the regulation of other sectors or problems. Of these, Directive *98/26/EC, of 19 May 1998, regarding settlement finality in payment and securities settlement systems* (Articles 6–9) and *Directive 2002/47/EC of 6 June 2002 on financial collateral arrangements* (one of the main objectives of which is to protect the beneficiary creditors of a financial guarantee from the risks of the insolvency of the debtor) are especially worthy of notice due to their importance in the area of insolvency.

> *Other rules*. A number of other Community texts also contain rules on insolvency or which may affect the area: *inter alia, Directive* 2000/74/EC on the Approximation of the Laws of the Member States relating to the Protection of Employees in the Event of the Insolvency of their Employer; *Directive* 90/314/EC regarding Package Travel, Package Holidays and Package Tours (Article 7); and *Directive* 97/9/EC regarding Investor Compensation Schemes. *Regulation* (EC) 2157/2001 regarding the European Company Statute does not modify the existing rules. According to Article 63, in the matter of insolvency proceedings, the European Company will receive the same treatment as a public limited-liability company set up in accordance with the law of the Member State in which its registered office is situated.

8. All of these legal texts make up a *system of cross-border insolvency*. Within this system, the Insolvency Regulation constitutes the *general rule*. It forms the backbone of the whole system and has been taken as the reference model for deciding whether to adopt the same solutions or to depart from them, when drafting special rules for certain kinds of debtors (e.g. in the case of the Directives regarding credit institutions and insurance undertakings) or for specific arrangements (e.g. in the case of the Directive on financial guarantee agreements). The Directives constitute *special rules*.

But they all form the "hermeneutic circle" within which interpretations should be made. The idea that all of these rules must be seen as parts of a consistent (although still unfinished) statutory scheme is important. As we shall see, the solution to some of the problems of interpretation presented by some of these rules must be looked for in the connection between them all (i.e. in *systemic arguments*).

Chapter 2

The Normative Model

1. APPROACHES TO THE CROSS-BORDER ASPECTS OF INSOLVENCY

1.1. Normative models: universality vs. territoriality

9. In this chapter, we shall explain the cross-border model adopted by the Insolvency Regulation. We will begin by analysing the two normative models which have inspired, to a different extent, the laws of the Member States: the *territorial* model and the *universal* model.[22] Each of these models provides a very different response to the problems presented by cross-border insolvencies. We will present them as "ideal models", i.e. not referred to the law of any given State. Then we will explain the basic features of the Insolvency Regulation's model.

10. The *territorial model*, in its most radical version, is a perfect reflection of the legal fragmentation which exists in the world: corporate international activity is conducted in a legally fragmented world, a world in which each State has its own legislation and in which each State can only guarantee the coercive implementation of rights within its own territory. The result of this in the sphere of international insolvency is easy to deduce: each State where the debtor has assets organises the insolvency according to its own law. This means that: (a) there are as many insolvency proceedings as there are States where the debtor has assets;[23] (b) each set of proceedings is governed by the law in force in that State; and (c) only the creditors from the State in question can participate in the proceedings. Both the body of creditors and the estate of the debtor are limited to the territory of each State.

From this starting point, the territorial model can be diluted and move towards *intermediate models*. Thus, e.g. (a) the opening of territorial proceedings can be determined by the existence of an establishment of the debtor in the territory of the State in question, i.e. the presence of an asset is not sufficient, but rather the permanent presence of the debtor in that State is required before insolvency proceedings can be opened against him; (b) foreign creditors can form part in the body of creditors, i.e. the estate of the debtor remains territorial, but the body of creditors is

---

[22] The most recent debate between the two models was put forward with especial intensity in the North American doctrine; by way of introduction, see GUZMAN, *passim*; LOPUCKI (2000), *passim*; WESTBROOK, *passim*.

[23] LOPUCKI (2000), p. 2218, "territoriality means that the bankruptcy courts of a country have jurisdiction over those portions of the company which are within its borders and not those portions that are outside them".

universal; and (c) mechanisms of cooperation are established between the various territorial proceedings in order to assure as far as possible a coordinated winding-up of the company or the international *par conditio concurrentium* of the creditors (e.g. the so-called "cooperative territorialism").

11. The *universal model*, on the other hand, stems from the *principle of symmetry* between legal regulation and economic activity:[24] Even though the economic activity of a company is conducted in various markets and, as a result, a plurality of creditors in different countries are affected by that activity, collective proceedings will be conducted under the authority of a single court and by a single insolvency administration for the entire activity and for all of those creditors. This means that: (a) a single procedure is opened in the debtor's "home country" which encompasses all of the assets of the debtor independently of where they are located; (b) a single national law is applied, both to procedural and substantive questions (i.e. the *lex fori concursus*); (c) all creditors, both national and foreign, can participate in the proceedings; and (d) the decisions taken in these proceedings are recognised and enforced in all other Member States. As someone once said, in the universal model "one court plays the tune, and everyone else dances" (LoPucki).

Furthermore, as is the case with the territorial model, the universal model can be modified and move towards *intermediate models*. Thus, for example: (a) by allowing certain subordinated territorial proceedings to run concurrently alongside the main insolvency process; (b) by allowing, under certain conditions, the opening of territorial proceedings without the need to open proceedings with universal scope; or (c) by establishing exceptions to the application of the *lex fori concursus*.

1.2. General policy considerations

1.2.1. The territorial model

12. Viewed from the perspective of the policies involved, the *territorial model* is basically justified for *two reasons*: one of which is substantive in nature and the other organisational.[25]

(a) It is a model suitable for providing protection for the interests of *local creditors*. Countries tend to be reluctant to accept the effects of foreign insolvency proceedings when these conflict with the interests of their local creditors, in particular "unsophisticated creditors" such as employees, consumers, small suppliers, etc. In the case of "sophisticated creditors" there are no serious problems: the cost of attending insolvency proceedings abroad is already reflected in the price of the credit they extended to the debtor.[26] When a national bank or a large company enters into an agreement with a foreign firm, it is capable of assessing the associated risks (e.g. the need to attend insolvency proceedings abroad or the application of a foreign law), so these risks will be taken into account in the form of a higher or, as the case

---

[24] WESTBROOK, p. 2283.
[25] LoPucki (2000), *passim.*
[26] GUZMAN, p. 2186.

may be, lower price. However, unsophisticated creditors are unable to make this adjustment. They are unable to adjust the terms of their transaction to reflect the risk which they are assuming (we can call these creditors *non-adjusting creditors*, to use the term which is beginning to gain widespread acceptance). This leads to certain inefficiencies arising from the "moral risk" and from the "adverse selection" which goes hand in hand with these situations: (i) debtors, insofar as they are not subject to close "scrutiny" by local creditors, lack any incentive to protect the solvency of the claim; and (ii) crossed subsidies are produced: high-risk debtors will borrow too much, while low-risk debtors will borrow too little, which can cause the latter (precisely the more solvent ones) to be driven out of the market.[27]

> *Example*. Let us imagine a commercial creditor who enters into an agreement with two foreign companies which are identical, except for the fact that each of them is subject to a different insolvency regime. One is subject to that of State F1 and the other to that of State F2. Let us imagine that according to the law of F1 commercial creditors are given no priority, while the law of F2 states that these creditors enjoy a preferential position (i.e. he is at the head of the scale of ranking of the claims). If the commercial creditor in our example is an unsophisticated creditor he will be incapable of reflecting this difference in the risks which he is assuming in the price. In other words, if the F1 company and the F2 company apply for credit at the same rate of interest, the result may be obviously inefficient as the F1 company is paying less for the credit than it should and vice versa. In fact, the F2 company is subsidising the F1 company. The first, due to the lower price, will request greater credit, and the second, less. The greater the difference between the insolvency regimes the greater the distortion will be.

The same line of argument has been invoked to justify local proceedings with regard to creditors with a privilege over an asset which is located in the territory of the State in question or with regard to public law claims. In these cases, the problem is not that the creditors ignore the risks they are assuming, but the possibility that the law of the State where the debtor's centre is situated and whose insolvency courts have worldwide jurisdiction (i.e. the debtor's "home country") does not recognise those creditors as having any priority or preferential status.

The situation may become even more complicated if we consider the possible strategies open to a debtor in the period prior to insolvency and the incentives to forum shopping inherent in a universalal system: as the insolvency court will apply its own law (or at least its own conflict of laws rules) debtors may change their domicile or centre (i.e. their "home country") opportunistically after credit has been extended, in order to take advantage of the differences in the national insolvency laws. The possibility of opening territorial insolvency proceedings operates as a kind of insurance against strategies of this kind.

(b) Furthermore, *in certain situations* the territorial insolvency *might facilitate the liquidation* of the assets of the debtor. Thus, for example, when in order to restructure the company it may be sufficient to liquidate some assets located abroad

---

[27] GUZMAN, p. 2184.

(e.g. to sell a division), it may also be sufficient to open territorial insolvency proceedings there, thus saving on the cost of opening universal proceedings. Just as there are situations where a general anaesthetic is not necessary when operating on a patient, and a local anaesthetic is sufficient, there are situations in which it is not necessary to open universal insolvency proceedings, and in which one (or more) territorial bankruptcies are sufficient. Lastly, there may be cases where it is very costly or complicated to conduct the entire proceedings from a single State and it is preferable to combine the main process with territorial proceedings. For example, when dealing with rights which have been created according to a law other than the law of the State of opening *(lex fori concursus)*, it may prove difficult to transpose them to the insolvency categories recognised by the latter. Or, from the procedural point of view, when the number of local creditors is high, segregating different sub-estates may facilitate the access and participation of local creditors and simplify negotiations. To continue using the same metaphor: when the situation is very complicated, the chief surgeon cannot do everything himself, but requires the assistance of other specialists to operate on different parts of the body.

13. Nevertheless, the territorial model contains serious *deficiencies*. With this model, the position of a creditor in the insolvency can vary depending on where the assets of the debtor are located.[28] This leads to numerous difficulties: (a) the distribution of the assets is difficult to predict, and this increases the price of the credit due to the greater uncertainty associated with it; (b) the debtor may be tempted, in collusion with certain creditors, to strategically transfer his assets from one country to another or to close the establishment which might constitute grounds for jurisdiction; (c) the costs of conducting the proceedings are multiplied because instead of a single process being held, there are as many processes as there are States in which the debtor has assets or establishments; and (d) it obstructs decisions aimed, not at winding-up the company, but at restructuring it. In general terms, it is easier to restructure a company when dealing with the whole than when dealing with each individual part.

1.2.2. The universal model

14. Set against this, the universal insolvency model reflects the symmetrical *advantages*: (a) the applicable law is easy to predict; (b) cross-border movements of assets are irrelevant, and this prevents asset forum shopping; (c) the process, because it is centralised, may reduce the administrative costs arising from a plurality of proceedings and can therefore be conducted more efficiently. As we have just seen, this last point is particularly relevant when the aim of the insolvency process is to restructure the company. The restructuring of any company requires a high degree of cooperation between the various parties. The administration and financial rescue of a company must be conducted in a centralised way, because the company, from an economic point of view, has to constitute an integrated whole. Only a universal

---

[28] That is why it has been said in these cases that: *"international bankruptcy is reduced to a game of musical chairs in which creditors cannot know in advance where the assets of the debtor will be located when the music stops"*, WESTBROOK, p. 2309.

model can guarantee this. And the same is true when the liquidation of the assets of the debtor proves more efficient through the sale of the company as a going concern. However much cooperation there is between the different territorial proceedings, they make it much more difficult to guarantee the efficiency of decisions regarding restructuring. The universal model increases the winding-up value of the company because it allows it to be sold as a whole.

Furthermore, (d) by reducing the uncertainty and the possibilities for opportunism, it allows *ex ante* for a more efficient assignment of capital, as it reduces the cost of the credit,[29] and it assigns that capital without distortions external to its economic profitability. (e) It reduces *ex post* the rush by the creditors to request the opening of insolvency proceedings (which can precipitate the insolvency itself). If the creditors know that the debtor can remove assets and place them in a State where the enforcement of their claims will be denied ("execution havens"), they will have an incentive to block and realise those assets as soon as possible. If the location of the assets is irrelevant (i.e. wherever the assets are located they will be encompassed by the main insolvency proceedings), this incentive no longer applies.

15. However, in turn, this universal model also has *drawbacks*. Together with the fact that there may be cases in which a territorial insolvency may be more efficient in organisational terms (*supra*, No. 12.b), the problem faced by the implementation of the universal model is that it requires a sincere attitude of inter-state cooperation. A State will not be willing to "sacrifice" its local creditors if it does not have a full guarantee that the other States will behave in a reciprocal manner.

16. The fact that it is not possible to design a "perfect model" or that, even if it were possible, it is not certain that States would adopt such a model unilaterally, explains why there was no uniform response to this question in the European national systems. Some States gear their solutions towards a universal model and others are more in favour of a territorial model. One of the fundamental objectives of the Insolvency Regulation is precisely to put an end to this legal diversity. The greatest difficulty of the Regulation was to seek a solution which balanced the two models.

2. MODEL OF THE INSOLVENCY REGULATION: MITIGATED UNIVERSALITY

17. Though we will look in more detail at the contents of each of the rules of the Regulation, it is helpful to summarise, from the very beginning, the normative model which underlies the EC text. To this end, it is usually said that the Regulation responds to a *model of modified or mitigated universality*.[30]

The Insolvency Regulation is based on a universal model in the sense that it permits the opening of insolvency proceedings in the State where the debtor has his

---

[29] GUZMAN, p. 2281.

[30] VIRGOS, p. 6; see also, LÜKE (1998), pp. 280–281, which discusses the different interpretations of the term universality in this context; TAUPITZ, pp. 324–325; DORDI, p. 339; FUMAGALLI, pp. 686–687; WIMMER (2002), pp. 2490–2491.

centre of main interests and gives this process universal scope, both in terms of the estate of the debtor and the body of creditors, on a *worldwide basis* (see *infra* No. 27b). In principle, all assets, wherever they are situated, become subject to these proceedings; and all creditors of the debtor, irrespective of their nationality, domicile, residence or registered office, can participate in them. Furthermore, for conflict of laws purposes, the Insolvency Regulation is based upon the application of a single law, the law of the State of opening (*lex fori concursus principalis*), to both the procedural and the substantive aspects of the insolvency.

18. The Insolvency Regulation establishes a series of rules which correct or mitigate the universality of the model. Basically, these rules can be divided into two types:

(a) On the one hand, rules which deal with the applicable law and establish a number of *exceptions* to the application of the *lex concursus*; certain positions or rights will not be subject to the law which governs the insolvency proceedings, but rather to a different national law via the operation of *special connecting factors*.

(b) On the other hand, rules whose purpose is to permit the opening of *territorial proceedings* (i.e. insolvency proceedings restricted to the assets of the debtor in a certain State); in turn, the Insolvency Regulation places a series of restrictions with regard to the opening of these territorial proceedings in order not to undermine the main criteria, i.e. the universality of the insolvency. Thus, (i) territorial proceedings can only be opened where the debtor has an establishment, (ii) the body of creditors is not limited territorially and (iii) the resulting proceedings are, to a certain extent, subordinated to the main proceedings, in the event that both types of proceedings are opened.

19. As a good understanding of the normative model which underlies the Regulation to a large extent facilitates the explanation of its rules, we shall now look at it in more detail.

20. The first possibility provided for by the Regulation is the opening of a *main insolvency process* with universal scope. The only courts with jurisdiction to open main insolvency proceedings are those of the State where the debtor has his centre of main interests. There can only be one set of main proceedings. These proceedings encompass all of the assets of the debtor, both inside and outside that State, and all creditors, both national and foreign, can participate in them. Therefore, both the estate of the debtor and the body of creditors are universal. For these universal proceedings to be effective, the decisions taken in them must of necessity be recognised and enforced in the other States. As we have said, in the case of non-Member States, the Regulation is powerless: effectiveness depends on the law of the non-Member State in question, including any international agreements or conventions in force. In the case of a Member State, the Regulation itself ensures the cross-border effectiveness of the insolvency proceedings through a system of mandatory recognition and enforcement of the decisions of the court of opening.

21. In principle, the law of the State of opening will apply to all *insolvency issues* (Article 4). However, there are several conflict of laws rules which follow a different solution (Article 5 *et seq.*): the effects of the insolvency proceedings on specific rights or relationships will be governed by a law other than that of the law of the

State of opening. These are to be interpreted and construed as *special rules* rather than as exceptions in the technical and legal sense. Although the scope of each may differ, as we shall see later, they all share certain common bases. The objective of these special rules is two-fold. On the one hand, substantive, as they seek to protect certain pre-insolvency rights or positions and, on the other hand, procedural, since they try to facilitate the administration and management of the estate.

22. The exception to the idea of a single set of insolvency proceedings with universal scope arises from the possibility provided by the Regulation of opening *territorial insolvency proceedings*. These proceedings, however, can only be opened where the debtor has an *establishment*. Unlike the stricter territorial model, the Regulation does not consider the presence of assets of the debtor to be sufficient grounds for permitting the opening of territorial proceedings, but rather requires a more stable and lasting presence. Furthermore, in these cases, even where the *"estate"* is strictly territorial (it only encompasses the assets of the debtor located in the State in question), the *"body of creditors"* is universal, the proceedings are open to any creditor of the debtor, whether national or foreign, and whether or not their claim has derived from the activities of that establishment.

Rationale. The reason for allowing a combination of universal proceedings and/or territorial proceedings can be explained in terms of information costs.[31] As we know, there may be cases in which a single set of main proceedings is efficient, others in which one or more territorial proceedings are efficient, and cases in which the combination of both is preferable: one size does not fit all (*supra* Nos 12 *et seq.*). What the Regulation aims to do is to allow those who possess the necessary information (e.g. the creditors or the main liquidator) to choose the model best suited to each specific case while, nevertheless, preventing this choice from being made from purely opportunistic motives. For this reason, it can be said that the Regulation "does not impose" a specific model, but rather allows those involved to select one.

23. These territorial insolvency proceedings can be characterised as either *secondary* or *independent* proceedings, depending on whether the main proceedings have been opened or not.

(a) The insolvency Regulation permits the opening of territorial proceedings in Member States, *even when no main proceedings are pending*. In such a case, the territorial proceedings operate independently. They deal with the insolvency of a part of the company, without the rest of the company being involved. "*Independent*" territorial proceedings can only be opened under two circumstances: either when so requested by "local creditors" or when it is not possible to open insolvency proceedings in the State where the debtor's centre of main interests is situated. In this way, the Regulation intends "that cases where territorial insolvency proceedings are requested before the main insolvency proceedings are [...] limited to what is

---

[31] See, VIRGÓS, pp. 6–7; LÜKE (1998), pp. 282–283.

absolutely necessary" (Recital 17).[32] Furthermore, if main insolvency proceedings are opened at a later point, these territorial proceedings become "secondary" proceedings, with the consequences that we will explain in the next paragraph. Independent territorial proceedings may be aimed at winding-up or restructuring.

> *Rationale.* As we already know, there may be reasons to justify the opening of territorial proceedings separately from the main proceedings, but this possibility also permits opportunistic behaviour. That is why the Regulation tries to restrict the opening of these proceedings as much as possible. The fact that any creditor can participate in these territorial proceedings may also act as a disincentive to opportunism on the part of local creditors.

(b) The Regulation also allows the opening of territorial insolvency proceedings *alongside the main proceedings opened* in another Member State. In this case, the territorial insolvency proceedings operate as *secondary* proceedings: they are conditioned by the main proceedings and may be subject to different measures of mandatory coordination, such as the obligation of the liquidators to cooperate and the directing role given to the liquidator of the main proceedings. Furthermore, the Regulation obliges any surplus assets remaining from territorial proceedings to be "transferred" to the main proceedings.

This unitary or cooperative view of the different proceedings also explains why secondary proceedings can only be winding-up proceedings (the definition of winding-up proceedings is, however, quite wide; see Article 2.c). These proceedings are listed in Annex B of the Regulation.

Territorial insolvency proceedings can meet certain needs such as the protection of local creditors or the more efficient administration of the debtor's assets; for example, there may be cases in which the assets of the debtor are too complex to be administered as a single unit or in which the differences between the legal systems are so acute that it is preferable to limit the role of the *lex concursus principalis* (see Recital 19). For this reason, the Insolvency Regulation does not impose any specific restriction upon the opening of territorial proceedings as secondary proceedings.

24. In contrast to the model of "modified" or "mitigated universality" provided by the Insolvency Regulation, Directive 2001/24/EC regarding the *reorganisation and winding-up of credit institutions* and Directive 2001/17/EC regarding the *reorganisation and winding-up of insurance undertakings* adopt a model of "full" universality. The reorganisation or winding-up is based on a single procedure with universal scope (see Articles 3 and 9, and 4 and 8, respectively), and no territorial proceedings are allowed. Jurisdiction corresponds exclusively to the State of origin or "home Member State" of the credit institution or insurance undertaking (Articles 2 paragraph I and 2.e, respectively; on this concept see *infra* No. 107 and 108). In both

---

[32] See BALZ (1996a), p. 949, who points out that the 1995 Insolvency Convention did not look favourably upon the opening of independent territorial proceedings; the same is true of the Insolvency Regulation.

cases a regime of exceptions is established to the application of the *lex fori concursus* which is parallel to that of the Insolvency Regulation.

Exception. The Directives on credit institutions and insurance undertakings, unlike the Insolvency Regulation, apply to companies from non-Member States which have branches in the European Community. The cross-border normative model with regard to these companies is not a model of full universality, since these Directives permit the opening of proceedings limited to a specific branch. Jurisdiction will correspond to the authorities of the Member State where the branch is located. Where the foreign (extra-Community) institution has several branches, each of them is dealt with separately, without prejudice to the duty to coordinate the actions of the respective authorities, which is established by the above-mentioned Directives (see Articles 8.2 and 19.3 of the Directive on credit institutions, and Article 30.2 of the Directive on insurance companies).

Chapter 3

Sphere of Application

1. PRELIMINARY

25. The purpose of this chapter is to explain the scope of operation of the Insolvency Regulation. This scope can be defined on the basis of five criteria: (a) the sphere of *territorial* application; (b) the sphere of *subjective* application; (c) the sphere of *substantive* application; (d) the sphere of application *in time*; and (e) the *relationship with international conventions* ratified by the Member States. As we will see below, the Regulations's scope is limited and needs to be complemented by national law.

2. SPHERE OF TERRITORIAL APPLICATION: THE "COMMUNITY CONNECTION"

26. The Insolvency Regulation deals primarily with intra-Community cooperation in insolvency matters. For this reason, the Regulation has a limited sphere of territorial application. Its rules do not have global scope, i.e. they are not applicable to any proceedings regardless of the State where the debtor or the creditors are located. The Regulation *only applies* to insolvency proceedings *opened in a Member State* against *community debtors* (i.e. a debtor, of whatever nationality, whose centre of main interests is in a Member State) and only governs the *intra-Community effects* of these proceedings (i.e. *vis-à-vis* the laws of other Member States). This link with the European Community which is required in order for the Insolvency Regulation to apply is known as the *"Community connection"*. The special position of *Denmark* which, for the purposes of the application of the Insolvency Regulation, is considered as a non-Member State, must be taken into account (see *supra* No. 3).

For insolvency proceedings not encompassed (i.e. those opened in a Member State against debtors not located in the European Community and those opened in non-Member States against any debtor), the national rules of Private International Law on insolvency matters of each State apply.

Rationale. This intra-Community limitation of the Regulation originated with the 1995 Convention on Insolvency Proceedings and at that time obeyed the strong desire of certain States (in particular, the United Kingdom) to reserve for themselves a degree of freedom with regard to non-Member States. The result is a complicated dual regime.

27. In order to specify this limitation, it is convenient to distinguish between the various groups of rules contained in the Insolvency Regulation and to address the question in a separate way for each of them: first the Insolvency Regulation itself,

and then, successively, the rules regarding international jurisdiction (Article 3), applicable law (Articles 4–15), recognition and enforcement of decisions (Articles 16–26), secondary proceedings (Articles 27–38), and finally, the rules regarding information for creditors and the filing of their claims (Articles 39–42).

(a) The Insolvency Regulation *only applies* when the debtor has his centre of main interests in the territory of a Member State. In this sense, the "centre of main interests" of Article 3 fulfils a *double function*: on the one hand, it determines when the Regulation is applicable and, on the other hand, it determines which Member State has international jurisdiction to open main insolvency proceedings. We shall look at this second function *infra* Chapter 4. It is the first function which interests us now. Recital 14 of the Regulation is very clear on this issue: *"This Regulation applies only to proceedings where the centre of the debtor's main interests is located in the Community"* (on the concept of "centre of main interests", see *infra* No. 44; in the case of a company, it is presumed to be the place of its registered office, see Article 3.1). It is important to state that, in order for the Insolvency Regulation to apply, the location of the debtor's centre of main interests in a Member State is enough. The Insolvency Regulation does not require, in addition to this, a connection with another Member State.[33] Furthermore, the nationality of the debtor or, in cases of companies and legal persons, the place of incorporation, is irrelevant. The Regulation applies to debtors whose centre of main interests are in a Member State even if they are nationals of non-Member States or companies incorporated in non-Member States. In the latter case, however, the company's registered office will function as presumption *iuris tantum* of the location of its centre of main interests (see Article 3.1). Any other solution would be inconsistent with the objectives of the Regulation, in particular with the proper functioning of the internal market, which demand that their rules govern the insolvency of all those debtors based in the Community.[34]

In the case of debtors whose centre of main interests is not in a Member State, the Private International Law rules of each State will apply. In this case, the fact that they have an establishment (or assets) in a Member State is not sufficient for the Insolvency Regulation to apply.[35]

Example. When a company has its centre of main interests in a Member State, the EC Regulation is applicable, even if the company has been incorporated under the laws of a non-Member State and has its registered office there. See, for instance, the case In re Branc Rent-a-car International Inc. decided by the English High Court, Chancery Division in year 2003; I this case the place of incorporation of the corporate debtor was Delaware but the centre of main interest was in England, where insolvency proceedings were opened.[36] On the other hand, the fact that the company has its registered office in a Member State is

---

[33] For a different view, see Duursma-Kepplinger/Duursma/Chalupsky, p. 82–83.

[34] National courts have decided affirmatively on this question, in particular, see in Re Brac Rent-A-Car International Inc [2003] EWHC 128 (ch); (2003) 2 All E.R. 201, and the decisions indicated by Wessels (2004), p. 9.

[35] Virgos, p. 9.

[36] (2003) ILP, p. 23.

a simple presumption *iuris tantum* that the company also has its centre of main interests there. However, if it is shown that the company has its centre of main interests outside the European Community (in Delaware, the Bahamas or anywhere else), the Insolvency Regulation ceases to be applicable. In such a case, national Private International Law rules will determine whether or not insolvency proceedings can be opened in that Member State against that debtor, or whether or not the decisions taken after the opening of proceedings abroad are going to be recognised.

(b) When the debtor's centre of main interests is located within the European Community, the Insolvency Regulation establishes the *international jurisdiction* of the courts of the Member States to open insolvency proceedings, regardless of the debtor's nationality or place of incorporation (for the same reasons stated in the previous paragraph). As far as international jurisdiction is concerned, the Insolvency Regulation does not limit the scope thereof to the Community, but establishes a true universal jurisdiction with worldwide scope (see *infra* No. 72).

Elaboration. The Insolvency Regulation has universal scope, i.e. its objective is to encompass all of the assets of the debtor, whether they are inside or outside the European Community. Universal scope outside the European Community is also deduced from Recital 12: "These proceedings have universal scope and *aim at* encompassing *all* the debtor's assets". Also, this point was discussed expressly during the negotiations which led to the 1995 Insolvency Convention and was reflected thus in the VIRGOS/SCHMIT Report, Margin No 19: "Assets located outside the State of opening are also included in the proceedings and sequestrated as from the opening of proceedings *on a world-wide basis*" (*emphasis added*). Obviously, the Insolvency Regulation is only binding on Member States. Therefore, its extra-Community effectiveness will depend upon the laws of the non-Member concerned Sate. In this case, account should be taken of any possible international conventions between Member and non-Member States, which the Insolvency Regulation does not affect.

(c) With regard its conflict of laws rules, the Insolvency Regulation contains a specific self-limitation: It does not seek to regulate the effects of the insolvency proceedings *vis-à-vis* non-Member States. In this respect, the Regulation only governs *intra-Community conflicts*. With regard to conflicts of laws with non-Member States (*extra-Community conflicts*, including Denmark), the Regulation defers to the national Private International Law on insolvency matters of the Member States themselves.

The problem, of course, lies in determining what makes a case *intra-Community*. The Insolvency Regulation is silent in this point, although the relevant criteria can easily be deduced from its rules: the debtor's centre of main interest is in the Community *and either* the asset in question is located in a Member State (for this purpose, the rules on location established in Article 2.g IR apply) *or* the law governing the claim or relationship itself (contract, etc.) is, according to the ordinary conflict of laws rules of the forum, that of a Member State.

This restriction is not obvious in the Insolvency Regulation, although it was alluded to in the Preamble of the 1995 Convention on Insolvency Proceedings, whose text was transformed into the text of the Regulation (see No. 2), and then further expanded upon in the Explanatory Report[37]: "*Where non-Member States are concerned, it is the responsibility of each Member State to define the appropriate conflict rules*". This explains why all of the exceptions to the application of the law of the State of opening (*lex fori concursus*), which is the basic conflict of laws rule in all cases in which the courts of a Member State have jurisdiction according to the Insolvency Regulation, are limited to situations governed by the law of a Member State. With regard to the laws of non-Member States, the Insolvency regulation defers to the national Private International Law of the Member State in question. This, in turn, may establish exceptions in favour of the laws of non-Member States in similar or different cases to those provided for in the Regulation (or the Directives on the reorganisation and winding-up of credit institutions and insurance undertakings, where applicable).

> *Further explanation.* Following its own terms, Article 4 of the Insolvency Regulation, which is the general conflict of laws rule, applies in all cases ("save as otherwise provided in this Regulation"). However, the exceptions (Articles 5–15) are drafted so as to restrict themselves to the law of *other* Member States. From the genetic argument we know that the historical legislator's intention was to allow the Member States to decide freely which rules they consider to be more appropriate in those cases in which the exceptions point not to another Member State, but to a non-Member State.[38] In other words, when Articles 5–15 of the Regulation are not applicable, then the Member States are free to decide, in the same cases as those contemplated by the said exceptions, whether they allow the same exceptions in favour of the laws of a non-Member State, or prefer a different solution. In this sense, Articles 5–15 would have a double function: to establish exceptions to the application of the law of the Member State of opening, and to open the door to the national conflicts of laws rules when those exceptions do not lead to the law of a Member State (i.e. the asset is not situated in a Member-State, the claim is not governed by the law of a Member State, or the lawsuit is not pending in a Member State).[39] For example, Article 8 of the Regulation governs the effects of the insolvency proceedings on contracts relating to immovable assets as an exception to the general application of the *lex fori concursus*. Nevertheless, this precept only applies when the immovable asset is located in a Member State. When the asset is located in a non-Member States, it is for the State of opening to decide, according to its law, if an equivalent exception should be made and under what conditions. The question is then whether Member States may introduce further exceptions in addition to those provided by the Regulation (or the Directives). Once again, the genetic argument would speak in favour of this possibility, albeit limited to *extra-Community* cases.

(d) The rules of the Insolvency Regulation on *recognition and enforcement* apply to all insolvency decisions handed down by the courts of a Member State in application of the Insolvency Regulation; this, again, presupposes that the debtor's centre of main interests is in the Community.

---

[37] VIRGOS/SCHMIT Report, Margin No. 44, p. 93; BALZ (1996b), 507; FLETCHER (1999), p. 265; DUURSMA-KEPPLINGER/DUURSMA/CHALUPSKY, p. 103.

[38] VIRGOS/SCHMIT Report, Margin No. 93.

[39] HUBER, 153; DUURSMA-KEPPLINGER/DUURSMA/CHALUPSKY, p. 103.

NB. The rules on recognition apply regardless of whether the conflict of laws rules applied by the court of origin were those of the Insolvency Regulation or, for the reasons explained above, those of its national Private International Law.

On the other hand, a decision rendered in a Member State in insolvency proceedings opened against an extra-Community debtor (i.e. a debtor whose centre of main interests is not located in a Member State) is not recognised in the other Member States pursuant to the Insolvency Regulation, but rather pursuant to the autonomous rules on recognition of each State. Nevertheless, as we will see (*infra* No. 70), the Insolvency Regulation's rules on international jurisdiction have an indirect effect on the solutions adopted by those national rules.

(e) The rules of the Insolvency Regulation regarding *territorial insolvency proceedings* are also determined by the fact that the debtor's centre of main interests is located in another Member State. In the case of *secondary* territorial proceedings, the rules of coordination contained in the Regulation apply to proceedings pending *in Member States*.

(f) Finally, the rules of the Insolvency Regulation concerning the *information* due to the creditors and the *lodgement* of their claims (Articles 39–42) only apply to creditors whose habitual residence, domicile or registered office is located in a Member State other than the one in which the proceedings are opened ("*Intra-Community creditors*"). The nationality of the creditor (of a Member or non-Member State) and, in the case of companies and legal persons, the place of incorporation, are irrelevant. For creditors with habitual residence, domicile or registered office in a non-Member State (i.e. *extra-Community creditors*) the rules of national law apply.

Tasks left to Member States. On the basis of the above statements we can summarise the sphere which the Regulation leaves to national Laws: (a) In the case of a *debtor* whose centre of interests is *located in a Member State*, the Insolvency Regulation applies, but needs to be complemented. The national rules of private international law will determine the applicable law in extra-Community conflicts of laws and, with regard to extra-Community creditors (those whose residence, domicile or registered office is not in a Member State), the rules governing the informing of creditors and the filing of their claims. (b) In the case of a *debtor* whose centre of main interests is *not located in a Member State*, the Insolvency Regulation does not apply and the national rules of Private International Law will determine: the international jurisdiction to open insolvency proceedings and the scope of these jurisdiction; the applicable law both for intra-Community and extra-Community conflicts; the recognition of the insolvency proceedings opened in other States, whether these are Member States or not; and the regime of coordination with insolvency proceedings opened in other States.

28. At any rate, it must be taken into account that the complex nature of this system (a regime of cross-border insolvency *ad intra* and another *ad extra* of the European Community) can be simplified in two ways: (a) by the unilateral action of the States; there may be powerful reasons, fundamentally relating to the internal coherence of the system, for the Member States to change their rules of Private International Law to adapt them to the Regulation and thereby establish, with the

necessary modifications, the same normative model *ad intra* and *ad extra*;[40] (b) by the action of the European Community itself, by extending the same rules with regard to non-Member States, if this sphere of jurisdiction is "communitarised".[41]

29. For their part, the *Directives on credit institutions* and *insurance undertakings* also have a limited sphere of territorial application (see Articles 1–2 of both). The most notable feature of these two texts, on account of their relationship with the Regulation, is that they extend their sphere of application also to those credit institutions or companies of non-Member States which have *branches* in the European Community. In these cases, the Directives establish the jurisdiction of each State where the branch is located to adopt restructuring or winding-up measures (see Articles 1.2, 8 and 19; and Articles 1.2 and 30, respectively). When the extra-Community institution or company possesses several branches in several Member States, each branch will be dealt with separately for the purposes of applying the said Directives, i.e. each branch will be subject to separate restructuring or winding-up proceedings, without prejudice to the duty to inform and coordinate between the competent authorities (see Recitals 21–22 and 28–29, respectively).

3. SPHERE OF SUBJECTIVE APPLICATION: ELIGIBILITY (ARTICLE 1.2)

3.1. Debtors covered by the Insolvency Regulation

30. The Insolvency Regulation does not provide a definition of "debtor", but defers this to the applicable national law (Article 4.2.a). The Regulation does not require any special nature on the part of the debtor; it makes no distinction as to the kind of debtor, whether individual or corporate, private or State-owned, etc. Neither does it make any distinction between the capacities in which the debtor may act (e.g. whether or not he is a trader or *commerçant*, see Recital 9). It corresponds to the national law (the *lex fori concursus*) designated by the Insolvency Regulation to determine who or what can be subject to insolvency proceedings. In addition to natural and juridical persons (whatever corporate or associative form they adopt), the concept of debtor includes partnerships and other unincorporated associations, and even separate funds or estates, provided that they can be subject to insolvency proceedings under the applicable national law.

Examples. An European economic interest grouping (EEIG) has capacity, in its own name, to have rights and obligations of all kinds and to sue and be sued (Article 1.2 Council Regulation 2137/85); however, it may not have legal personality, as this question is referred

---

[40] Hence, VIRGOS, p. 9; EIDENMÜLLER (2001a), p. 10 *et seq.*, modifying, admittedly, those extremes which obey the principles of mutual trust within the EC or, in general, the peculiarities of the phenomenon of European integration. On this thesis, see VIRGOS/GARCIMARTIN, pp. 81–82.

[41] On this point, see BORRAS, pp. 405–416; and also bear in mind the Council declaration included *infra* No. 41.

back to the national law (Article 1.3: "The Member States shall determine whether or not groupings registered ... at their registries have legal personality"). Nevertheless, it can be subject to insolvency proceedings (Article 36: "Groupings shall be subject to national laws governing insolvency and cessation of payments"). According to Section 11(2).1 of the German *Insolvenzornung*, insolvency proceedings may be opened for the assets owned by a company without legal personality, such as a limited partnership or a civil law company.

31. The Insolvency Regulation does not contain any specific rule with regard to *groups of companies*; for the Insolvency Regulation, each person or legal entity is a separate debtor. On this topic see *infra* No. 61 and ff.

3.2. *Debtors excluded: credit institutions, insurance companies, investment undertakings*

32. As we have already indicated, the Insolvency Regulation expressly excludes from this subjective sphere of application *insurance undertakings*, *credit institutions*, and *investment undertakings* which provide services involving the holding of funds or securities for third parties or qualify as collective investment undertakings. The concepts of "credit institution", "insurance undertaking", "investment undertaking" and "collective investment undertaking" have to be taken from other EC instruments.[42] Specifically, for the concept of *credit institution* we need to refer to Directive 2000/12, of 20 March 2000. For the concept of *insurance undertaking*, the relevant texts are Directives 73/239, of 24 July 1973, and 79/267/EC, of 5 March 1979. These Directives only apply to companies dealing in direct insurance. The Insolvency Regulation applies to Reinsurance companies if they do not transact direct insurance activities.[43] For the concept of *investment undertaking*, see Directive 2004/39, of 21 April 2004; and for the concept of *collective investment undertaking*, Directive 85/611, of 20 December 1985. In each case, the concept will need to be supplemented with the corresponding changes in Community legislation.[44]

Type of debtor and applicable rules. Both the Regulation and the Directives contain conflict of laws rules with regard to applicable law. Different rules will apply according to the type of debtor against which insolvency proceedings are opened (e.g. a business undertaking, a credit institution, or an insurance undertaking). In this respect we can say that the nature of the debtor "attracts" the conflict of laws rules which apply in the event of insolvency. For example, if the insolvent debtor is a banking entity, set-off is governed by Articles 3 or 10, and Articles 23 and 25 of Directive 2001/24/EC; if the insolvent entity is the counterpart (a business undertaking), set-off is governed by Articles 4 and 6 of the Insolvency Regulation. There is a clear legal risk inherent in this: if these conflict of laws rules are different, depending on which of the two parties of a same relationship enters into insolvency (e.g. the banking entity

---

[42] See VIRGOS/SCHMIT Report, Margin Nos 56–60.
[43] See MARKS, in MOSS/FLETCHER/ISAACS, p. 146.
[44] VIRGOS/SCHMIT Report, Margin Nos 57–60; FUMAGALLI, p. 684, footnote 21.

or its counterpart), the solution to the conflict of laws relating to the same problem (the possibility of set-off between the banking entity and its counterpart) would be different. This risk has been avoided by means of a conscious coordination of the conflict of laws rules contained in all EC texts. In spite of the diversity of sources, there is a systematic background unity in the way in which conflicts arising from the insolvency are dealt with. As we will see later, this idea of a "coherent whole" (or single system) is important for the interpretation of the different texts.

4. SPHERE OF SUBSTANTIVE APPLICATION: INSOLVENCY PROCEEDINGS INCLUDED (ARTICLE 1.1 AND ARTICLES 2.a AND 2.c)

33. The Insolvency Regulation applies both to *winding-up* procedures and *reorganisation* proceedings. Pre-insolvency voluntary restructuring negotiations and schemes aimed at preventing insolvency proceedings remain outside the sphere of application of the Regulation (e.g. the *règlement amiable* of French law).[45]

> *Rationale.* Although it was the subject of a certain amount of debate while the 1995 Convention on Insolvency Proceedings, the immediate predecessor of the Regulation, was being drawn up, the final solution by which the Regulation applies to both insolvency proceedings aimed at *winding-up* the assets of the debtor, and to those aimed at *restructuring* the company is very sensible.[46] Otherwise a large number of proceedings would have been left out and the solution would have been difficult to justify in practice. Nevertheless, the decision to include restructuring proceedings was taken when negotiations had already reached a very advanced stage, which explains why the regime of the Regulation is basically worded with a view to winding-up processes. In this sense, the winding-up proceedings are "the shadow under which the Regulation was drawn up".

34. However, the Insolvency Regulation only applies to those national insolvency proceedings which are expressly *listed in the Annexes* of the Regulation. To be included in these Annexes the proceedings must meet certain generic *conditions* which are established in Article 1.1.

35. According to this Article, Regulation *shall apply to collective insolvency proceedings which entail the partial or total divestment of a debtor and the appointment of a liquidator*. There are four relevant conditions:

(a) The proceedings must be *collective* proceedings, i.e. the regulation does not apply to procedures for the enforcement of individual claims, but only to those in which all of the creditors attempt to settle their claims on a joint basis.

(b) The proceedings must be based on the *insolvency* of the debtor; the Regulation does not specify this situation. The underlying idea is the situation of "financial crisis" of the debtor, but the exact nature of the conditions by which this

---

[45] BALZ (1996b), p. 948; LÜKE (1998), p. 284; GOTTWALD (1999), p. 154.

[46] For a more detailed treatment, VIRGOS, pp. 10–11; LÜKE, (1998), p. 284. On the need to regulate both alternatives, VON WILMOWSKY (2000), p. 203.

crisis manifests itself is established by national law[47] (on the role of the Annexes, see the following section).

(c) The proceedings must involve a *total or partial divestment* of the debtor, i.e. the transfer to another person, the insolvency representative, of the powers of administration and of disposal over all or part of his assets, or the limitation of those powers through the intervention and control of the debtor's actions.[48] The divestment may be partial with regard to the assets or with regard to the debtor's powers, denoting in both cases some degree of loss of control over his affairs (e.g. the debtor continues to operate the business but requires the authorization or supervision of a liquidator to carry out certain acts). The Regulation excludes any type of proceedings which leave the debtor in *full* control of his estate, with the consequence that the court does not appoint a liquidator or administrator once the proceedings commence (i.e. proceedings which fully adopt the "debtor in possession" principle).[49] The legal nature of that divestment according to the applicable national law is irrelevant.

(d) The proceedings must entail the appointment of a *liquidator*, which is the term that the Insolvency Regulation employs to refer to the person or body responsible for administering the estate or supervising the debtor's business. This latter requirement is a corollary of the previous one: the divestment must entail the appointment of a liquidator. The Regulation employs a very wide concept of "liquidator" (see Article 2.b): any person or body whose function is to administer or liquidate the assets of which the debtor has been divested, or to supervise the administration of his affaires. The purpose of this definition is to encompass *any person or body* upon which those functions are conferred. National insolvency laws refer to this person or body by a number of different titles (administrator, supervisor, receiver, trustee, commissioner, liquidator, etc.) and in comparative law the term "insolvency representative" is gaining acceptance. When this function is carried out by the court itself, this must be recorded in Annex C (*infra*).

> *Non-judicial proceedings.* Not all procedures included are of a judicial nature. The Insolvency Regulation does not even require the intervention of a *judicial or administrative authority*. It allows the non-judicial collective proceedings which are common in countries such as the United Kingdom or Ireland (e.g., the *creditors' voluntary winding-up*) to be included within its sphere of application. The practical importance of these proceedings and the fact that they offer procedural guarantees equivalent to those of judicial proceedings made it advisable to include them in the Regulation.[50]

36. Article 2.a requires the proceedings in question to have been expressly included in *Annexes A and B* of the Regulation. The reason behind this requirement

---

[47] VIRGOS/SCHMIT Report, Margin No. 49. When the same proceedings can fulfil different ends (as is the case with the *winding-up* proceedings of the British and Irish systems), they will only be included in the Insolvency Regulation when they are based on the insolvency of the debtor, *Ibid.* and EIDENMÜLLER (2001a), p. 4; WIMMER (2002), p. 2503.

[48] See VIRGOS/SCHMIT Report, Margin No. 49.

[49] BALZ (1996b), p. 502; FLETCHER, in MOSS/FLETCHER/ISAACS, p. 37; TORREMANS, p. 141.

[50] VIRGOS/SCHMIT Report, Margin No. 52; VIRGOS, p. 12; TORREMANS, p. 141.

is to avoid problems of characterisation: in a sector where national laws diverge considerably, a *closed-list system* provides security with regard to proceedings to which the Regulation applies. That is why only the proceedings expressly designated in the lists are considered as "insolvency proceedings" for the purposes of the Regulation and it only applies to them.[51] It is important to highlight that once the proceedings have been included in the list, the Regulation applies without any further review by the courts of other Member States. It is not necessary for the national courts to determine in every case whether or not a particular insolvency process satisfies the four conditions. The list system facilitates the application of the Regulation as, in practice, national courts and authorities will only have to examine whether or not the foreign proceedings are included in the list. Member States can modify the list of their proceedings by means of the revision mechanism provided for in Article 45.

37. The same is true in the case of *liquidators*; for equivalent reasons the Insolvency Regulation requires the States to indicate who, according to their law, can be considered as liquidators (*Annex C*).

38. The *Directives* on *credit institutions* and *insurance undertakings* apply to reorganisation measures and winding-up proceedings. Unlike the Regulation, the Directives expressly define the measures and proceedings to which they apply without reference to the situation of insolvency of the debtor and without requiring these measures and proceedings to be specifically included in any Annex. The significant aspect is the intervention of an administrative or judicial authority and the aim of the proceedings: that they are aimed either at maintaining or re-establishing the financial situation of an entity or company and affect the pre-existing rights of third parties (*reorganisation measures*); or that they entail the liquidation of the assets of the institution in question and the distribution of the result (*winding-up proceedings*). For more detail regarding the meaning and scope of these concepts, see Article 2 of both Directives.

5. Sphere of Application in Time (Articles 43 and 47)

39. The Regulation came into force on 31 May 2002 (Article 47). With regard to its sphere of application in time, the Regulation has no retroactive effects.

(a) The Regulation only applies to insolvency proceedings opened after its entry into force (Article 43). The time of the opening of proceedings is determined by the Regulation itself (Article 2.f): the time at which the decision of opening becomes effective (not the filing of the request for opening), regardless of whether or not the decision is final. This rule has absolute scope, which means that where insolvency proceedings against a specific debtor have been opened before the Regulation enters into force in a Member State, the proceedings which are thereafter opened against this same debtor, and for the same situation, shall not be subject to the provisions of the Regulation, regardless of whether the said later proceedings are main or secondary according to the rules of the Regulation.

---

[51] Virgos/Schmit Report, Margin No. 48; see also, Duursma-Kepplinger/Duursma, p. 507.

Example. If territorial proceedings have been opened against the debtor in a Member State before the Regulation enters into force, and main proceedings are opened in another different State after the Regulation enters into force, the regulation will not apply to either of the two proceedings. And vice versa: if main proceedings have been opened in a State prior to the Regulation entering into force and then territorial proceedings are opened in another, the Regulation will not apply either.[52] The Regulation will only apply when the first insolvency proceedings against a specific debtor have been opened *after* the Regulation has come into force.

On some occasions, national courts have based their rulings on an *"anticipated application"* of an EC law. This possibility is not incompatible with the Insolvency Regulation. The Regulation only imposes its application from the date on which it enters into force; the possibility of applying it before that date is, therefore, a question of national law. Anticipated application of a law which, while not yet in force, will come into in force in the near future has been used by Continental courts as a gap-filling hermeneutic recourse when there is no rule which provides for the case and the new rule fits into the existing system.[53] The legal system is a dynamic system and the use of this recourse facilitates transitions, i.e. it helps to reduce the brusqueness of changes in the law.

(b) The Insolvency Regulation does not modify the law applicable to acts carried out by the debtor before the entry into force of the Regulation. In order to be clear on this point, it is expressly laid down in Article 43 *in fine* that those acts *shall continue to be governed by the law which was applicable to them at the time they were done.*

Rationale. Article 43 *in fine* is a rule of prevention. It seeks a result similar to the first sentence: that there will be no retroactive effects with regard to the applicable conflict of laws rules. The first sentence refers to insolvency proceedings and indicates that the Regulation only applies to proceedings opened after it comes into force. The second sentence refers to juridical acts (e.g. contracts) and states that the conflict of laws rules which determined the law governing the legal acts of the debtor before the Regulation came into force (and, logically, before the opening of proceedings governed by the Regulation) continue to apply in determining their juridical regime. The safeguard which it establishes should not be interpreted any further than this; specifically, it should not be used to subject the *effects of an insolvency proceedings opened according to the Regulation* to a law other than that which is established by the Regulation itself, on the grounds that the acts were carried out before the regulation came into force. Article 43 *in fine* refers to the juridical acts themselves, not to the effects which the proceedings could have on them, as these are governed by the Regulation. To interpret it in any other way would lead to unacceptable results: in no system are the effects of the insolvency determined by reference to the moment the act is carried out, but rather (with some exceptions) by reference to the moment when the insolvency proceedings are opened. For this reason, to understand that Article 43 *in fine* governs the effects of the insolvency on acts carried out prior to the entry into force of the Regulation

---

[52] See VIRGOS/SCHMIT Report, Margin No. 304. It is true that this is not deduced from a first reading of Article 43, but it can be justified with a teleological interpretation: the *ratio* of the law is to prevent different insolvency proceedings dealing with the assets of the same debtor to be subject to different rules of *Private International Law*, see EIDENMÜLLER (2001a), p. 2, footnote 2; WIMMER (2002), p. 2531.

[53] For all, with further references, KRAMER, pp. 159–160. This has been the case in the Netherlands, see WESSELS, "Anticipation and Application of the EV Insolvency. Regulation in the Netherlands", in *Insolvency Law & Practice* (forthcoming).

would mean, *de facto*, that by imposing the earlier point in time, the rule on non-retroactivity would be modifying the rules previously in force in the Member States. Furthermore, to understand that Article 43 *in fine* safeguards the insolvency effects of the law which would apply to insolvency proceedings before the Regulation enters into force (but which have not been opened) would mean that the same insolvency proceedings would produce different effects according to the date of the legal acts affected.

40. For their part, the *Directives* on *credit institutions* and *insurance undertakings* establish an implementation phase in the Member States of three years for the former (up until 5 May 2004), and two years for the latter (up until 20 April 2003). The provisions adopted by Member States to enforce the Directives will only apply to restructuring measures or winding-up processes initiated after these dates (see Articles 34.1 II and 31.2, respectively).

6. Relationship with other Community Legal Instruments and International Conventions (Article 44)

41. The Insolvency Regulation replaces the *International Conventions* signed between *two or more Member States* in those matters governed by the former, provided that the proceedings have been opened after its entry into force. Article 44.1 lists the Conventions excluded.

Exception. Bilateral Treaties may still play a role in areas not covered by the Insolvency Regulation. For example, they can still deal with recognition issues with regard to insolvency proceedings opened in one of the contracting States concerning a branch of a company whose centre of main interests is outside the Community.[54]

The Regulation, on the other hand, does not replace the International Conventions between Member States and *non-Member States* concluded before its entry into force (Article 44.3). On this last point, the Council has included a declaration according to which a Member State may enter into agreements with non-Member States regarding the same area as the Regulation, when the agreement in question does not interfere with the functioning of the said Regulation (OJ, 30 June 2000, p. 1). The aim is to prevent any misunderstanding that the "communitarisation" of this area of law means that these agreements cannot be entered into.

Conventions concluded or ratified after the Regulation enters into force: The drawing up in different international fora, such as the Hague Conference or UNIDROIT, of conventions on specific matters which contain rules on insolvency can lead to problems of demarcation between the different texts. The above declaration by the Council provides guidelines for resolving these problems.[55] (a) Where there is no incompatibility or interference between both texts (e.g. when the new conventions only deal with substantive law), the possible

---

[54] Torremans, p. 146.

[55] See also Borras, pp. 405–415; Duursma-Kepplinger/Duursma, p. 511, with further references.

entering into of these agreements ceases to be a problem. (b) Where the texts are incompatible, individual States should refrain from entering into such agreements, otherwise they would jeopardise the uniformity imposed by the Regulation. The powers to ratify these agreements belong to the European Community. Once ratification has taken place, and unless expressly otherwise provided for in the Convention (e.g. by means of a clause regarding the relationship of texts), the convention will apply in place of the Regulation on the basis of the principle of *lex specialis derogat generalis*. (c) When the Regulation and a Convention are incompatible, and the latter has been ratified on an individual basis by one Member State, but not by all, (thereby contravening the above rule), the national judge must refrain from applying the Convention. Remember that the Regulation only applies to intra-Community judicial proceedings. The Convention may continue to play a role beyond this sphere, but not within it. In this case, the Regulation constitutes the *lex specialis*, without prejudice to any international liability incurred by the State in question.

42. The *UNCITRAL Model Law on cross-border insolvency* represents a truly international standard in the matter. It governs certain, fundamentally procedural, aspects of situations of international insolvency.[56] As its name indicates, it is a "model law". It is not a law with legal force, but rather a law which States can use as a model for designing their own international insolvency law. In this respect there is no risk of incompatibility or direct collision with the Insolvency Regulation. On the other hand, as recognised in the Guide to Enactment of the Model Law itself (paragraph 18), the Model Law has taken into account the solutions provided by the 1995 Convention on Insolvency Proceedings, the immediate predecessor of the Insolvency Regulation. This anticipates a high degree of compatibility between the solutions provided by the Insolvency Regulation and the laws in force in States that enact the UNCITRAL model law.

43. In principle, the Insolvency Regulation does not present problems of compatibility with other instruments of *Community legislation*. Any such problems which might arise would be resolved according to the general rules of Community law. In particular, their relationships with the Regulation on Jurisdiction and the Recognition and Enforcement of Judgements in civil and Commercial Matters (Regulation 44/2001, of 22 December 2000, also known as "Brussels I") are amicable because the latter text expressly excludes "bankruptcy, conventions between bankrupt and creditors and other similar proceedings" from its sphere of application (Article 1.2.b). The criteria for defining the limits of the respective spheres of substantive application were established by the ECJ. In order to prevent gaps or overlaps between the two texts, the Insolvency Regulation itself applies this same criterion. For more detail, see *infra* No. 76 and ff.

---

[56] See the text, together with the Guide to Enactment, in www.uncitral.org. Several States have enacted legislation based on the model law. On this topic see, WESSELS (2003), pp. 169–172.

Part II

The Main Insolvency Proceedings

Chapter 4

International Jurisdiction

1. The Centre of Main Interests: General Aspects (Article 3.1)

44. According to Article 3.1 of the Insolvency Regulation, *"The courts of the Member State within the territory of which the centre of a debtor's main interests is situated shall have jurisdiction to open insolvency proceedings"*. This provision enables the courts of the Member State where the centre of the debtor's main interests is located to open insolvency proceedings with the character of *"main proceedings"*. Such proceedings have universal scope and are intended to encompass all the debtor's assets on a worldwide basis and to affect all creditors, independently of where they are located. Only one main insolvency procedure may be opened under the Insolvency Regulation.[57]

45. The "centre of main interests" (*COMI*) is an *autonomous concept*, i.e. a concept peculiar to the Insolvency Regulation. As such, its meaning is uniform and independent of the national laws of the Member States; the latter may not modify that meaning. The method to determine the centre of main interests must be the same for all Member States.

> *Terminology.* An *"autonomous concept"* is understood to mean a concept peculiar to a text of uniform law (whether substantive, procedural or relating to Private International Law), which, given the international origin of the rule and the unifying function which it fulfils, must have a meaning which is also uniform and independent of the national law where this text is inserted. Otherwise the concepts become "nationalised" and the divergent national definitions reproduce the legislative divergence which the uniform text was supposed to eliminate

46. The relationship of the Insolvency Regulation to previous drafts and other international legal instruments sheds some light that is relevant for the understanding of this concept. On the one hand, the centre of the debtor's main interests is intended to represent the *focal point of the economic life* of the debtor. On the other hand, it presupposes a degree of *"institutionalised presence"* in the forum; and this explains the *prima facie* value which a formal connecting factor such as the registered office has for the purpose of determining the centre of the debtor's main interests (see the presumption established in Article 3.1, last sentence).

> *Origin.* The concept of the "centre of main interests" has its intellectual origin in the "real seat" principle (*Sitztheorie*) employed by the Company law of certain continental European

---

[57] Virgos/Schmit Report, Margin No. 73.

countries in order to identify the *lex societatis*.[58] What was sought was an objective criterion which revealed a real connection between a company and a specific State. The criterion which best expresses this connection was thought to be the place where the central
management and control of a company are exercised: the place where its actual head office
is established. This idea was adopted by the 1980 Draft Convention between the Member
States of the EC on bankruptcies, concordats and similar proceedings. Article 4 thereof
used the effective "centre of administration" as the criterion for international jurisdiction to
open insolvency proceedings. The draft failed and was abandoned. Later on, the 1990
Istanbul Convention was drawn up under the auspices of the Council of Europe and dealt
with certain international aspects of insolvency. In this later convention the decision was
taken to avoid the concept of centre of administration, which was too closely associated
with companies and legal persons, and the concept of "centre of main interests" was
coined to include individuals (see Article 4 thereof). The Insolvency Regulation combines
both experiences; it takes the concept of centre of main interests from the 1990 Istanbul
Convention and adds a definition very similar to that contained in the 1980 Draft regarding
the concept of actual centre of administration (which was understood to be *"the place
where the debtor usually administers his main interests"*).[59] This concept – the centre of
main interests – was also later adopted by the 1997 UNCITRAL Model Law on cross-border insolvency. According to its Article 2.b, a "foreign main proceedings" means a foreign
set of proceedings "taking place in the State where the debtor has the centre of its main
interests". Point 72 of the Guide to Enactment of the internal law of the Model Law,
expressly states that this concept is taken from the 1995 Convention on insolvency proceedings, the immediate predecessor of the Regulation.

47. The centre of main interests is a concept of *open character*. This open character gives it the advantage of flexibility: the concept can be applied to any class of
debtor and to any type of organisational structure of that debtor. This is reasonable,
because the Insolvency Regulation does not make distinctions on the basis of either
the capacity or nature of the debtor (trader or non-trader, public or private) or the
way it is structured (association, company, foundation, etc.). However, this same
open texture may also be its greatest weakness, because its practical application
implies a previous examination and evaluation of the debtor's circumstances. This
requires time and increases the risks of different conclusions being reached by different Courts. For this reason, the Insolvency Regulation does two important things:
(a) it provides the concept with a *legal definition*, which furnishes a single meaning
for all Member States and channels that examination: *"the centre of main interests
should correspond to the place where the debtor conducts the administration of his
interests on a regular basis and is therefore ascertainable by third parties"* (Recital 13);
and (b) it establishes a *presumption*, which simplifies the application of the rule:
*"In the case of a company or legal person, the place of the registered office shall be
presumed to be the centre of its main interests in the absence of proof to the
contrary"* (Article 3.1).

---

[58] GOTTWALD (1999), p. 155. The German doctrine is perhaps the one which has concerned itself most
with this concept; very comprehensive, PANTHEN, *passim*.
[59] See VIRGOS/SCHMIT Report, Margin No. 75. On the 1980 Draft see the LAMONTEY Report, p. 56 *et seq.*

2. THE CENTRE OF MAIN INTEREST: TEST OF APPLICATION

48. The *legal definition* of the centre of interests is contained in Recital 13 of the Preamble of the Insolvency Regulation. According to this definition, the centre of main interests should be understood to mean *"the place where the debtor conducts the administration of his interests on a regular basis and is therefore ascertainable by third parties"*.

Value of the definition. The concept of centre of main interests is not defined in the text of the Regulation, but rather in one of the recitals contained in the Preamble. The function of this definition is the same as that of the definitions contained in the Articles themselves (see Article 2): to establish the technical meaning of the concept in the context of the Regulation. Recitals do not contain normative provisions and do not have binding force. However, they form part of the legislation and are important for its interpretation as they state the reasons on which the legislative act is based and illustrate the purpose served by its rules or, as the case may be, its concepts. The European Court of Justice has held that a preamble to a Regulation may be referred to where the text of the Regulation is imprecise. Seen thus, this definition should have the same value as the definitions contained in Article 2. Neither the systematic argument nor the linguistic argument should be used to weaken this value.

(a) From the *systematic* point of view, the location of the definition in the preamble may appear strange, but it is due to *genetic reasons* related to the peculiar process of drawing up the Regulation; in no way does it respond to a legislative intention to "degrade", or to place some definitions on a lower hierarchical scale than others. As we have already explained (see No. 4) the text of the Insolvency Regulation stems from the text of the 1995 Convention on Insolvency Proceedings, which it practically reproduces without variations. The above-mentioned 1995 Convention on Insolvency Proceedings was accompanied by an explanatory report entrusted with explaining the concept of centre of main interests. The official nature with which this Report, which was also negotiated, was to be endowed explained this "delegation". When negotiating the transformation of the Convention into an EC Regulation, the Member States took two decisions. The *first* was to modify the text of the Convention only in very exceptional cases. In line with this decision, only those modifications which proved necessary in order to accommodate the text to its new role as a piece of EC legislation were accepted in practice, together with two changes in wording: one to clarify the fact that the concept of right *in rem* encompassed figures such as the *floating charges* of the laws of United Kingdom and Ireland; and another to clarify the use of languages in multi-lingual States. The *second* decision was to incorporate in the preamble of the Regulation those aspects of the Report which were considered especially relevant for the purposes of ensuring the correct understanding of its rules; this explains why the definition of the centre of main interests, initially delegated to the explanatory report, now reappears in the recitals of the Regulation.

(b) From the *linguistic* perspective, the wording of the definition is explained by its location in the preamble. In effect, Recital 13 of the Insolvency Regulation defines the centre of main interests by saying that the said centre *"should* correspond" to the place of administration. The use of the conditional "should" does not detract force from the definition when compared with other alternative wordings. No legal relevance should be attached to the formula used to introduce the definition; in particular, it should not be taken advantage of as a literal argument to interpret the legal definition as being an *"open* definition", which invites that meaning to be given to the concept of centre of interests, but does not prevent another different interpretation. The use of the verb in the conditional tense ("should") is a stylistic formula which is used in many other recitals in the Preamble to the Regulation by way of anticipating what, in accordance with the normative part of Regulation, "shall be". Thus,

Recital 9 states that the Regulation "should apply" regardless of whether the debtor is a natural person or a legal person, a trader or an individual; there is no doubt that the Regulation "applies" in all of these cases. The same can be said, for example, of Recitals 16, 21, 22, 23, 26, 28, 29, 30 and 31. There is no argument in favour of a different meaning. The genetic argument also speaks in favour of the legal irrelevance of the stylistic formula used. The Report of the 1995 Convention on Insolvency Proceedings, predecessor of the Regulation, clearly states that the concept of centre of main interests "must be interpreted" in this way. When drawing up the Preamble of the Regulation at no time was an attempt made to vary the character of the definition, but rather simply to insert it while respecting the style of the Preamble.

49. This definition results from the combination of *three fundamental ideas*: (a) the *primacy of the administrative connection*; (b) the *primacy of the external sphere*; and (c) the *principle of unity*. These three ideas – explained in more detail below – can also be reformulated as *directives* for determining, in each particular case, the centre of main interests of any given debtor. This will make adjudication more predictable.

2.1. First directive: the primacy of the "administrative connection"

50. According to the legal definition, the important factor when determining the centre of debtor's interests is the place where the interests are *administered*, not the place where those concrete interests are located. It is therefore the place from where the debtor conducts a certain activity, the administration of his main interests, that is relevant for defining jurisdiction. "Interest" is a very general term which can be employed to denote a right, claim, title or legal share in something. Here, it must be understood as referring to the debtor's *economic* affairs. "Administration" is intended to mean the *management and control* of those interests.

Rationale. Although not stated expressly anywhere in the Regulation, the drafters intentionally avoided words too suggestive of industrial, commercial or professional activities. The general term "interest" was considered appropriate, because it represents the only common denominator among the different debtors to whom the Regulation applies. In this way, the same criteria (centre of main interests) serves to establish international jurisdiction both over commercial and professional debtors, as well as over individuals and legal persons that do not conduct entrepreneurial activities. "Administration" is also a term sufficiently neutral to be applied to natural and juridical persons, for everyone administers his property. Hence, to speak of the administration of the "interests" is equivalent to speaking of the administration of the debtor's business, profession, or property.

51. Consequently, the *"administrative connection"* (which is established in the place of *management and control*) must take precedence over both the *"operational connection"* (which is established in the *place of business or operations*) and the *"asset connection"* (which is established in the place where the *property* is located). In layman's terms, what the definition tells us is that in order to establish international jurisdiction over a debtor what matters is where the "head" (i.e. the directing power) is located, not the "muscles" (i.e. the assets, the factors of production, the market, etc.).

Difficulty. According to the definition, the relevant factor is the place where the administration of the company or legal person in question is situated, not the place where the people or the shareholders who possess control *over* the company are located. Thus: (a) in the case of *subsidiary companies* the relevant connection will be the place where the centre of administration (i.e. the head office) of the subsidiary company is located. The fact that the decisions of this subsidiary are taken in accordance with instructions emanating from the parent company or from shareholders living elsewhere does not modify the rule of international jurisdiction over this company (with regard to corporate groups, see further No 61). (b) *Companies with "mobile" administration:* in the case of debtors which have a mobile organisational structure which transfers its management to the country of operations or rotates it periodically, the centre of interests is the one established at the moment the request for the opening of the proceedings is presented.

2.2. Second directive: the primacy of the "external sphere"

52. Another relevant aspect when determining the centre of main interests is the *external organisation* of the debtor: how the debtor manifests itself *on a regular basis* towards the outside world (i.e. in the market). This is why the definition requires that such place be *ascertainable by third parties*. The prevailing principle here is that of appearance or "visibility" (hence the relevance of "institutional" connections). In the case of companies and legal persons, the Insolvency Regulation does not expressly require any physical connections (e.g. premises or operational facilities); however, the legal definition presupposes a certain degree of *material presence* of the entity within the forum: "place" is a physical criterion denoting territorial location.

53. In a *positive* sense, this directive entails the prevalence of the representative sphere (i.e. the external manifestation) over the internal organisational sphere. In a *negative* sense, it means that, *vis-à-vis* creditors and third parties, the debtor cannot assert as his centre of main interests a place other than the place from which he is seen in the market as taking his decisions and centralising the management of his affairs. This should preclude a debtor from pleading that his true centre of main interests is in a different State from that in which external parties have been led to believe.[60]

Development. The term *on a regular basis* ("habitual" in other linguistic versions of the Insolvency Regulation) indicates a quality of presence. It suggests a degree of continuity being required and it implies an idea of normality (i.e. a reference to the way things are usually arranged). In order to determine if a given place complies with this requirement, the *duration* and the *continuity* of the contacts, both past and prospective, will be taken into account, as well as any other data which reveals, from the point of view of an external observer, a *stable link* with the forum.[61] It is worth adding that the term "regular" is used to express a degree of permanence, but not to implicitly impose a minimum time of prior presence in the forum (e.g. "more than six months") before the connection can be established. The trans-border *transfer* of debtor's centre is studied in No. 69.

---

[60] FLETCHER, in MOSS/FLETCHER/ISAACS, p. 40.

[61] See, albeit with reference to the concept of residence, Resolution No. 72 of 18 January 1972 of the Council of Ministers of the Council of Europe.

This directive of interpretation ensures that the connection can be anticipated by third parties (i.e. by potential creditors). The *objective ascertainability* of the centre of main interests is an important factor, as it enables creditors to calculate the commercial or financial risk they face in the event of the debtor's insolvency. In this way, they will be able to shape and adjust their transactions to the lesser or greater risks they are incurring in when they enter into agreements with "fixed" or "mobile" debtors.[62]

2.3. Third directive: the "principle of unity"

54. This directive is inherent to the very notion of *"centre"*, which is opposed to the idea of a debtor possessing several centres of main interests. The principle of unity implies that a debtor can have only one centre of main interests at any one time (hence the idea of focal point).[63] On the other hand, a centre of main interests must be assigned to all debtors.

55. The Insolvency Regulation enshrines a model based on a *sole* main insolvency procedure eventually supplemented by one or more territorial proceedings; functional considerations (the choice of the State whose courts are competent to open that universal process and whose law is applicable depends upon this criteria) and considerations of legal security (the restricting of forum shopping) justify this logic. Consequently, in the logic of the Insolvency Regulation there can only be a sole centre of main interests for each debtor established in the European Community. For this reason:

(a) If a corporate debtor has two (or more) places of management, it must be determined which of them appears as the *directing centre*, denoting the place where the executive or head office functions are carried out (hereafter place of *"central administration"*), as opposed to the day to day operation of the business.[64] These are functions which, by their very nature, require a single interlocutor, such as: (i) relationships with the providers of funds (shareholders and external financers), including the raising of capital and the publication of accounts; (ii) strategic decision-making and the establishing of policies and corporate objectives; (iii) general supervision of the business and approval of important operations; (iv) central treasury management; and (v) the provision of services which benefit from economies of scale or range for the organisation, in particular the entity's external authority or legal representation.

(b) Where the debtor's interests include activities of different types which are run from different places, the term *"main"* requires to consider both the scale and importance of the interest administered at each place. The one from which he administers his principal interests is the relevant one.

---

[62] VIRGOS/SCHMIT Report, Margin No. 75; VIRGOS, p. 13.

[63] TORREMANS, pp. 150–151.

[64] MOSS/SMITH, in MOSS/FLETCHER/ISAACS, p. 169.

(c) As a *rule of closure* the principle of unity translates into a procedural rule of *lispendens*: once a main procedure have been opened in a Member State, only territorial proceedings can be commenced in the other Member States (see further No. 70).

2.4. Application of the test

56. In principle, given the above explained directives, the following results may be anticipated from the application of the concept of center of main interests:[65]

(a) In the case of *corporate debtors*, the centre of main interests will correspond to the place that appears as its central administration; i.e. the place from which the main activities of the entity are controlled and the ultimate decisions at the highest level are actually made. But, as we will see, (No. 57), to facilitate the determination of the centre of main interests, the Insolvency Regulation establishes a presumption in favour of the place of the registered office.

(b) In the case of *partnerships* and *unincorporated associations* (provided that they can be subject to insolvency proceedings), if no place of administration can be identified, the "operational connections" will regain relevance and the centre of main interests will normally lead to the principal place of business or operations. The presumption established by the Insolvency Regulation may also be applicable (see No. 57).

(c) For *individuals*, if the debtor is engaged in an *independent* business or professional activity, the centre of main interests will normally correspond to the State where he has his business or professional centre (i.e. his "professional domicile"), provided that it is the business or professional activity that is at the root of the insolvency.[66] In other cases, it will be the individual's habitual residence.

Examples. If an *independent* professional has his personal habitual residence in one State and his place of business in another State, the latter is considered to be the centre of main interests. However, if a person has his habitual residence in one State and his *dependent* work in another, the former is considered to be his centre of main interests.

(d) For *separate funds or estates* (provided that they can be subject to insolvency proceedings), the centre of main interests will normally be the place where their external administration is located.

Insolvent estates of deceased persons. What matters is the place of the last domicile of the deceased, not the place of the domicile of the testamentary executor or trustee, which would constitute a new situation in the face of the deceased's creditors.

---

[65] VIRGOS/SCHMIT Report, Margin No. 75; BALZ (1996a), p. 949; TAUPITZ, pp. 326–327; LEIBLE/STAUDINGER (2000), pp. 543–544; WESSELS (2004), *passim*.

[66] VIRGOS/SCHMIT, Margin No. 75; MOSS/SMITH, in MOSS/FLETCHER/ISAACS, p. 169.

2.5. Companies and legal persons

2.5.1. Presumption in favour of the place of the registered office

57. In the case of companies or legal persons the Insolvency Regulation establishes a *presumption* in favour of the *registered office* (Article 3.1, last sentence). The term *"companies or legal persons"* must be understood in a wide sense as encompassing legal persons (whether corporations, associations or foundations) and those *unincorporated associations* and *partnerships* which, although do not have separate legal personality, are subject to insolvency proceedings.

58. We have already looked at the reason for this presumption. The concept of centre of main interests is an open character notion which needs to be specified in each case. In order to facilitate the application of the concept and the taking of decisions regarding international jurisdiction, the Insolvency Regulation establishes a presumption for the case which is considered most problematic, that of *companies* and *legal persons*. In this case, the place of the *registered office* it is presumed to be the centre its of main interests.[67]

> *Rationale.* The reasons in favour of the registered office as the basis of the presumption are *probabilistic*, the more common situation being where the registered office and the effective head office (central administration) coincide in the same State; and also *procedural*, as it is easier to demonstrate connections of a formal nature, such as the registered office, than connections based on factual criteria. Both the parties and the court are *addressees* of the presumption (on this point see No. 65).

59. The presumption is a presumption *iuris tantum*, which accepts proof to the contrary. The possibility of proof to the contrary means that the divergence between the functional realities (i.e. the "reality test") and the registered office (i.e. the "formal test") will be resolved in favour of the former.[68]

However, presumptions are a key instrument for *legal certainty*: In the absence of sufficient elements of proof to the contrary, the judge must accept as certain the legal proposition indicated by the presumption. Seen thus, the presumption fulfils two very important instrumental functions: (a) As a rule on the *burden of proof*. In the absence of elements in favour of another different location, the presumption is taken as valid and it is the registered office connection which counts; the burden of proof will rest upon any party wishing to displace its application (b) As a *rule for resolving doubts:* although other connections are claimed and proven, if the overall assessment of those connections does not provide a reasonably clear result in favour of the location of the centre of main interests in a State other than the State of the registered office, the presumption prevails.

---

[67] See, in spite of the good sense of the solution, LÜKE (1998), p. 288; LEIBLE/STAUDINGER (2000), p. 544.

[68] See Re Daisytek-ISA Ltd and others, English High Court, chancery division, 16 May 2003 (2003) LLpr, pp. 467–468; see, in relation with this case, WESSELS (2004), pp. 20–24, with further references,

Limits of the presumption. The circumstances of a particular debtor may be such that it is impossible to identify one State as the State where the centre of main interests is located even with the help of the presumption. It may occur, for example, that the presumption does not resolve the problem because the doubt is not between the State of the registered office and another State, but between two States other than the State of the registered office; this can occur if the connection with the State of the registered office is clearly weaker than the connection with any of the other two States. There is little sense in applying the presumption in order to resolve the doubt, as this will lead to an inappropriate State (i.e. to a State without material connections). These cases will have to be resolved using the directives of interpretation discussed previously, alone.

60. The term *"registered office"* is used in the English version, while the term *"statutory seat"* is used in other linguistic versions of the Insolvency Regulation (cfr. *"siège statutaire"*, *"satzungsmäßiger Sitz"*, *"sede statutaria"*, *"sede estatutária"*, *"domicilio social"*). These are autonomous concepts which make it unnecessary for a Member State to refer to its rules of private international law to locate the seat of a company or legal person. The "statutory seat" is the place designated by the founders or the members of a company or legal person as official address of the entity. The statutory seat is located at the place pointed out as such in the instrument of formation of the entity or its statutes, or in a separate document subject to the requirements of publication, if any, laid down by the law in accordance to which the entity is constituted.

The concept of statutory seat is known in the Company Laws of all Member States, but not in United Kingdom and Ireland, where the domestic concept of registered office is narrower. In the Insolvency Regulation both concepts, the registered office and the statutory seat, must be construed as *interchangeable*, in order to ensure the equality of rights and obligations deriving from Article 3 for all Member States and for all persons concerned.[69] This may give rise to problems, since the concepts of the Insolvency Regulation, although autonomous in their definition, must be applied to companies and legal persons governed by national laws. To solve a similar problem, Regulation 44/2001 on civil jurisdiction and enforcement incorporates a new rule which facilitates the application of the concept of statutory seat with regard to these two countries. According to its Article 60.2, *"For the purposes of the United Kingdom and Ireland "statutory seat" means the registered office, where there is no such office anywhere, the place of incorporation or, where there is no such place anywhere, the place under the law of which the formation took place"*.

The same rule can be applied by analogy for the purposes of the presumption established in Article 3 of the Insolvency Regulation, not only in the case of those legal systems in which the concept of statutory seat is unknown (e.g. Ireland or United Kingdom), but also in those cases in which the entity in question has not a "statutory seat" (as may happen with some civil companies or partnerships).

---

[69] The same terms are used in the different linguistic versions of Article 48, on the right of establishment of companies and firms, of the EC Treaty.

Rationale. The internal law of all Member States requires that companies and legal persons have their formal seat (statutory seat or registered office) in the State under whose laws they have been constituted (*lex societatis*). The statutory seat of a legal entity and the law under which it is constituted therefore point to the same State. As a consequence of this, both elements may be used as equivalent connecting factors for the purposes of the presumption. This result is consistent with the policies underlying Article 3. While the "centre of main interests" finds its inspiration in the "real seat" theory followed by several continental States for company law purposes (see *supra* No. 46), the statutory seat (and the registered office) finds its origin in the "State of incorporation" theory. For this reason, the combination of both connecting factors in Article 3 has been regarded as a "bridge" or compromise between both theories.

2.5.2. *Groups of companies and combines*

61. In the legal view of all Member States, insolvency is the inability to pay not of an organisation, but of a person, natural or juridical.[70] This is also the view taken by the Insolvency Regulation when it uses in Article 3 the term "debtor", which is a juridical concept denoting a person subject to liabilities. The Insolvency Regulation contains no rule concerning jurisdiction in the case of *groups of companies*, so that each debtor must be considered separately. Under the Insolvency Regulation the concept of centre of main interests refers to each debtor, not to the group.[71]

Rationale. There are reasons which support this approach from the point of view of both substantive law and conflict of laws. From a substantive law perspective, the international treatment of corporate groups faces two risks.[72] One is the risk of *fragmentation*, i.e. dealing in a segmented way with the reorganisation of a corporate combine made up of several companies which are legally independent but which are subject to some form of unified economic control, can prove inefficient. The other is the risk of *over-centralisation*, i.e. consolidating different companies because they have corporate structures linked by relationships of property or shareholder control contradicts the principles of risk diversification and asset partitioning which, for good reasons, form the basis of company law. One aspect of corporate law is the delimitation of the extent to which creditors of an entity have recourse against the *assets of the owners* or other beneficiaries of the entity; however, another essential aspect is the reverse of limited liability, namely, the shielding of the *assets of the entity* from claims by the creditors of the entity's owners or managers.[73] From the conflict of laws perspective, the risk of over-centralization exists if the centre of main interests of the parent company is deemed to be the centre of its subsidiaries.[74] It is difficult to give a reason to justify why the insolvency regime of a company which only operates in one State must be determined by the laws and courts of a State whose only link to the matter consists in the fact that the company's owner is established there. The COMI could not be ascertained by third parties without investigating the group structure; this would make it much more difficult for potential creditors to determine beforehand which insolvency regime would appply to the insolvency of a company. Furthermore, *ceteribus paribus*, a simple change in control would automatically modify that regime and the rights of all

---

[70] European Principles, General Commentary, § 1.

[71] VIRGOS/SCHMIT, Margin No. 74; see also EHRICKE (2002), *passim*; DUURSMA-KEPPLINGER/DUURSMA, pp. 509–510, with further references.

[72] LOPUCKI (2000) p. 2229 *et seq.*

[73] HANSMANN/KRAAKMAN, p. 390.

[74] See VAN GALEN, point 2, p. 3 ff.

creditors, creating strong incentives for forum shopping, since it would make it easier to shift the COMI from one Member State to another. Such a rule would also reduce the scope and effectiveness of the Insolvency Regulation. Member States would not be able to control the insolvency of subsidiaries of non-Member States' companies, even if the activities of the subsidiaries take place only whithin the Community. This would run against the goal of promoting the proper functioning of the internal market. This argument holds true even if it were possible to open secondary territorial proceedings in the Member State where the subsidiary is established: since the scope of these proceedings are limited to the territory of the State of opening, with regard to assets in other Member States, the insolvency of the subsidiary would be governed by the law of the non-Member State where the parent company's COMI is located.

62. To state that the Insolvency Regulation does not provide a special rule of international jurisdiction for these cases does not mean that the reciprocal relationships between persons and entities are not dealt with in the international sphere; it means that they must be dealt with in the framework provided by the general rules. Here it is convenient to distinguish between two different hypothesis.

(1) *Concentration* of centres of main interests in the same Member State:[75] This is the case when the subsidiary companies are incorporated in different States but their centre of main interests can be considered to be located at the group's centre (i.e. where the parent company has its own COMI). If a Member State has international jurisdiction over both the parent and the affiliated entities, it is free to consolidate the insolvency proceedings of them all. This includes substantive consolidation (i.e. the joining of the estates), if the national *lex fori concursus* so permits; and if it does this, other Member States will recognise and treat these proceedings as one main insolvency procedure.[76]

(2) *Dispersion* of centres of main interests: This is the case when the companies forming part of a group have their respective centre of main interests in different Member States. In this case, the problems presented when the insolvent company belongs to group, can be dealt with in different ways.

(a) *In a parent–subsidiary setting.* (i) *"Downwards"*, by *taking immediate control* of the subsidiaries, as the Regulation ensures the automatic recognition of the powers of the liquidator for the whole sphere of the European Community (except Denmark). (ii) *"Upwards"*, by means of possible *liability actions* against the parent company or its directors. Liability actions can be based on *insolvency law* (see ECJ case 133/78), in which case the courts of the insolvent subsidiary may have jurisdiction ex Article 3.1 of the Insolvency Regulation; or be based on *civil and commercial law* (e.g. where ordinary contract, tort or company law permit, under any legal theory, to impose liability on the parent or other members of the corporate group), in which case Regulation 44/2001 on Civil Jurisdiction and enforcement will determine the international jurisdiction (on questions of jurisdiction see *infra* Nos 86

---

[75] See VAN GALEN, with references to case law.
[76] BALZ (1996b), p. 503; VIRGOS/SCHMIT, Margin No. 76; EIDENMÜLLER (2001a), p. 4.

et seq.). Furthermore, if both the parent and the affiliate companies enter into insolvency proceedings, some of the rules of the Insolvency Regulation regarding coordination of parallel insolvency proceedings can be applied by analogy (see No. 424).

> *Subsidiaries used as an establishment of the parent company*. A different situation occurs when the subsidiary seeks to be dealt with as if it were an establishment of the parent company for the purposes of opening insolvency proceedings *over the latter* in the forum. It is accepted that a subsidiary does not, of itself, constitute an establishment or branch of its parent: it has a separate legal entity. However, such a solution could be acceptable in exceptional cases if the subsidiary *appears in the market operating as branch*; the insolvency proceedings (over the parent company) would have a purely territorial scope and would include only the assets of the parent company in the forum.[77]

(b) In a brother–sister setting. "Side-wards", if parallel insolvency proceedings are opened against two or more affiliated companies and international jurisdiction *ex* Article 3.1 IR over each of them corresponds to different States, by applying *by analogy* some of the rules of the Insolvency Regulation on the *coordination of proceedings*; the "common enterprise" is the reason which may justify this analogy. Naturally, given that the national proceedings opened will both be *main* proceedings, this analogical application must be sufficiently flexible (see No. 424).

3. INTERNAL TERRITORIAL JURISDICTION

63. The rule contained in Article 3.1 is a rule of international jurisdiction. *Territorial jurisdiction*, on the other hand, is determined by the law of each State. The language of the precept, which confers jurisdiction on the courts "of the State" (and not "of the place") in which the centre of main interests is located, and Recital 15 leave no room for doubt. In order to know specifically the competent court in the State indicated by Article 3.1, it will be necessary to consult the law of that country.

64. The Insolvency Regulation does not pronounce itself on the issue of internal conflicts, i.e. multi-unit States in which different territories have different insolvency laws. By virtue of the principle of *subsidiarity* (Article 5 of the EC Treaty), internal conflicts are a matter competence of the multi-unit Member State. The same applies when each territorial unit has its own courts. Accordingly, if a debtor's centre of main interests is located in Scotland but his registered office is situated in England, for example, then the Insolvency Regulation does not bar the possibility of opening the main insolvency proceedings in England, provided the internal rules of the United Kingdom allow it. In practice this means that the parties involved must carry out a "double consultation" to identify the competent courts: first they must identify *to which member State* the Insolvency Regulation points, and then they must turn to the law of that Member State to determine the relevant territorial unit.[78]

---

[77] See, GOTTWALD (1999), pp. 155–156; PAULUS, pp. 500–501; *cfr.* EHRICKE, pp. 105–107; DUURSMA-KEPPLINGER/DUURSMA, p. 509.

[78] See FLETCHER (2003), p. 176.

4. OTHER PROBLEMS

4.1. Examination as to jurisdiction

65. An examination of *the grounds of jurisdiction* must be conducted on its own motion (i.e. *ex officio*) by the national courts on the basis of the data supplied by the parties or which the court has a procedurally admissible record of.[79] The presumption contained in Article 3.1 II of the Insolvency Regulation also functions in the framework of this control. Unless the court expresses the reasons to the contrary, the centre of main interests will correspond to the registered office of the company.[80]

> *Rationale.* Although the Insolvency Regulation does not expressly establish this, the examination by the court of its own International Jurisdiction is the only solution consistent with two principles adopted by the regulation: the jurisdiction of the court which is dealing with the matter on the basis of Article 3.1 is exclusive (see No. 96) and the jurisdiction of that court may not be reviewed by the courts of other Member States (see No. 402-b). For the same reason, the national laws of the Member States must give the interested parties an opportunity to dispute the international jurisdiction of the court of opening.

66. In the decision to open insolvency proceedings the court must *expressly record* whether it bases its jurisdiction on Articles 3.1 or 3.2 of the Insolvency Regulation; i.e. it must disclose whether the proceedings in question are main proceedings or territorial proceedings (see Article 21.1).[81]

> *NB.* If the judge concludes that the centre of main interests is not in his State, this does not mean that he cannot open insolvency proceedings against that debtor. If the connection is valid as an establishment (in the sense provided for in Article 2.h), he can open territorial proceedings; and if the centre of interests is not located in the European Community, he will follow the national rules of his State regarding international jurisdiction (the Insolvency Regulation does not apply).

67. The Regulation does not recognise the institution of the *forum non conveniens*. The national judge cannot refuse the jurisdiction conferred upon him by Article 3 of the Insolvency Regulation on the grounds that he considers it more advisable for the proceedings to be opened in another State.

4.2. Reference date

68. The *relevant moment* to establish international jurisdiction is when the application to open insolvency proceedings is filed.[82] It is at this moment that the debtor's

---

[79] VIRGOS, p. 13.

[80] GOTTWALD (1999), p. 155.

[81] VIRGOS, p. 15; BALZ (1996a), p. 949.

[82] See, however, the case of *Geveran Trading Co. Ltd* v. *Kjell Tore Skejvesland*, (2202) EWHC 2898 (Ch), establishing the date at which the court decides to open insolvency proceedings, and WESSELS (2004), p. 12.

centre of main interests must be located in the forum. This is the only reference date that avoids the incentives for forum shopping that the Insolvency Regulation expressly tries to eliminate (see Recital No. 4; see also *infra* No. 70). Changes occurring afterwards have no influence on jurisdiction: the principle of *perpetuatio fori* applies, and thus (provided that proceedings have been opened) a *later transfer* of the debtor to a different State does not alter the jurisdiction of the court.[83]

69. A more delicate problem is presented when the transfer of the center of main interests from one State to another is a *prior transfer*, namely, a transfer which takes place prior to the application for insolvency proceedings, especially if it is *immediately* prior. In principle, a change of domicile, residence or head office is something which any creditor must expect within the European Community framework, where the basic principle is freedom of establishment. The Insolvency Regulation does not require a specific period of time to pass in order for the centre of main interests to serve as grounds for international jurisdiction. Nevertheless, this does not mean that mere nominal changes of location are sufficient. A *"reality test"* is implied in the definition of centre of main interests. This definition requires the new location to be genuine, i.e. it should be based on real facts: it should be the place where the debtor "conducts" a certain activity (*"the administration of his main interests"*) in a certain way (*"on a regular basis"*). It seems clear that a period of more than six months in the new location, for example, satisfies these requirements. But the Regulation does not establish a fixed time limit, and Member States cannot impose it either. Accordingly, the judge must look at the facts and circumstances in each case. Again, the open character of the definition permits its application to any type of debtor and to any type of organizational structure of the debtor.[84]

Rationale. From a theoretical point of view, in the case of a transfer of the centre of main interests there are three possibilities:[85] (a) to maintain the jurisdiction of the State in which the previous centre was located until the debtor has been in the new centre for a certain period of time; (b) to uphold the jurisdiction of the State where the debtor's new centre is located; or (c) to allow the alternative jurisdiction of both States until the debtor been in the new centre for a certain period of time. The Regulation, without saying so, opts for the second possibility; either of the other two solutions would have required an express legislative provision which the Regulation lacks (*cfr.* Article 6 of the 1980 EC Draft Convention on bankruptcy, winding-up, arrangements, compositions and similar proceedings). This solution should be inferred from the Regulation itself, not from a reference to national laws. Furthermore, the Regulation takes into account the moment when the claim is filed. It is true

---

[83] It is highly significant that Article 13 of the proposal for the Directive on the transfer of the registered office does not permit companies against which insolvency proceedings have been opened to transfer their registered office. With regard to the European Company (SE), see Article 8.15 of Regulation 2157/2001, pursuant to which the Company against which insolvency proceedings have been initiated may not transfer its registered office.

[84] National courts have reached different conclusions. Compare the rulings of the Court of Wuppertal, Germany, of 17 June 2003 (the German Supreme Court has required a preliminary decision to the ECS, see ZIP 2/2004, pp. 94ff), the Court of Appeal of Amsterdam of 17 June 2003, JOR 2003/186 and the Netherlands Supreme Court of 9 January 2004, quoted and studied by WESSELS, "Moving House: which court can open Insolvency Proceedings", available at www.iiiglobal.org.

[85] LAMONTEY Report, p. 61; see also HAUBOLD (2003), pp. 36–38 with further references.

that this solution does not make impossible strategic movements of the debtor looking for a favorable insolvency regime. Nevertheless, there are certain elements that reduce this kind of *forum shopping*. (a) First of all, the formulation of the connecting factor set forth by the Regulation. As we have already stated, the formulation in present tense ("conducts") together with the requirement of "regularity" in the administration of the main interests of the debtor imply a certain degree of temporal stability in the new location. If the debtor moves from State 1 to State 2, and immediately afterwards he requests to open the proceedings, it seems obvious that he is not administering his main interests in State 2 on a regular basis. In the case of companies and legal persons, the presumption in favor of the register office makes opportunistic behavior on the part of the debtor (i.e. *forum shopping* in search of a more favorable insolvency law) more difficult, because the cross-border transfer of a register office usually implies a change of the *lex societatis*. And a change of *lex societatis* is normally dependent on the adoption of special protective measures such as appraisal remedies for minority shareholders or the right of creditors to obtain adequate guarantees. Furthermore, the transfer of the head office or central administration of a company from one State to another is relatively costly, or at least more costly than moving other criteria; and if it is not accompanied by actual elements, the change will not be taken into account. (b) Second, the possibility of opening secondary proceedings based on the presence of an establishment and the exceptions to the *lex fori concursus* listed in Articles 5–15 may prevent the advantages associated with this kind of opportunistic behavior. (c) Third, in particular cases, the general rules on fraud may be invoked.

4.3. Conflicts of jurisdiction

70. Only a *single* main insolvency procedure may be opened with regard to the same debtor in the Community. International jurisdiction corresponds, exclusively, to the Member State where the centre of main interests of the debtor is located.[86] The "centre of main interests" is a uniform concept in all Member States, thereby making it necessary for the national court in which the opening of proceedings has been requested to verify its own jurisdiction in accordance with the Insolvency Regulation's test. However, there is always a possibility that different national judges faced with the same facts will interpret the concept of "centre of main interests" in disparate ways. In theory, this can give rise to two types of jurisdiction conflicts: positive conflicts (where two States consider the debtor's centre of main interests to be located in their territory) or negative conflicts (where the courts of the State where the registered office consider the centre of main interests to be located in another State, and the courts of the latter State deny this). In practice, this type of situation should not arise within the scope of the Insolvency Regulation since, as we will see, once the courts of a Member State have adopted a decision regarding their jurisdiction in accordance with the Regulation, this decision must be respected by all other States.[87]

(a) In the case of potential *positive conflicts*, the principle of *temporal priority* applies: when two national courts consider themselves competent to open main

---

[86] VIRGOS/SCHMIT Report, Margin No. 73.

[87] See Recital 22 *in fine* and MOSS/SMITH, in MOSS/FLETCHER/ISAACS, p. 171; REINHART (2003), pp. 872–873; WESSELS (2004), p. 14.

insolvency proceedings, the first procedure opened takes precedence over the second. This solution derives from the automatic recognition of decisions established in Article 16: once the court that deals with the matter first adopts the decision to open proceedings on the basis of the location of the centre of main interests in its territory, the courts of all other Member States are obliged to acknowledge this decision without these courts having the power to control the jurisdiction of the court of origin; i.e. they are compelled to admit that declaration of jurisdiction.[88] If a party in interest does not agree with the jurisdiction of the courts of the Member State that has opened the proceedings, then it must contest that jurisdiction through the means of appeal that exist in that State. The correct application of the Insolvency Regulation by the courts of justice of that State is guaranteed by the possibility of requesting a preliminary ruling on interpretation to the European Court of Justice (see No. 4). By "time of opening" the Regulation (see Article 2.f) understands the moment in which the decision to open proceedings produces effect, independently of whether it is definite or not.

> *Example.* The Daisytek cases are a good example. In May 2003 the high Court in Leeds, England, issued administration orders in respect of 14 group companies (the Daisytek group), ten of them in the United Kingdom, three in Germany and one in France. The English company is a holding for the European group of companies. The English court was satisfied that it had jurisdiction under Article 3.1 of the Insolvency Regulation, as all the companies were managed centrally from England, while the local functions of those companies were limited. This decision has to be recognised in other Member States, even though the issue has triggered a colorfull debate both in Germany and France, where competing applications for insolvency proceedings were made.[89]

Consequently, *lis pendens* problems must be solved in keeping with the following rules: (i) If, once main proceedings have been opened in Member State F1, the opening of main proceedings is requested in a different Member State F2, then this second petition must be rejected. (ii) If, lacking knowledge of the first proceedings, main proceedings are opened in F2, then these second proceedings must be dismissed or transformed into territorial proceedings. (iii) If the petition is first made in F1 and, before the proceedings are opened, it is also requested in F2, then the courts of the second State must wait to hear the decision of the courts of the first State (even when the Regulation takes the time of opening as general reference); this application of the "first in time" rule is justified, in order not to incentive the presentation of "competitive" requests in different Member States. This solution is parallel to the one given to the problems of *lis pendens* by Article 25 of Regulation 44/2001 on jurisdiction and the recognition and enforcement of judgments on civil and commercial matters. The complementary nature of both Regulations support this analogy. The Explanatory Report provides further authority for this interpretation: a reference to the 1968 Brussels Convention (now Regulation 44/2001) was expressly

---

[88] For a more detailed treatment see the VIRGÓS/SCHMIT Report, Margin No. 79; on the problems of determining this date, see LÜKE (1998), pp. 289–290; LEIBLE/STAUDINGER (2000), p. 545.

[89] For further details and references to this and other cases, see WESSELS (2004), points 13–15.

included in its Margin number 79 to suggest the courts to apply, where appropriate, the general solutions already established in the area of intra-Community judicial cooperation. Accordingly, any court other than the court first seised shall of its own motion stay its proceedings until such time as the jurisdiction of the court first seised is established, during which period it may only order provisional, including protective, measures.[90]

Non-Member States. As regards these States, the national rules on recognition and *lis pendens* hold sway, but these must respect the "useful effect" of the Regulation and this entails an important result. The rule that appears in Article 3.1 of the Regulation and establishes exclusive jurisdiction has universal scope. Exclusive jurisdiction must be controlled *ex officio* and produce a "reflex effect" in the national systems of recognition and *lis pendens*: foreign decisions and proceedings that infringe on the exclusive jurisdiction established in favour of Member States cannot be recognized. Consequently, the courts of the Member State before which the recognition of an insolvency proceedings of a third State is alleged must check that the centre of main interests, as defined in the Regulation, is located *neither in the forum nor in another Member State* (there is "community-wide" control on the international jurisdiction). If the latter is the case, then the foreign procedures cannot be recognized as the main proceedings. This control should also be exercised in cases of *litispendence*, so that main proceedings can be opened if the centre of main interests is located in the forum, even if a prior procedure that claims to be universal has been opened in a non Member State. Naturally, this is valid in the absence of an international agreement that might apply between the Member State and the third State (in which case see Article 44.3).

(b) With regard to *potential negative conflicts*, something similar occurs: when the court of a Member State rejects the request to open proceedings on the grounds of its lack of international jurisdiction, the courts of the other States cannot reject their own jurisdiction by claiming that, in their opinion, the court of the first State was the competent one to seize the case. The courts of the other Member States must "admit" this result (they must accept this negative) and take it into account when applying the rules of international jurisdiction of the Insolvency Regulation.

Example. In the case decided by the Svea Court in October 2002,[91] the court considered that a debtor who had stated that his habitual residence was in Spain and who according to the Swedish Register Office was recorded as emigrated to Spain, had no centre of main interest in Sweden. *Ceteris paribus*, if a request for insolvency proceedings is made in Spain, the Spanish Courts will have to accept this "no" and resolve the doubt on whether the COMI was in Sweden or Spain, in favour of the latter.

---

[90] For a different interpretation, see the decision taken by the Parma Civil and Criminal Court in February 19, 2004, in the EUROFOOD IFSC case (I.L.Pr, 2004, Part. 5, p. 273). EUROFOOD IFSC, a company with registered seat in Dublin, Ireland, acted as a financial vehicle for the Parmalat group of companies. Parmalat SpA, with its seat in Parma, Italy, was the parent company of the group. The Italian ruling holds that the fact that proceedings were pending in Ireland was not an obstacle to the admissibility of the petition for a declaration of insolvency of the same debtor in Italy, where it considered that the effective seat of EUROFOOD IFSC was situated, since the mere lodging of a petition in Ireland (where a provisional liquidator had been also appointed) was not sufficient.

[91] SWARTING/LIVIJN, *passim.*

5. SCOPE OF INTERNATIONAL JURISDICTION

71. In order to determine the scope of the international jurisdiction of the courts of the Member State where the debtor's centre of main interests is situated, we shall first address the question of *extra-territorial* scope and then try to define the *subject matter* scope.

5.1. Territorial scope: "world-wide" extension

72. The jurisdiction conferred by Article 3.1 permits the opening of both winding-up and restructuring procedures. In both cases the proceedings are *universal*. This means that they *aim to* encompass all of the debtor's assets and affect all creditors wherever they are, on a *world-wide* and not merely an EC-wide basis. This is a consequence inherent in the normative model chosen. A world-wide scope of the jurisdiction is essential in order to ensure the principle of collective action on an international level. Universal means capable of affecting *all*. Such a scope is *necessarily* implied in the Insolvency Regulation to give it practical effect in the light of its overall scheme and purpose. This extra-Community scope of the main insolvency proceedings is also a logical consequence of the *restriction* accepted by other Member States with regard to the opening of additional proceedings against insolvent debtors situated in the Community: a Member State other than the one where the centre of main interests is situated can only open insolvency proceedings if there is an establishment in the forum and these proceedings can only affect assets located in its territory. To compensate for this restriction, it is logical for the main proceedings to encompass as many assets as possible (i.e. the rest of them) in order to maximize the possibilities of the satisfaction of Community-based creditors. Otherwise, the Insolvency Regulation could self-impair this goal (or make it dependent upon national law), which would be an absurd result.[92] The teleological and genetic arguments also support this conclusion: corporate reorganisation cannot be easily conceived without a forum with universal jurisdiction; and the world-wide scope of the international jurisdiction conferred by Article 3 was *expressly* mentioned in the Explanatory Report for these reasons.[93]

73. Naturally, the Regulation can only guarantee universal scope within the space of the European Community. Outside the European Community the universal scope depends on whether the foreign States in question allow for this or not. Therefore, in order to know if the EC proceedings effectively extend to assets located outside the

---

[92] DEGUÉE, p. 261 (albeit in connection with the Directive on the restructuring and winding-up of credit institutions).

[93] VIRGOS/SCHMIT Report, Margin No. 73. The Regulation recognises the validity of the international conventions and agreements signed by EC States, so this scope can be restricted by the conventions in force (see Article 44.3 of the Insolvency Regulation). Recital No. 11 of the Regulation is not opposed to the statement made in the text; its aim is not to restrict the scope of the universal proceedings, but rather to explain why a full universal model of cross-border insolvency does not constitute an adequate solution within Europe.

European Community (or if they are recognised in other States as main proceedings) the laws of the foreign State in question must be consulted. Some Member States have a rather elaborate network of international treaties which will facilitate this extension. There is no need to labour this point. However, it is important to point out that the Regulation does not self-limit the international jurisdiction of the courts of the centre of main interests to the European Community sphere, nor does it leave this question to national laws.[94] In principle, proceedings ex Article 3.1 are both universal and main (or as universal and main as the non-Member States in question so permit), on a world-wide basis.

5.2. Substantive scope: Insolvency matters

5.2.1. Background

74. The question of what actions or disputes fall within the jurisdiction of the court of opening of the insolvency proceedings is a delicate one. Insolvency proceedings transform the debtor's world; they encompass his assets and influence all of his legal relationships. These broad effects explain why national laws adopt very different solutions on the extent of that jurisdiction, in particular, on the question of whether it is confined to the core procedure itself or extends to other ancillary actions related to the insolvency. This divergence, in turn, illustrates why it is important to establish a uniform criterion for defining the substantive scope of the international jurisdiction of the courts of the State of opening.

75. Article 3 of the Insolvency Regulation confers international jurisdiction on the courts of the debtor's centre of main interests in relation to insolvency proceedings but does not define the extent of this jurisdiction. However, the gap is only apparent. The silence of the Insolvency Regulation has to be understood in the context of the relationship of this Regulation to the prior state of Community law; basically to the 1968 Brussels Convention on Jurisdiction and the Enforcement of Judgments in Civil and Commercial Matters. This silence simply means that the criteria already established by Article 1(2)(b) of the 1968 Brussels Convention as interpreted by the European Court of Justice for the demarcation of civil and commercial disputes from insolvency matters will continue to operate.

76. This solution is supported by the genetic argument, as evidenced by the Explanatory Report,[95] Recital 6 of the Insolvency Regulation and, albeit indirectly, by Article 25. Its justification requires a previous clarification of important policy decisions adopted during the drafting of the Insolvency Regulation.[96]

---

[94] It must be made clear that the Regulation does not attempt to establish two categories of territorial proceedings, *Community-wide* territorial proceedings (ex Article 3.1) and *State-wide* territorial proceedings (ex Article 3.2), but a truly universal one (ex Article 3.1) which does not exclude the possibility of territorial proceedings (ex Article 3.2).

[95] VIRGOS/SCHMIT Report, Margin No. 77.

[96] See also LÜKE (1999), p. 481; HAUBOLD (2002), p. 161.

5.2.2. No regulatory loopholes between the Insolvency Regulation and the Regulation on Civil Jurisdiction and Enforcement

77. The question of the subject-matter scope of the international jurisdiction is linked to the question of the subject-matter scope of the rule which confers it. With respect to insolvency matters, this issue was dealt with by Article 1(2)(b) of the 1968 Brussels Convention and now by an equivalent provision in Regulation on Jurisdiction and the Recognition and Enforcement of Judgments in Civil and Commercial Matters (hereafter *Regulation 44/2001 on Civil Jurisdiction and Enforcement*). This Article excluded from its sphere of application "bankruptcy, proceedings relating to the winding-up of insolvent companies, judicial arrange-ments, compositions and analogous proceedings". As is well known, one of the pur-poses of the Insolvency Regulation was to close that particular gap left by the 1968 Brussels Convention in the Community system of judicial cooperation in civil mat-ters. With this in mind, it was the intention of the drafters of the Insolvency Regulation that this and the 1968 Brussels Convention (now Regulation 44/2001 on Civil Jurisdiction and Enforcement) should *dovetail*, without leaving any loopholes of uniform law *in between*.

78. This purpose could be achieved in two different ways. The *first*, by including a specific provision in the Insolvency Regulation establishing the desired criterion, whether the same or a new one. The *second*, by letting the criterion *already appli-cable* to continue operating. This criterion was established by the Court of Justice of the European Communities in 1979 in a preliminary ruling on the interpretation of the 1968 Brussels Convention (Case 133/78), in order to distinguish civil and com-mercial matters from insolvency matters, the latter being excluded from its scope of application. Article 1(2)(b) of the 1968 Brussels Convention excluded the core insol-vency proceedings themselves; and the European court of Justice clarified that other proceedings arising in the context of an insolvency will also be excluded if they derive directly from the bankruptcy or winding-up and are closely connected with the insolvency proceedings. This criterion is now applicable to Regulation 44/2001 on Civil Jurisdiction and Enforcement, the 1968 Brussels Convention in connection with Denmark, and the 1988 Lugano Convention. The *second* path was chosen. As a consequence of this, proceedings excluded from the 1968 Brussels Convention and Regulation 44/2001 on Civil Jurisdiction and Enforcement, as being characterised, according to the established criteria, as an insolvency matter, now fall under the Insolvency Regulation. In other words, for the purposes of establishing jurisdiction, the *test of exclusion* of "insolvency matters" from the Regulation 44/2001 on Civil Jurisdiction and Enforcement is the same as the *test of inclusion* in the Insolvency Regulation.

NB. This, naturally, only with regard to insolvency proceedings covered by the Insolvency Regulation. The Insolvency Regulation does not apply to all kinds of insolvency proceed-ings, but only to those listed in its Annexes; furthermore, certain debtors (credit institutions, insurance undertakings, investment undertakings) are excluded from its scope. If the insol-vency proceedings opened are not included in that list or the debtor is not an eligible debtor, the test of exclusion from the Regulation 44/2001 will be satisfied, but not the test of inclusion in the Insolvency Regulation. In such cases, the Directives on the restructuring and winding-up of credit institutions or insurance undertakings (regarding non-eligible debtors) or the Private International Law rules of the Member States (regarding unlisted proceedings) will be applicable.

5.2.3. No referral back to national law

79. The solution described above prevents turning to the law of the Member States (i.e. to the *lex fori*) to supplement Article 3 of the Insolvency Regulation in order to define the scope of the matters falling under the international jurisdiction of the court of opening of the insolvency proceedings. This is particularly important if it is taken into account that some authors, under different theories, have sustained a different view. In addition to the genetic argument, there are two reasons which justify why the Insolvency Regulation does not refer the scope of international jurisdiction to the national *lex fori* of the court hearing the case.

80. The *first* is coherence with the principles of Community law. Whenever the *scope* of the rules establishing the jurisdictional *fora* available to the parties has been the object of a preliminary ruling, the ECJ has consistently practised an "autonomous definition" of their concepts, interpreting them in the light of the objectives and scheme of the Community text and not by a referral to the law of one or another of the Member States in question. Any other interpretation would result in an infringement of a basic policy of the whole European system of cooperation in civil matters: that of ensuring as far as possible the equality and uniformity of the rights and obligations arising out of the Community legislation for the States and the persons concerned.

81. The *second* is an argument of "evaluative absurdity", given the unworkable consequences of a referral to national law[97] whereby: (a) some disputes *would fall* under the jurisdiction of the courts of the State of opening according to the Insolvency Regulation, but this Regulation *would not apply* to the recognition of the decisions taken by that very court; for example, when the *lex fori concursus* allows *vis attractiva* but the decisions rendered do not fall within the definition of Article 25.1 II; and (b) in the inverse situation, some disputes *would not fall* within the jurisdiction of the courts of the State of opening according to the Insolvency Regulation, but this Regulation *would apply* to the recognition of the decisions handed down by that court. It is difficult to see how such a solution would contribute to strengthening, within the Community, the legal protection of persons or can be reconciled with the particular aim of this Regulation, which is that cross-border insolvency proceedings should operate efficiently and effectively.

5.2.4. No adoption of a "vis attractiva concursus" principle

82. To varying degrees, the laws of some of the Member States follow the principle of the *vis attractiva concursus*, according to which the national court which

---

[97] Further, HAUBOLD (2002), p. 160.

opened the insolvency proceedings has sole jurisdiction to deal not only with the insolvency proceedings themselves, but also with any disputes arising from the insolvency. This principle, which provides for the concentration in the insolvency court of all litigation relating to the debtor, has not been adopted by the Insolvency Regulation.[98]

83. This was not the case of prior initiatives. The 1980 Draft Convention on bankruptcy, winding-up, arrangements, compositions and similar proceedings included a principle of *vis attractive concursus* in its Article 15: a broad spectrum of actions arising from the insolvency fell within the exclusive jurisdiction of the courts of the State of opening. By contrast with that Draft Convention, the Insolvency Regulation adopts a model of international jurisdiction which can be characterised as a model of non-*vis attractiva concursus*.

> *Rationale.* In Europe, some national laws confer extensive jurisdiction on the courts of the opening of insolvency proceedings, which permits them to deal not only with the insolvency proceedings themselves, but also to hear and determine other disputes to which the debtor (or the liquidator) is a party, thereby displacing other courts, whenever the outcome of those disputes could conceivably have an effect on the estate being administered in the insolvency proceedings. Take the example of a claim, the existence or amount of which is disputed between the parties:[99] a creditor files his claim in insolvency proceedings opened in State 1, where the said claim is contested by the liquidator on the basis of general contract law (for example, on the grounds of breach of the terms of the contract); the contract contained a clause submitting any dispute to the exclusive jurisdiction of the courts of State 2. Does the opening of insolvency proceedings in State 1 prevent the creditor from having recourse to the courts of State 2 to demonstrate that his claim is well founded? The answer depends on the system chosen by each State. A system following a strict *vis attractiva concursus* would require all civil claims against the debtor (or the liquidator) that may affect the estate to be brought before the insolvency courts. On the other hand, in a system without *vis attractiva*, the jurisdiction of the ordinary courts would not change.
>
> This second model is the one followed by the EC Insolvency Regulation. The result of not modifying the general rules of international jurisdiction except where this directly concerns the insolvency proceedings is the following; in our example, in the insolvency proceedings opened in Member State 1, the disputed claim would be accepted as a *conditional or contingent claim*. Meanwhile, the creditor may bring his case to the courts of Member State 2 and obtain a money judgment fixing the amount of his claim. This judgment cannot be directly enforced in State 2, because this State must recognise the insolvency proceedings opened in State 1 and the effects thereof, in particular the stay of executions by individual creditors. However, pursuant to Regulation 44/2001 the money judgment has, in its turn, to be recognised in the State 1, which means this claim must be admitted in the insolvency proceedings opened in State 1. A previous *exequatur* or registration is not necessary in this case, because what it is in question is the recognition of the adjudicated claim in the insolvency proceedings, not the enforcement of the judgment.

84. The exclusion, at the level of international jurisdiction, of the principle of *vis attractive concursus* was clearly affirmed in the Explanatory Report: "*neither this precept (Article 15 of the 1892 Draft Convention) nor this philosophy has been*

---

[98] See a reasoned range of arguments against such a solution in JAHR, *passim.*
[99] Taken from GRASMANN, p. 461.

adopted".[100] Incorporating a model of strict *vis attractiva concursus* would have required an *express rule*, given the radical shift of jurisdictional risks which it involves and given that such a model would have meant a fundamental change in the legal systems of several Member States; a change which it would be unreasonable to expect to occur implicitly.

> *Forum legis*. For this same reason, interpretations which lead to a similar result by *indirect means* must be discarded. Specifically, the idea that a *vis attractiva* of the jurisdiction of the courts of the State of opening can be deduced from the conflict of laws rule contained in Article 4 IR and, in particular, of its long list of matters governed by the *lex concursus*, must be discarded. This reasoning does not take into account the different functions fulfilled by Article 3 (jurisdiction) and Article 4 (law applicable). Article 4 is a uniform conflict of laws rule whose function is to ensure that, whichever court is competent, the law applied will be the same; in this respect it is aimed at *all courts* of the Member States. The question of international jurisdiction is prior to this and is related to the allocation of the burdens of claiming and defending in a given forum. Naturally, only the courts of the State of opening can deal with the opening, conduct and closure of the proceedings. However, the effects of the insolvency on the debtor's relationships is a question which can be raised as an incidental question in any dispute brought before other courts; in order to resolve this incidental question, these courts must apply the conflict of laws rules of the Regulation, including Article 4. The Insolvency Regulation does not follow a model of *forum legis* in which international jurisdiction depends on applicable law.

85. The Insolvency Regulation only deals with international jurisdiction and does not prejudge the solutions regarding jurisdiction in the internal or domestic sphere. If, according to the ordinary rules on international jurisdiction, the courts of the State of opening have jurisdiction to decide on a given action, the Insolvency Regulation does not oppose the possible concentration, in accordance with the applicable rules (internal law or other Regulations or conventions), of such cases before the same Court. In other words, a domestic *vis attractiva* is still possible.

5.2.5. *Matters under the jurisdiction of the court of opening*

86. In technical terms, Article 3 is not a forum of general jurisdiction (i.e. *dispute-blind*), but a forum of special jurisdiction (i.e. *dispute-specific*), albeit a very broad one. However, the Insolvency Regulation does not contain any express rule defining the scope of this jurisdiction or establishing criteria of characterisation. As a part of Community legislation, these criteria should be determined by turning to Community Law and to the objectives of the Insolvency Regulation itself, instead of the national law of the forum. In line with this, two considerations are relevant:

(a) The Court of Justice of the European Communities adopted in its ruling of 22 February 1979 (Case 133/78) a criterion to define the "insolvency exception" of Article 1.2.b of the 1968 Brussels Convention (now Regulation 44/2001), which was based on the nature of the action undertaken *and* the links of this action with the

---

[100] Virgos/Schmit Report, No. 77, *parenthesis added*; for a more detailed treatment, Herchen, pp. 219–229; see also Dordi, pp. 348–351; Wimmer (2002), p. 2504.

insolvency procedure: it is necessary, if decisions relating to bankruptcy and winding-up are to be excluded from the scope of the 1968 Brussels Convention, that *they must derive directly from the bankruptcy or winding-up and be closely connected with the proceedings*. Reasoning from the point of view of the legislative history of the Insolvency Regulation, we have already explained that this *test* must now operate to include those "insolvency matters" in the Insolvency Regulation and, therefore, to define the scope of application of its rules regarding international jurisdiction.

(b) Furthermore, the silence of the Insolvency Regulation with regard to this problem is only partial. Article 25.1 II reproduces the same criterion in order to clarify that foreign decisions characterised, according to it, as decisions relating to insolvency proceedings fall under the scope of the Insolvency Regulation, *even if they were handed down by another court*. We will come back to this provision later. At this point it is important to state that the Insolvency Regulation does not discriminate between the rules on jurisdiction and the rules on recognition with regard to the scope of the subject matter; they were drafted as parallel rules. Consequently, the distinction made by Article 25 between three different types of decisions according to their respective object can also be employed to clarify which applications or disputes fall under the competence of a court with jurisdiction under Article 3.

87. In accordance with this construction, jurisdiction under Article 3.1 encompasses:

(a) The *opening, conduct and closure* of insolvency proceedings and all questions strictly forming part of the core insolvency procedure itself. These include (but are not limited to) matters concerning: (i) the divestment of the debtor and the appointment of a liquidator; (ii) the formation and administration of the estate; (iii) the modification or termination of the stay; (iv) the admission, verification and ranking of claims; (v) the confirmation of compositions or plans; (vi) the collection and liquidation of assets of the estate; (vii) the distribution; (viii) the closure and discharge.

(b) *Actions* which, without forming part of the insolvency procedure itself, derive directly from the insolvency proceedings and which are closely linked with them.

(c) *Preservation measures* ancillary to either of the two previous categories.

88. The second group of cases may pose more problems of demarcation and deserve some additional clarification; the third group will be dealt with later.

89. The basic purpose of insolvency proceedings is not to resolve individual conflicts between the debtor and his creditors, but to collectively realise the rights of the latter and possibly of other interested parties. However, certain applications or disputes are so closely connected to the insolvency proceedings and to the policies of insolvency law that it is advisable for them to fall within the jurisdiction of the courts of opening. This is precisely the case of those applications or claims which fulfil the *double requirement* of both substantive and procedural nature established by the ECJ: (a) from the *substantive* perspective, the legal foundation of the action

sustained must be insolvency law (i.e. the outcome of the proceedings depends upon insolvency law);[101] and (b) from the *procedural* point of view, the action must be closely connected with the insolvency proceedings (i.e. it must be inextricably linked to the proceedings themselves). Only applications which satisfy this *double test* (i.e. fulfil the two requirements) fall under the jurisdiction of the courts designated by Article 3.[102]

> *Autonomous characterization.* Applications are based on national law. National law there-fore provides the juridical attributes of the actions involved; but whether or not a given action falls within the scope of Article 3 is a question of *characterisation*. And this question must be uniformly resolved in the context of Community law and in the light of the "sense and purpose" of the rules of the Regulation (i.e. by "*autonomous* characterisation"). In the above-mentioned case, the Court of Justice relied upon six factors which are relevant for that characterisation:[103] (a) the application can only be made to the insolvency court; (b) only the liquidator can make the application; (c) the time limit for the application is calculated by reference to a given date derived from the insolvency proceedings; (d) the general rules regarding burden of proof are modified in favour of the applicant; (e) if the application succeeds it is the general body of creditors which benefits; (f) if the person made responsible for the liabilities does not discharge them, the court may order the opening of insolvency proceedings against that person (in the case decided, the *de facto* manager) without having to verify whether or not he is insolvent.

90. Establishing a general conclusion on the scope of the jurisdiction of the insolvency courts always entails a risk, because characterisation must always be based on specific grounds, in the light of the action in question. With this reserva-tion, the following matters may be considered as insolvency matters which fall within the jurisdiction of the court designated by Article 3.1 of the Insolvency Regulation.

(a) Disputes between the liquidator and the debtor related to whether or not an asset belongs to the estate; (b) disputes related to the exercise of the powers of the liq-uidator, including any liability which may arise there from; (c) proceedings to deter-mine, avoid or recover preferences, fraudulent conveyances or other acts which are detrimental to the general body of creditors; (d) disputes concerning the ability of the liquidators to assume or reject executory contracts; (e) applications which, within the context of insolvency proceedings opened against a body-corporate, permit the court to decide, in the benefit of the general body of creditors, that the debts of the body-corporate will be borne, wholly or in part, by the managers (whether *de iure* or *de facto*) of the business, and which make it possible to open insolvency proceedings against them without having to verify whether they are unable to meet their liabilities (such as the French action which gave rise to ECJ case 133/78); (f) and, in general terms, those actions which are based on *insolvency law* and are *only possible* while the insolvency proceedings are open (i.e. are not conceivable outside insolvency).[104]

---

[101] The formal location of the rules is not important. What matters is that the legal reason for the rule.
[102] See TRUNK (1998), pp. 114–118.
[103] See LÜKE (1999), pp. 473–478.
[104] JAHR, p. 316.

Exception. Disputes concerning the recognition in another State of the insolvency proceedings or of the appointment of the liquidator are excluded, as well as disputes arising
from an infringement by the liquidator of the laws which govern the exercise of his powers
in other States (see Article 18 IR); jurisdiction to hear these cases belongs to the courts of
the Member State concerned.[105]

91. On the other hand, Article 3 of the Insolvency Regulation does not alter the
international jurisdiction which may correspond to the national courts *vis-à-vis* the
pathology of the specific relationships between the debtor and the creditors or other
interested parties (e.g. the debtor's debtors). These include, for instance: (a) actions
which seek to *determine* the extent, content, validity or amount of a claim (but not
actions which seek to avoid or recover preferences or fraudulent conveyances); (b)
actions to *recover debts* owing to the insolvent debtor; (c) actions for the recovery of
another's property in possession of the debtor; (d) claims to *separate assets* from the
estate based on a right *in rem* ex Article 5 or Article 7 IR; (e) disputes concerning the
right to *set-off* (except in cases of insolvency set-off of procedural nature, see *infra*
No. 182); (f) and, in more general terms, all actions which could have been undertaken even without the opening of insolvency proceedings. In all these cases jurisdiction is not modified by the Insolvency Regulation and follows the general rules.[106]

Rationale. In all of these cases, the object of the application or dispute concerns a contractual or proprietary issue where the insolvency effects are an incidental point and fall outside the scope of Article 3.1 of the Insolvency Regulation. The fact that a claim falls due
beforehand and must be addressed against the liquidator or that the possibilities of a set-
off with regard to a claim against the estate may be modified does not alter the overall
nature of the dispute or give rise to a specific need to modify the legal framework governing the international jurisdiction of the courts.

92. Once the administrator or liquidator comes into play, the contracts and transactions he concludes on behalf of the estate are also subject to the ordinary rules on
international jurisdiction (e.g. Regulation 44/2001);[107] but not disputes concerning
the use of his powers or the avoidance of his acts, which fall under the jurisdiction
of the court of opening, ex Article 3.1 IR.

93. Proceedings related to restructuring schemes and compositions entered into
by the debtor and his creditors *before the commencement* of insolvency proceedings,
also fall outside the scope of Article 3.1 of the Insolvency Regulation. These agreements are of a purely contractual nature and are subject to the ordinary rules regarding international jurisdiction.[108]

94. Applications and disputes *excluded* from the scope of Article 3 of the
Insolvency Regulation are subject to the general regime of international jurisdiction.
In principle, depending upon whether or not the defendant is domiciled in the
European Community, this general regime is provided by Regulation 44/2001 on

---

[105] VIRGOS/SCHMIT Report, Margin No. 166.
[106] VIRGOS/SCHMIT Report, Margin No. 196; TORREMANS, pp. 147–148.
[107] TORREMANS, p. 149.
[108] JENARD Report, p. 57.

Civil Jurisdiction and Enforcement, the 1968 Brussels Convention in the case of Denmark, the 1988 Lugano Convention on Jurisdiction and Enforcement of Judgements in Civil and Commercial Matters, in the case of Switzerland, Norway, and Iceland, or the *national* rules on international jurisdiction.

NB. When the *ordinary rules* on international jurisdiction of the national law are applicable (e.g. the defendant is not domiciled in a Member or Contracting State), this national law may provide for the *vis attractiva* of its insolvency courts. Because it is a dispute *excluded* from both Articles 3 and 25.1 II IR, such a solution will not clash with the rules of the Insolvency Regulation.

5.2.6. *Character of the jurisdiction: exclusive jurisdiction and its exceptions*

95. We have already explained that Article 3 of the Insolvency Regulation confers international jurisdiction with regard to: (a) the *opening, conduct and closure* of collective insolvency proceedings and disputes related to the proceedings themselves; (b) *actions* deriving directly from the insolvency proceedings and which are closely linked with them; and (c) preservation measures adopted in connection with any of the two previous cases.

96. The *character of the jurisdiction* is not the same in all the three cases: jurisdiction in cases (a) and (b) is *exclusive* in principle, while jurisdiction in case (c) is not exclusive but *alternative*, as we will explain later.

97. Furthermore, jurisdiction in case (a) is, by its own nature, *always exclusive* to the courts of the State of opening, while jurisdiction in case (b) is *relatively* exclusive, so that the courts of other States may also deal with the said actions.

The reason for this difference can be outlined here. The exclusive jurisdiction protects the estate and the objectives of the insolvency proceedings. However, in the case of ancillary actions deriving from the insolvency this character may be counterproductive. With regard to these kind of actions, the exclusive character of the jurisdiction must be considered a benefit which may be waived by the liquidator (or any other person legally empowered to do so on behalf of the estate). For this purpose, it is enough that the liquidator (or that other person) makes the application directly to the courts with ordinary jurisdiction; hence the characterisation as "relatively exclusive".

Development. This interpretation finds an indirect confirmation in the literal meaning of Article 25.1 IR. This Article establishes a parallel difference between decisions concerning the opening, conduct and closure of insolvency proceedings (which always emanate from the court of opening referred to in Article 16) and decisions deriving directly from the insolvency proceedings and closely linked to them. With regard to this second group of decisions, the provision contemplates two situations: that these decisions be issued by the court of opening of the insolvency proceedings or by a different court, without limiting this second possibility to the courts of the same Member State (i.e. to courts of the State of the opening). Obviously, Article 25.1 II IR presupposes that such "another court" has international jurisdiction to hear and determine that case.

98. The flexibility provided by this interpretation with regard to *actions deriving directly from the insolvency proceedings and which are closely linked with them* is necessary for different reasons.

99. *In the first place*, in the case of territorial insolvency proceedings, an exception to the exclusive jurisdiction of the courts of opening is already established by Article 18.2 IR. This exception is a natural consequence of Article 3.2 IR. According to this provision, the international jurisdiction of the court of the opening of the territorial proceedings is strictly limited to the sphere of that territory. This is why Article 18.2 of the Insolvency Regulation establishes that the liquidator of the territorial proceedings *"may claim in any other Member State through the courts or out of court, that moveable property was removed from the territory of the State of the opening of proceedings to the territory of that other Member State after the opening of the insolvency proceedings. He may also bring any action to set aside which is in the interest of the creditors"*. It is clear that to pursue the claim through the courts presupposes the international jurisdiction of the "other" Member State to decide on the action brought by the liquidator.

(a) For actions which seek to determine that moveable property was removed from the territory of the State of opening, Article 18.2 must be interpreted as conferring jurisdiction to the courts of the Member State to whose territory the property was transferred. Reasoning in terms of statutory interpretation, it is clear from the actual wording of the provision that an argument from "undisputed obvious meaning" justifies this conclusion.[109] Furthermore, the courts of the Member State where the property is situated are the best placed, for reasons of proximity, to ascertain the facts satisfactorily.

(b) For actions which seek to render juridical acts of the debtor ineffective as against the estate (i.e. actions to set-aside), Article 18.2 does not give any indication as to the competent courts. Given that jurisdiction cannot stem (ex hypothesis) from the same Article 3.2 on which the court of opening based its jurisdiction, the reference to "any other Member State" necessarily presupposes the applicability of other rules; and, in particular, the applicability of Regulation 44/2001 on Civil Jurisdiction and Enforcement. In this respect, the interpretation of Article 1.2 of the latter Regulation must be corrected in order to re-accommodate this type of actions and its rules should establish international jurisdiction.[110]

NB. The court entertaining the said action will apply Article 4 of the Insolvency Regulation, which designates the *lex concursus* of the State of opening as the law applicable (save where the exception provided for in Article 13 of the Insolvency Regulation comes into play) to the actions to set-aside.

100. *In the second place*, in the case of main proceedings, establishing the exclusive jurisdiction of the courts of the State of opening for insolvency-derived

---

[109] It also must be remember that Regulation 44/2001 does not establish any forum based upon the situation of *moveable* property, but refers actions concerning such property to the defendant's domicile.

[110] Article 1.2 of Regulation 44/2001 does not oppose this solution, because the relationship between the Insolvency Regulation and Regulation 44/2001 are to be decided from the point of view of the former, as the *lex specialis*. Actions to challenge transactions and juridical acts are characterized under Regulation 44/2001 as personal claims for which the jurisdiction lies, in principle, in the State of the defendant's domicile; see ECJ cases C-115/88 and C-261/90.

actions without leaving room for any further exception does not appear to be the most suitable solution, either.

With regard to assets or persons located in non-Member States, it would be counterproductive to establish the exclusive jurisdiction of the courts of opening ex Article 3.1 of the Insolvency Regulation in strict terms. On the one hand, those States are not bound by the Regulation; thus, there is no guarantee that this decision is going to be recognised and enforced in the foreign State in question. On the other hand, if the dispute is brought to that non-Member State and its courts decide the case, neither is there any guarantee that its decision will be recognised in the Community, due to the fact that the national rules on recognition will have to "defend", *vis-à-vis* judgments originating from non-Member States, the exclusive jurisdiction required by the Insolvency Regulation in favour of the courts of the Member State of opening (in the so called "reflex effect" of the exclusive jurisdiction).[111] Neither would it be convenient in *intra-Community* situations to claim the strictly exclusive character of the jurisdiction of the courts of opening, ex Article 3, for these actions. The consequence of such a claim would be to tie the hands of the liquidator with regard to applications based on non-insolvency law and made by creditors in the courts of other Member States. The liquidator would not be able, for example, to *counterclaim* by invoking the invalidity of the juridical act under insolvency law, *vis-à-vis* a claim brought by a creditor on the basis of common law.

> *Other way of explaining it.* An exclusive jurisdiction may result in an unnecessary increase in the *administrative costs* of the system of cross-border insolvency: in the cases in which the applicable law is not the *lex concursus* (see Article 9 for example), because to dispute in the State of opening increases both the explicit costs (foreign law has to be proved, etc.) and implicit costs (the risk of error increases) of the process; and, more generally, because the costs of recognition and enforceability in the other State (where the creditor and his assets are located) may have to be added to the costs of the process in the State of opening while it may be quicker and more economic to bring the action directly in the former State.

101. *In conclusion*, the Insolvency Regulation confers jurisdiction over insolvency-derived actions on the courts of opening, but does not prevent the liquidator (or other empowered persons) from deciding to waiver the possibility offered by the said Regulation and to bring the action before the normally competent courts, for the purposes of avoiding feared added costs or delays or for any other reason. Given that what the Insolvency Regulation does is allocate the jurisdictional risk to the creditor by imposing upon him the burden to defend at the insolvent debtor's place, while resorting to the ordinary *fora* releases him from this burden, it seems that no objection can be raised to this release without contravening the requirements of good faith; in fact the creditor will then be sued in his "natural" forum. In such cases, the international jurisdiction of the court seised with the matter will be determined by Regulation 44/2001 on civil jurisdiction, while the recognition of that court's decision

---

[111] It must be remembered that the system of recognition of the Insolvency Regulation would not be applicable as the ruling does not originate in a Member State.

will be governed by the Insolvency Regulation (see Article 25.1 II, which refers to the decisions of courts other than the court of opening of the insolvency proceedings). In this way equal treatment is guaranteed for all decisions falling within the scope of application of the Insolvency Regulation.

6. Preservation Measures

102. The Insolvency Regulation's regime of provisional orders or preservation measures is explained in detail in the Virgós/Schmidt Report.[112] The key to understanding this regime lies in the auxiliary nature of preservation measures. The Court of Justice has already pointed out that provisional or protective measures may serve to safeguard a variety of rights. As a consequence, their inclusion in the scope of each of the Regulations is not determined by their own nature, but by the nature of the rights they serve to protect. In our case, by the nature of the insolvency proceedings to which they relate.[113] When the main proceedings are insolvency proceedings subject to the Insolvency Regulation, they will also govern any preservation measures, whatever the specific nature of these may be.[114] In the case of insolvency proceedings subject to national law (e.g. when the debtor's centre of main interests is in a non-Member State) national law will also apply to the preservation measures.

> *Conditions for application.* In practice, this means that the Insolvency Regulation regime will apply provided that the following three conditions are satisfied: (a) that the provisional orders or preservation measures are aimed at ensuring the effectiveness of insolvency proceedings; (b) that the debtor has his centre of main interests in a Member State; and (c) that the said insolvency proceedings are included in the Annexes of the Regulation.

103. Within the sphere of application of the Insolvency Regulation, preservation measures can be ordered either by the courts with jurisdiction to open the main insolvency proceedings or by the courts of the Member State where the measure has to be put into effect (i.e. where it must be complied with).

(a) The jurisdiction of the courts of the debtor's centre of main interests encompasses jurisdiction to adopt preservation measures, regardless of where the assets or the persons affected are located (i.e. it has the same universal scope and the same limits indicated in Nos 72–73). These measures will be recognised and enforced in the other Member States in accordance with the provisions of Article 25.1 III of the Insolvency Regulation. It falls to national law to decide which preservation or provisional measures can be adopted.

Preservation measures may be ordered from the moment the request for the opening of insolvency proceedings is filed. Such measures may be demanded by the

---

[112] Margin Nos 78 and 201.
[113] See STJCE case 143/78.
[114] Virgos/Schmidt Report, Margin No. 199; Herchen, p. 159.

liquidator, including the temporary administrator, or any other person authorised according to the law of the State of opening.

Measures prior to the petition. There is a gap in the Insolvency Regulation. However, if the interpretation of Article 25 that we suggest in Chapter 9 (see *infra* No. 391) is accepted, jurisdiction under Article 3.1 will include the power to anticipate such preservation measures in accordance with the national applicable law.

(b) Together with this possibility, the courts of the place where the provisional orders or preservation measures have to be put into effect (e.g. the courts of the place where the asset is located, with the restriction established by Articles 5 and 7) also have jurisdiction to adopt them. In this case, the measures will have territorial scope and will be subject to the law of the State in question. As the aim of the measures is to ensure the effectiveness of the main proceedings, they may be requested by both the main liquidator and the temporary administrator (this is not the situation in which Article 38 applies). This auxiliary nature aimed at ensuring the effectiveness of the main proceedings explains why these measures are subordinated to the decisions of the courts of opening of the main proceedings. Pursuant to Articles 16 and 25, the court where the main proceedings are opened may order the lifting, modification or continuation of those preservation measures.[115]

Comparison with Regulation 44/2001. The system of provisional, including protective, relief provided for by the Insolvency Regulation is similar to that of Regulation 44/2001. This model offers two alternative possibilities: (a) to apply for the preservation measures to the court with jurisdiction according to Article 3.1; the measures ordered by this court will be recognised and enforced in accordance with Article 25.1 III by the Member States in which the person or asset subject to the measures is located (*formula*: "main forum + recognition"); (b) to apply directly for the preservation measures to the courts of the place where the person or asset that must be subject to the measures is located, in accordance with its national law (*formula*: "special forum" of the place where the measure is to take effect). This double system is necessary in order to ensure the immediate enforceability of the measure requested. The liquidator of the main proceedings (or any other empowered person) can use both possibilities indistinctly, depending on which is most convenient.

104. In addition, Article 38 of the Insolvency Regulation expressly empowers the *temporary liquidator* of the main proceedings to request those preservation measures of a general nature which specifically protect the effects of the opening of insolvency proceedings. On this rule see infra Nos 373 *et seq.*

105. In the case of *territorial insolvency proceedings*, jurisdiction to adopt provisional orders or preservation measures corresponds to the courts of the State which opens those proceedings.

7. SPECIAL REGIME FOR CREDIT INSTITUTIONS AND INSURANCE UNDERTAKINGS

106. *Credit institutions* and *insurance undertakings* are excluded from the sphere of application of the Insolvency Regulation. The legal framework which governs

---

[115] VIRGOS/SCHMIDT Report, Margin No. 78.

them is provided by Directive 2001/24/EC on the reorganisation and winding-up of credit institutions and Directive 2001/17/EC on the reorganisation and winding-up of insurance undertakings. In both cases the Directives modify the normative model of the Insolvency Regulation (which permits the opening of both main and territorial proceedings) and exclude the possibility of opening territorial proceedings against entities with registered offices in the European Community. On the other hand, both texts permit proceedings to be opened against branches in the Community of entities whose registered offices are outside its borders.

107. In the case of *credit institutions*, a distinction has to be made between two situations. (a) If the entity has its head office inside the European Community, jurisdiction to adopt restructuring measures or initiate winding-up procedures belongs exclusively to the *authorities of the Member State of origin*.[116] The Member State of origin is the State which authorised the credit institution to take up its activities. Pursuant to Directive 2000/12/EC relating to the taking-up and pursuit of the business of credit institutions, this authorisation is valid for all countries belonging to the European Community. Competence for conferring this authorisation corresponds to the State of the head office of the entity. (b) If the entity has its head office outside the European Community, but has a branch in a Member State, the Directive presupposes the jurisdiction of the host Member State of the branch to adopt restructuring or winding-up measures in connection with that branch (see Articles 8 and 19 and recital No. 21 of Directive 2001/24/EC). A branch is a place of business which forms a legally dependent part of a credit institution and which carries out transactions inherent in the business of credit institutions.

108. In the case of *insurance undertakings*, a distinction must also be made between two situations. (a) If the entity has its head office inside the European Community, jurisdiction to adopt restructuring measures or initiate winding-up procedures belongs exclusively to the *authorities of the Member State of origin*. The Member State of origin is the State which authorised the company to take up its activities, pursuant to Directive 73/239/EEC on the coordination of laws, regulations and administrative provisions relating to the taking-up and pursuit of the business of direct insurance other than life assurance, or Directive 79/267/EEC on the coordination of laws, regulations and administrative provisions relating to the taking up and pursuit of the business of direct life assurance. Competence for conferring this authorisation corresponds to the State of the head office of the undertaking. (b) If the entity has its head office outside the European Community, but has a branch office in a Member State, the Directive confers jurisdiction on the host Member State of the branch to adopt restructuring or winding-up measures in connection with that branch (see Article 30 Directive 2001/17/EC).

---

[116] In those cases where the authorities of the *host* Member State deem it necessary to implement within their territory reorganisation measures, they shall inform the complement authorities of the *home* Member State (see Article 5 of Directive 2001/24/EC and Article 12 of Directive 2000/12/EC), who are the only ones empowered to take them (see Article 3.1 Directive 2000/12/EC); on this point see DEGUÉE, p. 266.

Chapter 5

Applicable Law: The *Lex Fori Concursus* as General Rule

1. PRELIMINARY

109. In this section, we shall explain the general features of the scheme followed by the Insolvency Regulation with regard to the problems of the law applicable to the insolvency proceedings and to its effects.

110. Situations of insolvency give rise to a problem of collective action. Each creditor has an individual incentive to recover the largest possible amount of money to the detriment of other creditors. Competition among creditors to individually execute their claims on the debtor's property may lead to the piecemeal dismantling of the assets and to a loss of value for all parties, as well as making it impossible to find an alternative solution, whether this be an orderly liquidation or restructuring, even where such a solution would be more efficient in economic terms (it would maximise the total value measured in monetary terms). For this reason, the most important function of insolvency law is to provide a collective forum to sort out the rights of all parties in interest, in order to avoid such competition and facilitate cooperation between all parties.[117]

111. However, insolvency law does not create or govern creditor's claims. Debtor and creditors' rights and obligations are created and defined by the ordinary rules of civil, commercial, labour or public law. Insolvency law concerns itself instead with the process of collectivisation and with the consequences that derive therefrom, by determining the relative position of each of those rights in the insolvency of the debtor and, where appropriate, by establishing the restrictions and modifications which such rights and obligations must undergo in order to ensure the fulfilment of the collective aims of the insolvency proceedings.

112. This perception of insolvency law is also valid in the sphere of the conflict of laws. In fact, it provides a good explanation of the scheme followed by the Insolvency Regulation:

(a) The Insolvency Regulation's rules do not determine if and when a claim exists against a debtor or an estate. Whether a given right has been created, and the content thereof, is something that belongs to the realm of the ordinary conflict of laws rules. From the point of view of the Insolvency Regulation, this is a "*preliminary question*" that is not governed by its rules. It is the proper law of the contract that will determine if a contractual claim exists against the insolvent debtor and the

---

[117] JACKSON, pp. 7–19.

amount thereof; the *lex rei sitae* will tell us if a real security right has been created in favour of a specific creditor, and so on. In this sphere, each Member State will apply its own conflict of laws rules, including the international conventions in force (e.g. the 1980 Rome Convention on the law applicable to contractual obligations).

(b) The Insolvency Regulation concerns itself instead with the process of collectivisation which takes place through the opening of insolvency proceedings and with the effects of these proceedings in those rights and obligations. The Regulation tries to ensure that the principle of collective action (i.e. the change from an individual regime of remedies to a collective one) is also carried out on a Community-wide level and that the legal consequences of the opening of insolvency proceedings against a debtor located in a Member State are predictable for everybody.

> *Post-commencement claims.* This scheme is valid both for pre- and post-commencement claims (i.e. for insolvency claims and claims against the estate). In both cases the question of whether a claim arises against the debtor or the estate is determined in accordance with the ordinary conflict rules. After commencement, the debtor or the liquidator may enter into new contracts or cause new liabilities in the administration of the estate. The respective powers of the debtor and the liquidator will be determined by the Insolvency Regulation (i.e. by the *lex fori concursus*, see Article 4.2.c). The contract or the tort claim will be governed by the national law applicable to the contract or tort according to ordinary conflict of laws rules (e.g. in the case of a contractual claim, by the 1980 Rome Convention on the law applicable to contractual obligations). The treatment in the insolvency proceedings of the creditor's claim arising from that contract or tort will, in turn, be determined by the Insolvency Regulation (see Article 4.2.g; Articles 5, 6, 7, 13 and 15, are not applicable, since they only protect rights created or transactions entered into prior to the opening of insolvency proceedings).

113. To this end, the Insolvency Regulation does not unify insolvency law in Europe, but is content with standardizing the conflict of laws rules which determine the national law applicable to the insolvency proceedings and the effects thereof. The immediate purpose of these rules is to ensure that any problems of applicable law which may arise in insolvency proceedings are resolved in all of the Member States in accordance with the same rules; in other words, it strives to achieve international harmony of result.[118]

However, the Regulation also contains a series of rules of uniform *substantive* law. These rules have a complementary function with regard to the general system of the Regulation, which basically deals with Private International Law. They deal with matters such as informing the creditors and the filing of claims, a unified treatment of which was considered indispensable for the purposes of ensuring an adequate level of legal certainty in the Community. These rules apply directly and displace national law.

114. The conflict of laws rules contained in the Insolvency Regulation (Articles 4–15) follow a format of *rule-exception*. The formula "unless otherwise provided by" included in Article 4 IR, which establishes the general rule, reflects this idea. According to this Article, the law of the State of opening (*lex fori concursus*) governs the insolvency proceedings in all of its stages and in all of its effects. This

---

[118] BALZ (1996a), p. 950; VIRGOS, p. 16; TAUPITZ, p. 324.

NB. A useful scheme of the way the Insolvency Regulation operates is the following:

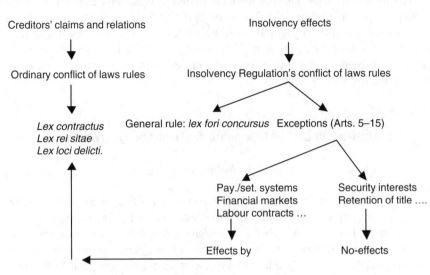

law establishes the position in the insolvency which corresponds to the different rights of the creditors (i.e. their relative value) and determines what interferences or modifications, if any, they must undergo to fulfil specific insolvency policies, regardless of the national law that governs the affected right (i.e. the *lex causae*).

The *exceptions* to the *lex concursus* are contained in Articles 5–15, which point to the application of a different national law, e.g. to the law governing the right in question itself (i.e. the *lex causae*), or, more radically, directly exempt certain rights from the effects of the insolvency proceedings. These exceptions constitute, as regards *intra-Community* cases (*infra* Nos 25 *et seq.*), a closed list.

115. The Insolvency Regulation excludes the *renvoi*.[119] When the conflict of laws rules contained in the Insolvency Regulation refer to the law of a Member State, they make reference to the *domestic law* of that State, irrespective of its rules of Private International Law.

The Insolvency Regulation remains silent on the question of public policy as an exception to the application of foreign law. This is an exception inherent to the systems of all Member States that the Regulation did not intend to eradicate. However, Member States cannot resort to public policy to render the system of exceptions to the *lex fori concursus* meaningless. These exceptions imply that it corresponds to the national law thereby designated, and not to the State of opening, to establish the insolvency policy which needs to be applied in each case.

---

[119] VIRGOS/SCHMIT Report, Margin No. 87; VIRGOS, p. 16; BALZ (1996b), p. 507; TAUPITZ, p. 329; LEIBLE/STAUDINGER (2000), p. 549; HUBER, p. 151; TORREMANS, p. 172.

116. The Insolvency Regulation does not offer a rule to deal with the problem of *States with more than one legal system*, in which different territorial units have different insolvency laws. This occurs in the United Kingdom, for example. By virtue of the principle of subsidiarity, this would imply that Member States are not bound to apply the Insolvency Regulation to conflicts solely between the laws of such units. Since this increases the complexity of the system, it would be advisable for multi-unit Member States to solve their internal conflicts with rules similar to those laid down by the Insolvency Regulation.

2. GENERAL RULE: THE LAW OF THE STATE OF OPENING (ARTICLE 4)

2.1. Justification

117. Article 4 of the Insolvency Regulation contains the general rule for determining the law applicable: "*the law applicable to insolvency proceedings and their effects shall be that of the Member state within the territory of which such proceedings are opened, hereafter referred as the 'State of the opening of proceedings*" (*lex fori concursus*). This rule applies both to the main proceedings and to territorial proceedings (see Recital 23 and Article 28). It presupposes that the court has jurisdiction to open insolvency proceedings according to the Regulation, which means that the rules of international jurisdiction (Articles 3.1 and 3.2) end up fulfilling a *double function*: they determine the competent jurisdiction directly and the applicable law indirectly.

118. The application as a general rule of the law of the state of opening (*lex fori concursus*) constitutes one of the principles of comparative international insolvency law.[120] Three *arguments* tend to be put forward to support this solution:[121] (a) In a world with different insolvency visions, it allows a single set of insolvency policies to be pursued. Collective action is only possible within a coherent and predictable legal framework, which is an argument in favour of the *lex fori concursus* providing this. It enables the parties to readily identify their rights and obligations, and consequently to bargain "in the shadow of" a single legal system. (b) It facilitates the administration of the proceedings as it makes *forum* and *ius* coincide, and thereby avoids the costs associated with the application of a foreign law (problems of legal adjustment, information on foreign law, etc.). This argument is particularly strong in those proceedings, such as insolvency proceedings, where the procedural aspects and the substantive aspects are closely linked. (c) It ensures, from the conflict of laws perspective, the *par conditio creditorum*: all of the creditors of the same insolvent debtor are subject to the same proceedings and to the same legal system.

---

[120] LÜER (1992), p. 112; VON WILMOWSKY (1996), p. 281.

[121] LÜKE (1998), p. 282; ESPLUGUES, p. 29; VON WILMOWSKY (1996), pp. 281–282; HERCHEN, p. 47; CALVO/CARRASCOSA, p. 447.

2.2. *Scope of applicable law*

119. In accordance with Article 4, *"save as otherwise provided in this Regulation, the law applicable to insolvency proceedings and their effects shall be that of the Member State within the territory of which such proceedings are opened, hereafter referred to as the State of the opening of proceedings"*. This is a very broad and general description which includes both the *opening, conduct* and *closure* of the insolvency proceedings as well as their *effects*, both *procedural* and *substantive*,[122] on the rights and obligations of all the concerned parties.

Insolvency effects. Under all national laws, insolvency proceedings may interfere and bring about abrupt changes in the legal position of the debtor and the creditors. The effects referred to the competence of the law of the State of opening (*lex fori concursus*) are those which are linked to specific insolvency law policies. They encompass those legal consequences and legal variations which the procedural and substantive rights of the debtor and the creditors must undergo in order to achieve the objectives of the insolvency proceedings, as set forth by the *lex fori concursus*. From this perspective, the *lex fori concursus* displaces, in so far as insolvency policy requires, the law governing the affected act or right itself. We shall refer to these insolvency policy-founded effects as *"insolvency effects"*. These effects may be greater or lesser depending on the legislative policy decisions of each State. There are systems which significantly alter the positions of the parties and there are others which respect those positions as far as possible. In other words, there are systems which are more "interventionist" than others. In terms of insolvency policies the Regulation itself is *neutral*; it respects national diversity and admits, in its Annexes, insolvency proceedings with a very different degree of "interventionism". It is the task of the national *lex fori concursus* to establish the degree to which the insolvency proceedings need to interfere in the rights and relationships of the parties; i.e. the modifications or restrictions ("redistributions") which are necessary for the insolvency to achieve its collective objectives. That is why the starting point is always "what is required by" the *lex concursus*. However, two qualifications are necessary: (a) In the first place, the *lex fori concursus* may only interfere with the law governing the act or right itself *for insolvency law reasons*. It determines the impact of the insolvency proceedings on those acts or rights; but it must *only* apply to the extent required by insolvency law policies. The *lex causae* continues to apply to other civil law consequences not connected with insolvency policies. On many occasions the application of this criterion requires the decision as to whether or not a given effect is founded on insolvency law policies to be inferred from the "sense and purpose" of the rule which establishes it. If such is the case, the *lex fori concursus* takes precedence over the *lex causae*; if not, then the latter continues to apply. (b) In the second place, the Insolvency Regulation establishes some safeguards against an excessive "interventionism" by the *lex concursus*: (i) the exceptions in favour of a different national law expressly established in Articles 5–15; (ii) the possibility of opening territorial proceedings, which will entail a different *lex concursus* being applied; (iii) and, in extreme cases, the public policy clause.

120. Article 4.2 contains a list of specific matters which are subject to the law of the State of opening: *"the conditions for the opening of those proceedings, their conduct and their closure"*. And, more specifically: *"(a) against which debtors insolvency*

---

[122] VIRGOS, p. 17; HOMANN, p. 361; TAUPITZ, p. 325; DORDI, p. 351; KEMPER, p. 1615; REINHART (2003), pp. 876–877. The fact that both types of effects are subject to the same law reduces the difficulties of legal application because it eliminates problems of characterisation and adjustment.

proceedings may be brought on account of their capacity; (b) the assets which form part of the estate and the treatment of assets acquired by or devolving on the debtor after the opening of the insolvency proceedings; (c) the respective powers of the debtor and the liquidator; (d) the conditions under which set-offs may be invoked; (e) the effects of insolvency proceedings on current contracts to which the debtor is party; (f) the effects of the insolvency proceedings on proceedings brought by individual creditors, with the exception of lawsuits pending; (g) the claims which are to be lodged against the debtor's estate and the treatment of claims arising after the opening of insolvency proceedings; (h) the rules governing the lodging, verification and admission of claims; (i) the rules governing the distribution of proceeds from the realisation of assets, the ranking of claims and the rights of creditors who have obtained partial satisfaction after the opening of insolvency proceedings by virtue of a right in rem or through a set-off; (j) the conditions for and the effects of closure of insolvency proceedings, in particular by composition; (k) creditors' rights after the closure of insolvency proceedings; (l) who is to bear the costs and expenses incurred in the insolvency proceedings; (m) the rules relating to the voidness, voidability or unenforceability of legal acts detrimental to all the creditors".

121. This list is not exclusive. Its function is to facilitate the interpretation of the general rule contained in Article 4.1 and to resolve any problems of characterisation or doubts which may arise with regard to its application. Thus, this rule clarifies the fact that the *lex fori concursus* will determine the following.

(a) *The debtors that may be subject to insolvency proceedings;* including the question as to whether a specific debtor can be subject to insolvency proceedings on account of his capacity (merchant, consumer, etc.), form (corporate or unincorporated) or ownership (private or State-owned).

NB. With regard to this issue, bear in mind Article 3.4, which permits a territorial insolvency to be opened precisely in those cases in which the law of the State where the debtor has its centre of main interests does not permit it; and Article 16.1 II, whereby the fact that according to the law of the State where the recognition of the insolvency proceedings is requested the debtor, on account of his capacity, cannot be subject to insolvency proceedings is not admissible as a reason for refusing to recognise those proceedings.

(b) The commencement standards, the type of proceedings that may be opened (e.g. liquidation or reorganization), the parties that may apply (e.g. debtor, creditors, authorities) and the time from which the effects of the judgment opening proceedings begin to apply.

Conditions for opening. The laws of the Member States differ on the specific standards that must be satisfied before insolvency proceedings can be opened. The *lex fori concursus* determines the commencement standard and the presumptions that may facilitate its proof. This law will decide whether the standard for commencement is the *liquidity or cash-flow test* (i.e. the inability to meet liabilities as they come due in the ordinary course of business), the *balance-sheet test* (i.e. excess of liabilities over assets) or a combination of both. It will also decide whether or not *imminent insolvency* or prospective inability to pay permits commencement. When it comes to applying these tests, it must be taken into account that, in principle, in cases of cross-border insolvency, the framework for evaluating the insolvency is not the national framework but the international one. This means, for instance, that the inadequacy of the company's assets to meet its liabilities – when the *lex fori concursus* employs the balance-sheet test – should be established by reference to all of the debtor's assets, and not only to the assets located in a specific State. Inability to meet liabilities as they come due must likewise be established by reference to the debtor's creditors as a whole, including those located in other States, and not only local ones.[123] However, the presumptions and specific tests that the national laws establish to facilitate creditor's applications also apply here. Evidence of specific observable events may be then enough; for example, failure to pay in the forum essential business costs (e.g. taxes or salaries), failure to pay a matured debt within a specified period of time after a demand for payment has been made, disappearance of the debtor from his domicile, etc. Morover, in some jurisdictions the uncontested application of the debtor justifies the opening of insolvency proceedings, so this problem does not arise. For *territorial insolvency proceedings* see No. 315 and the exception established in Article 27.

(c) The notice of the application for opening or of the opening of insolvency proceedings. The *lex fori concursus* will also determine the manner in which notice must be given: through delivery of a personal notice (i.e. to the debtor in the case of a creditor's application), through publication of the opening in an official gazette or newspaper, etc. Article 40 establishes a uniform duty to inform known creditors of the commencement by means of an individual notice. Publication and registration in other Member States of the judgement opening proceedings are dealt with in Articles 21 and 22.

(d) The provisional and protective measures available between an application for opening and the opening itself, including the appointment of an interim administrator.

(e) The partial or total *divestment of the debtor*, the appointment of an insolvency representative ("*liquidator*" in the terminology of the Regulation) and the *respective powers* of the debtor and the liquidator. The *lex fori concursus* determines the extent to which the debtor retains control of the business, the acts the debtor can and cannot do and the consequences of acts which breach these restrictions. The exception provided for in Article 14 IR regarding the protection of third-party purchasers must be taken into account. The *lex fori concursus* specifies the duties and functions of the liquidator, the person or entity that can be appointed (including whether a legal person can qualify), the qualifications required, the remuneration and the liability of the liquidator.

(f) The *assets which form part of the insolvency estate* and the treatment of assets acquired by or devolving upon the debtor after the opening of insolvency proceedings. The *lex fori concursus* will determine, for example, the extent to which certain assets belonging to or vested in the debtor are not comprised by the estate in order to allow him the necessary means to carry on his professional work and satisfy his personal and familial vital needs.

NB. Specific assets may be excluded from enforcement actions for different reasons and to varying levels according to the national law which governs the asset in question (e.g. in so

---

[123] MANKOWSKI, p. 1650 *et seq.*, albeit with reference to German law; VIRGOS, p. 17.

far as is necessary for the continued functioning of a public service); these are non-insolvency law limitations which the *lex concursus* has to respect.

(g) Protection of the assets of the debtor against collection actions of the creditors, in particular by application of a *suspension or stay* on the commencement or continuation of individual actions or proceedings concerning the assets or the rights and obligations of the debtor. According to Article 4.2.f, the *lex fori concursus* determines "the effects of the insolvency proceedings on proceedings brought by individual creditors, with the exception of lawsuits pending" (about which see Article 15). Insolvency proceedings are designed to provide a collective forum, a solution that avoids competition by creditors for the debtor's assets and allows for the orderly examination of the debtor's and the creditor's rights. Article 4.2.f protects this function. The *lex fori concursus* will therefore decide to which extent individual actions by creditors to enforce their claims through collection efforts, adjudication, execution or otherwise are to be suspended or enjoined. The term "proceedings" is broad enough to encompass all kinds of procedures brought about by individual creditors, including arbitration proceedings[124] and enforcement measures initiated by creditors outside the court system, where allowed.

> *Remark.* The language of the provision varies in the different linguistic versions of the Regulation (e.g. "proceedings brought by individual creditors", "ejecuciones invididuales", "poursuites individuelles", "Rechtsverfolgungsmassnahmen einzelner Gläubiger", "azioni giudiciarie individuali"). However, this divergence should not give rise to difficulties of interpretation. The list of matters mentioned in Article 4.2 is non-exhaustive, and the basic rule remains the same: unless otherwise provided for in the Insolvency Regulation, the *lex fori concursus* governs all the effects of the insolvency proceedings.

To understand this provision and its exception (Article 15 IR), a distinction must be made between *individual enforcement actions* and *lawsuits*. Examples of the former are measures such as the realisation of an asset or the foreclosure of a security right. Examples of the latter are actions which seek to determine the existence, validity, content or amount of a claim. Accordingly:

(i) The effects on individual enforcement actions, both pending and future, are always determined by the *lex fori concursus*,[125] including preservation measures. A stay on the normal methods of enforcement against the debtor and his assets is common to all Member States.

---

[124] On a similar conclusion see the UNCITRAL guide to the enactment of the Model Law on cross border insolvencies, No. 145. This result is not contrary to the 1958 New York Convention on the Recognition and Enforcement of Foreign Arbitral Awards, to which all Member States are party.

[125] VIRGOS/SCHMIT Report, Margin Nos 91 and 142.

Exequatur or registration. The *lex fori concursus* can stay a procedure of *exequatur* or registration commenced under Article 38 of Regulation 44/2001. This may be reasonable: although the *exequatur* or registration procedure established therein is not really an enforcement process which may immediately prejudice the estate, in a system of automatic recognition of decisions, which is what the said Regulation seeks, it is difficult to imagine what legitimate interest the holder of a decision dictate could have for requesting its *exequatur* in a Member State when insolvency proceedings have been opened which suspend in all Member States individual creditors' enforcement actions.

European Enforcement Order. The insolvency stay of individual enforcement actions also applies to judgements, court settlements and authentic instruments certified as an European Enforcement Order.[126]

Preservation measures. The effects of the insolvency proceedings on provisional and protective measures adopted in favour of a creditor may give rise to doubts. The most reasonable thing is for these proceedings to follow the same regime as enforcement actions because, although they do not lead directly to the realisation of the asset, they do "insulate" it, i.e. make it more difficult for it to be included in the estate of the insolvency and be administered by the liquidator, and this is prejudicial to the successful conclusion of the insolvency proceedings.[127]

(ii) The effects on the continuation of *lawsuits pending* at the moment of the opening of the insolvency proceedings, are, by way of exception, determined by the law of the State where the lawsuit is pending (Article 15).

(iii) The effects on the commencement, after the opening of insolvency proceedings, of *new lawsuits* are governed by the *lex fori concursus*, with one important exception: international jurisdiction. The *lex concursus* will determine the necessary procedural modifications which result from the divestment of the debtor (e.g. actions will have to be filed by or against the liquidator) and may impose a temporary stay to enable the liquidator to make an inventory of the debtor's position. But the international jurisdiction to entertain new actions will be determined by the Insolvency Regulation itself, in the case of insolvency-derived actions, or by the ordinary rules, including the Regulation 44/2001 on civil jurisdiction and other international instruments, in other cases.

The *exceptions* to the application of the *lex fori concursus* established in Articles 5 (rights in rem), 6 (right to set-off), 7 (retention of title) and 9 (payment systems and financial markets) also operate in this context.

(h) The claims which are to be filed against the debtor's estate (*insolvency claims*) and the treatment of claims arising after the opening of insolvency proceedings (*estate liabilities*); the latter include the expenses of the proceeding and also debts and liabilities arising from the administration of the estate as a result of new contracts or torts.

(i) The rules regarding the *filing, verification and admission* of claims. The *lex fori concursus* will determine, for example, whether or not a foreign claim, given its public law nature, is admissible in the insolvency of the debtor and whether or not it

---

[126] See Regulation 805/2004 of the European Parliament and of the Council of 21 April 2004 creating a European Enforcement Order for uncontested claims.

[127] LÜKE (1998), pp. 313–314.

enjoys a special status. The *lex fori concursus* also determines the consequences of the failure to present or admit a claim (see also Article 4.2.k).[128] We should here remember that Chapter 4 of the Insolvency Regulation also contains a set of uniform rules which govern various questions directly and which displace national law. Thus, for example, it is important to point out that Article 39 IR establishes the admissibility of certain *public law claims* on the part of the Member States (see *infra* No. 281).

> *Recognition and admission of claims.* Two common questions in the area of cross-border insolvencies are the *"recognition"* of rights acquired according to a law other than the law of the State of opening and the *admission and treatment* of those rights in the insolvency proceedings. In cases where the national law governing the insolvency proceedings and the national law governing the right or claim are different, a distinction should be made between these two aspects: (a) Recognition of a right or claim acquired in accordance with a foreign law constitutes a *"preliminary question"* with regard to its admission in the insolvency proceedings. Here the issue to be determined is the validity and effectiveness of the acquisition in question. This issue is resolved by the normal conflict of laws rules of the forum;[129] the law applicable in accordance with these rules will tell us whether or not the creditor is the holder of a validly acquired right. This is a non-insolvency matter. (b) A second question is whether the right thus acquired is admitted or not and what is its relative position in the insolvency proceedings. This is an insolvency matter. It falls to the law governing the proceedings, the *lex fori concursus*, to determine this issue; this law will determine, for example, if the said claim, given its nature and conditions, is admissible in the insolvency of the debtor and the ranking of the claim. This in turn may give rise to what is known in technical terms as a problem of *"substitution"* (see infra letter o).[130]

(j) The extent to which and the conditions under which *set-off or netting* may be enforced or protected, notwithstanding the opening of insolvency proceedings. Article 6 IR, which increases the possibilities of set-off or netting for creditors, may also come into play.

(k) The effects of the insolvency proceedings on *current contracts* to which the debtor is party. Article 8 (contracts relating to immovable property), Article 9 (payment systems and financial markets), and Article 10 (contracts of employment) must be taken into account, as they establish exceptions to this rule.

(l) The rules regarding the voidness, voidability or unenforceability of *acts which are detrimental to the creditors as a whole*. The *lex fori concursus* determines if and who must apply for a declaration by the courts invalidating those acts or if the order opening the proceedings entails such invalidation. In any case it must be remembered that Article 13 IR on detrimental acts and Article 9.2 IR on payment systems and financial markets, establish exceptions to the application of the *lex fori concursus*.

---

[128] For example, the eventual discharge of the claim if it is not filed in a timely manner, in the way provided for by French Law (see Article 53 Loi No. 85–98 *relative au redressement et à la liquidation judiciaires des entreprises*); see GOTTWALD (1997), p. 31; TAUPITZ, p. 327, note 65.

[129] See TROCHU, p. 160 *et seq*; TAUPITZ, pp. 330–331; SIEHR, p. 815; GOODE, p. 502.

[130] VON WILMOWSKY (1996), pp. 285–286; SIEHR, p. 815.

In the case of *territorial proceedings*, the rules regarding set-aside are only applicable insofar as the debtor's assets in the said State have been affected.[131]

(m) *Creditors participation* in the insolvency proceedings. The laws of the Member States differ on the authorised degree of creditor involvement in the decision-making process in insolvency proceedings. The *lex fori concursus* determines the extent of creditors' participation and the form that this participation may take: direct (i.e. through creditors meetings) or indirect (i.e. through the formation of a creditor committee, or the election or appointment of a creditor representative).

(n) The manner in which the liquidator may use or dispose of assets of the estate. Nevertheless, Article 18.3 must be taken into account.

(o) The *ranking* of claims. Just as one of the pivotal questions of any insolvency system is the *ranking of claims*, one of the key objectives of any insolvency law is the establishment of clear and predictable rules regarding priority. The ranking of a claim in the insolvency proceedings is determined by the law of the State of opening, irrespective of the law governing the claim itself. The *lex fori concursus* determines whether or not a claim enjoys any priority or privilege, and also what claims may be subject to subordination. In cases of contractual subordination, the agreement itself will be governed by the proper law of the contract, but its effect on the insolvency priority scheme will be determined by the *lex fori concursus*.

Problems of "substitution". These problems arise when the law governing the ranking of claims and the law governing the claim are different. The categories of privileges and priorities that exist and the ranking of claims is always established by the *lex fori concursus*. Normally, when establishing these categories and this ranking, the national legislator takes into account the rights *as and how* they exist in his own legal system. However, the right of a creditor may have been constituted in accordance with a foreign law. In this case, it is necessary to determine which claims or rights created under foreign law qualify as equivalent to domestic claims or rights conferring certain privileges or priorities; i.e. it is necessary to examine if the kind of right created under foreign law is "equivalent" to the kind of right upon which the *lex concursus* confers a special status in the insolvency.[132] The test to apply is whether or not both rights, given their essential content and function, correspond to the extent that they can be considered as "functionally interchangeable". If the answer is affirmative, they must be considered as equivalent and receive the same treatment in the insolvency proceedings.

Subrogation. Where a third party satisfies a creditor in lieu of the debtor, the admissibility of a subrogation to a creditor's priority is also determined by the *lex fori concursus*. For example, in the case of public institutions or equivalent social systems which are obliged to meet the claims of certain preferential creditors (e.g. public guarantee schemes with regard to workers salaries), whether or not these institutions can benefit from the same priority that the satisfied claims enjoyed is determined by the *lex fori concursus*. However, the preliminary question regarding whether or not a right of subrogation exists (i.e. whether the public institution is entitled to exercise against the debtor the rights which the creditor had against that debtor) is determined by the law which governs the third party's (i.e. the

---

[131] VIRGOS/SCHMIT Report, Margin No. 91 *in fine*.

[132] SIEHR, p. 815: A well-known problem of Private International Law may also be met with in bankruptcy proceedings. "Which claims or rights created under foreign law qualify as equivalents to domestic claims or rights conferring certain privileges or preferences?".

public institution's) duty to satisfy the creditor. Article 11 of the Directive on insurance undertakings contains a special rule regarding guarantee schemes.

The Insolvency Regulation permits the opening of parallel proceedings against the same debtor. As the *lex fori concursus* is applied by virtue of Article 4 in each set of main and secondary proceedings opened, different proceedings will be governed by different applicable laws; for this reason, the ranking of the same claim may be different in each of the proceedings opened.

> *Credit institutions and insurance undertakings.* The Directive 2001/24/EC on credit institutions and the Directive 2001/17/EC of insurance undertakings follow a stricter model of universalism: only one insolvency procedure may be opened when the institution or undertaking has its head office in the Community. Both directives establish a principle of *equal treatment of equivalent claims*: claims by creditors not resident in the State of the opening should be treated in the same way as equivalent claims in that State, without any discrimination (see Article 16 both Directives). According to the Directive on insurance undertakings, Member States should ensure special treatment for insurance creditors. For this purpose, they have to choose one of two optional methods provided for: (a) granting insurance claims absolute precedence over any other claim with respect to assets representing the technical provisions; or (b) granting insurance claims a special rank which may only be preceded by claims on salaries, social security, taxes and rights.

(p) The *distribution of proceeds* from the realisation of assets, including the rights of creditors who have obtained partial satisfaction after the opening of the insolvency proceedings pursuant to a right *in rem* or due to the effect of a *set-off*.[133]

(q) In the case of a *reorganisation*, the *lex fori concursus* will determine the range of possibilities available (e.g. from a simple composition to an insolvency plan where the corporate form, the capital structure or the membership of the debtor will be affected) and their limits (e.g. whether the statutory scheme of priorities has to be maintained in reorganisation), the parties affected (e.g. whether the plan can affect secured creditors or equity holders), the procedures for approval, the effects of an approved plan, the possibilities of amendments, the implementation of a plan and, in case of substantial breach, the conversion to liquidation.

(r) The conditions and the effects of the *closure of the insolvency proceedings*. In the case of territorial proceedings, the limits imposed by Articles 17.2 and 34.2 must be taken into account.

(s) The rights of the creditors after the closure of the insolvency proceedings, including the eventual *discharge* of the residual debt. In the case of territorial proceedings, Articles 17.2, 34.2 and 35 must be taken into account.

(t) The *costs* of the proceedings.

---

[133] See VIRGOS/SCHMIT Report, Margin No. 91; also on this point, TAUPITZ, p. 328.

2.3. *Particular issues regarding the insolvency of companies*

2.3.1. *General overview*

122. In situations of company insolvency, particular problems of conflict of laws may arise when the national law applicable to the insolvency of the company (*lex fori concursus*) and the national law applicable to the company itself (*lex societatis*) do not coincide. This may typically occur when the place of incorporation of the company and the centros of main interests are located in different States (i.e. in cases in which the presumption contained in Article 3 IR in favour of the registered office is rebutted) and the forum State determines the *lex societatis* on the basis of the former. In this case, it will be necessary to delimit the respective scope of application of the *lex concursus* and the *lex societatis*.

> *Centre of main interests and lex societatis.* It is important to state that the fact that the Insolvency Regulation bases the jurisdiction to open insolvency proceedings on the debtor's centre of main interests, a concept which may be viewed as a "new version" of the real seat for companies, has no bearing on the question of the law applicable to the company. Companies maintain their original status (*i.e.* the *lex societatis* remains the same) even if the centre of main interest lies within the forum for the purposes of commencing insolvency proceedings. For example, the question of whether a company incorporated in a Member State should be treated as a limited company has to be determined according to the law of its incorporation.[134]

123. As we have already explained, insolvency law "interferes" in the rights and obligations of debtors and creditors, displacing, in so far as insolvency policy requires, the normally applicable rules. In line with this view, the Insolvency Regulation, but for a limited number of exceptions, subjects all "insolvency effects" (on this concept see No. 119) to the *lex fori concursus*. By applying this criterion to those cases in which the debtor is a company or a firm, we can reach the following conclusions:

(a) The fact that the insolvency of the company can extend automatically to the members, as may be the case in certain legal systems with personal business associations, is subject to the *lex fori concursus*, not to the *lex societatis*. The insolvency nature of the rule can be defended insofar as its purpose is to protect the rights of the creditors in the face of the insolvency of the entity.[135] The *preliminary question* of whether the members have unlimited liability for the company's debt is governed by the *lex societatis*. Having said this, as is the case with groups of companies, only if the court dealing with the insolvency of the company also has international jurisdiction over the member or members of the company, is it able to subject that member or members to insolvency proceedings in the forum.

---

[134] No other solution is consistent with the EC Treaty and the freedom of establishment of companies formed in accordance with the law of a Member State and having their registered office, central administration or principal place of business within the Community. See European Court of Justice judgments in cases C-212/97 ("*Centros*"), C-208/00 ("*Überseering*"), and C-167/01 ("*Inspire Art*").

[135] TROCHU, pp. 239–240.

(b) The *lex fori concursus* determines the eventual liability of the administrators of a company with regard to the body of creditors, arising from the insolvency of the company.

(c) The changes brought about by the declaration of opening on the general regime of company administration (e.g. supervision by, or transfer to, an outside administrator or liquidator who replaces the company's directors) are likewise subject to the *lex fori concursus*.

(d) The changes brought about by the declaration of opening on the claims of the company against its shareholders (e.g. only the liquidator can demand payment) and of the shareholders against the company are also subject to the *lex fori concursus*.

(e) When the *lex fori concursus* imposes upon the corporate directors the duty to petition for insolvency, this duty must be respected as it fulfils a purpose inherent to the insolvency, that of establishing the obligations of the persons involved in cases of insolvency when the debtor is a legal person. This kind of rules determines when the fiduciary duties that corporate directors ordinarily owe to shareholders "shift" to creditors when the corporation approaches insolvency; and this is typically an insolvency-related policy. An application to the competent court as determined by Article 3 of the Regulation (e.g. that of the company's registered seat or, when it is elsewhere, of the center of main interest) shall discharge this duty.

(f) However, the possible dissolution of the company is subject to the *lex societatis*. Considering that it does not respond to a specific need of insolvency law (i.e. the measure is not aimed at protecting any purpose of insolvency law), this question must be subject to the *lex societatis*.[136]

(g) On the effects of reorganisation plans in the corporate sphere, see also Nos 126 *et seq.*

124. Territorial insolvencies are subject to the same principles. The *lex fori concursus* applies, although its rules must now *be adjusted* to the limited scope of this type of proceedings. The territorial insolvency encompasses the establishment and the assets located in that State, but not the rest of the company. Consequently, the measures provided for by the *lex fori concursus* which are aimed at the debtor as a natural or a legal person must also be restricted to the territory of the State of opening, and no further. Thus, for example, the debtor's powers of administration and disposal over the establishment and the assets located in the territory of that State may be restricted, but not his powers in respect of the rest of his assets. Nor may those rules be applied which, in the case of legal persons, entail the restriction or destitution of boards of directors beyond that which may concern the branch affected.

2.3.2. *Directors disqualifications*

125. *Directors disqualifications* deserve a more detailed explanation. In general, the *lex fori concursus* determines the regime of sanctions, if any, which may be imposed upon bankrupts and their directors; for example, restrictions on administering

---

[136] TROCHU, p. 239; WIMMER (2002), p. 2484.

assets for a specified period of time after the insolvency. However, the disqualifications of the bankrupts or their directors (e.g. the prohibition from becoming a company director for a period of, e.g. 6 years) can be seen in two ways: (a) as a
"sanction" deriving from the insolvency; but (b) also as a rule for the protection of
the public. By excluding certain people from becoming directors of a company, corporate law establishes a standard of due care in the administration of legal persons.
In the first case, that of legal sanctions founded on the insolvency of the company,
the *lex concursus* applies and if the insolvency proceedings are opened in another
Member State, the problem is classed as a question of recognition: disqualifications
associated with and deriving from the insolvency proceedings are recognised insofar as the insolvency proceedings themselves are recognised. In the second case,
regarding rules for the protection of the public, the applicable law would be the *lex
societatis*, because it concerns a problem of who can be director of a company.

> *Rationale*. In the sphere of Private International Law where there is a potential double func-
> tion of a given rule, there is also a potential *"double characterisation"*: insolvency-related
> because disqualification is associated with a policy of insolvency law; or company-related
> because it is associated with a policy of company law. This entails consulting, in this order,
> first the *lex concursus* (ex Article 4 IR) with regard to the first function, and second the *lex
> societatis* (to be determined according to the conflict of laws rules of the forum) with regard
> to the second.
>
> *Example*. In the event that a bankrupt in State F1 seeks to be a company director in F2,
> the following would occur: (a) if the *lex concursus* of F1 provides for the disqualification of
> the debtor and of his directors *as an effect of the insolvency*, this effect will be recognised
> in the same terms provided for by the law of F1 by applying Articles 16 *et seq* IR. (b) even
> though the law of F1 does not provide for the said effect, if the law of F2, which is the *lex
> societatis*, excludes bankrupts and their directors from becoming directors of companies
> incorporated under its law, the *company-law disqualification* established by the *lex soci-
> etatis* will apply *if* it considers the insolvency proceedings opened in another Member State
> to be functionally "equivalent" to the national insolvency.

2.3.3. Reorganisation plans and compositions

126. According to Article 4.2.j, *"the conditions for and the effects of closure of
insolvency proceedings, in particular by composition"* are subject to the law of the
State of opening. Article 2.k, in turn, also subjects to this law the *"creditors' rights
after the closure of insolvency proceedings"*. This means that once insolvency
proceedings have been opened in accordance with the Insolvency Regulation, all of
the available alternatives with regard to that procedure are governed by the law of the
State of opening. The *lex fori concursus* will determine whether and under what
conditions it is possible to propose, approve and implement a reorganisation plan,
a composition or a comparable measure. This law will establish the parties permitted to propose the plan or composition, the procedures for approval, the plan or
composition's content and effects, and the persons who may be affected (i.e. debtor,
creditors and equity holders).

> *Third parties*. In principle, a composition or a reorganisation does not affect the rights of
> creditors against third parties, such as *joint debtors* or *guarantors*. Such rights may have

been created precisely to protect creditors against the event of the insolvency of the debtor. The general rule is that the consequences which the insolvency of the debtor may have on those rights are determined by the law governing the right in question (*i.e.* the *lex causae*), not by the law of the State of opening (*lex fori concursus*). In so far as no insolvency policy or purpose is involved, such consequences cannot be characterised as insolvency effects. Whether the rights of recourse which those third parties may have against the insolvent debtor are affected by the plan is, however, governed by the *lex fori concursus*.[137]

127. The Insolvency Regulation is based on a model whereby restructuring normally has to be dealt with from the *main insolvency proceedings*. Therefore, it contains a battery of measures aimed at making a global restructuring plan possible on an international or, at least, a Community-wide scale. On the other hand, the Regulation also accepts that secondary proceedings may also end in a composition, plan or equivalent measure (see the wide definition of winding-up proceedings given in Article 2.c); however, this composition or plan must not disrupt any plans for composition or restructuring in the State of the main proceedings. These measures also facilitate the possibility of proposing a single plan covering both the main and the secondary estate (see No. 452).

Elaboration. Although those measures will be explained with more detail in Chapter 10, it is worth mentioning that: (a) the liquidator in the secondary proceedings is obliged to give the main liquidator the opportunity to propose uses for the assets in the secondary proceedings (Article 31.3); (b) winding-up operations in the secondary proceedings may be stayed at the request of the main liquidator (Article 33) and during this time only the main liquidator may propose measures of this type (Article 34.3); (c) if the secondary proceedings were opened before the main proceedings and are aimed at restructuring, they may be converted into winding-up proceedings at the request of the main liquidator (Article 37); (d) a composition or reorganisation plan is only admissible in secondary proceedings if the liquidator in the main proceedings gives his consent thereto or, in the absence of such consent, if the composition or reorganisation plan does not affect the financial interests of the creditors participating in the main proceedings (Article 34.1 II).

128. The composition approved by the court or competent authority is *recognised automatically* in other Member States (see Chapter 9), which means that it extends its effects there without any additional formalities. In the case of main proceedings, the opening of territorial proceedings entails a limit to this recognition, albeit compensated for by the rules on coordination described in the above paragraph. In the case of territorial proceedings, Article 17.2 excludes the extension of their effects to other Member States; an exclusion which runs parallel to the limitation of the effects of the territorial proceedings to the sphere of the State in which the territorial proceedings are opened.

129. Reorganisation usually involves a mixture of organisational, commercial and legal measures. In practice, it takes place on the basis of a comprehensive scheme or plan which states the kind, manner and extent of the restructuring of the debtor's business. A reorganisation plan will certainly address the restructuring of

---

[137] On a comparative basis, see Principles of European Insolvency Law.

the liabilities of the debtor, and, depending on the law applicable, it may include other additional measures such as: (a) the reordering of the composition of participations or shares in the corporate debtor, including the issue of new shares and the participation of new partners; (b) the adjustment of the terms and conditions of existing contracts and positions to the new conditions; or (c) the taking up of new loans.[138] In other words, a reorganisation plan may typically combine insolvency measures, such as arrangements regarding the liabilities of the debtor (e.g. a reduction of the debt or a restructuring of the payment schedule), with corporate measures (e.g. share capital reductions and increases to allow new members, debt-equity conversions, mergers or spin-offs). From the conflict of laws perspective this raises the question of the relative role which corresponds to the law governing the insolvency proceedings (*lex concursus*) and to the law governing the company or legal entity (*lex societatis*), when they are different.

130.   The Insolvency Regulation neither contains a special rule for resolving this problem nor does it establish any specific exception to the application of the *lex fori concursus*. The basis for resolving the problem is the same as we have seen above: in principle, the functioning of the internal structure of a company and the managers' and members' respective rights are all questions governed by the *lex societatis*. However, the *lex fori concursus* may interfere in that functioning and those rights to the extent necessary to achieve the objectives of the insolvency proceedings (a reorganisation may be viewed as sale to the creditors). It corresponds to the *lex fori concursus* to determine the degree of *interference* which insolvency policy requires.

Explanation. A degree of interference by the *lex fori concursus* is inevitable under the Regulation. The divestment of a corporate debtor may imply, for example, that the administrator or liquidator assumes all of the powers necessary for the management of the company and the continuation of the debtor's business, thereby replacing or supervising the company's normal bodies. If the *lex fori concursus* allows further interferences in the corporate organisation which are justified by specific insolvency policies, these interferences may be characterized as insolvency effects and, thus, be governed by the *lex concursus* as designed by Article 4 IR.[139]

131.   As a consequence of this, the line of demarcation between *lex concursus* and *lex societatis* cannot be drawn in the abstract, but depends on the insolvency policies adopted by the former. This risk of interference by the *lex concursus* in the structure of a company is a risk associated with the place where the company decides to establish its centre of main interests (e.g. its actual head office), and therefore, a risk under its sphere of control.

In keeping with this scheme, the law of the State of opening (*lex fori concursus*) is responsible for determining the effects that, for *insolvency reasons*, the reorganisation

---

[138] European Principles, § 9.2.

[139] TRUNK (1998), p. 228. Community law may limit the options of the national legislator, see ECJ ruling of 30 May 1991 (joint cases C-19/90 and 20/90).

plan can have on the insolvent company or firm. Thus, the *lex fori concursus* decides whether a reorganisation plan adopted in conformity with insolvency law can have a bearing on the legal regime of the legal person, thereby modifying his organisational, financial or capital structure. However, even when the *lex fori concursus* admits such direct action, the nature of things imposes a limit: the plan can establish any corporate measure known to the *lex societatis* (provided that measure is necessary for reorganisation purposes), but not others.

> *Explanation.* As we have already pointed out, the reorganization of a corporate debtor entails different types of measures, i.e. insolvency law measures (e.g. debt reductions or deferments) and corporate law measures (e.g. capital increases or reductions, modifications of the articles of association, mergers). The former concerns creditors, the latter equity holders. National insolvency systems follow two normative models. In the *first model* the "insolvency sphere" and the "corporate sphere" remain apart. Under this model, the plan or composition regulates the relationship between creditors and the corporate debtor and, eventually, establishes the corporate measures required to implement the plan. But the plan or composition cannot have a direct bearing over the corporate sphere. It is therefore necessary that the measures contemplated therein be approved (where the debtor's management proposes the plan, this may have been already approved by the equity holders) and implemented by the company organs in accordance with the corporate regime established by the *lex societatis*. In this model the *decision* regarding what is to be done corresponds to the reorganisation plan or composition, but the *manner* in which it is executed and the *organs* that must approve it fall under the competence of the *lex societatis*. In these cases, the coordination between the reorganisation plan and the operation of the society can be done by conditioning the approval of the plan to the execution in the corporate sphere of the measures provided for in the plan. In the *second model*, the insolvency sphere can interfere in the corporate sphere, so that the reorganisation plan can establish measures that directly affect the organisational (e.g. a modification of the articles) or capital structure (e.g. a reduction and increase of capital) of the insolvent company. In this model, not only does the decision on which corporate measures to adopt fall under the reorganisation plan, but also the adoption of the measures themselves. This faces a limit inherent in the fact that the company is governed by a different national law: the *lex societatis* limits the range of available corporate measures. Thus, the plan cannot establish measures that are unknown to that legal system or that run contrary to its corporate principles.

132. As a matter of principle, *corporate measures* are not suitable to be adopted in *territorial proceedings*.

133. *Consensual restructurings and private workouts* remain outside the scope of the Insolvency Regulation (which only applies to the *proceedings* listed in its Annexes). Corporate workouts are financial restructuring agreements between the company and its principal creditors that take place outside the confines of insolvency law. They are based on general contract and property law and are governed by the general conflict of laws rules.[140]

> *NB.* Frameworks in the form of guidelines have been developed to encourage the use of workouts. In the United Kingdom, with the involvement of the Bank of England, this

---

[140] EIDENMÜLLER (1999), p. 921 *et seq.*

framework is defined by the so called *"London Approach"*, which consists of a set of principles of how banks respond to the financial difficulties of one of their corporate customers
(see www.bankofengland.co.uk). INSOL international, in turn, have developed a set of principles of best practices for workouts, the *Statement of Principles for a global approach to
Multi-creditor workouts* (see www.insol.org).

In practice, however, hybrid restructuring mechanisms have developed which
seek to combine the advantages of private arrangements with those of formal
proceedings: negotiations concerning the composition or reorganisation plan take
place outside and prior to court proceedings, the opening of which is requested later
in order to benefit from the stay of individual enforcements, from the rules which
permit the pre-negotiated composition or reorganisation plan to be approved by
majority (and not by unanimous vote) and from other benefits (such as any tax benefits). It may be that, with regard to proceedings included in the Regulation, national
legislation allows for a proposed composition or reorganisation plan (along the lines
of what is known in practice as a *"pre-packaged bankruptcy"*), and even bind itself
to it (by way of a *"pre-voted prepack"*), in such a way that the said proposal is presented along with the request for the opening of proceedings or is admitted in the
early stages of the proceedings with a view to speeding up the conduct thereof and
allowing a fast way out from the situation of insolvency of the debtor. In these cases,
it seems logical to apply the Regulation (and not the national rules of Private
International Law), so that these agreements are governed from the outset by the law
of the State of the (future) opening of insolvency proceedings, by way of putative or
hypothetically applicable law (ex Article 4 in connection with Article 3).

NB. Financial distress is a dynamic process that covers everything from the initial stages in
which a firm experiences financial problems that can be coped with at the corporate level
to the stages when the firm is no longer viable from an economic point of view and must
be winded-up. A useful scheme of this process and its status in terms of conflict of laws is
the following:[141]

1		2		3		4
Emerging Problems: management led correction	→	Worsening problems: private workout	→	Insolvency with likely viability: reorganisation	→	Insolvency with unlikely viability: liquidation

Conflict of laws reflection						
lex societatis		*lex contractus*		*lex fori concursus*		*lex fori concursus*

As a matter of principle, the Insolvency Regulation only applies to stages 3 and 4 of this
scheme. Some Member States may also offer formal structured procedures before insolvency; these are not covered by the Insolvency Regulation either (see No. 33); usually they
will also be governed, according to the national conflict rules, by the *lex fori concursus*.

---

[141] Taken from the document *"Insolvency arrangement and contract enforceability"*, September 2002,
prepared by the Contact Group on the legal and institutional underpinnings of the international financial
system under the auspices of the European Central Bank (see www.ecb.int).

2.4. *Credit institutions and insurance companies*

134. The *Directives* on the reorganisation and winding-up of *credit institutions* and *insurance companies* contain an equivalent rule. Here the basic choice of law rule points to the application of the Law of the *home* Member State or *lex domus* (Articles 3.2 and 10 of the Directive on credit institutions and Articles 4.1 and 9 of the Directive on insurance companies, respectively).

NB. Jurisdiction to adopt reorganisation measures corresponds to the authorities of the *home* Member State (i.e. *State of origin*) and will take place in accordance with the laws, regulations and procedures applicable in that Member State. Jurisdiction to wind up also corresponds to the authorities of the *home* Member State and the institution will be wound up in accordance with the laws, regulations and procedures applicable in that Member State (Articles 3, 9 and 10 of the Directive on credit institutions, together with Recital 8 of this same Directive; Articles 4, 8 and 9 of the Directive on insurance companies). A series of specific matters are then added which are subject in particular to the competence of the law of that *home* Member State; see Article 10 of the Directive on credit institutions and Article 9 of the Directive on insurance companies. The list is practically identical to the one in Article 4 of the Insolvency Regulation.

Chapter 6

Applicable Law: Exceptions to the *Lex Fori Concursus*

1. INTRODUCTION

135. Articles 5–15 of the Insolvency Regulation establish a series of exceptions to the application of the *lex fori concursus*. These exceptions subject the effects of the insolvency proceedings on certain rights or entitlements to some other national law (e.g. to the same law that governs the right or entitlement in question) or establish that they are not affected by the opening of the proceedings (e.g. see Article 5). In general, there is a twofold reason for the existence of these exceptions: on the one hand, they enable the preservation of rights or interests specially protected by the laws of Member States from the uncertainties or inconsistencies in policy that may result from the application of a foreign *lex concursus*; and on the other hand, they respond to the need to reduce the overall complexity of the insolvency proceedings (see Recital 11).

(a) The first reason is *substantive* in nature. The application of a sole legal regime, that of the State of opening, to govern the insolvency proceedings and their effects is desirable in terms of collectivisation, but has consequences in other States. For example, it may affect the legal framework for secured lending, introducing a factor of instability that may increase the domestic cost of finance. If foreign proceedings intrude upon local security rights even when the insolvency law of the State where the collateral is situated does not permit such a result, the value of that security right may be seriously impaired; a simple transfer of the debtor's centre to a different State can bring about a radical change in the position of the secured party. This example shows that there is an inherent tension in establishing a single standard to govern the debtor's insolvency (the *lex fori concursus*), and thereby introducing an element of unpredictability or extra costs into commercial dealings in other States. Seen from this perspective, the exceptions to the application of the *lex fori concursus* can be explained in terms of legal certainty and protection of legitimate expectations.

> *Rationale.* As we know, claims arise and circulate on the basis of the expectation that they will be satisfied. The parties shape their relationships "in the shadow" of a specific legal environment; an environment that includes the degree of "resistance" of these rights in the event of the insolvency of the debtor, which is the most typical risk faced by any creditor. The application of the law under which the right in question was created is, in general, less costly to inform oneself about and more difficult for the debtor to manipulate *ex post* than the application of the law of his centre of main interest. It therefore seems reasonable, under certain circumstances, to permit and foster reliance on this law.[142] For example, in order to reflect in the conflict of laws the greater intensity with which substantive laws insulate certain

---

[142] See VIRGOS/SCHMIT Report, Margin No. 92; VIRGOS, pp. 16 and 18.

positions from the risk of insolvency. This is the case, according to the laws of several Member States, of security rights (e.g. insolvency proceedings may not affect the rights and remedies of those who hold a security interest or who own property which is in the possession of the debtor). Furthermore, there are areas of the law whose normative function is to ensure legal certainty as to the holder of a right over an asset (hence the rules regarding property registers) or to provide certainty and liquidity to their exchange (hence the rules regarding securities markets). These functions require the legal regime to be both stable and uniform. The Land Register, for instance, cannot fulfil its function if the protection it grants depends on the actual domicile of the holder. None of these qualities can be guaranteed by Article 4. In the first place, because it determines the applicable law on the basis of a factor, namely the debtor's centre of main interests, which is extrinsic to the interests protected by these rules; in the second place, because a change in the debtor's centre translates of necessity into a change of applicable law.

(b) A *procedural argument* also comes into play. Insolvency proceedings are relatively complex and costly to administrate. As we shall see, certain solutions contained in the Insolvency Regulation are justified by the need to minimize costs and facilitate a global solution in a timely fashion. A reduction of costs may privilege certain creditors but may well end up benefiting all of them insofar as the total costs (including time) of the administration of the proceedings are reduced. Take the example of Article 5 IR concerning rights *in rem*. The solution it gives was not adopted because it is the best solution in terms of abstract legislative policy, but because it was thought to represent the best way of balancing the need to meet those objectives, on the one hand, and of ensuring simplicity in the application of the rules, on the other. Restricting the added complexity of the insolvency proceedings arising from international aspects and reducing the costs associated with this specific complexity form part of the *institutional goals* of the Insolvency Regulation.

136. The combination of these two arguments enables us to understand the *different scope* of the exceptions to the *lex concursus*.[143] The Insolvency Regulation follows three main formulas: (a) in some cases *it excludes* from the effects of the insolvency proceedings certain rights located abroad; by means of a "negative" conflict of laws rule it treats the right as if there was no insolvency. This is the case of Articles 5 and 7, for example. As we shall see, the search for simple solutions explains the radical nature of this solution. (b) In other cases, the Regulation subjects the effects of the insolvency proceedings not to the law of the State of opening (*lex concursus*), but to the national law which governs the right in question (*lex causae*). In this way, the effects of insolvency proceedings opened in a Member State on a right whose applicable law is that of a different Member State will be the same as if the insolvency proceedings had been opened in this latter State. This is the case of Articles 8–10. (c) Finally, the Regulation combines the application of the law of the State of opening with the national law which governs the right in question. Articles 11 and 13 represent two variations on this idea. In the latter two cases (b and c), the idea of protecting legitimate expectations is dominant.

---

[143] See Virgos/Schmit Report, Margin No. 92; Virgos, p. 18; Taupitz, p. 329; Flessner (1998), p. 283; Leible/Staudinger (2000), p. 550.

Problem: effects according to a different national law. When Regulation rules establish that the effects, or some of the effects, of the insolvency proceedings should be governed by the law of a State (F2) different from the State of opening (F1), then the problem arises of specifying which effects correspond to those proceedings according to the law of that other State (F2). This problem should be solved in keeping with the principle of equivalence: the applicable effects will be those befitting an equivalent national procedure, from among those listed for that State (F2) in the Annexes to the Regulation (since it operates with a "closed list system" of procedures, see No. 35). If the procedure opened in F1 is of a reorganisation type, then it must be attributed the effects which according to the law of F2 correspond to a reorganisation procedure (listed in Annex A for this State). If the procedure opened in F1 is of a liquidation nature, then the effects should be those of a liquidation procedure in F2 (listed in Annex B of the Regulation).

137. Each of the special rules provided for by the Regulation will be analysed in greater detail below. For reasons which we have already explained (*supra* No. 27-b), they only apply when the case is linked with another Member State. With regard to non-Member States (including Denmark), national conflict of laws rules apply. The premise that these special rules only function when the designated law is that of another Member State (or in Articles 5 and 7, when the asset is located in a Member State) is expressly included in all of the provisions except for Articles 6 and 14. A literal interpretation of this omission could lead one to think that the exceptions established in these two Articles have a more general scope. However, this silence should simply be attributed to a question of wording. The reason for this is that the Regulation restricts itself to governing intra-Community conflicts, and neither a genetic nor a teleological analysis support any special reason to deviate from this self-limitation in the cases regulated by these two Articles.[144] In any case, what must be made clear here is that this restriction does not authorise, by means of a merely literal *argumentum a contrario*, any interpretation with regard to non-Member States whereby the Regulation orders or permits an unrestricted application of the *lex fori concursus*; it simply does not govern the question.[145]

2. THIRD-PARTY RIGHTS IN REM AND RETENTION OF TITLE

2.1. *Rights in rem of creditors or third parties (Article 5)*

2.1.1. *The rule*

138. Article 5 of the Insolvency Regulation establishes that "*the opening of insolvency proceedings shall not affect the rights in rem of creditors or third parties in respect of tangible or intangible, moveable or immoveable assets – both specific assets and collections of indefinite assets as a whole which change from time to time – belonging to the debtor which are situated within the territory of another Member State at the time of the opening of proceedings*".

---

[144] VIRGOS/SCHMIT Report, Margin No. 93; BALZ (1996a), p. 950; TAUPITZ, p. 343; LEIBLE/STAUDINGER (2000), p. 554; HUBER, p. 152; VIRGOS, p. 18.

[145] VIRGOS/SCHMIT Report, Margin No. 93 II.

139. The treatment of rights *in rem* is a central theme in all insolvency systems. Rights *in rem* provide creditors with an efficient instrument for reducing or eliminating the risk of the insolvency of the debtor and fulfil an important function by promoting the availability of low-cost credit both in personal and business financing.

140. The conflict of laws problem arises because the treatment of these rights in the insolvency of the debtor (e.g. the degree to which they survive the debtor's insolvency unaltered) differs from one country to another. In particular, the problem will arise when the encumbered assets are situated in a State other than the State of the opening of the insolvency proceedings, because in this case the national law applicable to the insolvency proceedings (*lex fori concursus*) and the national law applicable to the right *in rem* (e.g. the *lex rei sitae*[146]) will be different.

141. In theory, *three general solutions* may be given to the problem of the insolvency treatment of rights *in rem* in respect of assets belonging to the debtor, which are situated in the territory of a State other than the State of the opening of insolvency proceedings.[147]

(a) To maintain the principle of universality in its strictest terms and, consequently, subject the treatment of these rights in the insolvency to the *lex fori concursus*. The meaning of this solution is as follows: without prejudice to the recognition of rights *in rem* constituted abroad (which, from the point of view of insolvency law, is a preliminary question), the restrictions and alterations that these rights may suffer in the insolvency of the debtor are determined by the *lex fori concursus*. This means that the *position* of the security rights in the insolvency proceedings (whether or not they are affected and to what extent) is established by the *lex fori concursus*. We have already looked at the arguments which tend to be put forward in favour of this solution. The problem presented by this solution is that the intervention of the *lex concursus* may lead to gaps in protection which are inconsistent with the security function that these rights must provide according their national applicable law. This will occur, e.g. when the *lex concursus* imposes restrictions on the enforcement of rights *in rem* or gives priority over the collateral to the claims of another party which do not exist in the *lex rei sitae*. It is not easy to justify the fact that a real security right validly created over assets located in the forum is secure *vis-à-vis* domestic insolvency proceedings but vulnerable in the face of foreign insolvency proceedings; a factor external to the real security right, such as the transfer of the domicile of the debtor to another State, would be enough to devalue the rights of the creditor over a collateral which always remains located in the same jurisdiction.

(b) To let the law that governs the right *in rem* (e.g. the *lex rei sitae*) also determine the treatment thereof in the event of the insolvency of the debtor. This solution

---

[146] For the sake of simplicity, we will consider that security rights are always governed by the *lex rei sitae*, because this is the general rule. However, the arguments are still valid even when a different conflict of laws rule is applicable.

[147] See TROCHU, pp. 172–173, 184 *et seq*; FAVOCCIA, pp. 22–26; DROBNIG (1992), pp. 178–179; VIRGOS, p. 20; SANCHEZ LORENZO, pp. 57, 137–146; HANISCH (1993), pp. 66 *et seq*; TAUPITZ, pp. 330–333; FLESSNER (1998), p. 279; VON WILMOWSKY (1996), pp. 285–292; HERCHEN, p. 75; HUBER, p. 153 (all with references to the possible combinations of connections).

means that the law governing the right *in rem* would determine not only its creation and general validity, but also its effectiveness in the case of the opening of insolvency proceedings. The *position* of the real security right *in the insolvency proceedings* opened abroad will be established by the insolvency rules of the national law applicable to the security right (the *lex rei sitae*). This exception to the play of the *lex fori concursus* tends to be justified in two ways: (i) by the need to ensure the stability and universality of these rights, in keeping with their *erga omnes* character; and (ii) by the immediate control which the authorities of the location have over the asset, which could make it more difficult to implement foreign insolvency rules.[148] The problem is that this solution can significantly increase the administrative costs of the proceedings. This is due to the complexity arising from the fact that the effects of the same insolvency proceedings would be governed by different laws, depending on the location of the collateral. This complexity is reflected both in the sphere of information, as it will be necessary to consult as many national laws as there are countries in which the debtor's assets are located, and in the substantive sphere, due to the problems of the adjustment which will be necessary in order to accommodate the insolvency proceedings to the variety of different effects ordered by the different national laws in question.

(c) To exclude rights *in rem* from the effects of the insolvency proceedings: to apply neither the *lex fori concursus* nor the insolvency law of the *lex rei sitae*. The rights *in rem* become *immunised or shielded* in the face of the insolvency, both in their substantive aspect (the right of preference in respect of the value of the asset), and in their procedural aspect (the right to a separate or individual enforcement). The reasons for this solution are based on the reduction of administrative costs by simplifying the administration of the insolvency.

Summary of the alternative solutions. Let us imagine main insolvency proceedings opened in Germany and a pledge perfected under Spanish law in favour of a given creditor over assets located in Spain. The first solution would mean that the position of the secured creditor in the insolvency proceedings is determined by German insolvency rules. According to the second solution, the position in the insolvency would be determined by Spanish insolvency rules. And according to the third, by neither the one nor the other: the insolvency proceedings opened in Germany do not affect the position of the secured creditor. He can dispose of the assets in accordance with the out-of-insolvency provisions of Spanish law regarding security interests.

142. Article 5 of the Insolvency Regulation is geared towards this latter solution, as it establishes a rule of *non-alteration* of the rights *in rem* of creditors or third parties in respect of those assets of the debtor which are located in a State other than the State of opening. It is often said that Article 5 IR is a rule of *relative immunity*, as it does not prevent the opening of *territorial proceedings* in the State where the asset is located provided that the debtor has an establishment there. In such a case, the liquidator of the main insolvency can request the opening of secondary insolvency

---

[148] Siehr, pp. 814–815; Taupitz, p. 331.

proceedings. If the law applicable to these proceedings enables the said rights to be affected, then the liquidator of the main proceedings can take advantage of this possibility.[149] If the debtor does not have an establishment in the State where the collateral is situated, then Article 5 IR operates as a rule of absolute immunity. Actions to set-aside follow a different regime (see No. 175).

143. In order to analyse Article 5 in more detail we are going to follow the usual pattern: first we will look at the conditions for the application of the rule and then at its legal consequences. With regard to the latter, we will consider the reasonableness of the solution contained in Article 5 of the Insolvency Regulation.

2.1.2. Condition of application: rights in rem in respect of assets located in a Member State other than the State of opening

2.1.2.1. Meaning of "rights in rem"

144. When it comes to understanding how this provision works, the greatest difficulties lie in the definition of the term *"rights in rem"*. To clarify this concept three ideas have to be taken into account: (a) Article 5 of the Regulation is not a rule which attributes new rights: it is a rule which simply recognises and protects rights *in rem* acquired, before the opening, according to the applicable non-insolvency national law; (b) Article 5 is not a "blank cheque" rule of recognition; it only recognises authentic rights *in rem*; and (c) as a rule of recognition, Article 5 cannot be used to confer more powers upon the holder of a right *in rem* than those which he would have according to non-insolvency law. Let us now look at the significance and scope of each of these ideas in more detail.

(a) First idea: Article 5 is a rule of recognition of rights

145. Article 5 of the Insolvency Regulation is not a rule which confers rights, but a rule which simply respects and protects the rights *in rem* acquired according to national laws. In this respect, what this provision tells us is that whoever has perfected a right *in rem* before the declaration of opening (i.e. has a pre-insolvency position protected by a right *in rem*) is not affected by the opening of insolvency proceedings in another Member State.

146. From the conflict of laws perspective, the application of Article 5 presents a problem of *preliminary question*. Article 5 does not confer rights *in rem*; these are conferred by national laws. Consequently, the application of this provision requires prior clarification as to whether or not we are dealing with a *right in rem*. To resolve this question we have to start from the premise that rights are created according to national laws, and that the attributes of any right are determined by the national law which governs this right. In the case of rights *in rem*, the basic solution tends to coincide in all legal systems: the *lex rei sitae* is applied.[150] Consequently, it will be this law which tells us whether or not the holder has a right *in rem* and the scope

---

[149] VIRGOS/SCHMIT Report, Margin No. 98; VIRGOS, p. 19; TAUPITZ, pp. 333, 336–337; FLETCHER, p. 273; HERCHEN, pp. 73 *et seq.*; HUBER, p. 156; KEMPER, p. 1616.
[150] See VIRGOS/SCHMIT Report, Margin No. 100; see also, TAUPITZ, p. 335; KOLMANN, p. 574.

thereof. Only if the holder has a right *in rem* under the national law applicable will his position be protected in the event of insolvency by Article 5 of the Regulation.[151]

Variable connecting factors ("conflict mobile"). The problem of the so-called *conflict mobile* arises when, at the time the right *in rem* is created, the asset is located in one State (e.g. Germany) and at the time the insolvency proceedings are opened the asset is located in a different State (e.g. France or Spain).[152] In order to resolve these problems it is necessary to differentiate two aspects: (a) the continued existence in the new *situs* of the right *in rem* created under the *lex situs originis* and (b) its effectiveness in the insolvency proceedings. The general conflict of laws rules are used to resolve the *preliminary question*: in this case, the question of whether or not, in the event of a change of *situs* of the collateral, the holder continues to enjoy a right *in rem* (e.g. a security interests). For this reason, the problem of mobile conflict is resolved as if the insolvency proceedings had not been opened. In principle, where the collateral moves to a new *situs* (e.g. Spain) the impact of subsequent events (including failure to observe a re-perfection requirement, such a registration in a local register) on a right *in rem* validly created under the law of the first *situs* (e.g. Germany) is determined by the law of the new *situs* (in our example, Spanish law).[153] If, in accordance with these general rules, the response to the preliminary question is favourable, i.e. the holder enjoys a right *in rem*, then Article 5 of the Insolvency Regulation applies if, *at the time of the opening of the proceedings* and in accordance with the rules of location of the Regulation itself, the collateral is located in a Member State other than the State of opening.

Liens in respect of claims and assignments by way of guarantee. The Insolvency Regulation expressly includes in its catalogue of rights protected by Article 5 the lien and the assignment of claims (Article 5.2.b). The Regulation does not govern the *preliminary question* of if and how a lien in respect of the claim or an assignment by way of guarantee is created. This question is regulated by the non-insolvency conflict rules; for example, in the case of a contractual claim, Article 12 of the 1980 Rome Convention will govern its assigment.[154] Once the lien or assignment by way of guarantee has been created in accordance with the applicable national law, Article 5 guarantees the non-alteration of this right in spite of the opening of the insolvency proceedings, when the *debitor debitoris* or "account debtor" has his domicile in a State other than the State of opening (see Article 2.g III).

(b) Second idea: Article 5 is not is a "blank cheque" rule

147. In spite of the fact that the Insolvency Regulation refers to national laws to determine when we are dealing with a right *in rem*, this is not a "blank cheque" referral. Article 5 only covers *rights in rem in the strict sense of this concept.* This is

---

[151] VIRGOS/SCHMIT Report, Margin No. 95; TAUPITZ, pp. 334–335; DROBNIG (1992), pp. 177–178; HANISCH (1993) pp. 63 *et seq.*; GOODE, p. 502; FLETCHER, p. 270; HERCHEN, p. 55; EIDENMÜLLER (2001a), p. 6, note 29; LEIBLE/STAUDINGER (2000) p. 551; HUBER, p. 154.

[152] On this problem in the sphere of insolvency, see HANISCH (1993), pp. 63 *et seq.*; FLETCHER, p. 271; HERCHEN, pp. 55–56.

[153] DROBNIG (1981), pp. 299 *et seq.*

[154] Although the interpretation of this Article is debatable; in the future, the UNCITRAL Convention on the assignment of receivables in international trade may play a fundamental role (see the state of the question in *www.uncitral.org*

deduced from Article 5.2 and the VIRGOS/SCHMIT Report.[155] In other words, Member States remain free to determine according to their own laws when a right is a right *in rem*. However, it is for the Insolvency Regulation to determine the limits within which the Member States may have recourse to that concept for the purposes of Article 5.

148. It is in this context that Article 5, paragraphs 2 and 3 come into play. According to Article 5.2, a "right in rem" shall in particular mean: "*(a) the right to dispose of assets or have them disposed of and to obtain satisfaction from the proceeds of or income from those assets, in particular by virtue of a lien or a mortgage; (b) the exclusive right to have a claim met, in particular a right guaranteed by a lien in respect of the claim or by assignment of the claim by way of a guarantee; (c) the right to demand the assets from, and/or to require restitution by, anyone having possession or use of them contrary to the wishes of the party so entitled; (d) a right in rem (in the above sense) to the beneficial use of assets.* Article 5.3 complements this description it by adding: "*The right, recorded in a public register and enforceable against third parties, under which a right in rem within the meaning of paragraph 1 may be obtained, shall be considered a right in rem*".

149. The purpose of these provisions is not to give a Community definition of the expression "right *in rem*" but, simply, to facilitate the operation of Article 5, by establishing clear and predictable criteria for its application. Article 5.2 contains a typological description of what is meant by a right *in rem* for the purposes of Article. 5 [156] Its function is to operate as a limit to the characterization of a right as a right *in rem* for the purposes of Article 5. Only those rights conferred by national laws that conform to its *typological characterisation* are protected by Article 5.1 of the Regulation.

150. Article 5.2 covers all the "normal types" of rights *in rem* which exist in the laws of the Member States. The list of attributes contained in Article 5.2 is *not exclusive*. The expression "in particular" reflects this idea. However, any later judicial development thereof must be carried out in accordance with the aim of covering only strict rights *in rem*, not personal rights, even if these are reinforced by some kind of priority in the event of enforcement. Intermediate forms between personal rights and rights *in rem* are excluded from Article 5.1 of the Regulation. Article 5.3 which recognises as a right *in rem* for the purposes of Article 5 a right recorded in a public register and enforceable against third parties *to obtain* a right *in rem*, reflects this idea (by an argument *a contrario*).

151. Supplementary guidance can be found in the Explanatory Report. According to the Report, Article 5 was drafted under the assumption that a right *in rem* has basically two characteristics: (a) its *direct and immediate relationship* with the asset, which remains linked to the satisfaction of its holder, without depending upon the

---

[155] VIRGOS/SCHMIT Report, Margin No. 103; see also HERCHEN, pp. 115–119; TAUPITZ, p. 333; FLETCHER, pp. 270, 271–273; HUBER, p. 155.

[156] BALZ (1996b), p. 508, note 98; see also HUBER, p. 155.

asset belonging to the estate of a specific person, nor on the relationship of its holder with another person; and (b) the *absolute nature* of the allocation of the right to the holder. This means that these rights are effective with respect to anyone (i.e. *erga omnes*). Expressions of this character are, for example, the fact that the holder is protected by a right of pursuit or that the right can be asserted in the face of attempted enforcements by third parties or in situations of insolvency (because it confers upon its holder a right of separation or to individual satisfaction). To sum up, a right *in rem* is a right *over*, and exercisable *against*, an asset.

> *Justification.* This restriction is perfectly reasonable.[157] Article 5 constitutes an exception not only to Article 4 (i.e. to the application of the *lex fori concursus*) but also to the principle of universality which underlies the Regulation: in practice, the most common effect of the said provision will be to place the assets affected by a right *in rem* outside the estate of the insolvency. Although only the right *in rem*, and not the collateral as such, is excluded by Article 5 from the effects of the opening, the exercise thereof will mean, in the majority of cases, that the separate enforcement of the asset and/or payment to the secured creditor will exhaust its economic value. This is particularly serious if we also remember that the mere presence of assets is not sufficient grounds for opening territorial proceedings; it is also necessary for the debtor to have an establishment in the State in question. When this is not the case, Article 5 becomes a rule of absolute immunity: it neither responds to a universal model nor to a territorial model. For this reason, an unrestricted *lege causae* characterisation would entail the risk that the States use an unreasonably broad definition of the concept "right *in rem*". The inclusion under this term of any type of priority or privilege of payment could end up frustrating not only the principle of universality of the main proceedings, but all of the principles which underlie Insolvency law; as the Report itself warns, it would drain the Regulation of content.[158]

152. For the purposes of the Insolvency Regulation, Article 5.3 establishes that *"the right, recordered in a public register and enforceable against third parties, under which a right in rem ... may be obtained, shall be considered a right in rem"*.[159] In this latter case, it is understood that when the registration confers upon its holder, or permits the conferral of, powers analogous to those of a right *in rem*, it must be covered by the rule contained in Article 5. That is to say, it is understood that the position conferred upon the holder by the registration, although a *minus* with regard to the right *in rem* itself, is comparable in terms of value and must be covered by Article 5.

153. By contrast, *priorities* and *"privileges"* do not count as rights *in rem* for the purposes of Article 5. A privilege is not an independent right, but a quality associated with a claim which gives it a better ranking of payment compared with other creditors; and there is no doubt whatsoever that the scheme of distribution and the priorities are subject to the *lex fori concursus* (Article 4.2.i; see also Recital 11). It falls to this law, and not to the *lex causae*, to determine which kinds of priorities and privileges exist in the insolvency of the debtor and what type of claims benefit therefrom. This is also true for the so-called "special privileges": the mere fact that a

---

[157] See VIRGOS/SCHMIT Report, Margin No. 102; HUBER, p. 155.

[158] Margin No. 102, *in fine*.

[159] BALZ (1996a), p. 950; TAUPITZ, p. 333; HERCHEN, p. 119; LEIBLE/STAUDINGER (2000), p. 552.

priority is linked to a specific asset of the debtor as part of his estate does not mean that it becomes a right *in rem* in the sense of Article 5, nor that the holder of the privilege may benefit from it. Otherwise, there would be a serious risk of the universal scope of the main proceedings being frustrated.[160]

> *Explanation.* The category of "privilege" is a very broad category which national laws use in different ways. The Regulation does not enter into this use. It simply states that, in order to benefit from Article 5, a right must be a right *in rem* in the sense explained above. Therefore, only if a national law protects a privileged claim by granting its holder a right *in rem* (e.g. the maritime privileges covered by the 1926 Brussels Convention, which "follow the ship, even if there is a change in owner"), will the right of this holder be protected by Article 5 IR.
>
> *Problem: "Superprivileges".* These are superpriorities in the sense that they confer on their holder a priority even in respect of secured creditors. They are normally used for the purposes of social protection (such as to ensure the payment of wages up until a multiple of the minimum salary) or to protect a public interest. Thus, in some Member States, unpaid wages and taxes came ahead of security rights in the distribution of the proceeds from the sale of property subject to a security interest. Superprivileges are, like other priorities, accessory qualities of a claim and not independent rights. These superprivileges do not confer rights over specific assets nor establish any direct entitlement to the debtor's assets; they rather operate as preferences in payment over other creditors of the debtor, and apply both in insolvency and non-insolvency situations. In so far as they do not confer a security right they are not covered by Article 5. This, without prejudice to the possibility of opening territorial insolvency proceedings (Article 3.2, *supra*).[161] In fact, one of the arguments put forward to defend the possibility of opening territorial insolvencies was to ensure that this type of superprivilege was effective in situations where the law of the State of the debtor's centre of main interests does not recognise such a priority. The possibility of triggering the opening of secondary proceedings is also a negotiating tool. If the national law so permits, the liquidator or administrator in the main proceedings may agree to recognise that preference in exchange for those benefiting from the superprivilege not requesting the opening of secondary proceedings. On the relationship between superprivileges and rights *in rem* protected by Article 5, see also No. 154.

(c) Third idea: Article 5 does not confer "more" than that which corresponds to the "non-insolvency" situation

154. Article 5 cannot be used to confer more powers on the holder of a right *in rem* than those which he would enjoy in a non-insolvency situation. Article 5

---

[160] See also POTTHAST, pp. 175 *et seq.*

[161] See Recital 28 of the Regulation and VIRGOS/SCHMIT Report, Margin No. 128; see also FLETCHER, p. 279; GARRIDO, p. 90. A different means of providing protection for employees is followed by Directive 80/987/EEC, modified by Directive 2002/74/EC on the approximation of the laws of Member States relating to the protection of employees in the event of the insolvency of their employees. This Directive establishes a body which guarantees payment of the outstanding claims of the employees concerned. According to Article 8a, when an undertaking with activities in at least two Member States is in a state of insolvency, the guarantee institution responsible for meeting employees' outstanding claims will be that of the Member State in whose territory they work or habitually work. The extent of employees' rights will also be determined by the law governing that institution.

recognises the rights *in rem* acquired prior to the declaration of opening and protect them against the effects of the insolvency proceedings. But it cannot be used to improve the *non-insolvency position* of the holder of a right *in rem*. Therefore, Article 5 respects the separate right of enforcement which the holder of a right *in rem* may have over the asset affected, but does not alter the regime of priorities which governs this right outside the insolvency. The law governing the right *in rem* (i.e. the security interest) will determine the priorities of payment between the secured creditor and any preferential creditors;[162] if there are liens or privileges which have precedence over the security right in non-insolvency situations, they continue to apply in the normal terms.

> *Example: "superprivileges"*. This is relevant in the case of the so-called "superprivileges", i.e. creditors who have a right to payment which has priority over secured creditors and which is also effective in non-insolvency situations. For example, workers, in accordance with Article 32.1 of the Spanish Workers Code (*Estatuto de los Trabajadores*), had a privilege of payment for their outstanding claims, which, where necessary, took precedence over creditors secured with a right *in rem*. The practical application of this rule in the context of the Regulation would be as follows (and the analysis is valid for similar rights in other States): if a creditor secured by a right *in rem* over an asset located in Spain intends to enforce his right, he may do so even if insolvency proceedings have been opened against the debtor in another Member State. Article 5 protects this right. Having said that, if this same debtor has employees working in Spain, these, in spite of the insolvency proceedings opened abroad, may prove their claim in the enforcement procedure initiated by the secured creditor in Spain[163] and receive payment out of the proceeds of the realisation of the collateral, up to the limit provided for by the privilege. In this case, the employees would be exercising a right they enjoy even if no insolvency proceedings had been opened. The compatibility of this solution with Article 4 and with the idea, expressed in the VIRGOS/SCHMIDT Report (Margin No. 128), that superprivileges are subject to the *lex fori concursus*, may be debatable, but only at first sight. The fact that the application of the *lex fori concursus* can be excluded through Article 5 is inevitable, because otherwise the secured creditor would receive an extra benefit for no reason whatsoever: the secured creditor would be exempt from the preference which the superprivileged creditors have *in non-insolvency situations*. With Article 5, the secured creditor may expect not to be affected by the insolvency of the debtor, but not to improve upon his non-insolvency rights.
>
> If a creditor with an insolvency claim (e.g. the employees) obtain total or partial satisfaction thereof, there are reasons for respecting this satisfaction (by not applying Article 20.1 IR, which imposes an obligation to return what has been obtained outside an insolvency proceedings), but also likewise to apply by analogy the provisions of Article 20.2 IR on imputation, in connection with the dividend which would correspond to that creditor in the insolvency proceedings.

2.1.2.2. The time factor

155. Article 5 only applies to those rights *in rem* constituted *before* the proceedings were opened (regarding this moment, see Article 2.f). The teleology of the provision would require, when various steps are necessary for perfection according to

---

[162] ISAACS/TOUBE/MARSHALL, in MOSS/FLETCHER/ISAACS, p. 113.

[163] Take into account that the *lex concursus* cannot affect rights *in rem* protected by Article 5 IR; and this protection includes their procedural prerogatives (i.e. the privilege of separate realisation).

the applicable law, that all of the necessary acts be completed prior to the opening of the proceedings (bearing in mind, however, Article 5.3).[164] Floating charges also benefit from this rule; once the creditor complies with all perfection requirements in accordance with the applicable law, the security interest is brought into being and may be described as "present security".[165] Under a floating charge, the security right is attached, in the first instance, to a shifting fund of assets, even though it is only in the end that it crystallises and fastens on specific assets; but no new security interest is created by crystallisation.[166]

If the right *in rem* has been constituted *after* this time, Article 4 applies.[167] In other words, creditors who have not succeeded in perfecting a pre-insolvency right *in rem* under the national applicable law before the opening of insolvency proceedings in another Member State, will not benefit from the "non-effects" rule established in Article 5. Consequently, the *lex fori concursus* will determine the effects of the insolvency proceedings on subsequently created rights. This, without prejudice to the possible application of Article 14. This provision establishes an exception of a different nature to the play of the *lex fori concursus* in order to protect third-party purchasers.[168]

156. Furthermore, Article 5 only applies when the right *in rem* concerns an asset (or a collection of them) which is situated in a Member State other than the State of opening. Again, the relevant time at which the *situation of an asset* is to be determined is the opening of insolvency proceedings. Article 5 comes into play if the asset (i.e. the collateral) is situated in another Member State at that time. Subsequent changes of location do not alter this result.

2.1.2.3. *Property protected by Article 5*

157. A key to any efficient regime governing security rights is to enable the grantors thereof to use the value inherent in their property to the maximum extent possible for the purposes of obtaining credit.[169] In order to resolve possible problems arising from the strict conception of right *in rem* which underlies Article 5, the text itself expressly introduces several clarifications. The main reason for these clarifications is to extend the sphere of application of Article 5 of the Regulation to rights in respect of "*assets*" which are not things in the strict sense of the word but which, from an economic perspective, can fulfil an equivalent function as security.

Consequently, Article 5 recognises rights *in rem* over all types of property: "*tangible or intangible, moveable or immoveable assets – both specific assets and collections of indefinite assets as a whole which change from time to time –*". This

---

[164] See FLETCHER, p. 272; HERCHEN, pp. 122–124; LEIBLE/STAUDINGER (2000), pp. 550–551.

[165] For English law, see GOODE (1988), p. 50.

[166] GOODE (1997), p.15.

[167] VIRGOS/SCHMIT Report, Margin No. 96.

[168] VIRGOS/SCHMIT Report, Margin No. 96; TAUPITZ, p. 341; LEIBLE/STAUDINGER (2000), p. 550.

[169] UNCITRAL, Draft Legislative guide on secured transactions. Report of the Secretary-General (document A/CN.9/W G.VI/WP/2./add.1), p. 5.

description includes *intellectual and industrial property rights*; *claims and receivables* (see Article 5.2.b which deals with liens in respect of claims and the assignment of claims by way of guarantee); *shifting pools of assets*, meaning that, for example, the *floating charges* of the laws of Great Britain and Ireland are protected, together with equivalent figures in other legal systems;[170] and the *beneficial use* of an asset (see Article 5.2.d).

> *Present and future assets.* The wording of Article 5 presupposes the existence of the assets *at the time of the opening.* The distinction between an existing and a future asset may pose difficulties. In principle, present property is considered to include potential property (property not yet in existence but growing out of property which is in existence). The concept of potential property applies both to tangibles (growing crops in a piece of land) and intangibles (the right to receive sums payable in the future under existing contracts). The important thing about this distinction is that the grant of security over the potential property will be treated as a present assignment of existing property.[171] Thus, an assignment by way of guarantee of the right to receive sums payable in the future under a contract already concluded by the time the insolvency proceedings are opened, benefits from Article 5; but not the assignment of sums payable under future contracts (or other claims that may arise from a future activity of the assignor). Article 5 only protects pre-existing rights: only securities which give rise, before the opening, to a *present* right *in rem* are encompassed. Article 5.3 reinforces this idea.

2.1.2.4. The situs of assets

158. As already stated, in order for the rule contained in Article 5 to come into play it is necessary for the asset (i.e. the collateral) to be located in a *Member State other* than the State of the opening of the proceedings. If the assets are located in a non-Member State, the national conflict of law rules, apply.[172]

We will study the rules for determining the *location* of an asset in Chapter VIII and the same applies here (see Article 2.g). However, in order to explain how Article 5 functions, we will anticipate here the treatment of claims, means of transport and *res in transitu.*

159. A claim is a right to payment of a monetary sum or to performance of a non-monetary obligation. Claims are located at the place where the third party required to meet them (*debitor debitoris*) has his centre of his main interests (Article 2.g). In practice this will be the domicile of that party. In the case of bank accounts see, however, No. 312. The concept of control underlies this location. Article 5 applies to liens in respect of claims (*e.g.* debt charges and receivables) and assignments of claims by way of guarantee, when the debtor's debtor (*debitor debitoris*), has his domicile in a State other than the State of opening. Example: a Spanish company (A) is the holder of a claim against a German company (B). According to the rules on the location of assets (Article 2.g III), this claim is considered to be located in Germany. The Spanish company then assigns this claim by way of guarantee to a third

---

[170] Virgos/Schmit Report, Margin No. 104.
[171] Goode (1995), p. 682.
[172] Virgos/Schmit Report, Margin No. 94; Leible/Staudinger (2000), p. 551; Fumagalli, p. 700.

party (C). If insolvency proceedings against A are opened in Spain (*ex* Article 3.1), the assignee of the claim (C) is protected by Article 5 of the Regulation.

> *NB.* Two specific cases deserve further comment: (a) When the *debitor debitoris* is situated in a different Member State but the law applicable to the security interest is the law of the State of opening. From a teleological point of view it seems plausible to practice an *interpretative reduction* of article 5 and exempt this case from its benefit; none of the reasons which justify the solution given by Article 5 (i.e. protection of legitimate expectations and simplicity of results) are present here. (b) When the *debitor debitoris* has his domicile in the State of opening, the *lex fori concursus* will determine the effects of the insolvency on that lien or assignment even if the law applicable to that lien or assignment is not the law of the State of opening. In this case, an *extensive interpretation* of Article 5 is not justified; the policy on simplicity of results could be alleged in favour, but not the protection of expectations, as these expectations would point to the State of opening.

160. *Means of transport* and *res in transitu* give rise to specific problems.[173] To understand how the Regulation deals with these assets, we can distinguish between two issues: the creation of a right *in rem* and the treatment of such a right in situations of insolvency.

(a) The first issue is, in technical terms, a *preliminary question*. Insofar as Article 5 does not confer rights, but rather recognises those rights *in rem* acquired according to non-insolvency laws, the location of those assets, for the purposes of deciding the preliminary question of whether or not the holder enjoys a right *in rem*, must be based on the ordinary conflict of laws rules of each State.

(b) The second issue requires a more detailed analysis. If the answer to the first question is affirmative, the decision as to whether the asset is located in a Member State other than the State of opening for the purposes of Article 5 must be based on the Insolvency Regulation's rules concerning location (i.e. Article 2.g). The rules contained in the Regulation take into account the possibilities of realisation and, therefore, are based on the idea of control or immediate power over the assets. For the purposes of Article 2.g this entails, e.g. in the case of tangible assets, looking to the place of the physical presence or registration of the assets and, in principle, not considering other locations. Nevertheless, it is clear that the place of physical presence is not a reasonable location in the case of goods in transit, even under the theory of ultimate control. In such a case it is necessary to resort to some kind of "*fictional* location" (e.g. the place of origin, the place of destination, etc.).

> *Rationale.* Let us suppose that France is the State where the main insolvency proceedings are opened; at the time of the opening, the assets are being transported through Spain in transit to Portugal. In this case it does not seem reasonable to treat the assets as if they were situated in Spain for the purposes of the Regulation. There are two arguments to support this: (a) in the case of goods in transit, all Member States permit an exception to the *lex rei sitae* in non-insolvency situations; the actual location being considered a casual

---

[173] HERCHEN, pp. 112–115.

location and therefore irrelevant, other connecting factors are preferred (e.g. the place of origin or the place of destination). In this context, it would make little sense for the Insolvency Regulation to go back to the *situs naturalis* in detriment to these other connecting factors; and (b) the inconsistency of such a solution is easy to detect if Article 5 were worded in a positive rather than in a negative sense, by stating that the law of the place of location will determine the effects of the insolvency proceedings on the rights *in rem* of creditors and third parties. It would then be difficult to justify in policy terms the application of the law of the State through the territory of which the asset is being transported at the time of the opening; in our example, Spanish law. The obvious conclusion is, therefore, that in the case of goods in transit the physical location is irrelevant.

The problem is that the Regulation does not contain a uniform rule on this question. A reasonable option is to apply the rules concerning the location of goods in transit (*res in transitu*) of the State of the opening of the main proceedings, which are the only proceedings with universal jurisdiction. This solution allows a uniform result and prevents conflicts among Member States as to the location of goods in transit. If only independent territorial proceedings are opened, their rules regarding location can be applied (see No. 310).

Means of transport. With regard to means of transport (ships, aircraft, railways, etc.) the international conventions ratified by the Member States must be taken into account, as they may contain rules regarding both the constitution of rights in respect of these assets and their location. If, in accordance with these rules, the holder has perfected a right *in rem* over an asset and that asset is deemed to be situated outside the State of opening, Article 5 of the Insolvency Regulation will apply.

NB. Several international conventions are currently being drafted which may contain rules regarding the law applicable in situations of insolvency. For example, the UNCITRAL Convention on the assignment of receivables in international trade;[174] the UNIDROIT Conventions on International Factoring; the Convention on International Interests in Mobile Equipment and the Protocol on Matters Specific to Aircraft Equipment promoted by UNIDROIT and the International Civil Association Organisation;[175] or the Convention on the law applicable to certain rights in respect of securities held with an intermediary of the Hague Conference on Private International Law.[176]

161. For the regime governing rights *in rem* over *negotiable securities* see infra No. 311.

2.1.3. Legal consequence: non-alteration of the right in rem

162. The legal consequence provided for by Article 5 is that the main insolvency proceedings cannot interfere with security rights held over assets located outside the State where the insolvency proceedings are opened: "*the opening of insolvency proceedings shall not affect the rights in rem of creditors or third parties*". The scope of this provision deserves a detailed explanation.

---

[174] See www.uncitral.org
[175] See www.unidroit.org
[176] See www.hcch.net

As we know, Article 3.1 establishes the principle of the universality of the main insolvency proceedings. But for the opening of territorial proceedings, all the assets and all the creditors, wherever they are, are subject to them. Consequently, it falls to the law of the State of the opening (*lex fori concursus*) to determine which assets form part of the estate of the main proceedings and which are excluded (Article 4.2.b). However, even though an asset is included in the estate in accordance with Article 4, Article 5 establishes an exception to this rule with regard to rights *in rem*. Its rationale is to preserve the security rights of creditors or third parties over assets belonging to the debtor which, at the moment of opening, are situated in a Member State other than the State of opening.

This means, e.g. that the holder of a security right can exercise and enforce that security in accordance with the proper law of the security regardless of whether or not the law of the State of opening permits this. For example, it would be inconsistent with Article 5 that the court of opening grants an injunction to restrain a creditor from taking action to enforce a security interest abroad over an asset protected by Article 5.[177]

163. Article 5 does not operate as a normal conflict of laws rule. It does not state that the effects of the insolvency proceedings on the rights *in rem* will be governed by one or other national law (i.e. the *lex fori concursus* or the *lex rei sitae*). It operates rather as a *negative conflict rule*: the opening of insolvency proceedings will not impinge upon those rights. The purpose of this is to ensure that the holders of rights *in rem* are not subject to *insolvency-law restrictions* arising from either the law governing the main insolvency proceedings or the law governing the security interest (e.g. the law of the place where the collateral is located).[178]

> Secured claim. It has been suggested that even if main proceedings cannot affect the *security interests* (i.e. the right *in rem*) as such, it may affect the underlying *secured claim*, for example, providing for the discharge of the obligations of the debtor in all States.[179] However, this interpretation is inconsistent with the teleology of Articles 5 and 7, because it would render the security function of rights *in rem* worthless. For this reason it can be considered an infringement of their policy.

164. In fact, the "non-effect" formula employed means there are no insolvency restrictions, either procedural or substantive, on these rights, even were such restrictions do exist in accordance with the law of the State of opening *and* the law of the State governing the security interest. For this reason, Article 5 functions more as a rule of substantive law than as a simple conflict rule and, when compared with the

---

[177] Isaacs/Toube/Segal/Marshall, in Moss/Fletcher/Isaacs, p. 112.

[178] Virgos/Schmit Report, Margin Nos 94–99; Virgos, p. 19; Balz (1996a), p. 950; Von Wilmowsky (1996), p. 298; Krings, p. 667; Herchen, p. 80; Leible/Staudinger (2000), p. 551; Beltran Sanchez, p. 38; Huber, p. 157; Garrido, p. 87; Kemper, p. 1616; Fumagalli, p. 701; Wimmer (2002), p. 2507; Reinhart (2003), p. 880; *cfr.* Flessner (1998), *passim.* Nor, when the acquisition of the right in rem is dependent upon the validity of the underlying obligation, the insolvency restrictions arising from the *lex contractus.*

[179] Identifying the question, Isaacs/Toube/Segal/Marshall, in Moss/Fletcher/Isaacs, p. 103.

national laws concerned, it may afford a stronger level of protection against the insolvency of the debtor than that which these national laws demand; in this sense, the rule may "overprotect" secured creditors.[180]

Reasonableness of Article 5: "overprotection versus simplification". The protection which this provision confers on the holder of a right *in rem* is highly debatable. Unlike other exceptions contained in the Regulation, Article 5 does not refer the effects of the insolvency proceedings to the insolvency law of the law which governs the right in question (e.g. to the insolvency law of the State where the asset is located). What it establishes is a rule of immunity; with the limits that will be later explained, for the holder of the right *in rem* it is as if the insolvency had not occurred. It is true that a territorial insolvency may be opened. But this possibility does not exist when the debtor does not have an establishment in the State where the asset is located, which can mean a rule of total immunity. The holder of a right *in rem* can, for instance, exercise an individual enforcement of the asset, even when he could not do so under either the *lex concursus principalis* or the *lex rei sitae*. This goes beyond what appears to be the principal *ratio* of this provision, i.e. the protection of expectations and the general certainty of trade. As the Explanatory Report itself indicates: "The fundamental policy pursued is to protect trade in the State where the assets are situated and legal certainty regarding the rights over them. Rights *in rem* have a very important function with regard to credit and the mobilisation of wealth. They insulate their holders against the risk of insolvency of the debtor and the interference of third parties [....] Rights *in rem* can only properly fulfil their function insofar as they are not more affected by the opening of insolvency proceedings in other Contracting States than they would be by the opening of national insolvency proceedings".[181] Because the holder of a right *in rem*, when constituting it, normally anticipates its resistance to insolvency on the basis of the law of the place where the asset is located, then the application of a foreign law could frustrate these expectations and *ex ante* make credit more expensive to obtain. In order to prevent this risk a rule similar to that of Articles 8 *et seq* would have been sufficient, i.e. a rule which stated that the effects of insolvency proceedings will be determined by the law of the State where the asset is located.[182]

However, the solution provided by the Regulation goes further because it does not impose insolvency limits on the right *in rem* even though both the *lex concursus principalis* and the *lex rei sitae* do impose such limits. For this reason, the overprotection offered by the Regulation can only be understood if we resort to a second argument: the simplification of the administration of the insolvency proceedings. As the Explanatory Report adds, it was the search for a solution which was simple and easy to apply which gave rise to the rule of Article 5 whereby rights *in rem* would not be affected.[183] This rule prevents problems arising

---

[180] For more detail on the substantive or conflictual nature of this rule, see HERCHEN, pp. 76–81; see also, FLESSNER (1998), pp. 280 and 283–284.

[181] VIRGOS/SCHMIT Report, Margin No. 97; see, however, TAUPITZ, pp. 330–331 and HERCHEN, pp. 124–130 (who put forward arguments in favour of the application of the *lex fori concursus principalis*)

[182] In fact, the application of the insolvency rules of the place where the asset is located has been quite a widely supported proposal; see DROBNIG (1992), p. 179 *et seq.* And this is the reason why the majority of commentators agree that Article 5 goes beyond its substantive foundation, see FLESSNER, pp. 277 *et seq.;* HANISCH, 1993, p. 69; HERCHEN, p. 92; LEIBLE/STAUDINGER (2000), p. 552; HUBER, p. 157; SIEHR is also critical, p. 815 with further references.

[183] See VIRGOS/SCHMIT Report, Margin No. 97, where it indicates how the proposal to apply the insolvency law of the *lex rei sitae* was considered and rejected during the process, BALZ (1996a), p. 950; *Id.* (1996b), p. 509; and for a more detailed treatment, VIRGOS, pp. 19–20. For the arguments in favour of this solution see also TAUPITZ, p. 332. The argument of seeking to simplify the proceedings even at the cost of immunising the holders of a right *in rem* was widely employed in the reform of German insolvency law, FLESSNER (1998), p. 279.

from the interplay of institutions and effects of one Member State with the *lex concursus* of another, which would arise from the rule of subjecting the effects of the insolvency proceedings to the provisions of the law which governs the right *in rem* itself (normally, the *lex rei sitae*); for instance, the problems of combining an English floating charge with a continental *lex concursus*. It also avoids the costs associated with the realisation of this right *in rem* by the liquidator in another Member State. Given the level of protection provided to the holders of rights *in rem* by the majority of national laws in the event of an insolvency, the reduction of costs associated with the simplification of the proceedings will be considered as offsetting any gains arising from the alternative rule of subjecting the effects to the law governing the right *in rem*. As already explained, simplification of the trans-border aspects of insolvency proceedings is one of the objectives pursed by the Insolvency Regulation and, as such, constitutes, therefore, an "institutional goal" against which arguments in favour of a different interpretation of Articles 5 and 7 have to be balanced.

165. This "overprotection" which Article 5 provides to the holders of rights *in rem* explains why, in the light of the term "does not affect", the commentaries on this provision have tried to reduce its influence in different ways,[184] in particular:

(a) by limiting the scope of the exception to the *lex concursus* by excluding the application of Article 5 in proceedings which are aimed not at winding-up but at restructuring the company.

> *Rationale.* This may seem a strong argument. In rehabilitation proceedings, where the ultimate objective is to enable the debtor to continue his affairs, the removal of significant assets by the secured creditors may prevent this reorganisation to the detriment of the creditors as a whole. However, this is only true in the case of those assets which are essential to running the business. And it is unlikely that this will be the case of those assets to which Article 5 applies: assets not integrated either in the debtor's main centre or in the debtor's establishments (because in the latter case local insolvency proceedings may be opened, see Article 3.2). Furthermore, in a number of States insolvency proceedings have no effect on secured creditors and this has not prevented reorganisations from taking place.

(b) By defending the conflictual and non-substantive nature of the rule, which would justify an interpretative exception to Article 5 when both laws (*lex fori concursus* and *lex rei sitae*) allow the right *in rem* to be affected by the opening of insolvency proceedings.

(c) By widening the concept of "establishment" in order to facilitate the opening of territorial proceedings.

(d) By defending a restriction of Article 5 based upon an argument of literal interpretation. The argument would be as follows: what Article 5 states is that the declaration of opening does not affect the rights *in rem* of third parties in respect of

---

[184] FLESSNER (1998), p. 281 *et seq.* (defending this conflictual nature of the rule); HERCHEN, pp. 94–107 (limiting the effects of Articles 5 and 7 to the decision opening proceedings, but not to any other decisions which may be adopted in the main proceedings, especially when they are aimed at restructuring, such as the reduction of the amount of the claims; in this case, the only restriction is the public policy clause); LEIBLE/STAUDINGER (2000), p. 551. See also TAUPITZ, pp. 338–339 (widening the notion of "establishment" in order to facilitate the opening of secondary proceedings) and HUBER, p. 157 (*idem*).

assets located outside the State of opening. *A sensu contrario*, what this would mean is that they can be affected by other decisions taken after the declaration of opening, e.g. a decision which suspends the right of separate enforcement for a certain period of time. The declaration of opening would not affect them, but later decisions would.

> *Objection.* This reading would appear to be confirmed by other Articles of the Regulation which use the expression "the effects of the insolvency proceedings" (e.g. Articles 8, 9, 10, 11 or 15). However, this interpretation must be rejected: on the one hand, it is clearly incompatible with the legislative intention, and on the other hand, neither is it acceptable in terms of a strict literal interpretation of the provision. Articles 5 and 7 do not refer to the "declaration opening insolvency proceedings", but rather to "the opening of insolvency proceedings". In Articles 5 and 7, the Regulation establishes a rule of immunity in the face of insolvency proceedings. In other provisions (Articles 8–11 for example), the opening of insolvency proceedings does affect the rights involved. The natural thing in these cases is that later decisions also affect them, and that is why the Regulation speaks of "the effects of the proceedings" and not of the effects of the opening of proceedings.

166. All these interpretations are methodologically dubious, because they are not in harmony with the genesis and teleology of the rule[185] and neither do they pay the proper attention to the mechanisms envisaged by the Regulation itself to prevent some of the "excesses of protection" which may arise from the exception established in Article 5:[186]

(a) First, we have to take into account the fact that the rule of "non-alteration" only covers the right *in rem* over an asset, not the asset itself.[187] The inclusion of the asset covered by this right *in rem* in the estate of the insolvency is governed by the *lex fori concursus* (Article 4.2 b). For this reason, the liquidator can decide on the immediate payment of the secured claim and thus prevent the loss of value which certain assets may undergo when they are realised individually, or can adopt any other measure in respect of the asset, provided that the right *in rem* of the holder is not prejudiced thereby.[188] And vice versa; the general clause regarding the exercise of rights in accordance with the requirements of good faith will oblige the creditor to take that fact into account when exercising his powers.

(b) Secondly, due to the fact that the asset itself forms part of the estate, when the value of the asset given as collateral exceeds the value of the claim guaranteed by the right *in rem*, the creditor is obliged to surrender to the estate any surplus arising from the enforcement in respect of the asset (Recital 25 *in fine*).[189]

---

[185] In detail, Virgos, pp. 19–20; Balz (1996b), p. 509.

[186] Very eloquent Taupitz, p. 342, by concluding, after analysing these routes: *"Zusammenfassend ist festzuhalten, daß Article 5 EuInsÜ mit seiner Territorialisierung dinglicher Sicherungsrechte kein terroristisches Konzept, sondern eine durchaus akzeptable Lösung enthält"*.

[187] Virgos/Schmit Report, Margin No. 99; Virgos, p. 20; Taupitz, p. 339; Flessner (1998), p. 285; Herchen, pp. 67–68, 81–111 (developing this idea); Leible/Staudinger (2000), p. 553; Huber, pp. 154, 158–159; Reinhart (2003), p. 881.

[188] Virgos/Schmit Report Margin No. 99; Wess, in Moss/Fletcher/Isaacs, p. 183.

[189] Virgos/Schmit Report, Margin No. 99; Virgos, p. 20; Herchen, pp. 132–133.

NB. When, on the other hand, the value of the asset does not cover the whole of the claim, the position of the creditor with regard to the remainder is subject to the *lex fori concursus* (Article 4.2.i).[190]

(c) Third, the Regulation always accepts the possibility of territorial proceedings in the State where the asset is located, assuming that the debtor has an establishment there. In this case, the liquidator of the main insolvency may request the opening of secondary insolvency proceedings which permit the liquidator to affect these rights in the same conditions as he would do so in accordance with purely internal proceedings.

And, *in the final analysis*, it is always possible to challenge acts which are detrimental to the body of creditors in accordance with the *lex rei sitae* in the conditions provided for by Article 13 IR.

2.2. Retention of title (Article 7)

167. Title finance is often used as an alternative to security. Here, the financer has title or ownership of the assets, as opposed to a security interest in assets which belong to another person (a right *in re aliena*). Forms of title finance may include hire purchase, finance leases, the factoring of commercial receivables, sale and leaseback, sale and repurchase agreements. Assets belonging to creditors are not encompassed in the estate, but the rights of the debtor over those assets are included and may be affected by the insolvency proceedings.

The Insolvency Regulation only addresses the reservation of title, which has been of longstanding importance in Europe. This relevance has been reinforced by Article 4 of Directive 2000/35 on combating late payment in commercial transactions. The Directive should ensure that creditors are in a position to exercise reservation of title on a non-discriminatory basis throughout the Community, if the reservation of title clause is valid under the applicable national provisions designated by Private International Law (Recital 21).

> *Recharacterisation*. Title finance involves a peculiar risk, the so-called "recharacterisation risk", as some jurisdictions consider this kind of transaction to be, in essence, a security, with the result that the rules on security interests are then applied (see Article 5). This depends totally on the law applicable to the right in question (in principle, the *lex rei sitae*).

168. The figure of reservation of title entails the right of the seller of an asset to recover it in the event of a failure on the part of the purchaser to pay. In spite of the fact that the majority of legal systems recognise this figure, not all of them recognise the same scope in case of insolvency. The aim of introducing a specific rule to protect these situations is to reduce the uncertainty associated with this diversity and to adjust the response of the Regulation to the specific nature of the figure. Article 7 contains a similar rule to that of Article 5. It excludes from the effects of the

---

[190] See VIRGOS/SCHMIT Report, Margin No. 175; HERCHEN, p. 131.

insolvency proceedings reservations of title in respect of assets located in a Member State other than the State of opening (with regard to the *situs* of assets, see No. 158 ff). Article 7 only applies to reservations of title constituted before the opening of insolvency proceedings (with regard to the *time factor*, see Nos 155–156).

169. The tenor of Article 7 is based on *two different hypotheses*: those situations in which the insolvent debtor is the purchaser of the asset; and those in which he is the seller.

170. The first section allows the seller, when *insolvency* proceedings have been opened against the *purchaser* of an asset, to retain his rights based on the reservation of title: *"the opening of insolvency proceedings against the purchaser of an asset shall not affect the seller's rights based on a reservation of title where at the time of the opening of proceedings the asset is situated within the territory of a Member State other than the State of opening of proceedings"*.

This provision protects the seller in the event that the *lex fori concursus* were to consider these rights to be unenforceable against the liquidator of the insolvency. This is the reason why the rule has similar scope to that of Article 5: the opening of the insolvency proceedings *does not affect* these rights on the part of the seller. In this case also, the asset, at the time the main insolvency proceedings are opened, must be located in the territory of a State other than the State of opening.[191]

171. The second section governs the event of the *insolvency* of the *seller* after delivering the asset which has been sold: *the opening of insolvency proceedings against the seller of an asset, after delivery of the asset, shall not constitute grounds for rescinding or terminating the sale and shall not prevent the purchaser from acquiring title where at the time of the opening of proceedings the asset sold is situated within the territory of a Member State other than the State of the opening of proceedings.*

The purpose of this provision is to protect the purchaser in the event that the *lex fori concursus* were to consider the asset as forming part of the estate of the debtor and to oblige the purchaser to return it or to allow the contract to be rescinded. In this case, Article 7.2 establishes an exception to the general rule whereby the effects of the insolvency proceedings on contracts are subject to the *lex fori concursus* (Article 4.2.e). Article 7.2 protects the rights of the *purchaser* by allowing the sale to continue having effects in spite of the insolvency of the seller. This means that if the purchaser continues to make the corresponding payments he will, at the end of the period established in the contract, acquire – or consolidate – ownership of the thing which has been sold.[192] Article 7.2 protects the expectant right of the purchaser (i.e. his *"Anwartschaftsrecht"*) as if it were a right *in rem*, because it ensures that the acquisition or consolidation of the property of the asset depends exclusively on the purchaser paying the price. Furthermore, in these cases it is a requirement that

---

[191] Which significantly reduces the practical importance of this rule as the assets will usually be in the domicile of the debtor, EIDENMÜLLER (2001a), p. 6, note 31.

[192] In spite of the fact that Article 7.2 uses the expression "acquiring title", the text is neutral with regard to the legal nature of the reservation of title; what it means is simply that the opening of the insolvency proceedings against the seller does not alter the rights of the purchaser.

the asset be located in a Member State other than the State of opening, and also that it has been *delivered* to the purchaser or the person by this designated.

172. The majority of commentators deduce from the tenor of Article 7 that it only applies to *simple reservations of title*, not to more complex figures such as "prolonged" or "extended" reservation of title; this clearly without prejudice to the fact that when these figures are protected as rights *in rem* they can be covered by Article.5.[193]

> *Explanation.* Prolonged reservations of title are really a *combination* of two distinct operations: a reservation of title with authorisation to sell and an anticipated assignment by way of guarantee of the claim resulting from this sale. Article 7 would apply to the reservation of title and Article 5 to the anticipated assignment by way of guarantee, where appropriate.

173. Article 7 presupposes the existence of this right, i.e. that title to the asset has been validly retained under the applicable law. This is a *preliminary question* that has to be determined according to the ordinary conflict of laws rules (e.g. in the case of movables, according to the *lex rei sitae*). If a valid retention of title has been constituted, what Article 7 excludes is the possible interference of the insolvency rules of the *lex fori concursus*, the *lex rei sitae* and *lex contractus* (= rule of non-alteration, see, *mutatis mutandis*, No. 162 ff). In this respect, as is also the case with Article 5, we are dealing with a rule of substantive rather than conflictual scope.[194]

> *NB.* The agreement on retention of title has *dual significance*, both contractual and real: the guarantee for the seller/supplier consists of the possibility of cancelling the sale and recovering the object which has been sold. Article 7 ensures the protection of both the real aspects and the contractual aspects of the agreement on retention of title;[195] i.e. it ensures that the declaration of the opening of the insolvency proceedings does not interfere with the effectiveness of the agreement in either of its two spheres.

2.3. Detrimental acts

174. Both Article 5 and Article 7 are based on the *non-fraudulent* location of the assets;[196] the Regulation does not cover fraud in the location of the asset so, in such cases, we must look to the general rule: the application of the *lex fori concursus*.

175. *Actions to set-aside* (i.e. actions of voidness, voidability or unenforceability of acts which are detrimental to the body of creditors) rights *in rem* covered by Article 5 and reservations of title protected by Article 7 are subject to the *lex fori concursus*. This is expressly stated both in Articles 5.4 and 7.3. However, Article 13 may also come into play. This provision allows the application of the *lex fori*

---

[193] HERSCHEN, pp. 120–121; LEIBLE/STAUDINGER (2000), p. 553 (based on Article 4.1 of Directive 2000/35, dated June 29).

[194] VIRGOS, p. 19.

[195] See TAUPITZ, p. 342; HUBER, p. 160.

[196] VIRGOS/SCHMIT Report, Margin No. 105; TAUPITZ, p. 341.

concursus to be excluded if the beneficiary of the act in question proves that the said act is, according to the law which governs it (*lex causae*), legally unquestionable. We shall examine this regime in more detail when commenting on Article 13.

2.4. Credit institutions and insurance undertakings

176. The Directives on the reorganisation and winding-up of credit institutions and insurance companies contain rules which are similar to those of Articles 5 and 7 of the Insolvency Regulation (Articles 21 and 22; and 20 and 21, respectively). In this case, the importance of this exception to the play of the law of the State of origin is greater insofar as these Directives do not provide for the possibility of opening territorial proceedings. The Directive on credit institutions also establishes a special rule for repurchase agreements (Article 26).

3. SET-OFF (ARTICLES 4 AND 6)

177. Set-off may be described as the discharge of reciprocal obligations to the extent of the smaller obligation.[197] Set-off presupposes the existence of two distinct claims, the *primary claim*, which is the claim owed to the insolvent debtor, and the *cross claim*, which is the claim owed to the creditor, that are set against each other to produce a single balance.

The Insolvency Regulation alludes to set-off in two provisions. Article 4.2.d subjects "*the conditions under which set-offs may be invoked*" to the *lex fori concursus*. And Article 6 states that "*the opening of insolvency proceedings shall not affect the right of creditors to demand the set-off of their claims against the claims of the debtor, where such a set-off is permitted by the law applicable to the insolvent debtor's claim*".

178. Traditionally, there has been some debate as to which law governs the set-off of claims in the event of commencement of insolvency proceedings. In comparative law, several solutions have been proposed:[198] (a) the *lex* fori *concursus*; (b) the proper law of the claim to be discharged, total or partially, by set-off (the insolvent debtor's claim); or (c) either of the two laws, alternatively. In this matter, the Insolvency Regulation leans towards the third solution; that is to say, towards an *alternative solution*. The combination of Articles 4 and 6 ends up permitting set-off in accordance with either of these two laws: the law of the State of opening (*lex fori concursus*) or the law governing the insolvent debtor's claim (the *primary claim*).

179. The relationship between Articles 4 and 6 of the Insolvency Regulation is explained as follows. Article 4 establishes the application of the *lex fori concursus* as the basic rule of the system. Insolvency law can be seen as a part of the general system of discharge of obligations; this explains why set-off, as a special mechanism to effect

---

[197] WOOD, p. 71.
[198] HANISCH (1985), p. 1238; FLESSNER (1997), p. 223; recently, and with further references, VON WILMOWSKY (1998), p. 343.

Example:		
Insolvent Debtor	*Lex fori concursus (Spanish law)*	**Creditor**
as creditor	──────────────────────▶	as debtor
	primary claim (German law)	
as debtor	◀──────────────────────	as creditor
	cross claim	

If we add both provisions (Articles 4 and 6) the result is, in fact, an alternative application of both laws: if, according to the *lex fori concursus* (Spanish law), the German creditor can set off, Article 4 permits him to set off; and if, according to the rules of German law, the creditor can set off, Article 6 permits him to set off, even though the *lex fori concursus* would not permit this.

such a discharge, is, in situations of insolvency, subject to the *lex fori concursus* on equal terms for all of the creditors. However logical this solution may be, it means that any party who wishes to calculate the consequences of the insolvency of the counterpart must first anticipate (by means of Article 3) which State is "destined" to become the forum of the insolvency proceedings (i.e. where the debtor's centre of main interests, or a debtor's establishment, will presumably be situated at the time of requesting the opening of insolvency proceedings).[199] This result is not coherent with the function performed by set-off in a number of Member states, where it operates, in substance, as a form of security. For this reason, Article 6 establishes an exception to Article 4 in order "to protect legitimate expectations and the certainty of transactions" (Recital 24). Article 6 permits set-off if this is possible, *in cases of insolvency*, in accordance with the law governing the claim where the insolvent debtor is the creditor in relation to the other party (i.e. the insolvent debtor's claim). This provision crystallizes the right to set-off in a national law which is predictable from the very moment of contracting, even though the debtor may become insolvent at a later date under a different national law. In conclusion, in Article 4, set-off is regarded primarily as a means of discharging or settling claims, whereas in Article 6 it is seen more as a means of guarantee.

3.1. Article 4: set-off under the lex fori concursus

180. The starting point is the general rule contained in Article 4: the *lex fori concursus* applies to set-off in the insolvency. This rule derives not so much from Article 4.2.d of the Insolvency Regulation, which has a specific function which we shall examine later, as from the character of Article 4 as a general rule: unless another rule of the Regulation establishes an exception, the *lex fori concursus* governs the insolvency proceedings and all of its effects, both procedural and substantive, in respect of the rights and positions of the parties. The admission, extension or reduction of set-off is one of these effects and, consequently, unless another rule of the Regulation establishes an exception, it is determined by the *lex fori concursus*. This

---

[199] FLETCHER (1999), p. 274.

law must always be consulted in order to know if two claims may or may not be set off in spite of the insolvency of the debtor, and what the requirements for this are.

NB. The VIRGOS/SCHMIDT Report (Margin No. 109) serves to clarify this: "The laws of some Contracting States altogether restrict or prohibit set-off in insolvency. Article 4 subjects insolvency set-off to the competence of the law of the State of the opening of the insolvency proceedings. [...] it falls therefore to the *"lex concursus"* to govern admissibility and the conditions under which set-off can be exercised against a claim of the debtor. If the *"lex concursus"* allows for set-off, no problem will arise and Article 4 should be applied in order to claim the set-off as provided for by the law. On the other hand, if the *"lex concursus"* does not allow for set-off (e.g. since it requires both claims to be liquidated, matured and payable prior to a certain date), then Article 6 constitutes an exception to the general application of that law in this respect...". It seems quite clear these statements can only be fully understood if the interpretation of Article 4 is the one being defended here.

181. However, when listing the issues which are subject to the *lex fori concursus*, Article 4.2.d indicates "*the conditions under which set-offs may be invoked*". In spite of its apparent simplicity, this provision has given rise to a problem of interpretation fuelled by the different language versions. The English text of the Regulation is more neutral as compared to other linguistic versions: "condiciones de *oponibilidad* de una compensación", "les conditions *d'opposabilité* d'une compensation"; "die *Voraussetzungen für die Wirksamkeit* einer Aufrechnung"; etc. This probably explains why the controversy has not arisen to the same extent in Great Britain or Ireland.

In effect, if we take the first section literally and in isolation, Article 4.2.d seems to restrict the role of the *lex fori concursus* to determining the conditions of effectiveness, against the estate, of a previously existent non-insolvency right to set-off. For some authors, Article 4.2.d establishes the "general model" for the treatment of the set-off by the *lex fori concursus*. According to this model, the Insolvency Regulation would require a distinction to be made between the "*existence*" of a right to set-off and its "*efficacy*" in the case of insolvency, with only the latter being governed by the lex *fori concursus* and the former being governed by the law applicable to the claim in question (*lex causae*).[200] This interpretation works in the context of Article 4.2.d but it is too narrow for Article 4 as a whole, and cannot be regarded as the "general model" for the treatment of set-off under the Insolvency Regulation, but only as one of the possibilities it affords.[201]

Explanation. It has been suggested that the necessary point of departure for understanding the treatment of set-off is to distinguish between the *existence* of the right to set-off and the efficacy of this right in the insolvency proceedings. The lex fori concursus only governs the possibility of enforcing the right to set-off in the insolvency, but not the existence of this

---

[200] VON WILMOWSKY (1998), pp. 358–360; HERCHEN, pp. 134–137; see also HANISCH (1993), p. 71; REINHART (2003), p. 877. On the complexities and the problems of adjustment which can arise from this interpretation, HANISCH (1985), p. 1238; ADERHOLD, pp. 285 *et seq.*

[201] On the different interpretations, see BALZ (1996a), p. 950; GOTTWALD (1997), p. 36; TAUPITZ, pp. 343–344; EIDENMÜLLER (2001a), p. 6, note 33; LEIBLE/STAUDINGER (2000), p. 555; FLETCHER, p. 274; GARCIA GUTIERREZ, *passim.*

right. The right to set-off constitutes a *"preliminary question"* to be decided by the national law which governs the claim to be set off. Consequently, if, in accordance with the non-insolvency rules of the national law which governs this claim, the creditor can discharge his obligation by way of a set-off, the conditions under which this right may be invoked in the insolvency of the debtor are determined by the *lex fori concursus*. Only if we obtain a "yes" under the law governing the preliminary question, will the second question (efficacy in the insolvency proceedings) arise. Essentially, the pre-insolvency right to set-off is subject to its applicable law, but whether this right can be invoked or not in the insolvency of the counterpart (and whether or not specific conditions are required for this to be possible) is subject to the *lex fori concursus*. The problem is that according to this construction the Regulation would be imposing a given normative model of insolvency set-off, when what the Regulation seeks to do, as we shall see, is not to interfere with the national models of set-off.

182. In order to interpret Article 4.2.d correctly, we have to bear in mind two points: first, its relationship with Article 4.1 (*systemic argument*); second, its relationship with the different national systems of set-off (*comparative law argument*). From the perspective of the first, it is clear that the purpose of the list of issues contained in Article 4.2 is not to limit the role of the law of the State of opening (*lex fori concursus*), but rather simply to give examples of its application. It serves to eliminate doubts concerning the scope of Article 4.1, but does not replace it. From the perspective of second argument, it is also clear that solutions to the problem of set-off in the Member States vary significantly. Seen in this context, the function of Article 4.2.d is not to "reproduce" a given national model on a European Community scale (and thereby reduce the scope of Article 4.1 with regard to set-off) but, on the contrary, to preserve the *"neutrality"* of Article 4 in the face of the different models of set-off which exist in the Member States.

In order to understand this last statement it is essential to distinguish between the different approaches to set-off that exist in Europe. Under English law, for example, set-off is treated as a mandatory process which must be applied to all insolvency proceedings opened in England.[202] "Insolvency set-off" functions as an autonomous institution. It requires the mutual debts between the parties to be taken into account. Then, even if the claims are completely unrelated to each other, set-off takes place by operation of the law. This results in the extinction of the two claims and only the aggregate result is payable. "Insolvency set-off" tends to be justified on the grounds that it facilitates a proper and orderly administration of the insolvent's estate. There is no doubt that Article 4.1 applies to this *"procedural model"* of set-off and that the *lex fori concursus* determines, in this case, both the possibility (*"existence"*) of set-off and the conditions under which it may be enforced (*"efficacy"*).

In other systems, insolvency set-off is not an institution related to the administration of the insolvent's estate, but simply a "prolongation" or extension of the pre-insolvency right to set-off. The question in these systems is whether or not that pre-existing right to set-off can be invoked and enforced once insolvency proceedings have commenced in the same way as it exists *outside the insolvency of the*

---

[202] See Rule 4.90, Insolvency Rules 1986.

debtor, and whether or not to impose certain restrictions upon the exercise thereof. Article 4.2.d was drafted with this model in view. Let us take the example of German law. Paragraph 94 of its *Insolvenzordnung* states that "if an insolvency creditor has, at the time the insolvency proceedings are opened, a right to set-off derived from the law or from a set-off agreement, this right shall not be affected by the proceedings". This provision means that set-off is also governed in the insolvency of the debtor by the general rules of the Civil Code and that the insolvency rules are limited to establishing certain restrictions upon the exercise thereof. In other words, the insolvency rules recognise and respect the right to set-off just as it exists according to the general *non-insolvency* regime;[203] and this ordinary *non-insolvency* regime, is determined by the ordinary conflict of laws rules. Technically, the existence of the right to set-off constitutes a *preliminary question*, governed by the ordinary conflict rules. Thus, Article 4.2.d ensures that, in the States which follow this model, the *lex fori concursus* is not applied beyond what it demands. There is no reason for the Insolvency Regulation to interfere with this "substantive model", causing the *lex fori concursus* to have other effects distinct from those sought by the national legislator (e.g. by applying the non-insolvency set-off rules of the German Civil Code even if the insolvent's debtor *claim* is governed by a different national law, merely because the insolvency proceedings are opened in Germany).

183. In conclusion, Article 4.2.d. does not monopolise the way set-off is dealt with, either within the framework of the Insolvency Regulation (see Articles 9 and 6, for example) or within the framework of Article 4 itself. Thus, Article 4 must be considered as a whole which contains, in reality, *two rules* regarding set-off.[204] The first rule is the general rule whereby the insolvency proceedings and their effects are governed by the *lex fori concursus* (Article 4.1). Insofar as this law so requires, it will govern both the possibility and the conditions of set-off in the event of insolvency. This is the case, for example, with the insolvency set-off of English law. The second rule (Article 4.2.d) operates when the *lex fori concursus* does not contain a specific model of insolvency set-off, but simply allows the ordinary regime of non-insolvency set-off to apply and establishes (or not) limits or exceptions to its application. The pattern of application provided for in Article 4.2.d permits, therefore, the substantive model of the national law to be respected. In other words, the Regulation does not impose a model, but recognises the model established by the *lex concursus*; it is the latter which decides, not the former.

3.2. *Article 6: set-off under the law governing the insolvent debtor's claim ("primary claim")*

184. Alongside this possibility, Article 6.1 of the Insolvency Regulation establishes an *alternative rule*: even when set-off is not possible through the application

---

[203] Albeit after establishing some restrictions on the exercise thereof in paragraph 96 InsO.
[204] In this respect, GARCIA GUTIERREZ, *passim*.

of the *lex fori concursus*, it would still be possible when the law which governs the insolvency debtor's claim (or *"primary claim"*) permits set-off in spite of the insolvency of the debtor (or precisely because of it). For this reason, Article 6.1 establishes that *"the opening of insolvency proceedings shall not affect the right of creditors to demand the set-off of their claims against the claim of the debtor, where such a set-off is permitted by the law applicable to the insolvent debtor's claim"*.

185. As we have already stated, in Article 6 set-off is perceived as a security-like device. The possibility of a set-off in insolvency, as allowed by the laws of some Member States, gives the parties a degree of confidence equivalent to that of a security interest. It reflects the idea that the parties were transacting in reliance upon their ability to secure payment and that it would be unfair to deprive the solvent party of this security to the extent of the set-off. The purpose of Article 6 is to protect this guarantee function. For this reason, it permits the acquisition of a right to set-off in accordance with a law that can be determined at the very moment of contracting or incurring the obligation (the law governing the primary claim), and ensures that this right will be recognised in the insolvency of the debtor.[205] This provision is very important for commercial predictability and availability of credit within the European market.

186. Article 6.1 not only protects the rights of set-off from the insolvency effects established by the *lex fori concursus*, but also contains a uniform conflict rule on the law applicable to the right of set-off itself (see Recital 26). The existence of this right of set-off is determined by the law which governs the *insolvent debtor's claim* (i.e. the primary claim).[206] This uniform rule displaces the national rules of Private International Law.

187. The referral made by Article 6.1 to the law of the insolvent debtor's claim includes the insolvency rules of that legal system. The question which must be asked is whether, according to the law which governs this claim, the creditor has the right to demand set-off in the event that insolvency proceedings are opened against the debtor. The Report is very clear on this point: "… Article 6 constitutes an exception to the general application of that law in this respect, by permitting the set-off according to *the conditions established for insolvency set-off* by the law applicable to the insolvent debtor's claim"[207] (our italics).

Difference between Articles 5 (right in rem) and 6 (set-off). This difference is easy to appreciate. Basically, what Article 5 says is that the creditor has the same position he would have *under non-insolvency* according to the national law which governs his right *in rem*; and Article 6 says that the creditor has the same position he would have *under insolvency* according to the national law governing the set-off.

---

[205] VIRGOS/SCHMIT Report, Margin No. 109 *in fine*; VIRGOS, p. 21; FLESSNER (1997), p. 223; TAUPITZ, p. 343.

[206] VIRGOS/SCHMIT Report, Margin No. 108; HERCHEN, p. 134; TAUPITZ, p. 344; in detail VON WILMOWSKY (1998), pp. 346 *et seq.*

[207] VIRGOS/SCHMIT Report, Margin No. 109; VIRGOS, p. 21; also HERCHEN, p. 136; VON WILMOWSKY (1998), pp. 360–361; EIDENMÜLLER (2001a), p. 7 note 35; LEIBLE/STAUDINGER (2000), p. 555; but see, FLESSNER (1997), p. 223; BELTRAN, p. 38.

188. Article 6 applies in respect of mutual claims incurred prior to the opening of the insolvency proceedings (i.e. claims existing before that moment). If the claims are incurred afterwards, Article 6 does not operate and the *lex fori concursus* (ex Article 4) governs both the possibility and the conditions of set-off.[208]

NB. This requirement must be interpreted in the light of the sense and purpose of the provision: to protect the expectations of set-off on the part of the solvent creditor when these expectations arose before the declaration of opening. For this reason, Article 6 applies when the claims arose out of contracts or other dealings entered into prior to the opening of the insolvency proceedings, even if they were, at that moment, mature or unmature, contingent or not.

189. The wording of the provision does not require that the law in question be the law of a *Member State*, but this requirement is implied as a result of the intra-Community limitation of the Insolvency Regulation itself.[209]

190. The regime of *actions to set-aside* (i.e. the actions of voidness, voidability or unenforceability of those acts which are detrimental to the creditors as a whole) which might affect a set-off protected by Article 6 is subject to the *lex fori concursus* by virtue of the referral made by Articles 6.2 to 4.2.m. It must be remembered, however, that Article 13 permits the application thereof to be excluded if the beneficiary of the act in question proves that the said act is legally unquestionable according to the national law which governs it (i.e. the *lex causae*). We shall examine this regime in more detail when commenting upon Article 13.

NB. In payment systems and financial markets, actions to set-aside are governed by the provisions of the law applicable to the system itself or to the market in question (Article 9.2).

3.3. Contractual set-off

191. *Contractual set-off* enables parties dealing with each other to combine an account in credit with an account in debt and to restrict liabilities to the payment of the resulting balance. Contractual set-off is governed by the law applicable to the contract establishing the set-off arrangement. As a general rule, this law is determined in accordance with the Rome Convention of 19 June 1980 on the law applicable to contractual obligations. This solution is implicit in Article 6 (the drafting of which is better adjusted to set-off in law) as the Explanatory Report confirms without any doubt: "*contractual set-off implies an agreement subject to its own applicable law according to the 1980 Rome Convention*".[210] Accordingly, under Article 6, the opening of insolvency proceedings will not affect the right of a creditor to set-off

---

[208] VIRGOS/SCHMIT Report, Margin No. 110; VIRGOS, p. 21; TAUPITZ, p. 343 note 148; HERCHEN, p. 134.

[209] VIRGOS/SCHMIT Report, Margin No. 93. With regard to non-Member States, the national rules of Private International Law apply. Dissenting: TORREMANS, p. 179; REINHART (2003), p. 882.

[210] VIRGOS/SCHMIT Report, Margin No. 110. This reference to contractual set-off was expressly requested by some Member States during the discussion of the Explanatory Report.

his claims against the claims of the debtor, where such set-off is permitted by the law applicable (including its insolvency rules) to the set-off agreement that governs the transactions between them.

> *NB*. Article 6.2 IR establishes an exception to this rule: actions to set-aside detrimental acts would remain the competence of the *lex fori concursus*, although subject, in turn, to the restriction provided for by Article 13 IR.

192. Article 6 is applicable to agreements which, according to the law of the State that governs them,[211] enable their participants to manage their credit exposures arising from all kinds of transactions on a net basis, by setting off reciprocal claims to produce a single amount due or owed.

The set-off agreement may be a provision contained in the same contract out of which the insolvent debtor's claim arises or may constitute an autonomous agreement. In a typical arrangement, a number of transactions are subject to a master agreement that functions as an umbrella governing the relationships between the parties and imposes common terms on the underlying transactions, including set-off or netting arrangements. This master agreement will have its own applicable law, which may be different from that of the underlying transactions. In the latter case, the law applicable to the set-off arrangement might be different from the law which governs each of the underlying claims. If the law applicable to the master agreement allows the set-off to operate successfully in the event of the insolvency of the counterpart, then Article 6 protects this result and the set-off operates successfully in respect of all the underlying transactions. For this reason the Report stated that "the same rationale on which Article 5 (security rights) is based explains that in the event of a contractual set-off covering different claims between two parties, the law of the Contracting State applicable to that agreement will continue to govern the set-off of claims covered by the agreement and incurred prior to the opening of the insolvency proceedings".[212]

> *Development*. Under Article 3 of the 1980 Rome Convention, the parties to a contract may freely choose the national law which better suits their interests. This means that the law applicable to the primary claim referred to in Article 6 may be the law expressly chosen by the parties. This is the situation which Article 6 is contemplating: the set-off agreement as an *accessory pact* within the main contract, the law of which governs both the claim and the set-off agreement. However, under Article 3 of the 1980 Rome Convention, the parties may select different national laws to govern separable parts of the contract. This means that the parties can choose the same law to govern the contract and the set-off agreement, but can also choose different laws to govern each of them, as distinct and separable parts of the contract (*content* v. *discharge*). It may be the case that the set-off agreement is concluded as a *separate* or *autonomous agreement*, subject to its own *lex contractus*, and that this law does not coincide with the one which governs the insolvent debtor's claim – in the example given above, because the parties have entered into a master set-off agreement

---

[211] In our view, the law of a *Member* State, see No. 189.
[212] Parenthesis added, VIRGOS/SCHMIT Report, Margin No. 110.

encompassing several transactions, each one of them with its own *lex contractus*. This result is both consistent which the teleology of Article 6 and with the possibilities allowed for by the 1980 Rome Convention. Article 6 focuses on the function of the set-off as a form of guarantee and, in these cases, this function does not derive from the law which governs the primary claim, but from the master agreement in which it is inserted. For this reason, and taking into account the freedom to choose the applicable law in contractual matters, Article 6 should be understood as deferring, in the case of an autonomous set-off agreement, to the proper law of this agreement. The accuracy of this interpretation is confirmed by the fact that this is the solution which is expressly included in the Directive on the reorganisation and winding-up of credit institutions (see Article 25). To reject this interpretation and claim that Article 25 of the Directive and Article 6 of the Insolvency Regulation provide different solutions would give rise to a paradoxical situation: that in the case of an agreement between a credit institution and an ordinary debtor, whether or not the set-off arrangement would be valid would depend on which of the parties of the set-off agreement was declared insolvent, the bank or the ordinary debtor, because the national law applicable to the set-off agreement would be different in each case.

193. The conditions for applying the set-off will be those agreed by the parties within the framework of the autonomy which the national applicable law allows them. In contractual set-off it falls to the parties themselves to establish the circumstances and the conditions in which set-off applies. Article 6 does not establish any specific condition or limit to set-off agreements different from those established by the national applicable law. For this reason, Article 6 may protect not only "simple" contractual set-off clauses (those that cover reciprocal monetary claims), but also more "complex" set-off agreements which contain special contractual provisions to convert non-monetary obligations (i.e. an obligation to deliver commodities) into monetary obligations or to close-out open contracts and net all obligations arising out of those contracts. In other words, Article 6 also covers "netting agreements".[213] This broad interpretation of the scope of Article 6 is also necessary given the absence of a specific exception for financial contracts in the Insolvency Regulation. Contractual set-off and netting play a central role in effective credit and systemic risk management, which, in turn, is essential for liquidity and market efficiency. For this reason, all Member States recognise contractual set-off and netting clauses in financial contracts, either by application of general insolvency rules or by special carve-outs provisions. Legal certainty and consistency require that this state of things be also recognised at the conflict of laws level. Article 6, in combination with the national applicable law, make it possible for these agreements to operate also in cross border situations. However, Article 6 does not limit its protection to financial contracts since it does not establish any subject-matter limitation in its sphere of application.

Rationale. In international practice, it is normal for set-off agreements to include contractual provisions which ensure that the set-off is completed before a specified date through

---

[213] Netting is a term of art developed to describe different types of arrangements, the common purpose of which is to combine different transactions or accounts to produce a single balance due or owed. See Wood (1995), p. 152: "Netting is often merely another term for set-off. But the term netting is used by the markets because in many cases the process involves more than just a set-off of debts".

acceleration or cancellation clauses; or to establish that the claims resulting from all of the transactions included are consolidated and replaced by a single debtor or creditor claim, so that the parties can only demand the resulting net balance; or for non-monetary obligations to be converted into monetary obligations so that the set-off can be applied.[214] The problem lies in determining whether these contractual devices designed to produce or facilitate set-off are also protected by Article 6 as components of the set-off arrangement or whether they fall under the general competence of Article 4 IR, since, as general rule, the effects of the insolvency proceedings on current contracts are determined by the *lex fori concursus*. Take the example of "close-out netting" agreements. This form of netting embraces two steps: "termination" of all open contracts and the set-off of all obligations arising out of those contracts on an aggregate basis. However, the clauses on termination and set-off are pieces of a single risk management mechanism that cannot be separated the one from the other without impinging on the function they perform. In financial transactions, counterparties typically hedge their risks by entering into contracts with third parties. Without the ability to close out, net and set-off defaulted contracts, failure of a party could lead the counterparty to be unable to perform its related financial contracts, resulting in a series of defaults in back-to-back transactions (= *"interdependence risk"*); this would hinder hedging against market fluctuations and risk management, reducing credit availability. For this reason, the close-out contractual provisions constitute a vital part of the "security structures" based on set-off which have gained great practical significance in financial transactions, and this security function is, *precisely*, what the Insolvency Regulation seeks to protect (see Recital 26). Article 6 was conceived to promote commercial and financial predictability by respecting these structures, not to change them; it should therefore be applicable to determine the set-off or netting arrangements that are enforceable in the insolvency of the debtor and their scope. The result is that the provisions of the set-off or netting agreement will be enforceable in accordance with their own terms against the insolvent party *if and insofar* as the national law applicable to the agreement so allows. Not only the teleological argument speaks in favour of this interpretation. The parallelism that exist between the Insolvency Regulation and the Directive on reorganisation and winding up of credit institutions as parts of a Community law provide a further reason (a *systemic argument*). In effect, Article 25 of the Directive expressly admits set-off and netting, including close-out netting, regardless of who the counterpart to the agreement is: another credit institution or an ordinary debtor. If the insolvency Regulation and the Directive were not in accordance, netting would or would not be possible depending on which of the parties becomes insolvent; a result that cannot be admitted. This is also consistent with the view taken by Directive 2002/47 on Financial Collateral Arrangements on analogous close-out provisions forming part of security interest structures. According to its Article 7, Member States shall ensure that close-out netting provisions can take place in accordance with their terms regardless of the commencement of insolvency proceedings. The conflict of laws reflection of this rule is the application of the law governing the agreement itself to determine its validity and enforceability in the event of the insolvency of the counterparty.

194. The *Directives* on reorganisation and winding up of *credit institutions* and *insurance companies* contain similar rules. Set-off is allowed: (a) if it is permitted by the *lex fori concursus* (see Articles 10.2.c and 9.2.c, respectively); or (b) if it is contemplated by the law that governs the primary claim (Articles 23 and 22, respectively). In addition to this, Article 25 of the Directive on credit institutions[215] contains a special rule regarding *contractual set-off*. According to this provision, the

---

[214] For an explanation of these mechanisms, see GOODE (1997), p. 178.
[215] On this Directive, DEGUE, No. 41 ff. and 66.

effects of the opening of insolvency proceedings on netting agreements (and *a fortiori*, simple set-off agreements) *"shall be governed solely by the law applicable to the contract which governs such agreements"*. Unlike the Regulation, Article 25 does not expressly reserve the application of the *lex fori concursus* for actions to set-aside (as do Articles 6.2 IR or 23.2 of the Directive).

> *Difficulty: actions to set-aside.* The parallels between the solutions provided by the Regulation and those provided by the Directive are justified on the grounds of general validity except on one point, where the solution provided by the Directive responds to the specific needs of financial entities, i.e. actions to set-aside. The Regulation subjects this regime (Article 6.2) to the general rules (Article 4.2.m in relation with Article 13, see No. 190), and the explanatory report, which is careful to adapt the solution of Article 6 to contractual set-off agreements, is silent on this point. This indicates that the general regime continues to apply. However, Article 25 of the Directive subjects these agreements *exclusively* to the law of the contract, without making any provision for the application of the *lex fori concursus*, as Article 23 does with regard to the set-off in law.[216] The aim of this is to show that actions to set-aside do not follow the general regime of the *lex fori concursus*, but are rather governed by the same law as the netting arrangement. The foundation for this special regime lies in the vital role played by set-off and netting in facilitating control of the solvency ratio of the credit institutions, which is a matter of public interest. This is why Article 25 of the Directive simplifies the conflict of laws solution and provides immediate legal certainty as compared to the Insolvency Regulation, where the interplay of Articles 4.2.m and 13 provides a less immediate answer. This foundation applies specifically to credit institutions, and cannot be extrapolated and applied to the Regulation in order to create a general exception to Article 6.2. However, when the set-off agreement is between an ordinary debtor and a credit entity, it seems justifiable to apply the solution provided for in Article 25 of the Directive, as the *lex specialis*. Firstly, because the law applicable to the set-off agreement should not vary according to the procedural position of the parties (i.e. according to which of them is declared insolvent); such a solution would be incompatible with the function which these agreements fulfil in commercial transactions and inconsistent with the teleology of Article 25 of the Directive. Secondly, because it would be paradoxical for the rules which protect a public interest (facilitate controls on solvency and reduce systemic risks) to insulate credit institutions against the risk of the insolvency of the counterpart to a lesser extent in the case of those debtors where the risk of insolvency is greater (ordinary debtors) than in the case of those other debtors where the risk of insolvency is, at least in theory, lower (other credit entities).

195. With regard to the set-off regime of *payment* and *settlement systems*, see *infra* Nos 211 *et seq.*

4. EFFECTS ON CONTRACTS

4.1. *General rule:* Lex fori concursus *(Article 4.2.e)*

196. In principle, the rights and duties of the parties and the dynamics of a contract (i.e. performance, termination and discharge) are subject to the law governing

---

[216] DEGUE, No. 66.

the contract itself (*lex contractus*) as determined in accordance with the ordinary conflict of laws rules. The 1980 Rome Convention on the Law Applicable to Contractual Obligations provides the general rule. Seen from the perspective of the contract, the insolvency of one of the parties is an event which, like other events which may occur over the lifetime of the contract, will have the consequences determined by the contract and/or by the law which governs it.

However, insolvency law may allow for interference with current contracts to the extent necessary to fulfil the policy objectives of the insolvency proceedings. Thus, it is usual to establish a special regime in the case of contracts pending execution by both parties (*executory contracts*), thereby allowing the liquidator to adopt or reject the contract on the basis of a cost-benefit analysis of the best interests of the body of creditors. The purpose of these insolvency rules is to protect the estate from the duty to comply with certain contracts which might prove onerous in the light of the new situation, or to prevent the mere fact of the declaration of the opening of the insolvency proceedings from terminating contracts which may be necessary for the continuation of the business.[217]

197. This interference of *insolvency rules* in the *general regime of contracts* poses a problem of applicable law. In principle, there are two theoretical solutions:[218] (a) to apply the *lex fori concursus*; (b) to apply the *lex contractus*, including its insolvency rules. The Regulation follows the first option. According to Article 4.2.e it falls to the law of the State of opening (*lex fori concursus*) to determine "*the effects of insolvency proceedings on current contracts to which the debtor is party*".[219]

> *Rationale.* There is an inherent tension between achieving insolvency objectives (e.g. promoting the survival of the debtor when its value as a going concern exceeds its liquidation value) and supporting certainty in commercial and non-commercial transactions (e.g. having contracts enforced according to their terms). Both policies must be balanced against each other. Article 4.1.e of the Insolvency Regulation implies that the competence to decide on that balance corresponds to the *lex fori concursus* – with, however, an implicit limitation: the interference of insolvency law with the ordinary contractual regime is only allowed to the extent needed to fulfil an insolvency policy (i.e. to achieve an objective of the insolvency proceedings) and not for other reasons.

These "*insolvency effects*" interfere with and overrule the ordinary regime of the contract deriving from the law applicable according to the non-insolvency conflict of laws rules (e.g. the 1980 Rome Convention). The *lex fori concursus* will determine, for example, whether the declaration of opening modifies the possibilities of terminating the contracts (e.g. whether or not "*ipso facto*" clauses cancelling the contract in the event of insolvency are effective) and the powers of the liquidator to choose to continue or disclaim contracts. And it will also establish the position in the insolvency which corresponds to the creditor in each case. Beyond those modifications specifically required by an insolvency-law policy, the *lex contractus* will continue to apply.

---

[217] Virgos/Schmit Report, Margin No. 116.
[218] Schollmeyer, pp. 150–176.
[219] Virgos, p. 21; Taupitz, p. 344.

NB. Unless the *lex fori concursus* provides otherwise for insolvency reasons, the termination in the event of insolvency of individual contracts due to their personal or *intuitu personae* nature is subject to the *lex contractus*. The dissolution of a partnership or a corporate body is subject to the *lex societatis* (*supra* No. 123-f). On the other hand, in the case of contracts subject to a public law regime (e.g. administrative contracts) the law of the State in question must be taken into account.

198. The Directives on *credit institutions* and *insurance companies* contain a similar rule (Article 10.2.d and 9.2.d, respectively).

4.2. *Exceptions to the* lex fori concursus

199. The Insolvency Regulation contains *special rules* for two types of contracts: contracts relating to *immovable property* (Article 8) and contracts of *employment* (Article 10).[220] The scope of the special rule is similar in both Articles. The effects of the insolvency on current contracts are not subject to the *lex fori concursus* but, respectively, to the insolvency rules of the law where the property is located or of the *lex contractus*. This is why both Articles use the adverb *"solely"*.[221]

NB. The scope of the special conflict of laws rules provided for in Articles 8 and 10 differs from the cases we have seen up until now. They are "positive" conflict of laws rules, because the insolvency rules of the *lex contractus* do apply, unlike the "negative" conflict of laws rule of Article 5. Neither do the insolvency rules of the *lex fori concursus* apply alternately, in contrast to the case of Article 6 which operates together with Article 4, as they *only* refer to the *lex contractus*. This explains why, in the case of employees, no alternative application should be sought between the *lex fori concursus and* the *lex contractus*: the latter is applied even though, *in casu*, the former may be more favourable to their interests. This solution reduces the complexity involved in the application of the rules because it avoids any process of comparison between legal systems.

200. Both Article 8 and Article 10 must be considered in relation to Article 4.2.e (effects of the insolvency proceedings on current contracts) to which they constitute an exception. This is important in order to understand that both Articles represent "narrow" exceptions to the application of the *lex fori concursus*; i.e. they constitute exceptions only with regard to their effects on current contracts, but not with regard to other aspects regulated by Article 4. Issues such as the ranking of the resulting claims (Article 4.2.i), the voidness, voidability or unenforceability of acts which are detrimental to the creditors as a whole (Articles 4.2.m + 13), the rights of the creditors after the proceedings are closed (Article 4.2.k), *inter alia*, remain beyond the scope of these two provisions and continue to be governed by the *lex fori concursus*.

201. The exceptions to the play of the *lex fori concursus* contained in Articles 8 and 10 arise from the desire to prevent conflicts between legislative policies. In the

---

[220] SCHOLLMEYER, pp. 176–199.
[221] VIRGOS/SCHMIT Report, Margin No. 118 *in fine*; TAUPITZ, pp. 344–345; FLETCHER, p. 277.

majority of Member States, these two types of contracts are subject to mandatory rules, whose aim is to protect general or social interests linked to a particular State; this has traditionally been the case with the position of lessees of immovable assets or employees.[222] These exceptions serve to prevent possible conflicts between those policies and the *lex fori concursus*.

> *Consumer contracts*. The Regulation does not establish any special connection for contracts with *consumers*. This type of contracts are not usually relational or long-term contracts (except in the case of contracts relating to immovable property which are already included for other reasons). However, it must be remembered that there are EC laws regarding consumption which contain special substantive rules to protect consumers in the event of the insolvency of the counterpart (see, e.g. Article 7 of Directive 90/314 regarding package trips).

202. Both provisions require the applicable law to be that of a *Member State*. In the case of non-Member States, the provisions of the rules of Private International Law of each State must be consulted.[223]

4.2.1. Contracts relating to immovable property (Article 8)

203. *Article 8* of the Insolvency Regulation establishes that *"the effects of the insolvency proceedings on a contract which confers a right to make use of or acquire immovable property shall be governed solely by the law of the Member State within the territory of which the immovable property is situated"*. This referral includes the insolvency rules of that State.[224] The provision applies not only to contracts covering the use of the property (e.g. rental or *leasing*), but also to those covering the transfer of the asset (e.g. purchase and sale).[225]

204. As we have indicated, the purpose of this special connection is to respect the specific rules which each State usually establishes to satisfy different interests: those of the contracting parties (e.g. the interests of leaseholders in the continuation of the contract) and the general interests protected by the State where the property is located.[226]

> *Explanation*. This teleology explains why the Regulation refers not to the *lex contractus* but directly to the *lex rei sitae*. The Rome Convention of 19 June 1980 permits the *lex contractus* to be chosen without any express restriction and the *lex rei sitae* is referred to only by default; see Articles 3 and 4.3. The direct referral in Article 8 to the *lex rei sitae* is due to the fact that some delegations tried to ensure the application, in all cases of insolvency, of the rules provided for in their legislation to the property located in their territory.[227]

---

[222] VIRGOS/SCHMIT Report, Margin Nos 118 and 125; SCHOLLMEYER, p. 176.

[223] VIRGOS/SCHMIT Report, Margin No. 93; FLETCHER, p. 277.

[224] VIRGOS/SCHMIT Report, Margin No. 118; VIRGOS, 21; TAUPITZ, p. 345; HUBER, p. 163.

[225] VIRGOS/SCHMIT Report, Margin No. 119; BALZ (1996a), p. 950; TAUPITZ, p. 345; HUBER, p. 163; WIMMER (2002), p. 2508.

[226] VIRGOS/SCHMIT Report, Margin No. 118.

[227] VIRGOS, p. 22; TAUPITZ, p. 345.

205. Actions to set-aside arising from the insolvency follow the general regime (Articles 4.2.m and 13).

206. The Directives on *credit institutions* and *insurance companies* contains a similar exception (Articles 20.b and 19.b, respectively). The only addition, in the case of the first, consists of a referral to the *lex rei sitae* itself in order to resolve a problem of characterisation: *"that law shall determine whether property is movable or immovable"*.

4.2.2. Employment contracts and relationships (Article 10)

207. Article 10 establishes that *"the effects of insolvency proceedings on employment contracts and relationships shall be governed solely by the law of the Member State applicable to the contract of employment"*. The purpose of Article 10 is to safeguard certain aspects of employee and labour relations from the application of a foreign insolvency law other than the one which governs the relationship between the employer and the employees.[228] To that end, it establishes an exception to the application of the *lex fori concursus* and subjects the effects of the insolvency proceedings on employment contracts and relationships to the *lex contractus, including its insolvency rules.*[229] The term "solely" is an attempt to highlight the fact that the only applicable rules are the insolvency rules of the law which governs the contract.

The continuance of the business either in the State of the opening or in other Member States will be decided in the main proceedings. However, the law governing the employment contract or relationship will be the one to determine the effects of the insolvency proceedings on these contracts and relationships, as if the insolvency proceedings had been opened in that State. This law will determine, for example, the effects of the opening of insolvency proceedings on the continuation or termination of employment (including the ability of the liquidator to enforce or cancel contracts) and the specific conditions or administrative procedures which must be applied; it will also determine the effects of the opening on the rights and obligations of all parties to such employment (see Recital 28). The expression "on employment contracts and relationships" makes it clear that the special connection protects not only the effects on the contract itself, but also on the rights and obligations as a whole (many of them arising *ex lege* or from a collective bargaining agreement) deriving therefrom.

208. The exception envisaged by Article 10 only covers the effects of the insolvency proceedings on employment relationships. Any other insolvency questions, such as whether or not employment claims are protected (and to what extent) by preferential rights and what status or ranking the preferential rights may have in the proceedings, are subject to the law of the State of opening (*lex fori concursus*).

209. The application of Article 10 involves a *"preliminary question"*: i.e. how to determine when we are dealing with an *employment contract* and the law which

---

[228] VIRGOS/SCHMIT Report, Margin No. 125.

[229] VIRGOS/SCHMIT Report, Margin No. 125; HUBER, p. 162; TORREMANS, p. 181.

governs that contract (*lex contractus*). The characterisation of a relationship as an employment relationship for the purposes of Article 10 is an "*autonomous charac-terisation*", i.e. a characterisation which derives from the sense and purpose of the Regulation itself and from the EC context in which it is situated (for specific details see, *inter alia*, ECJ Cases 75/63, 66/85 or 266/85). In contrast to what we saw with regard to Article 8, it is not the Insolvency Regulation which determines the law applicable to this relationship, but the ordinary rules of Private International Law of the Member States; specifically, the 1980 Rome Convention on the law applicable to contractual obligations (see Article 6 thereof).

> *Explanation.* Article 6 of the 1980 Rome Convention establishes the application of the *lex loci laboris* to the employment contract. This means that, in principle, the law of the State where the employee performs his work is the *lex contractus*.[230] However, we must take into account the possible exceptions to this rule when there is not a fixed place of work or when the employment contract is more closely linked with the law of another country (Article 6.2 *in fine*). When there is a choice of applicable law, and this law does not coincide with the *lex loci laboris* (or with another law with closer connections), the 1980 Rome Convention basically allows the application of that law which is most favourable to the claims of the employee: the law chosen or the law applicable in the absence of a choice. This possibility also functions in the sphere of insolvency. What is not possible, as we have already stated, is an alternate application of the law of the State of opening (*lex fori concursus*).

210. The Directives on *credit institutions* and *insurance companies* also contain a similar rule for employment contracts (see Articles 20.a and 19.a, respectively).

5. Payment Systems and Financial Markets (Article 9)

211. Article 9 establishes that "*without prejudice to Article 5, the effects of insolvency proceedings on the rights and obligations of the parties to a payment or settlement system or to a financial market shall be governed solely by the law of the Member State applicable to that system or market*".

The purpose of this article is to protect transactions carried out in *payment and settlement systems* or within the framework of *organised financial markets* from the effects of the declaration of insolvency. To that end it establishes that the effects of insolvency proceedings are not subject to the *lex fori concursus*, but to the law which governs the said system or market. This solution seeks to promote general confidence in these institutions and protect the smooth operation of the systems. It prevents the possibility of mechanisms for the settlement of transactions and payments being affected in the event of the insolvency of a business partner by a law other than the one governing the system (Recital 27). It also allows a single focal point for the assessment of risk: in order to determine the risks of insolvency which an operator assumes, it is not necessary to look individually at each of the national laws of the

---

[230] Virgos/Schmit Report, Margin No. 126; Taupitz, p. 344; Huber, p. 162.

other operators, as it is enough to look at a single law, the law of the State under which the system or market was organised.[231]

> *Rationale: the systemic risk.* Payment systems and financial markets are particularly sensitive to the risks of insolvency. A number of different operators participate in them, giving orders to the system. The volume of orders is very high. The systemic risk associated with these situations is the so-called "domino" or cascade effect: the insolvency of one of the participants might mean that his creditors are, in turn, unable to meet their payments, and this could end up spreading the situation of insolvency throughout the entire system or market. This is the reason why the national laws of all Member States permit different mechanisms to reduce these risks and to try to protect, as far as possible, the smooth operation of these systems in the face of the incapacity to pay of one of the participants therein. This has a clear conflictual consequence: the exception to the application of the *lex fori concursus* ensures the application of the law which governs the system or market, and this significantly reduces the transaction costs. The participants know that their position in event of the insolvency of another participant is not determined by the law of the latter (which would mean that, in order to assess and protect themselves against this risk, they would have to consult the individual law governing each of the other participants), but by the law of the system or market itself.
>
> *Participants.* Direct participation in payment systems or organised financial markets tends to be limited to credit or investment institutions. These institutions can participate in the said systems and markets either on their own account or on behalf of third parties. As the Insolvency Regulation does not apply to the insolvency of either credit institutions or investment companies, Article 9 will be mainly relevant in order to protect system and market transactions from any interference when these institutions are acting on behalf of third parties who become insolvent. For the response of the Directive on credit institutions, which is similar, see *infra* No. 220.

212. Article 9 of the Insolvency Regulation is closely linked to *Directive 98/26/EC on settlement finality in payment and securities settlement systems* (see Recital 27)[232]. The fundamental objective of the Directive on finality is the same as that of Article 9 of the Insolvency Regulation, "to minimise the disruption to a system caused by insolvency proceedings against a participant in that system" (Recital 4 of Directive 98/26/EC and Recital 27 *in fine* of the Insolvency Regulation). One of the cornerstones of the said Directive is Article 8, which contains a similar rule to that of Article 9 of the Insolvency Regulation: the effects of a declaration of insolvency on the rights and obligations of a participant in the said systems are subject to the law applicable to that system. The Directive is a *lex specialis* in relation to the Regulation (see Recital 27 of the latter), therefore: (a) national provisions dictated on the basis of this Directive take precedence over the general rules of the Regulation; and (b) the Directive will provide the hermeneutic reference necessary in order to clarify the concepts used in Article 9 of the Regulation.

---

[231] VIRGOS/SCHMIT Report, Margin No. 120; VIRGOS, p. 23; BALZ (1996a), 950; TAUPITZ, p. 345; BELTRAN SANCHEZ, p. 39; FLETCHER (1999), pp. 274–275; TORREMANS, p. 181; WIMMER (2002), p. 2508; REINHART (2003), pp. 884–885. On European payment and settlement systems, see ECB, *Blue Book,* August 2002.

[232] The Directive also applies to transactions by the Central Banks of the Member States and European Central Bank.

213. Article 9 distinguishes between *"payment or settlement systems"*, on the one hand, and *"financial markets"*, on the other.

214. The term *payment or settlement systems* is directly linked to Directive 98/26/EC on Settlement Finality. Consequently, it must be interpreted in a broad sense, to encompass both payment systems and securities settlement systems. The definition of these systems must be taken from the Directive on settlement finality, specifically from Article 2.a thereof: a system shall mean a formal agreement between two or more participants with common rules and standardised arrangements for the execution of transfer orders between the participants, be governed by the law of a Member State, and be designated as a system by that Member State (and the Commission has been notified to that effect).

Payment and settlement systems fulfil a basic function for the operation of the markets. They permit a large volume of standardised transactions to be carried out in a short space of time. For that reason, the protection established by Article 9 extends to the full range of activities which may be involved in the finalisation of a transaction (confirmation, clearance, settlement). The relevant mechanisms include the irrevocability of transfer orders; closing out contracts (displacing Article 4.2.e with regard to the effects of the insolvency on current contracts); and netting (displacing Article 6 with regard to set-off).

> *NB*. The relationship between the concepts of "payment or settlement systems" and "financial market", used in Article 9, is explained by historical reasons. Originally, Article 9 only referred to "financial markets"; the reference to payment or settlement systems was included as a result of the proposal of the Directive on finality. This reference ensured close coordination with the Directive on finality. The concept of "financial market" is wider than that of payment or settlement systems. These are a cornerstone in the operation of financial markets, but not the only one.

215. Along with these systems, Article 9 protects *"financial markets"* in general. Although no definition is offered, for the purposes of Article 9 a financial market is a market in financial instruments (e.g. shares and equivalents, bonds and other forms of negotiable debt instruments) or financial transactions (e.g. futures contracts and options), with a formally established exchange, characterised by regular trading and standardised conditions of operation and access, which are recognised and governed by the law of a Member State.

> *Regulated markets*. The term *"financial market"* used by the Insolvency Regulation is not necessarily equivalent to the term *"regulated market"* used by other EC instruments. Article 27 of the Directive on credit institutions contains a rule parallel to that of Article 9 of the Insolvency Regulation, which refers to "regulated markets", and Article 2 thereof defines this concept by referring to Directive 93/22 regarding investment services in the securities field. In this text, the concept of "regulated market" does not include markets in commodity derivatives. However, the definition of "financial market" provided in the Explanatory Report is broader.[233] According to this definition, "a financial market [....] is understood to

---

[233] See VIRGOS/SCHMIT Report, Margin N° 120 *in fine*.

be a market in a Contracting State where financial instruments, other financial assets or commodity futures and options are traded. It is characterised by regular trading and conditions of operation and access and it is subject to the law of the relevant Contracting State, including appropriate supervision, if any (*sic*), by the regular authorities of that Contracting State". As a result of this interpretation, any financial market that fulfils these characteristics and is recognised by a Member State can be considered a "financial market" for the purposes of Article 9 of the Insolvency Regulation, whether or not it is included in the list of regulated markets derived from Directive 93/22 on investment services.[234] Article 9 of the Regulation was meant to include, for instance, markets such as the *London Metal Exchange* or the *International Petroleum Exchange*. They are organised markets, recognised by a Member State, where futures and options contracts are traded. Both the origin of the rule (proposed by Great Britain) and its sense and purpose (to protect the expectations of operators in an organised financial market against the intrusion of a foreign *lex concursus*) advocate this interpretation. The same can be said of the Spanish FC & M market for futures and options on citrus products. Directive 93/22/EEC has been repealed by Directive 2004/39/EC on markets on financial instruments (*OJ* L-145, dated 30.04.2004), with effect from April 2006. The new Directive gives a broader definition of market which follows along the lines sketched by the Explanatory Report. It now includes markets in a wide spectrum of financial instruments (including, *inter alia*, derivatives relating to commodities, climatic variables, freight rates, emission allowances, inflation rates or other economic statistics). The Directive also recognises the emergence of a new generation of organised trading systems, the so called "multilateral trading facilities" (MTF) that, in so far as they present the same problems, should also be covered by Article 9 of the Regulation.

Transactions protected. The term "financial market" does not protect any transaction linked to these markets, but only the orders and transactions which are conducted *within* the *operational structures* of the market. i.e. it protects transactions between those who participate *directly* in the market (even when they do so on behalf of third parties). As far as transactions which are conducted outside the market are concerned (e.g. donation, hereditary transfer, direct purchase and sale, etc.) they will only be protected if and from the moment in which they are executed through a payment and settlement system.

216. Article 9 protects these operations against the scope of the *lex fori concursus*. Having said that, the exception to the general rule established by Article 9 is similar in nature to those of Articles 8 and 10. None of these transactions are immunised against the declaration of insolvency, as was the case with regard to the rights *in rem* protected by Article 5, but are rather subject to the *insolvency rules* of the State whose law governs the system or market.[235]

217. Actions to set-aside acts which are detrimental to the body of creditors are also excluded from the competence of the *lex fori concursus* (Article 4.2.m) and subject to Article 9. In order to protect as far as possible the confidence of the participants in these systems, section 2 of Article 9 establishes that any action for voidness,

---

[234] The Commission publishes a list of all regulated markets in the *Official Journal of the European Union* and at its website. The periodically updated version of the list can be consulted at: www.europa.eu.int/comm/internal_market/in/finances/mobil/isdlist_is.pdf.

[235] Virgos/Schmit Report, Margin No. 121; Balz (1996a), p. 951. This conflict rule and the substantive rules contained in Directive 98/26/EC on settlement finality and Directive 2002/47/EC on financial collateral arrangements, provide for a high degree of isolation from the insolvency risk.

voidability or unenforceability of the payments or transactions conducted in the said systems or markets and which might prove detrimental to the creditors as a whole, is also subject to the law which governs the system or market, not to the law governing the insolvency proceedings. In this respect, the connection provided for in Article 9 moves away from the general regime applicable to these actions under the Insolvency Regulation.

218. Article 9 expressly preserves the applicability of Article 5 concerning rights *in rem*. This exception is aimed at protecting any possible rights *in rem* which might be constituted within the framework of these systems; typically, security rights over accounts of negotiable securities or money.[236] It is normal for the parties, between themselves or with the system itself, to endow, as a mechanism to guarantee the liabilities arising out of the market transactions, a set of security rights. Article 5 protects these security rights and, consequently, when the collateral is located in a Member State other than the State of opening, they are not affected by either the *lex fori concursus* (pursuant to Article 5) or by the insolvency rules of the law which governs the system (because Article 9 reserves the application of Article 5).[237] However, the risk that the creation of the security right may be challenged by invoking the actions to set aside detrimental acts afforded by the *lex fori concursus* (Article 4.2.m with the restriction imposed by Article 13), makes it advisable to also apply Article 9.2 to this case (i.e. when the collateral is situated in the State of the market or system), thereby subjecting the actions to set-aside also to the insolvency rules of the law which governs the system or market in question.[238]

219. This rule only applies to systems of payment and settlement and financial markets subject to the law of a *Member State*. In the case of third-party States, national Private International Law applies.

220. The *Directive on credit institutions* contains a more detailed regulation on this type of question. Alongside a rule similar to that of Article 9 of the Insolvency Regulation (Article 27), it contains two special rules: one concerning the constitution of rights *in rem* in respect of registered or recorded negotiable securities (Article 24); and another for repurchase agreements (Article 25).

(a) Article 27 establishes a general rule for "regulated markets" (on this concept, see *supra* No. 215): transactions carried out in the context of a regulated market are governed exclusively by the law applicable to the contract governing the said transactions.

NB. Unlike Article 9 of the Insolvency Regulation, Article 27 of the Directive on credit institutions does not refer to the law which governs the market but to the law which governs the transaction. This should not present excessive problems as it is normal for the law which governs a transaction carried out in a regulated market to be the law which governs that market. This is one of the typical cases in which the exception provided for in Article 4.5 of the 1980 Rome Convention will come into play.

---

[236] Virgos/Schmit Report, Margin No. 124; Taupitz, p. 345.
[237] Virgos/Schmit Report, Margin No. 124.
[238] Virgos, p. 23.

(b) For its part, Article 24 contains the special rule for the enforcement of proprietary rights or other rights in respect of *financial instruments* whose existence presupposes a *record* in a register, in an account or in a centralised deposit system: the law of the State where the register, account or centralised deposit system in which those rights are recorded is held or located will apply (*PRIMA rule, infra* No. 311).

(c) Article 25 contains a rule for *repurchase agreements,* i.e. agreements by which negotiable securities or other assets are sold for cash, with the simultaneous agreement to repurchase the negotiable securities or equivalent assets at a specific price at a future date or upon request (*"repos"*). Without prejudice to the provisions of Article 24, these will be governed solely by the law of the contract which governs the said agreements.

221. The Directive on *insurance companies* restricts itself to establishing a rule for regulated markets similar to that of Article 9 of the Regulation (Article 23).

6. EFFECTS ON RIGHTS SUBJECT TO REGISTRATION (ARTICLE 11)

222. *Article 11* establishes a more limited *exception* to the application of the law of the State of opening (*lex fori concursus*). According to this provision, *"the effects of insolvency proceedings on the rights of the debtor in immoveable property, a ship or an aircraft subject to registration in a public register shall be determined by the law of the Member State under the authority of which the register is kept".*

There is a dual purpose to this exception:[239] (a) on the one hand, it seeks to prevent conflicts between the *lex fori concursus* and the law of the State of registration, for example in the case where the former law provides for effects or consequences which differ from those of, or do not exist in, the system of the State of registration and, consequently, difficult to implement; and (b) on the other hand, it seeks to protect trade and legal certainty; general confidence in the content of the registers and in their consequences must be protected under equal conditions both if the insolvency proceedings are opened in the State of registration and if they are opened abroad.

223. Article 11 does not protect creditors or third parties' rights but the system of registration as such and the level of legal certainty that it ensures. It is for this reason that Article 11 establishes an exception of lesser scope than those provided for in Articles 8, 9 and 10. In order to realise this, we have to take note of the fact that Article 11 does not use the adverb "solely" (it does not say, like the other provisions, "…shall be determined solely by the law of the member State…"). This means that Article 11 gives competence to the law of the State of the Register but does not exclude the application of the law of the State of opening (*lex fori concursus*). A kind of *cumulative* application of both laws is therefore implied in Article 11.[240] The law

---

[239] VIRGOS/SCHMIT Report, Margin Nos 129–130; VIRGOS, p. 22; TAUPITZ, p. 346.

[240] VIRGOS/SCHMIT Report, Margin No. 130; VIRGOS, p. 22; TAUPITZ, p. 346; LEIBLE/STAUDINGER (2000), p. 557.

of the State of the Register cannot impose effects which are not required by the *lex fori concursus* and the *lex fori concursus* cannot order effects which are inadmissible or do not exist in the law of the State of the Register (e.g. a general mortgage in the estate may be incompatible with the law of the Register). The resulting solution follows this idea: (a) the *lex fori concursus* determines what effects the insolvency proceedings seek to produce on the debtor's rights over registered assets; (b) the law of the register determines the admissibility and registrability (*"Eintragungsfähigkeit"*) of these effects: whether or not such effects can actually be admitted "as they stand" or whether a transposition into a functionally equivalent national concept is necessary, which entries are to be made when insolvency proceedings are opened, and the legal consequences of such an entry (or the absence thereof).[241]

224. The complexity associated with this rule and the inconvenience of finding ourselves faced with different effects in each State explains why its application has been limited to the registers of *immovable property, ships and aircraft*.

225. The term *register* must be understood in a broad sense.[242] The systems of registration vary in Europe. There are systems which directly register rights over assets and systems which only register the deeds regarding the creation, transfer or cancellation of rights over those assets. Article 11 encompasses all systems (e.g. the German Land Register and the Registry of Deeds which exists in Ireland). On the other hand, the term public does not refer to the authority which keeps the register, but to its legal function: disclosure of either title and rights *in rem* or juridical acts regarding the creation, transfer or cancellation of such rights and their effects *vis-à-vis* third parties. Article 11 includes private registers with these characteristics which are recognised by the national legal system in question.

As in the other cases, Article 11 only affects registers which are subject to the law of a *Member State*. For third-party States, the rules of national Private International Law apply.

226. Finally, we have to take into account the fact that Article 11 only governs the effects of the insolvency proceedings on the rights *of the debtor*. With regard to the rights *in rem*, whether they are registered or not, of *creditors* or *third parties* acquired before the declaration of opening, the more radical provisions of Article 5 apply.[243]

227. The *Directives* on *credit institutions* and *insurance companies* contain a parallel rule to that of Article 11 of the Insolvency Regulation (Articles 20.c and 19.c, respectively).

Differences. However, in the case of the Directive on credit institutions (Article 20.c), there are certain differences in the way the rules are drawn up. Specifically, there are two which should be pointed out: (a) it does not expressly mention that it concerns the rights of the

---

[241] VIRGOS/SCHMIT Report, Margin No. 130; BALZ (1996a), p. 950; VIRGOS, p. 22; HUBER, p. 164 (all with reference to the limits which might arise, for example, from a system of *numerus clausus*); TAUPITZ, pp. 346–347 (defending the need to "adapt" the foreign figures so as not to frustrate the play of the main rule); see also FLESSNER (1997), pp. 225–226; ADERHOLD, pp. 257–258; WIMMER (2002), p. 2509.

[242] VIRGOS/SCHMIT Report, Margin Nos 131–132; TAUPITZ, p. 346.

[243] VIRGOS/SCHMIT Report, Margin No. 131; TAUPITZ, p. 346.

debtor, i.e. of the credit institution, and (b) it includes the adverb "solely". The first omission should not present problems as it can be implicitly understood from the context of the text: the rights of third parties will normally be rights *in rem* and these are regulated in the following Article (Article 21). The second, in contrast, is important as it excludes the cumulative application of the law of the register and the *lex fori concursus*. In the Directive on insurance companies, the exception is equivalent to the exception made in Articles 8 and 10 of the Regulation (see Article 19.c thereof). This Directive does not contain the adverb "solely". Given that there is no reason to explain the difference in treatment in the case of credit institutions (what the provision seeks to protect is the register system) it must be due to a "lapse" while transcribing the general rule, and should be corrected accordingly for the purposes of interpretation.

7. COMMUNITY PATENTS AND TRADEMARKS (ARTICLE 12)

228. In spite of the fact that it is systematically situated among the exceptions, Article 12 of the Regulation does not constitute a true exception to the general rule of Article 4, but rather a *substantive rule* which performs a function similar to that of the rules assigning a *situs* to the different assets of the debtor: to determine which assets belong to the estate of the main proceedings and which to the territorial proceedings. What this provision establishes is that EC patents, EC trademarks and any other similar right established by an EC provision may be included only in proceedings with universal scope (i.e. those opened *ex* Article 3.1).

229. The aim of this provision is to correct the imbalance which is produced between rights which cover the whole of the EC territory and the possibility of opening territorial proceedings. As these proceedings have a scope which is limited to the assets located in the territory of the State in question, it is perfectly reasonable for those rights to be excluded. Such rights may only be included in the main proceedings.

Relation with other rules. Article 12 of the Insolvency Regulation seeks to modify the solutions provided for in Article 41 of the 1989 Agreement on Community Patents, Article 21 of the 1993 Regulation on the Community Trademark of 1993, and Article 25 of the 1994 Regulation on Plant Variety Rights. These three provisions establish that these rights may only be included in the first insolvency proceedings to be opened in an EC State. The relevant criterion was based purely on time factors, and it was a sensible solution insofar as there was a lack of common regulations dealing with insolvency proceedings. Now that regulations are available, these rules are no longer appropriate.[244] However, they continue to operate when the centre of main interests is located in a third-party State as the Insolvency Regulation will not apply in this case.[245] Article 31 of the 6/2002 Regulation on Community Designs establishes a solution which coincides with Article 12 of the Insolvency Regulation. The same can be said of the proposed Regulation on Community Patents (see Article 18.l).

230. The Directives on *credit institutions* and *insurance companies do not* contain a rule equivalent to Article 12 of the Regulation. The reason for this is easy to

---

[244] VIRGOS/SCHMIT Report, Margin No. 133; BALZ (1996a), p. 950.
[245] VIRGOS/SCHMIT Report, Margin No. 134.

understand: as the possibility of opening territorial proceedings is not provided for, such a rule would be unnecessary.

8. Detrimental Acts (Articles 4.2.m and 13)

231. In all Member States, the law provides for the avoidance or cancellation of fraudulent or preferential transactions enabling the recapture, for the benefit of the creditors as a whole, of assets transferred or encumbered by the debtor in the period prior to the commencement of insolvency proceedings.

There are basically *three* possible solutions for determining the law applicable to actions to set-aside in insolvency: (a) to apply the law which governs the act whose effectiveness is being challenged; (b) to apply the *lex fori concursus*; or (c) to apply a combination of both.[246] The Insolvency Regulation leans towards the third of these solutions. The Regulation starts out by applying the *lex fori concursus* (Article 4.2.m) but allows the law which governs the act or transaction whose effectiveness is being challenged to be invoked in order to "veto" the possibility of setting aside the legal act provided for by the former (Article 13).

232. This conflict of laws regime (Articles 4.2.m + 13) has *general scope* within the Insolvency Regulation and also applies in the case of relationships or rights protected by Article 5 (third-party rights *in rem*), Article 6 (set-off), Article 7 (reservation of title), Article 8 (contracts relating to immovable property), and Article 10 (contracts of employment).

> *Explanation*. The importance of the rules for the avoidance of detrimental acts is such that the Regulation expressly reserves the application of the *lex fori concursus* in Articles 5.4, 6.2 and 7.3, thereby establishing a kind of "exception to the exceptions" to the general competence of the *lex fori concursus*.[247] The justification for this rule is not to increase the estate, because to do that it would have been sufficient to remove the protection provided by Articles 5, 6 and 7, but rather to ensure that the rights protected by these Articles were not acquired in a fraudulent or challengeable way. The sense and purpose of this regime is to prevent the collective interests of the creditors from being prejudiced by intentionally prejudicial transfers, gifts, transactions at undervalue or preferences (eve-of-insolvency transfers which benefit some creditors at the expense of others, thereby distorting the pro rata sharing rule of insolvency law). What the Regulation does is ensure a conflictual *par conditio creditorum* (all creditors are subject to the same standards set by the *lex fori concursus*) by repressing this behaviour.[248] For that reason, what Articles 5, 6 and 7 are really protecting are the rights acquired in accordance with a law other than the law of the State of opening, *provided that* this acquisition is not subject to challenge; and it is the law of the State of opening (*lex fori concursus*), with the restriction provided by Article 13, which tells us what is challengeable and what is not challengeable. The same can be said in the case of Articles 8 and 10, though in these cases an express exception to Article 4.2.m was not

---

[246] For a more detailed treatment, Siehr, pp. 812–813; Aderhold, pp. 264–265; Herchen, pp. 168–169.

[247] See Herchen, p. 69.

[248] Herchen, pp. 71–73.

necessary. The reason for this is that both provisions must be understood as exceptions limited to Article 4.2.e and not as general exceptions to Article 4; i.e. as exceptions to the rule whereby the effects on current contracts are governed by the law of the State of opening, but not as exceptions to the application of the *lex concursus* to govern other questions.

On the other hand, Articles 4.2.m and 13 do not apply to situations protected by Article 9 regarding transactions carried out within the framework of *payment or settlement systems* and *financial markets*; in these cases the insolvency set-aside is also governed by the provisions of the law applicable to the payment system or financial market in question.

233. The Insolvency Regulation is based upon the application as a general rule of the law of the State of opening. According to Article 4.2.m, the *lex fori concursus* determines *"the rules relating to the voidness, voidability or unenforceability of legal acts detrimental to all the creditors"*. The reason for this is clear. These rules seek to protect the estate from transfers which diminish the assets available to the general body of creditors (e.g. fraudulent or undervalued transfers) and also to ensure that creditors are treated equally when the debtor's insolvency is already on the horizon. It is perfectly reasonable for these rules to be subject to the *lex fori concursus*. This law will determine the conditions to be met and the legal consequences of the voidness, voidability or unenforceability of the transaction (including the position in the insolvency which corresponds to the third party affected by this set-aside).[249]

234. Article 4.m contemplates actions to set-aside arising from the insolvency. Whether these actions are specific to insolvency law or are an insolvency version of a more general remedy (such as the *Actio Pauliana*) is immaterial. Ordinary actions of civil and commercial law for the avoidance or cancellation of transactions follow the general conflict of laws rules. However, these ordinary actions are only admissible if and insofar as the *lex fori concursus* so permits.[250]

235. *Article 13* establishes the *exception* to the application of the *lex fori concursus*. According to this provision: *"Article 4(2)(m) shall not apply where the person who benefited from an act detrimental to all the creditors provides proof that: (a) the said act is subject to the law of a Member State other than that of the State of the opening of proceedings; and (b) that law does not allow any means of challenging that act in the relevant case.*

236. This rule seeks to uphold the legitimate expectations of creditors or third parties regarding the validity of the act: those who confide in its validity according to the normally applicable national law, including the insolvency rules of that law, should not find themselves surprised by the application of a foreign insolvency law.[251]

---

[249] Virgos/Schmit Report, Margin No. 135; Balz (1996a), p. 951; Taupitz, p. 328; Herchen, pp. 69–70.

[250] Virgos/Schmit Report, Margin No. 91 m.

[251] Virgos/Schmit Report, Margin No. 138; Virgos, p. 22; Taupitz, p. 328; Huber, p. 165; see also, on the reasonableness of this type of exception, Henckel, p. 93; Aderhold, pp. 276–277.

237. The term "legal act" allows for a very wide interpretation of this provision, which includes unilateral or bilateral acts (payments, transfers, gifts, contracts, etc.), including acts of a procedural nature.[252]

238. Article 13 concerns acts carried out *prior* to the opening of the insolvency proceedings and threatened by either the retroactive nature of the proceedings opened in another country or actions to set-aside on the part of the liquidator. This explains why Article 13 does not apply to acts carried out *after* the decision to open proceedings.[253]

239. Specifically, Article 13 provides that the law of the State of opening shall not apply when the person who has benefited from the contested act provides proof that: (a) the said act is subject to the law of a Member State other than that of the State of opening; and that, furthermore, (b) that law does not allow any means of challenging that act in the relevant case.

240. This provision contains three expressions which are worth considering. The reference to the fact that "*the person who benefited ...provides proof*" implies that this is a question that the Court cannot decide on its own motion, but that the beneficiary must allege. Furthermore, the burden of proof falls upon him.[254] In other words, Article 13 contains an exception to the play of the *lex fori concursus* which the person in question must enforce.

Second, "*in the relevant case*" means that the act is open to challenge in fact, *i.e.* after taking into account all of the specific circumstances of the case; it is not enough to determine if it can be challenged in the abstract.[255]

Finally, the expression "*any means*" is understood to mean that the act must not be capable of being challenged using either the insolvency rules or the general rules of the national law applicable to the said act. The general rules include all kinds of civil, commercial and public rules affecting the validity in law of the act in question.[256] It is irrelevant that the consequences envisaged in each case are different than those provided for by the *lex fori concursus*. The main thing is that the act is really unassailable according to the law which governs it.[257]

NB. Some authors[258] exclude the rules on *prescription and limitation of actions*. In reality, there are no convincing reasons for this exclusion. The rules on prescription form part of the regime for the avoidance of acts; see, for a comparable example, Article 10.d of the 1980 Rome Convention. If the act was capable of being challenged according to the *lex causae* but the time for bringing an action has lapsed, there is no reason to consider the act as challengeable

---

[252] HERCHEN, pp. 70, 167–168.

[253] VIRGOS/SCHMIT Report, Margin No. 138.

[254] On the role of the *lex fori*, HENCKEL, p. 172.

[255] VIRGOS/SCHMIT Report, Margin No. 137.

[256] VIRGOS/SCHMIT Report, Margin No. 137; BALZ (1996a), p. 951; GOTTWALD (1999), p. 165; HABSCHEID (1998), p. 499; LAIBLE/STAUDINGER (2000), p. 557; HUBER, p. 165; FUMAGALLI, p. 701; against, HERCHEN, p. 173.

[257] BALZ (1996a), p. 951.

[258] BALZ (1996a), p. 951.

241. Article 13 permits the party concerned to enforce a kind of "veto" against the invalidity or unenforceability of the act decreed by the law of the State of opening: the rules of this law determining the voidness, voidability or unenforceability of a given act will not apply when the beneficiary of the said act proves that the act is legally unassailable according to the law which governs it. The law governing the act in question intervenes solely to determine whether or not the act is challengeable. If the beneficiary of the act proves that, according to this law, there are no specific means allowing the act in question to be challenged, the application of the *lex concursus* is discarded and the validity of the act is respected. Otherwise, Article 4 operates normally and the *lex fori concursus* applies; the regime of the challenge and its consequences are solely those which are provided for by this law.[259]

Rationale. This formula is easier to apply than other solutions based on the cumulative application of the two laws.[260] It is now clear that all the conditions for and consequences of the avoidance are determined by the *lex fori concursus*. The only function of Article 13 IR is to reject the application of that law in a given case.[261] If the act in question can be challenged according to the law which governs it, the "veto" does not operate and Article 4 2.m applies without exception.

242. In the case of territorial insolvency proceedings, the rules of the local *lex fori concursus* on the set-aside of detrimental acts only apply insofar as damage has been caused to the debtor's assets which were located in the State in question at the relevant time.[262] The location of assets is established by Article 2.g of the Regulation (*supra* Nos 306 *et seq.*).

243. Article 13 only comes into play when the law applicable to the act is that of a *Member State*. In all other cases, the national rules of Private International Law will apply.

244. The *Directives* on *credit institutions* and *insurance companies* establish a similar regime to that of the Regulation (see Articles 3.2, 10.2.1 and 30 of the first; see Articles 4.2, 9.2.1 and 24 of the second.

NB: The different wording of the corresponding provisions in the two directives arises from purely systematic reasons. In the case of reorganisation and not winding-up proceedings, the "veto" on challenging a detrimental act by invoking the law which governs that act is found in Article 30.2 of the Directive on credit institutions and Article 4.2 of the Directive on insurance companies.

---

[259] Balz (1996b), p. 512; Herchen, p. 171; Duursma-Kepplinger/Duursma/Chalupsky (2002), p. 320.

[260] Balz (1996a), p. 951; Taupitz, p. 328; Gottwald (1999), p. 165; Herchen, p. 169, who is critical of this solution and who considers the exception of public policy as sufficient defence, see Taupitz, p. 328, note 70 *et seq.*

[261] Virgos/Schmit Report, Margin No. 136.

[262] Virgos/Schmit Report, Margin No. 91 *in fine*.

9. PROTECTION OF THIRD-PARTY PURCHASERS (ARTICLE 14)

245. *Article 14* refers to *acts of disposal* concluded by the debtor *after* the opening of the main proceedings. Under the national law of all Member States, one of the typical effects of the opening of insolvency proceedings is for the debtor to be deprived of his powers of administration and disposal to a greater or a lesser extent.[263] These powers are transferred to the liquidator or subject to different kinds of restrictions according to the national law applicable. In fact, the partial or total divestment of the debtor is one of the key features used by the Regulation itself to define its sphere of application (Article 1.1). Improper acts of disposal by the debtor may, according to the applicable *lex fori concursus*, be either immediately ineffective or be subject to a possible challenge by the liquidator.

However, the enforceability of this ineffectiveness on third parties may conflict with the need to protect legal certainty and the reliance interests of third parties acting in good faith in other States, particularly when this confidence arises from the information provided in a public register in the said State.

246. Article 14 seeks to guarantee confidence in the integrity of public registers. For this reason, it states that *where, by an act concluded after the opening of insolvency proceedings, the debtor disposes, for consideration, of: (a) an immoveable asset, or (b) a ship or an aircraft subject to registration in a public register, or (c) securities whose existence presupposes registration in a register laid down by law, the validity of that act shall be governed by the law of the State within the territory of which the immoveable asset is situated or under the authority of which the register is kept.*

247. As in the previous cases, this Article is dependent upon the register or immovable asset being located in a *Member State.*[264]

248. The referral made by Article 14 to the national law is limited to the validity of the act of disposal for consideration, to the third party, but it includes, within that scope, the insolvency rules of that State; in this sense, the protection provided in the event of foreign proceedings cannot go beyond the protection provided in the case of comparable domestic proceedings.[265]

Difficulty. The requirement that the register must be "laid down by law" poses problems in the case of accounts of rights in respect of securities held with an intermediary. If according to the law governing the register or account, its entries have effect on the transfer and protection of the right, then the register is "recognised by law" as performing an equivalent function and Article 14 should therefore apply. This interpretation is consistent with the developments brought about in Community law. The relevant criterion should be that the right be recorded in a register, an account or a centralised deposit system governed by the law of a Member State; see Directive 98/26/EC (Article 9.2), Directive 2001/17/EC (Article 25), Directive 2001/24/EC (Articles 24 and 31) and Directive 2002/47/EC (Article 9).

---

[263] VIRGOS/SCHMIT Report, Margin No. 141; HERCHEN, p. 57.

[264] Although not expressly required by the provision, the reasons are the same as in No. 27.

[265] VIRGOS/SCHMIT Report, Margin No. 141; HERCHEN, pp. 60–61; LEIBLE/STAUDINGER (2000), pp. 557–558.

249. The sense and purpose of this exception to the *lex fori concursus* is, as we have said, to uphold the confidence of third parties in the content of public registers *vis-à-vis* the effects of the *lex concursus* (e.g. restrictions upon the debtor's power of disposal). The typical case which was contemplated is where the declaration of insolvency in another Member State has still not been reflected in the local register and the debtor disposes of an asset to a third party who is unaware of the opening. In this case, it seems reasonable that protection of the third party acting in good faith from the risks resulting from the debtor's insolvency be no different in respect of foreign insolvency proceedings than of domestic ones. For that reason, the validity of the said act of disposal is not subject to the foreign *lex fori concursus*, but to the law of the State where the immovable asset is located or the State under whose authority the register is kept.[266]

NB. There are close parallels between this solution and the one provided in Article 24 for the honouring of obligations in favour of the insolvent debtor. The difference between the two provisions is that in Article 24 the Insolvency Regulation establishes a substantive rule: the good faith of the third-party debtor of the insolvent is upheld by means of a presumption *iuris tantum:* the person honouring the obligation to the insolvent is presumed to have been unaware of the opening of insolvency proceedings as long as the foreign declaration of insolvency has not been made public there. Article 14, in contrast, establishes a conflict of laws rule: it is the law of the State where the immovable asset is located or under the authority of which the register is kept which will determine who is protected when the opening of the insolvency proceedings or the restrictions on the debtor have not yet been entered or referred to in the register in question, and any presumptions regarding good or bad faith.[267]

250. This provision only applies to acts of disposal for *consideration* (not those which are free of charge).The protection afforded by this Article includes not only the transfer of ownership, but also the constitution or transfer of other rights *in rem* in respect of those assets.[268]

With regard to acts of disposal concluded after the opening and which do not fall into these categories, the general rule of Article 4 (the *lex fori concursus*) continues to apply.

251. The *Directives* on *credit institutions* and *insurance companies* contain an equivalent rule (see Articles 31 and 25, respectively).

NB. The tenor of the two provisions differs from Article 14 of the Insolvency Regulation in that it expressly includes the requirement that the immovable asset or register be located in a Member State and in the extension of the section to encompass financial instruments and rights in such instruments the existence or transfer of which presupposes their being recorded in a register, an account or a centralised deposit system. This second difference makes it clear that security accounts maintained by financial intermediaries are also included. "Instrument" means the financial instruments referred to in Section B of the Annex

---

[266] VIRGOS/SCHMIT Report, Margin No. 141; VIRGOS, p. 23; FLETCHER, p. 281; HERCHEN, pp. 57, 60; LEIBLE/STAUDINGER (2000), p. 558.

[267] See also, HERCHEN, p. 61; PIELORZ, p. 244.

[268] VIRGOS/SCHMIT Report, Margin No. 141 *in fine*.

to Directive 93/22/EEC: transferable securities (e.g. shares, bonds and other forms of negotiable debts instruments) and other financial instruments or assets such as units in collective investment undertakings, money-market instruments, financial futures contracts,
forward interest-rate agreements, interest rates, currency and equity swaps, and options to
acquire any of the said instruments.

10. EFFECTS ON LAWSUITS PENDING (ARTICLE 15)

252. The laws of the Member States differ from one another with regard to the
effects of insolvency proceedings on a pending lawsuit to which the debtor is a party.
Differences concern not only the suspension of proceedings which may be necessary
to preserve the *status quo* but also the possible removal of litigation from the ordinary courts into the exclusive control of the insolvency court, under the principle
known as *vis attractiva concursus*.[269]

253. By regulating the effects of the insolvency proceedings on lawsuits pending,
the Regulation distinguishes between enforcement actions and litigation on the
merits of a case. Article 15 concerns the second: *"The effects of insolvency proceedings on a lawsuit pending concerning an asset or a right of which the debtor has
been divested shall be governed solely by the law of the Member State in which that
lawsuit is pending"*.

254. The effects of the opening of insolvency proceedings on individual enforcement actions by creditors (such as distress, execution, attachment or sequestration)
are governed by the law of the State of the opening, according to Article 4.2.f. The
main insolvency proceedings can stay (if they have already started) or prevent (if not
yet started) any individual enforcement actions brought by the creditors against the
debtor's assets in other States (see No. 121).[270]

255. However, the effects of the insolvency proceedings on *lawsuits pending*
regarding assets or rights of which the debtor has been divested are subject to the law
of the State where the lawsuit is pending (*lex fori processus*). This exception to the
application of the law governing the insolvency proceedings has a twofold explanation:
the fact that, as no enforcement action is involved, the principle of collective action
inherent in the insolvency proceedings is not impaired; and the close link with the procedural laws of each State resulting from the fact that the lawsuit is already in course.

Further explanation. The difference between subjecting individual enforcements to the *lex
fori concursus* and subjecting ordinary processes to the *lex fori processus* is sufficiently
explained if we consider the different consequences of each on the insolvent debtor's
estate. In the first case, the creditor satisfies his interest directly. In the second case, he
obtains a decision on the merits which does no more than allow him to join the body of
creditors with an established claim.

---

[269] FLETCHER, in MOSS/FLETCHER/ISAACS, p. 65.
[270] VIRGOS/SCHMIT Report, Margin No. 142; HERCHEN, pp. 209 *et seq.*; LEIBLE/STAUDINGER (2000), p. 561;
DUURSMA-KEPPLINGER/DUURSMA/CHALUPSKY (2002), p. 347.

256. The use of the term *"solely"* is aimed at preventing the cumulative application of different national laws. The meaning of this provision is to refer all questions
concerning the possible effect of the opening of insolvency proceedings on lawsuits
to the *procedural law* of the State where litigation is pending (or *lex fori processus*).
This law will decide whether the proceedings are to be suspended or may continue
subject to any procedural modification necessary in order to reflect the loss or the
restriction of the powers of disposal and administration of the debtor, and the intervention of the liquidator in his place, which all Member States must recognise under
Article 16.[271] However, this referral does not extend to the costs of the procedure: the
payment of costs *vis-à-vis* the estate is in any case subject to the *lex fori concursus*.[272]

257. The referral by Article 15 to the law of the litigation forum does not extend
to questions of international jurisdiction, which are subject to a uniform regime. The
Insolvency Regulation is based on the inadmissibility of the *vis attractiva* in the international arena, the decision opening insolvency proceedings does not affect the jurisdiction of the court which is dealing with the lawsuit pending, even when the national
law of the litigation forum *(lex fori processus)* provides for the concentration of all
litigation involving the debtor in the insolvency court *(vis attractiva concursus)*.[273]

258. Furthermore, application of Article 15 depends on the subject matter of the
process: *"an asset or a right of which the debtor has been divested"*. Article 15 operates regardless of the procedural position of the parties, both if the debtor is the plaintiff and if he is the defendant.[274] In any case, the divestment of the debtor and the scope
thereof is not determined by the *lex fori processus* but by the *lex fori concursus*. If an
asset is excluded from the effects of the insolvency proceedings according to the *lex
concursus*, it will also be unaffected by Article 15.[275]

Articles 5 and 7. Although the law governing the main proceedings may claim local assets
belonging to the debtor as parts of the estate in those proceedings, the rights *in rem* of
creditors or third parties with regard to those assets cannot be affected. In the case of a
dispute concerning the rights over those assets, both Articles 15 and 5 (or 7) come into
play; consequently, the application of the law of the litigation forum ex Article 15 has to
respect the rule of non-alteration of the creditor or third party's right *in rem*.

---

[271] BALZ (1996b), p. 513. It corresponds to the *lex concursus* to determine if and to what extent the
decision opening the insolvency proceedings limits the *powers of administration and disposal* of the
debtor or affect his *procedural capacity* (Article 4.2.c).

[272] VIRGOS/SCHMIT Report, Margin No. 142; HERCHEN, p. 196 (indicating that the rules of Private
International Law have to be excluded from this referral: the effect of insolvency proceedings opened in
another State on a lawsuit pending in the forum is the same as the effect which insolvency proceedings
opened in the forum would have) and pp. 207–208 (indicating that Article 15 does not cover the effects
of the insolvency on the contractual relationships of the debtor with his lawyers, but does cover the effects
of the insolvency on the procedural aspects of these relationships; e.g. the effects on the scope of the
procedural powers of attorney); HUBER, p. 166.

[273] BALZ (1996b), p. 513.

[274] BALZ (1996a), p. 951; LÜKE (1998), pp. 310–311; LEIBLE/STAUDINGER (2000), pp. 558–559 (which
also analyses the problems which have arisen in German procedural law); see also HERCHEN, pp. 189
et seq.

[275] FLETCHER, in MOSS/FLETCHER/ISAACS, p. 65.

259. The *time factor* is here obviously relevant. Article 15 refers to lawsuits *pending* at the time the insolvency proceedings are declared open. The concept of *"pending"* means that the plaintiff has concluded the necessary actions, which depend on him, for the process to begin prior to the opening of the insolvency proceedings.[276]

260. Article 15 only contemplates lawsuits pending in Member States. In the case of proceedings brought in non-Member States, the national conflict of laws rule will apply.

261. The Insolvency Regulation does not make any express reference to the effects of the insolvency proceedings on lawsuits pending before arbitral tribunals in member States. Arbitration is not excluded from the general effects of the *lex concursus* under Article 4 and the literal wording of Article 15 is broad enough to include them in its exception to the application of that law. Arbitration proceedings are equivalent substitutes to ordinary legal proceedings in all Member States, and there is no substantive or procedural reason justifying a different solution.

262. The *Directives* on *credit institutions* and *insurance companies* contain a similar regime to that of the Regulation. The effects of reorganisation measures or winding-up proceedings on lawsuits pending will be governed by the law of the Member State in which the process is pending, as an exception to the *lex fori concursus* (see Recitals 32 and 36, respectively); but the effects of such measures and proceedings on the enforcement of the decisions resulting from those lawsuits will be governed by the law of the Member State of origin (i.e. the *lex fori concursus*).

---

[276] HERCHEN, pp. 198–200.

Chapter 7

Applicable Law: Uniform Rules

263. In addition to the conflict of laws rules, the Insolvency Regulation also establishes a series of *uniform substantive rules*. These rules are directly applicable and prevail over the provisions of national law.

1. PUBLICATION AND REGISTRATION (ARTICLES 21–22)

264. The international publication of the declaration of insolvency is not a pre-requisite for the recognition of the insolvency proceedings in other Member States. However, creditors and other parties (e.g. debtor's debtors) have a direct interest in receiving notice of the proceedings, as their rights or duties may be affected. Furthermore, publication may be relevant for other purposes. It can have legal importance when judging the conduct of the people affected, both in the context of the Insolvency Regulation (see, e.g. Article 24 concerning payments to the debtor instead of to the liquidator) and in the context of the applicable national law. For this reason, the Regulation contains certain *rules on publicity* for the purpose of giving notice of the legal situation of the insolvent debtor in those countries where the insolvent debtor carries out economic activities through an established place of business. The Regulation also contains specific rules concerning registration in a public register in other Member States. The general aim of these rules is to protect the general public (which includes future, and not only present, creditors) and the reliance interests of third parties (e.g. debtors of the insolvent) in other States.[277]

265. The *costs* incurred by the publication and registration measures provided for in Articles 21 and 22 are considered as costs of the proceedings (Article 23).

1.1. Publication

266. The Insolvency Regulation contains *three rules* regarding the publication of the opening of the insolvency proceedings which is necessary in order to inform creditors and the general public (i.e. debtors, potential new creditors, third parties): (a) Publication of the declaration in the *State of opening* (Article 4.1) *and* in *non-Member States* is determined by the *lex fori concursus*. This rule applies to both the main proceedings and to territorial proceedings. (b) Publication *in other Member*

---

[277] VIRGOS, p. 23; LEIBLE/STAUDINGER (2000), p. 564.

States is optional and is governed by the provisions of Article 21.1. This rule applies to both the main proceedings and to territorial proceedings. (c) Publication in a Member State *where the debtor has an establishment* may be obligatory, if the law of the Member State in question expressly requires this. In this case, publication is governed by the provisions of Article 21.2. This rule only applies to the main proceedings.

267. According to Article 21.1, publication *in other Member States* of the decision opening the proceedings is optional: "*the liquidator may request that notice of the judgment opening insolvency proceedings and, where appropriate, the decision appointing him, be published in any other Member State in accordance with the publication procedures provided for in that State. Such publication shall also specify the liquidator appointed and whether the jurisdiction rule applied is that pursuant to Articles 3(1) or 3(2).*

The Insolvency Regulation leaves the publication decision to the *liquidator*: it falls to him to decide whether or not it is appropriate to publish in other States the decision opening insolvency proceedings and his appointment as liquidator (Article 21.1). Naturally, this does not prevent the courts of the State of opening from ordering, in their own motion, this publication to take place, if their national law so permits.[278] The question of what is appropriate in a particular case will involve considerations such as the geographical scope of the activities of the insolvent debtor and cost effectiveness. It also has to take into account that Article 40 requires individual notification for known creditors established in other Member States.

The Regulation does not establish uniform rules with regard to the *means of publication* (publication in an official gazette or in newspapers, etc.) but refers to the rules provided for by the law of each State where publication must take place. This referral encompasses the *language* in which that publication must be made. However, the Regulation does establish a uniform rule regarding the *content* of the publication, i.e. the information which must be provided, which consists of the following: (a) the basic content of the decision to open the insolvency proceedings; (b) the liquidator appointed and, if appropriate, the decision appointing him; (c) the rule of jurisdiction which has been applied, i.e. whether the proceedings are pursuant to Article 3.1 (main) or Article 3.2 (territorial). This content is the *minimum* content which must be provided in all cases, but it does not mean the publication cannot include further additional information of interest.

268. Pursuant to Article 21.2, the publication of the decision opening proceedings in another Member State *where the debtor has an establishment* is mandatory, if this is an express requirement of the law of this Member State: *any Member State within the territory of which the debtor has an establishment may require mandatory publication. In such cases, the liquidator or any authority empowered to that effect in the Member State where the proceedings referred to in Article 3(1) are opened shall take all necessary measures to ensure such publication.*

---

[278] Virgos/Schmit Report, Margin No. 179.

NB. Regard may be had to Council Directive 89/666/EEC of 21 December 1989 concerning disclosure requirements in respect of branches opened in a Member State by certain types of company governed by the law of another State. In order to ensure the protection of persons who deal with companies through the intermediary of branches, Article 2 of this Directive provides for the mandatory disclosure in the Member State in which a branch is situated of any insolvency proceedings to which the company is subject.

The mandatory publication required by the law of the State where the debtor has an establishment must be arranged by the liquidator himself or by the authority empowered to that effect in the Member State where the main proceedings have been opened. States cannot make publication a pre-condition for the recognition of the decision opening the proceedings. The sanction for the breach of this requirement cannot be a refusal to recognise, but can lead to liability on the part of the liquidator according to the rules of the State which imposes this obligation upon him.[279]

With regard to the means of publication, the language and the content of the publication, the contents of the previous paragraph apply, with one important exception; in this case, the mandatory content required by the Member State of the establishment may not go beyond the information mentioned in Article 21.1. While for the State of the opening of the insolvency proceedings it constituted the *minimum* content to be published in other Member States, here, for the Member State where the debtor has an establishment, it is the *maximum* content of the obligation which that State can impose.[280]

1.2. Registration

269. In addition to these general rules of publication, the Regulation contains a special rule regarding *publication in a public registry*. Public registries fulfil an essential function for upholding confidence and protecting trade security. The Regulation also contains three rules regarding registration: (a) Registration in the *State of opening* (Article 4.1 IR) and in *non-Member States* is governed by the *lex fori concursus*. This rule applies to both the main proceedings and to territorial proceedings. (b) Registration in *other Member States* is, in principle, *optional* and is governed by the provisions of Article 22.1 IR. This rule only applies to the main proceedings. (c) However, registration in a Member State *may be mandatory* if the law of this Member State expressly requires it. This rule only applies to the main proceedings.

270. Pursuant to Article 22.1 the registration of the decision opening proceedings in Member States other than the State of the opening of the insolvency proceedings is *optional: the liquidator may request that the judgment opening the proceedings referred to in Article 3(1) be registered in the land register, the trade register and any other public register kept in the other Member States.*

---

[279] VIRGOS/SCHMIT Report, Margin No. 180; VIRGOS, p. 24; LEIBLE/STAUDINGER (2000), p. 565.
[280] VIRGOS/SCHMIT Report, Margin No. 181.

Article 22.1 empowers the liquidator to request the registration of the decision opening main proceedings in the land registry, in the trade registry or in any other public registry in the other Member States. This possibility only refers to the main proceedings, because territorial proceedings do not produce effects on assets located outside the opening proceedings. In accordance with this rule, the Member States are obliged to permit the registration of insolvency proceedings opened in another Member State in accordance with the Insolvency Regulation, under conditions similar to those applied to the registration of national proceedings; the form and content of that registration must respect the requirements of the law of the authority which keeps the register.[281]

271. According to Article 22.2, the registration of the decision opening proceedings in another Member State may be *obligatory* if the law of that Member State expressly requires it: *any Member State may require mandatory registration. In such cases, the liquidator or any authority empowered to that effect in the Member State where the proceedings referred to in Article 3(1) have been opened shall take all necessary measures to ensure such registration.*

In this case, the liquidator or any other authority empowered to that effect in the Member State where the main proceedings have been opened must take the necessary measures to ensure that this registration is carried out. The States cannot make prior registration in their registers a pre-condition for recognition of the decision opening proceedings. The sanction for the breach of the duty to register cannot be a refusal to recognise the foreign decision, but can lead to liability on the part of the liquidator according to the rules of the State which imposes this obligation upon him.[282]

1.3. Credit institutions and insurance companies

272. The *Directives* on the reorganisation and winding-up of *credit institutions* and *insurance companies* also contain uniform rules regarding publication and registration. Given that these entities are subject to prudential supervision, their rules also take this fact into consideration.

Explanation. In the case of *reorganisation* proceedings, the Directive on *credit institutions* establishes the obligation to inform the authorities of the host Member State, if possible *before* the adoption of any reorganisation measure and, if not, immediately afterwards (Article 4.1). It also provides for a special regime of publication in the Official Journal of the European Communities and in two national daily newspapers in the host Member State, when the reorganisation measures might affect the rights of third parties in the host Member State and it is possible to file an appeal in the Member State of origin against the decision ordering those measures (Article 6 of the Directive on credit institutions). The Directive on *insurance companies* establishes the obligation of the competent authorities of the Member State of origin to urgently inform the supervisory authorities of this same State, who will be

---

[281] VIRGOS/SCHMIT Report, Margin No. 182, *in fine*.
[282] VIRGOS/SCHMITReport, Margin No. 180; VIRGOS, p. 24; LEIBLE/STAUDINGER (2000), p. 565; DUURSMA-KEPPLINGER/DUURSMA/CHALUPSKY (2002), p. 412.

responsible for informing the supervisory authorities of the other Member States (Article 5). It also provides for a special regime of publication in the Official Journal of the European Communities, accompanied by the national publicity which the supervisory authorities of the other States decide on (Article 6).

In the case of *winding-up* proceedings, the Directive on *credit institutions* establishes the obligation to publish the decision of opening by placing an extract in the Official Journal of the European Communities and in two national daily newspapers in the host Member State (Article 13). The Directive on *insurance companies* establishes a similar obligation although it refers national publication to the supervisory authorities of the Member States (Article 14).

In *both cases*, the administrator, the liquidator or any authority of the State of origin may request the registration of a restructuring measure or the decision to commence winding-up proceedings in the Land Register, the Mercantile Registers or in any other public register kept in the other Member States. However, all Member States may stipulate registration to take place *ex oficio*. Here also, the costs and expenses are considered as costs of the proceedings (Article 29 of the Directive on credit institutions; and Article 28 of the Directive on insurance companies).

2. HONOURING AN OBLIGATION TO THE DEBTOR (ARTICLE 24)

273. One of the typical effects of the declaration of insolvency is the divestment of the debtor. Third parties who are under an obligation to the debtor are now under an obligation to the liquidator, as administrator of the estate. The risk associated with this effect is that any payment made to the debtor instead of to the liquidator is not considered as having been discharged. Insofar as the Insolvency Regulation does not impose a mandatory system of publication of the decision opening the insolvency proceedings prior to its recognition in other Member States, situations may arise in which third parties affected (e.g. the insolvent debtor's debtors) are unaware of the opening of proceedings and may act in good faith but in a way which is inappropriate given the new circumstances: they make a payment to the debtor when in fact they should have made the payment to the foreign liquidator. To consider this payment not to have been discharged would appear unjustified (see Recital 30).

Article 24 of the Regulation aims to prevent this from happening. The first paragraph establishes that *where an obligation has been honoured in a Member State for the benefit of a debtor who is subject to insolvency proceedings opened in another Member State, when it should have been honoured for the benefit of the liquidator in those proceedings, the person honouring the obligation shall be deemed to have discharged it if he was unaware of the opening of proceedings.*[283]

274. Paragraph 2 of this same provision establishes a *presumption iuris tantum* the aim of which it is to allocate the burden of proof:[284] if the obligation is honoured prior to the publication provided for in Article 21 in the relevant State (i.e. the State where the person honouring the obligation is established or the State where the

---

[283] In this provision, the place where an obligation is honoured must be understood as the place where, in fact, the obligation has been performed by its debtor, VIRGOS/SCHMIT Report, Margin No. 188.

[284] VIRGOS/SCHMIT Report, Margin No. 187; LEIBLE/STAUDINGER (2000), p. 565.

payment is made, as the case may be),[285] the person concerned is presumed to have acted without knowledge of the commencement of insolvency proceedings in another Member State. If the obligation is honoured after publication, the opposite is presumed.

275. The regime of publication of the Directives on the reorganisation and winding-up of *credit institutions* and *insurance companies* is mandatory and stricter than that of the Insolvency Regulation. That is why only the Directive on the reorganisation and winding-up of credit institutions contains an equivalent rule, which operates in the case of credit institutions which are not legal persons (Article 15).

3. Provision of Information for Creditors and Lodgement of their Claims (Articles 39–42)

276. The Regulation contains a series of uniform rules regarding the informing of creditors and the filing of their claims (Articles 39–42). These rules apply to those creditors who have their habitual residence, domicile or registered office in *Member States* other than the State of opening. Their nationality (whether or not they belong to a Member State) is irrelevant for the application of these rules. With regard to creditors established in the State of the opening of the insolvency proceedings and creditors established in *non-Member States*, the national law of the State of opening applies (see Article 4).[286]

3.1. Duty to inform

277. In order to guarantee the exercise of the rights of the creditors, the Regulation imposes a series of *duties to inform*. Specifically, Article 40 establishes that "*as soon as insolvency proceedings are opened in a Member state, the court of that State having jurisdiction or the liquidator appointed by it shall immediately inform known creditors who have their habitual residence, domicile or registered office in the other Member States.*" "Known creditors" are those creditors that appear in the debtor's books and documents, such as they are received or found by the liquidator.[287] The aim of this rule is to protect intra-Community creditors situated outside the State of opening. Notification of creditors established in the State of opening or in non-Member States is subject to national law. The duty to inform covers known creditors. The Regulation does not establish any Community obligation to inform debtors.

278. This same Article establishes the manner of notification and the minimum content which the information must respect. Specifically, Article 40.2 requires an *individual communication*, in the form of a *notice*, for each known creditor.

---

[285] Moss/Fletcher/Isaacs, p. 208.
[286] Virgos/Schmit Report, Margin No. 269.
[287] Vallens (1995), p. 236; Bureau, p. 954.

With regard to time, notice has to be given promptly to the creditors: "*as soon as insolvency proceedings are opened*", the court or the liquidator "shall *immediately* inform" known creditors established in the Member States. With regard to the manner of giving notice, Article 40 does not require that a specific method be adopted. Notice can be made available to the creditor by personal delivery or by mail, including electronic means, directed to the last known address of the creditor.

NB. Articles 40 and 42.1 of the Insolvency Regulation set up a special system of notice to creditors. Council regulation (EC) No. 1348/2000 on the service in the Member States of judicial and extrajudicial documents in civil or commercial matters, which applies where a judicial or extrajudicial document has to be transmitted from one Member State to another for service there, does not operate with regard to such notice.

279. The notice to creditors must state at least: (a) time limits; (b) the penalties laid down for failing to meet those time limits; (c) the body or authority empowered to accept the lodgement of claims and other measures laid down to that effect; (d) it must also specify whether creditors whose claims are preferential or claims secured *in rem* need lodge their claim. As this is a rule of *minimum uniform content*, national law may stipulate the inclusion of additional information for the benefit of the creditors. What it cannot do is reduce this content.[288]

Special position of certain creditors. As we have seen, Articles 5 and 7 establish a rule of non-alteration of rights *in rem* or rights based on a retention of title in respect of assets of the debtor which are located in a State other than the State of opening. This rule applies to the rights, not to the assets themselves, which form part of the estate. That is why it also makes sense to ask these creditors to lodge their claims. However, both Articles operate on an unconditional basis. Take the example of Article 5. If the creditor fails to inform the liquidator of the proceedings of his right and of the asset covered by that right, he runs the risk that errors may occur (e.g. the collateral may be realised); but national law cannot "penalise" him with the loss or alteration of his right *in rem*. This means that the requirement referred to in Article 40.1 only really concerns: (a) those creditors who reside outside of the State of opening but whose right *in rem* covers an asset located in this latter State; or (b) those creditors who reside outside the State of opening and whose right *in rem* covers an asset also located outside this latter State, but who wish to participate in the main proceedings in the expectation that the realisation of the right *in rem* will not be sufficient to satisfy their claim.

Article 6 also operates on an unconditional basis. Creditors benefiting of a set-off do not need to lodge their claims, unless the national law applicable to set-off provides otherwise.

With regard to the *language* in which the information is worded, Article 42.1 states that it must be in an official language (the one which corresponds according to its internal rules) of the State of opening of the proceedings, not in the language of the addressees; the onus is in the creditors to obtain a translation. However, in order to help make creditors aware of the nature of the notice and the possible consequences that derive therefrom, the provision requires the information notice to be

---

[288] VIRGOS/SCHMIT Report, Margin No. 272.

headed "Invitation to lodge a claim. Time limits to be observed." This heading is to appear in all the official languages of the institutions of the European Union.

3.2. Lodgement of claims

280. In principle, pursuant to Article 4, the lodgement of claims is subject to the *lex fori concursus*; this law governs the verification and admission of claims and determines the procedure by which a creditor must establish his claim in order to have it admitted to the proceedings.[289] However, the Regulation contains rules which affect both the right to file claims (and participate in the proceedings) and the way they must be filed. These are uniform rules which prevail over the said national law. The special position of Articles 5, 6 and 7 must be taken into account (see No. 278).

281. With regard to the *right to lodge* claims, pursuant to Article 39, *"Any creditor who has his habitual residence, domicile or registered office in a Member State other than the State of the opening of proceedings, including the tax authorities and social security authorities of Member States, shall have the right to lodge their claims in the insolvency proceedings in writing."* This rule has a dual content, because it not only states how claims are to be lodged, but also who has the right to do so. Article 39 makes it very clear that the claims indicated therein cannot be excluded from the proceedings on the grounds that the creditor is foreign, is established in another Member State, or is governed by (another Member State's) *public law*.[290]

Public Law claims. Although Article 39 only expressly recognises the "right to lodge" claims of these creditors, it is undeniable that they cannot be discriminated against with regard to their participation and payment; this would go directly against the *ratio* of the rule.[291] This is particularly important in the case of tax and social security claims. The right to lodge these claims and participate in insolvency proceedings opened in another Member State derives from the Insolvency Regulation itself. However, it falls to the *lex fori concursus* to determine the position of those claims in the *ranking* of claims. Here the question is whether a State can privilege the claims of its own authorities but treat the equivalent claims of the authorities of other Member States as ordinary claims. On this point, the Directives on reorganisation and winding up of credit institutions and insurance undertakings establish a principle of equal treatment for claims of Member States' public authorities: these claims shall be treated in the same way and accorded the same ranking as claims of an equivalent nature lodgeable by public authorities of the Member State of the opening (see Article 16 Directive on credit institutions, and more clearly Article 16 of the Directive on insurance undertakings). Given the step taken by these two directives, a strong argument can be made in favour of extending this solution to the Insolvency Regulation. It would seem contrary to the coherence of the Community law system to allow any other solution in the context of this Regulation: there is no obligation to give any special status to public claims, but once a national legislator decides to privilege the claim of its public authorities, the principle of equal treatment of equivalent claims applies and a similar rank should also be accorded to the claims

---

[289] Virgos/Schmit Report, Margin No. 274; Virgos, p. 25; Leible/Staudinger (2000), p. 571.

[290] Virgos/Schmit Report, Margin No. 266; Virgos, p. 25; Balz (1996a), p. 955 (in reference to some problems which may arise from this referral to public law); Leible/Staudinger, p. 571.

[291] Fletcher, p. 259.

lodged by the public authorities of other Member States. The same argument can be made in favour of admitting claims of Member States' public authorities other than tax or social security authorities.

Article 39 applies to the lodgement of claims. The evidence that may be required for the verification of claims or the procedures for contesting claims are governed by the *lex fori concursus*.

This rule is limited to creditors established in Member States and to tax authorities and social security authorities of Member States. The position of non-EC creditors (i.e. those who have their habitual residence, domicile or registered office in a non-Member State or in Denmark, and the authorities of non-Member States) is determined by national law, not by the Insolvency Regulation.

282. On the lodgement itself: With regard to the *form*, Article 39 confers on creditors who have their habitual residence, domicile or registered office in a Member State other that the State of opening the right to file their claims *in writing*. This rule does not prevent national law from permitting claims to be filed in another more favourable form.[292]

With regard to *content*, Article 41 establishes a uniform standard. The requirements of this provision are intended to facilitate the identification of the claim which a creditor wishes to file. The requirements of Article 41 *vis-à-vis* content are of a maximum character: national law cannot impose supplementary conditions. Specifically, the content of the filing of a claim will include: (i) the nature of the claim; (ii) the date on which it arose; (iii) the amount; (iv) an indication of whether the creditor alleges any preferential ranking, security right or reservation of title, as well as the assets to which such ranking, security or reservation refer; and (v) a copy of the supporting documents in the possession of the creditor.

With regard to the *language*, the creditors who have their habitual residence, domicile or registered office in a Member State other than the State of opening of the proceedings may file their claims in their own language. However, the statement must be headed "Lodgement of claim" in the official language or in one of the official languages of the State in which the proceedings are opened. Creditors may later be required to provide a translation into the official language or one of the official languages of the State of the insolvency proceedings. This possibility is contemplated as an exception, if "*deemed necessary*"; the idea of the Regulation is that the normal procedure will be to allow claims to be filed in the language of the creditor.[293]

With regard to cross-filing, see *infra* No 429 and 430.

3.3. Credit institutions and insurance undertakings

283. The *Directives* on the reorganisation and winding-up of *credit institutions* and *insurance companies* also contain a set of rules of uniform law concerning the duty to inform the creditors and the right to file claims.

---

[292] Virgos/Schmit Report, Margin No. 270.
[293] Virgos/Schmit Report, Margin No. 277.

Rationale. The basic principle is also that of non-discrimination or equal treatment: creditors whose habitual residence, domicile or registered office is situated in a Member State other than the State of origin may file their claims or submit observations concerning their claims in writing under the same conditions as local creditors (Articles 7.2 and 16 of the Directive on credit institutions and the Directive on insurance companies). Arrangements concerning the notification of known creditors (Articles 7.1, 14 and 18 of the Directive on credit institutions; Articles 7.1 and 15 of the Directive on insurance companies), the formal filing of claims (Article 16.3 of the Directive on credit institutions and of the of insurance companies); and the languages which may be used (Article 17 of the Directive on credit institutions and the Directive on insurance companies) are likewise established.

Part III

Territorial Proceedings

Chapter 8

Territorial Insolvency Proceedings: Jurisdiction and Applicable Law

1. INTRODUCTION

1.1. Functions of the territorial insolvency proceedings

284. Different cross-border models are conceivable in the context of insolvency law; these have been described in Chapter 2. The normative model which inspires the Insolvency Regulation is a model of "mitigated universality". One of the principal features of this model is that it permits, under certain conditions, the opening of *local insolvency proceedings*, the effects of which are limited territorially. According to Article 3.2 IR, *where the centre of a debtor's main interests is situated within the territory of a Member State, the courts of another Member State shall have jurisdiction to open insolvency proceedings against that debtor only if he possesses an establishment within the territory of that other Member State. The effects of those proceedings shall be restricted to the assets of the debtor situated in the territory of the latter Member State.*

285. In this chapter, we are going to analyse the regime of territorial proceedings in general. The regime of coordination between parallel insolvency proceedings will be looked at in Chapter 10. Many of the issues raised by the opening of territorial proceedings have already been analysed in the previous chapters. In order to avoid unnecessary repetitions we will, where appropriate, refer back to the corresponding point.

286. In order to adequately understand the regime of the territorial proceedings it is worth establishing, in the first place, what function these proceedings perform within the model of the Regulation.

287. The basic principle of this model is that of the universality of the proceedings: a single insolvency procedure in the State where the debtor has his centre of main interests, encompassing all of the debtor's assets, and in which all of the creditors can participate. This solution permits the maximum advantages associated with a centralised collective procedure. However, the possibility of opening territorial insolvency proceedings can still be justified for different reasons and this has lead to their admission by the Regulation. During the negotiations leading up to the Insolvency Convention, there were two types of argument put forward in favour of leaving open the possibility of opening territorial proceedings.[294]

---

[294] VIRGOS/SCHMIT Report, Margin Nos 32–33.

(a) On the one hand, the idea of protecting local creditors. This is a defensive *function*. The commencement of local proceedings implies the application of a different *lex fori concursus*, since the basic conflict rule of the Insolvency Regulation, Article 4, makes the law of the State of opening applicable. This means that the effects of the insolvency will be determined not by the law of the State where the debtor's centre of main interests is located, but by the law of the State where the establishment (and assets) are situated. In this way, the possibility of opening territorial proceedings ensures that foreign debtors who operate through a local establishment can be subject to the same insolvency rules as domestic debtors. Hence, future creditors will not have to worry, if they enter into a contract through a local establishment, about the domestic or foreign quality of the company with which they are dealing: the risk of insolvency will, in principle, be the same.[295] This defensive function is very important because the scope of application of the Regulation is very broad with regard to the type of proceedings to be encompassed. The Regulation applies to both winding-up and restructuring proceedings and is "neutral" on the question of which insolvency policies those proceedings may be aimed at. Once a national procedure is included in the lists of the Regulation, other Member States must recognise it and its effects, which may imply a very different degree of "interventionism" in the respective rights of the debtor and creditors. The possibility of opening local insolvency proceedings according to the domestic law of the State in question serves to palliate that broad scope and it was this which facilitated agreement among the Member States. Facilitating the participation of small creditors in the proceedings was also one of the arguments given by some Member States to justify the possibility of secondary proceedings. Furthermore, territorial proceedings also act as a defence against the "mobility" of the debtor, who can legitimately change his centre of main interests from time to time.

(b) On the other hand, the idea that territorial proceedings facilitate the administration of the insolvency proceedings and the realisation of the debtor's assets. This is an *auxiliary function*. The fact that the company has decided to open an establishment in another State presupposes that there are economic motives which justify a certain degree of decentralisation in its operations or business administration. These motives can be reflected in the insolvency proceedings. In general, the insolvency proceedings must retain a certain symmetry with the business activity: in the case of a centralised business activity in a single State (where the centre of main interests is located) then a sole set of proceedings is justified; on the other hand, in the case of a decentralised activity, several sets of insolvency proceedings *may* be justified. Reasons of procedural economy and access to justice may also play a role; for example, when the number of domestic creditors involved is high, local proceedings organised from the State where the establishment is located may be more convenient than centralising everything in the State where the main insolvency has been opened. Furthermore, in the case of the Regulation, territorial proceedings can be used to affect the rights *in rem* of third parties over assets which are located

---

[295] VIRGOS/SCHMIT Report, Margin No. 32.

outside the State where the main proceedings are opened and which would otherwise remain unaffected.

288. Having said this, the very possibility of commencing territorial proceedings can undermine the advantages of the universal nature of the main proceedings and, in addition, encourage opportunistic behaviour on the part of certain creditors (*supra* No. 13). This explains why the Insolvency Regulation has been very careful when it comes to determining if, and under what conditions, territorial proceedings can be opened.

1.2. Secondary and independent territorial insolvency proceedings

289. The Insolvency Regulation permits the opening of territorial insolvency proceedings either *previously* or *subsequently* to the opening of main insolvency proceedings in another Member State (see Articles 3.3 and 3.4). In both cases the debtor is required to have an establishment in the State in question. However, the way territorial proceedings are treated depends on whether they are opened before or after the main proceedings. Once main insolvency proceedings have been opened in a Member State, any territorial proceedings opened or due to open subsequently in other Member States are treated as "secondary" proceedings. Secondary proceedings are legally linked to the main proceedings. This link consists of a set of rules establishing the mandatory coordination of secondary proceedings with the main proceedings and implies a certain degree of subordination to the latter. In other words, the local insolvency proceedings are regarded as satellites of the "planet" of the main proceedings. If no main insolvency proceedings are opened (or until they are opened), the territorial proceedings are treated as "independent" proceedings; in other words, they are viewed as "small planets" in their own right. We will address the differences in treatment below.

290. As explained above, the Insolvency Regulation permits the commencement of territorial proceedings *before* any main proceedings have been opened (Article 3.4). Insofar as there are no main proceedings, the territorial proceedings are *independent*.

Nevertheless, the Regulation contemplates this possibility with a certain distrust.[296] In these circumstances there are still no main proceedings, there is no possibility of coordination within the framework of centralised EC proceedings and, as a result, the risks associated with the opening of territorial proceedings are greater.[297] This explains why the Regulation has only admitted the possibility of opening independent territorial proceedings as a mechanism for covering certain gaps in protection which may arise within a model of sole universal proceedings. In this respect, *independent* territorial proceedings fulfil, in addition to the generic defensive (albeit anticipated) function indicated above, a specific *supplementary function*: they serve to palliate the impossibility of requesting the opening of insolvency proceedings in application of the law of the State of the debtor's centre of main interests which,

---

[296] BALZ (1996), p. 949.
[297] See VIRGOS/SCHMIT Report, Margin No. 30.

however, could be opened in application of the law of the State where the establishment is located.[298] This supplementary function on the part of independent territorial proceedings explains why they can be aimed at both *winding-up* and *restructuring*.

291. A subsequent opening of main insolvency proceedings *converts* the independent proceedings into secondary proceedings, with some special rules addressing this question. In accordance to Article 36, *"Where the proceedings referred to in Article 3(1) are opened following the opening of the proceedings referred to in Article 3(2) in another Member State, Articles 31–35* (on secondary proceedings) *shall apply to those opened first, in so far as the progress of those proceedings so permits"* (parenthesis added; see also Article 37).

292. The Insolvency Regulation also permits the opening of territorial insolvency proceedings after the main insolvency proceedings have been already opened. These territorial proceedings are *secondary* proceedings. The possibility of local insolvency proceedings following the opening of the main proceedings is not regarded with the same distrust as the reverse situation of a prior opening of the local proceedings. Insofar as the Insolvency Regulation ensures that there is coordination between the local and the main proceedings, territorial proceedings can place themselves at the service of the main proceedings. For this reason, secondary insolvency proceedings can fulfil, in addition to a defensive function of the protection of local interests, important *auxiliary functions* for the main proceedings.[299] In this second sense, local proceedings can be used to facilitate the administration and realisation of the insolvent debtor's assets. As we shall see, the Regulation aims to reflect these circumstances by widening the circle of people authorised to request the opening, or by exempting them from the need to examine the insolvency of the debtor in other States once the main insolvency proceedings have been opened. However, the predominance of the defensive function in these proceedings explains, in addition to operational simplicity, why they can only be *winding-up* proceedings.

2. JURISDICTION: ARTICLES 3.2, 2.g AND 27

2.1. The concept of "establishment"

293. The *jurisdiction* to open *territorial insolvency proceedings* corresponds to the courts of the Member State where the debtor (whose centre of main interests must be located in a different Member State) has an establishment (Article 3.2). In the event that the debtor has his centre of main interests outside the Community the rules of Private International Law (in a broad sense, including international procedural law) of each State will apply.

This rule of jurisdiction is valid for any territorial proceedings, be they *independent* or *secondary* (Articles 3.2, 3.3. and 27).

---

[298] For all, MANKOWSKY, pp. 1652–1653; WIMMER (1998), p. 985; see also VIRGOS/SCHMIT Report, Margin No. 32.

[299] See VIRGOS/SCHMIT Report, Margin No. 33.

294. The *relevant moment* to establish international jurisdiction is when the application for insolvency proceedings is filed. It is at this moment that the debtor's establishment must be located in the forum. This is the only reference date that avoids incentives for forum shopping, which is one of the aims of the Insolvency Regulation itself (see Recital 4). Changes occurring afterwards have no influence on jurisdiction: the principle of *perpetuatio fori* applies, and thus (provided that proceedings are opened) a later modification (e.g. the closing of the establishment by the debtor) has no effect.

295. As in the case with the main proceedings, the Regulation only determines the *international jurisdiction* of the courts of the State where the establishment is situated. The *territorial jurisdiction* within that State will be determined by its national law. The lack of a specific rule on territorial jurisdiction cannot be invoked to deny jurisdiction to open insolvency proceedings, as this would frustrate the "*effet utile*" of the Insolvency Regulation.[300] When this circumstance arises, the most appropriate course of action is to attribute a "double function" to the rule of international jurisdiction contained in the Regulation: the location of the establishment determines both international and internal jurisdiction.

Explanation. It may occur that the law of the country where the debtor's establishment is located does not contain rules for determining territorial jurisdiction. If this is the case, what cannot be done is to invoke this gap in order not to open territorial proceedings. On the contrary, the solution can be taken from the same rule of jurisdiction contained in the Regulation and, consequently, the courts of the place where the establishment is located can be considered to have territorial jurisdiction. If the debtor has more than one establishment in the same State, the most appropriate course of action is to consider that the courts of any of them have territorial jurisdiction, with the choice of court to be made by the person initiating the proceedings.

296. The concept of *establishment* is an *autonomous* concept defined in the Insolvency Regulation itself (Article 2.h). This fact, together with the genesis of the provision, is very significant as it tells us that this definition is independent not only from definitions contained in national law, but also from any contained in other Community texts, and in particular, from the definition of the term "establishment" which the ECJ has been applying in its interpretation of Article 5.5 of the 1968 Brussels Convention, today Regulation 44/2001 on civil jurisdiction and enforcement.

Rationale. The fact that the Insolvency Regulation has its own definition of establishment entails an exception to any principle of "continuity of concepts" within EC law. The reasons for this exception are explained in the VIRGOS/SCHMIT Report.[301] During the negotiations leading up to the Insolvency Convention, various States defended the possibility of the opening of territorial proceedings being based on the mere presence of assets of the debtor, without the need for the latter to have an establishment. With the aim of achieving

---

[300] See VIRGOS/SCHMIT Report, Margin No. 222: "States shall ensure that their legislation designates the court which has jurisdiction to open secondary proceedings."
[301] Margin No. 70; see also VIRGOS, p. 15; WIMMER (1998), p. 985; LÜKE (1998), p. 299; LEIBLE/STAUDINGER (2000), pp. 546–547; HUBER, p. 142; WESSELS (2004), pp. 10–11.

a global consensus on the Convention, these States agreed to renounce the presence of assets as a basis for jurisdiction on the condition that the concept of establishment was interpreted *widely*. This explains the refusal to resort to Article 5.5 of the Brussels Convention, now Regulation 44/2001. The Court of Justice has insisted that the special jurisdictions provided for in its Article 5 should be *interpreted strictly*, as they are exceptions to the general forum of the domicile of the defendant. Resorting to this jurisprudence involved the risk of introducing a restrictive interpretation of the concept of establishment into the Insolvency Regulation, which was just the opposite of what the majority of the group wanted. This is why the decision was taken to provide a definition which was specific to the Insolvency Regulation.

NB. While there can only be one "centre of main interests", the same debtor may have several establishments located in different countries. In this case, there is no risk of jurisdictional conflicts (e.g. the courts of two States claiming that the centre of main interests is located in their respective jurisdiction), as each establishment only gives rise to proceedings with a territorial scope. What this situation may do is present problems of coordination between paralell proceedings (see Chapter 10).

297. The concept of "establishment" as used by the Insolvency Regulation is *neutral* with regard to the nature of the debtor (an individual or a legal person) or the capacity (merchant, professional, etc.) in which he may act. The function of this criterion is solely to confer jurisdiction upon the courts of the State in question, and therefore, in principle, any natural or legal person, whether or not a trader, can have an establishment for the purposes of the Regulation.[302] This prevails over national rules which may reserve the use of the concept of establishment to specific persons (legal persons, traders, etc.).

298. According to the Regulation, an establishment is *"any place of operations where the debtor carries out a non-transitory economic activity with human means and goods"* (Article 2.h).[303] The definition provided by the Regulation is, thus, a relatively open definition, based on the combination of *two elements*: (a) a *place of business* or *operations*, (b) with a certain degree of *organization and permanence* in time.

299. The following directives of interpretation can serve to determine an establishment for the purposes of claiming jurisdiction to open territorial proceedings:

300. *First directive*: from an *external* point of view, an establishment must involve a *distinct presence* on the part of the debtor in the market of the State in question. Or, in other words, for a debtor of any one State (F1), what represents an establishment in another different State (F2) is that the debtor is operating in the market *not from his own State (F1), but from the territory of that second State (F2)*.

The Insolvency Regulation expresses this idea through the two basic elements upon which it builds the definition of establishment. As we saw previously, an establishment for the purposes of the Regulation is a place of operations with human means and goods, where the debtor carries out a non-transitory economic activity. *Place of operations* means a place from which the debtor conducts commercial,

---

[302] Implicitly, Virgos/Schmit Report, Margin No. 71.
[303] This definition has been incorporated into the UNCITRAL Model Law, Article 2.f.

industrial or professional activities in the market (i.e. externally).[304] The reference to *human means and goods* expresses the requirement of some form of organisational presence in the forum (a branch, an office, a factory, a workshop, etc.). From the time element of the definition, a *"non-transitory* economic activity*"*, it follows that a certain degree of stability and iteration with the forum is needed.[305]

> *Time requirements.* A place of business clearly set up for a short temporary purpose does not qualify as an establishment. On the other hand, the Regulation does not require a *permanent* establishment, i.e. an establishment open on an indefinite time basis. Thus, if the debtor opens a place of operations of a stable nature, it can qualify as an establishment although it has a limited time horizon (e.g. the time of a building project). However, in this case, the usefulness of the establishment as a connection is limited. Potential creditors contracting through the local establishment should assess the insolvency risks they are assuming by reference to the local law only in relation to short-term transactions; once the establishment is closed, if insolvency proceedings have not been opened (see No. 294), the basis for jurisdiction disappears. The Insolvency Regulation requires the connection employed in Article 3 as basis for jurisdiction to be genuine. The definition it gives of establishment is fact-oriented and the test to determine when there is an establishment, a "reality test". Fictions that may exists in national laws are not applicable (e.g. the rule that a person is treated as continuing the business in the forum until he settles his business debts).[306]

The formulation of these elements is not rigid. The definition of establishment does not require it to carry out the same activity as the main centre, nor to have a specified degree of involvement in its operations with third parties (e.g. to have the authority to conclude contracts or be responsible for supervising or ensuring compliance). Neither does it require the human means or the goods to be the direct property of the debtor. All of these elements have to be specified in the light of the general idea: the requierement that the place of operations represents a certain degree of *external business activity* on the part of the debtor, in or from that State.

> *Negative definition.* The formula used by the Regulation is relatively open and it leaves an important role for the judiciary in the way it is interpreted. This means that the rule can be adapted and evolve so as to keep up with changes in the way businesses are organised. Nevertheless, the formula which is used permits certain situations to be excluded. Thus, for example, the following cannot be considered as establishments for the purposes of the Regulation: (a) the mere presence of assets of the debtor, even when they are immovable; (b) the presence of permanent elements which lack a certain degree of organisation (e.g. a postal address or an Internet web site); (c) the presence of permanent elements linked to the business activity but which do not have an external presence in the market of the State in question (e.g. a storage facility or a computer server used for storing databases or web sites); (d) the sporadic presence of the debtor or his representatives, even when in possession of assets and human resources (e.g. when attending an international trade fair).

301. *Second directive*: from the *internal* point of view, the establishment must *form part of or be an extension of the operational structure* of the debtor. The

---

[304] VIRGOS/SCHMIT Report, Margin No. 71.

[305] The expression "non-transitory" seeks to avoid minimum time requirements, VIRGOS/SCHMIT Report, Margin No. 71.

[306] WESSELS (2004), pp. 12–13; but see FLETCHER (2003), pp. 179–180.

Regulation expresses this directive by saying that the debtor must "*possess*" an establishment. The term "possession" is not used in a technical or legal sense. It is immaterial whether the facilities are owned, or rented by, or are otherwise at the disposal of the debtor. What matters is that, in one way or another, the establishment must be subject to a certain degree of *control and direction* on the part of the debtor. The Regulation does not lay down the legal configuration of this requirement, and this could give rise to some difficulties of interpretation. The simplest case is when the establishment does not have its own legal personality: legally, it is a part of the debtor and, as a result, there is no doubt that it is under the control of the latter.

302. *Third directive*: As was the case with the concept of centre of main interests, *the external sphere prevails over the internal one*. The decisive factor for these elements is how they are manifested externally and not the subjective intention of the debtor.[307] This means that if the debtor appears by acting through an establishment and thus creates the impression in the market that the said establishment is an extension of or forms part of his organisational structure, it can be considered as an establishment for the purposes of the Regulation.

Subsidiaries. The Insolvency Regulation treats each legal entity as a different debtor. Therefore, a subsidiary company or an independent agent acting in the ordinary course of their business cannot constitute an establishment of the parent company of the principal. The typical premise for the application of Articles 2.h and 3.2 of the Regulation is the case of an establishment of the debtor with no legal personality. However, under special circumstances, a subsidiary (and the same can apply to an independent agent) may be deemed to constitute an establishment of the parent company.[308] This can be the case, for instance, if the subsidiary behaves in the market as a branch, performing activities that belong, in economic terms, to the sphere of the parent rather than to their own business operations. In such a case, the subsidiary appears in the market as an operational extension of the parent company. The fundamental reason for extending application is that the debtor is better placed to prevent the risk of confusion than are third parties. Third parties base their decisions on the information which they receive, not on what is really happening in a given company's "black box". In fact, the way in which the debtor organises his company is, in principle, something which it is difficult for third parties to obtain a clear idea about. That is why the most reasonable course of action is to impute the risk to the person who can control it at the lowest cost. If it is the debtor who is in a position to create confusion in the market (e.g. by using the same name and acting in fact as an agent of the parent company), it must fall to him to prevent it. In this case, the "establishment" would be taken as a basis for opening proceedings against the *parent* company and it would only extend to the assets of the *parent* company located in the State of opening (e.g. the shares of the subsidiary used as if it was an establishment).

2.2. Scope of the international jurisdiction

303. The jurisdiction of these courts is *territorial*: it only covers the assets of the debtor which are located in the territory of the State of opening (Article 3.2 *in fine*).

---

[307] VIRGOS/SCHMIT Report, Margin No. 71.
[308] *Cfr.* VALLENS, p. 308; HUBER, p. 143; on this matter, See also EHRICKE (2002), pp. 106–107.

Whether or not the assets are linked to the economic activities of the establishment is irrelevant.[309] This rule limiting jurisdiction applies to any territorial proceedings, whether *independent* or *secondary* (Article 3.2 *in fine*), and is reflected in the effects of the proceedings, which are also limited to the assets of the debtor which are located in the territory of the Member State in question (Article 27 *in fine*).

304. A special application of this rule is found in two provisions of the Regulation. The first is Article 17.2, regarding both *independent and secondary* insolvency proceedings, according to which any *restriction of the rights* of the creditors, in particular a stay or discharge, does not produce effects *vis-à-vis* assets situated in other Member States, unless the creditor gives his consent thereto. The second is Article 34.2, which operates in the case of a rescue plan, a composition or a comparable measure approved in *secondary* proceedings, and requires the consent of all the creditors having an interest, if the plan or composition is to affect assets outside the State of opening (see *infra* Nos 332 *et seq.* for further explanation).

305. The jurisdiction to adopt preservation measures in the case of territorial proceedings belongs solely to the courts of the State of opening. The reason being that territorial proceedings can only affect assets located in that State, so that the State of opening is the same as the State where the preservation measure is to be implemented (see No. 103).

2.3. Uniform rules of location

2.3.1. Meaning

306. Territorial proceedings only affect assets located in the territory of the State of opening. In order to resolve the uncertainties presented by the territorial location of certain assets, the Regulation establishes a series of *uniform rules of location* (Article 2.g).

307. The *relevant point of time* for determining the location of the assets is the time the proceedings are opened.[310] The liquidator of the territorial proceedings has the right to act outside his territory in order to recover an asset which has been removed from the said State after the opening of the proceedings or with the intention of defrauding the creditors of those proceedings (Article 18.2, *infra* No. 363).

308. With regard to the *uniform rules of location* contained in the Regulation, there are three general facts which are worth mentioning.

(a) First, these rules constitute a mechanism for preventing conflicts. It must not be forgotten that the situation faced by the Insolvency Regulation was one of normative diversity. Every national law had, and still has, its own rules regarding the

---

[309] Critical, in the face of the possibility that a secondary winding-up proceedings affects assets which are directly linked to the activities of the main centre and are necessary for the restructuring of the company, LÜKE (1998), p. 300; LEIBLE/STAUDINGER (2000), p. 546, note 95. The scope of this objection is relative given that these results can be partly avoided by using the mechanisms for coordination; *supra* Part IV.

[310] VIRGOS/SCHMIT Report, Margin No. 224.

location of specific assets. These rules operate as "legal fictions" in some cases, to move away from the physical location of the asset when this does not represent a reasonable solution (this occurs, e.g. in the case of assets which are *in transitu* or in the case of means of transport), and in other cases, to locate assets which do not physically exist (this is the case, e.g., with claims). These fictions vary from one legal system to the other. Consequently, if the national solutions had been retained, there would have been a risk of *positive conflicts*, i.e. that a same asset was considered to be located in two States at the same time; and, also, of *negative conflicts*, i.e. that an asset was not considered to be located in any State. This would make it more difficult to delimit the scope of territorial insolvency proceedings, both with regard to other territorial proceedings and to the main proceedings. In order to prevent these conflicts, the Regulation has established a series of uniform solutions which are common for all the Member States. As with any other uniform solution, interpretation thereof by the courts is also subject to the canon of uniformity.

(b) In the second place, the rules on location provided by the Regulation respond to a *"logic of enforcement"*. The determining factor for deciding the location of an asset is the idea of control or immediate power: whether or not it is possible to impose direct enforcement measures over the asset or, in the case of claims, over the person who is under the obligation to pay or perform. This solution is understandable if we accept the idea that the ultimate consequence which insolvency proceedings can produce is the winding-up of the debtor's assets. In this sense, insolvency proceedings are nothing but enforcement proceedings of a collective nature. The 1995 Convention on Insolvency Proceedings, from which the Insolvency Regulation stems, was drawn up in the shadow of this hypothesis: the idea of insolvency proceedings as winding-up proceedings. Only at a later stage of the negotiation was the Convention extended to encompass proceedings aimed at restructuring the debtor. However, the rules regarding location remained the same. The Insolvency Regulation inherited this approach. This is why the idea of "immediate power" or "direct domain" over the assets or rights is more important for the purposes of location than any idea based on the doctrines of "centre of gravity" or "closer and most real connection".

This approach has an additional virtue: it offers clear and simple solutions. As the rules on location of the assets are drawn up according to the *"logic of enforcement,"* legal fictions can be reduced to a minimum and, consequently, simple and easy to apply rules can be offered. This is particularly important in the sphere of insolvency, as both the liquidator and the creditors have a great deal of interest in determining as directly as possible which assets are covered by the proceedings.

(c) In the third place, the universal scope of the main proceedings implies that, but for their localization in a secondary forum, debtor's assets will fall under the realm of the main proceedings. Unclear cases might be resolved according to this directive.

2.3.2. *The rules*

309. The Regulation establishes three rules of location regarding tangible assets, rights subject to registration, and claims in Article 2.g: *"The Member State in which*

assets are situated 'shall mean, in the case of:

> – *tangible property, the Member State within the territory of which the property is situated,*
> – *property and rights ownership of or entitlement to which must be entered in a public register, the Member State under the authority of which the register is kept,*
> – *claims, the Member State within the territory of which the third party required to meet them has the centre of his main interests, as determined in Article 3(1)".*

310. According to this rule, *tangible assets* are located in the place where they are physically situated (i.e. the *situs naturalis*). This physical location prevails over any legal fiction and, in principle, is applicable to any asset except for *goods in transit*. While the goods are in the course of transport, their varying physical location reveals no meaningful link to the State through which they are passing and should not be used as a connecting point. The Regulation does not alter this idea. The problem is that it lacks any specific rule. As we have already explained, this gap has to be filled by referring to the rules regarding the location of goods in transit of the State of opening. Consequently: (a) if only independent territorial proceedings are opened, then this State's rules regarding location will tell us if the goods are considered to be situated in this State or not; (b) if main proceedings are opened while the goods are in transit, then the rules regarding location of this State, which is the only State with universal jurisdiction, prevail in order to decide where those goods are deemed to be situated for the purposes of the Regulation.

In the case of *means of transport*, the possible effect of special international conventions needs to be taken into account (e.g., Article 18.3 of the Convention on international railway transport, of 9 May 1980; see also next paragraph).

311. *Property and rights the ownership or entitlement to which must be entered in a public register* are located in the Member State under the authority of which the register is kept. This section includes rights over *ships* or *aircraft*,[311] *intellectual property rights* (e.g. patents, trademarks) and rights over *securities* represented through *book-entry* systems. As an exception to this rule, in the case of Community patents, trademarks and other similar rights established by *Community law*, Article 12 subjects these rights to the exclusive jurisdiction of the courts of the debtor's centre of main interests *ex* Article 3.1.

Registers. Two points have to be made here:[312] (a) The State *under the authority of* which the register is kept is not necessarily the State where the register is physically located; it can be a consular register, for example. In the case of *international registers*, the location of the assets must be considered in the light of the nature and function of the register in question. In each case, the international convention governing the system must be consulted. Thus, e.g., in the field of intellectual property, there are international registers which provide for the filing of a single international application with effect in several States, instead of filing several separate national and/or regional applications. This ensures that one international registration will have effect in any of the participating States as if the trademark or

---

[311] In this case, the legal location prevails over the physical location (as also occurs in Article 14, *supra*).
[312] Virgos/Schmit Report, Margin No. 68.

right had been filed therein directly: see, for instance, the 1977 Budapest Treaty on the International Recognition of the Deposit of Microorganisms for the Purposes of Patent Procedure; the Hague Agreement Concerning the International Deposit of Industrial Designs; the 1958 Lisbon Agreement for the Protection of Appellations of Origin and their International Registration; the 1891 Madrid Agreement concerning the international regis-tration of marks; and the Washington 1970 Patent Cooperation Treaty. The asset must therefore be considered as located in the State (or States) in which protection has been required by means of the international register. (b) The concept of *public register* makes no reference to the public or private ownership thereof, but to its function: that of providing legal certainty by giving information regarding ownership of or other rights over certain assets; information on which third parties can rely. This includes private registers with these characteristics, recognised by the national legal system in question. Whether third parties are authorised to consult the register directly (e.g. anyone can inspect its content) or knowl-edge of the content of the register is only made effective through certificates issued by the register (at the owner's request, as may be the case in the case of securities, for example) is irrelevant for these purposes.

Negotiable securities held through "indirect holding" systems. The location of *"directly held"* securities (i.e. securities which, evidenced by book entries, are included in a register maintained by the issuer or a person mandated by the issuer) poses no particular problems: in principle, they are located in the State where the securities records of the issuer or its offi-cial record holder (or depository) are situated. However, when securities are held through one or more intermediaries (i.e *"indirectly held"* securities), their location is not established by referring to the issuer or the initial depository, but to the financial intermediary maintaining the account to which the securities are credited. This might deserve some clarifi-cation. On the matter of international dispositions of securities title to which is evidenced by entries in a register or account, very specific holding and transfer structures have been developed in practice: the so-called indirect holding systems. These systems are characterized by the fact that the securities are held through multiple tiers of intermediaries. The investor no longer has a direct relationship with the issuer; rather, the investor's interest in respect of the under-lying securities is recorded on the books of an intermediary (a broker, nominee company, bank, custodian or depository) which, in turn, has its interests recorded with another inter-mediary and so on up the chain until some intermediary either (*i*) is recorded as the registred owner on the books of the issuer or the issuer's official recordholder or (*ii*) holds the certifi-cates or other documents of title representing the securities.[313] These systems have sim-plified the flow of securities across borders and facilitate their use as collateral (e.g. diversified portfolios of securities can be easily provided as collateral), and this explains their great relevance in practice. Under these schemes, in a typical transaction there are a number of intermediaries between the issuer and the investor. Negotiable securities circu-late by means of records in the registers or book accounts of each of those financial inter-mediaries, but without any communication between them. Each intermediary, from the issuer to the final investor, only has contact with the links in the chain on either side of him. Thus, when the initial issue is carried out, the negotiable securities are immobilised or recorded in the registers of the issuer or of a central depository (which is normally national but can be international, e.g. CLEARSTREAM); this register records the holder of the nego-tiable securities (Bank X, for example); in turn these negotiable securities may be recorded in the registers or book accounts of the latter under the name of another entity (investment company Y, for example); and recorded, in the registers or book accounts of this latter, under the name of a fourth party, and so on until the last investor. Each link in the chain is only connected to the immediate previous link, but not to the one which preceded it. The record which shows that the final investor in Spain, for example, is the holder of negotiable

---

[313] BERNASCONI Report, p. 2, in www.hcch.net

securities initially recorded in Japan, only resides in the registry or book account of his Spanish bank or investment company; but neither the Japanese issuer, nor the Japanese central deposit, nor the collaborating institutions (i.e. those which have an account at this central deposit), nor the rest of the financial intermediaries (e.g. CLEARSTREAM) up to the Spanish bank or investment company, know about or have any record of the existence of the Spanish investor. In reality, this means that what we are dealing with are derived assets ("rights in respect of negotiable securities"), and it is these rights – and not the underlying negotiable securities – which are the relevant *res* for the purposes of seeking the *situs*. For this reason, it is the location of the intermediary maintaining the register or account in which the entries are made that matters: the "Place of the Relevant InterMediary Approach (or "*PRIMA rule*").

PRIMA has been already adopted in the Community context, in particular in Article 9.2 of the 1998/26/EC Directive on settlement finality in payment and securities settlement systems, Article 24 of the 2001/24/EC Directive on the reorganisation and winding up of credit institutions, and Article 9 of the 2002/47/EC Directive on financial collateral arrangements.[314] The rules contained in these Directives are in line with the general pattern of location of assets adopted by the Insolvency Regulation, and they serve to complement it. According to the Directives, collateral consisting of book-entry securities will be deemed to be located in the State where the "relevant account" (i.e. the register or account in which the entries are made by which that book entry securities collateral is provided to the collateral taker) is maintained. When indirectly held securities are taken as collateral, the investor and the secured creditor must, therefore, rely exclusively on bookkeeping records to identify their interests in such securities.

The 2002 Hague Convention on the Law Applicable to Certain Rights in respect of Securities Held with an Intermediary also adopts a version of the PRIMA rule. When the intermediary has offices in several States, the determination of the relevant office may give raise to difficulties. For this reason, the Convention makes it possible for the parties to the account agreement (i.e. the account holder and its intermediary) to choose the law applicable to the account, subject to a "reality test". This test provides that the chosen law has a connection with the relevant intermediary: the intermediary must have an office in the State whose law has been chosen, and that office must engage in a regular activity of maintaining security accounts. In the absence of agreement, the Convention points out to the State in which the particular office of the intermediary through which the account agreement was entered is located; and, if this cannot be determined, to the State under which the relevant intermediary is incorporated (see Articles 4 and 5).[315] For the purposes of the Insolvency Regulation, the account will be considered located in the State whose law is applicable in accordance with the above mentioned rule.

312. Third: *claims and receivables* are understood to be located in the territory where the centre of main interests of the debtor of the claim (*debitor debitoris* or account debtor) is situated. When it comes to locating rights to tangible assets (rights *in rem*), the task is facilitated by the laws of physics: the right is located where the asset in question is itself located (*situs naturalis*). In contrast, the location of a claim which does not physically exist *per se* and is not linked to a tangible asset is pure legal fiction. This explains why we can find very different solutions to this question in national laws.[316] The Insolvency Regulation establishes a uniform solution, which

---

[314] For a more detailed treatment, POTOCK (ed.) *passim*; for Spain, PAZ-ARES/GARCIMARTIN, *passim*.
[315] See the convention at www.hcch.net
[316] A recent summary can be seen in GEIMER, Margin Nos. 3211–3212.

prevents possible conflicts. The specific solution contained in the Regulation is well explained in that "logic of enforcement" which motivates Article 2.g: in principle, the courts of the State where the debtor of the bankrupt (*debitor debitoris* or account debtor) has his centre of main interests are those which are best suited to impose payment of the claim.[317] With regard to the concept of "centre of main interests" what was stated *supra* Nos 44 *et seq.* applies also here.

> *Bank accounts and "separate entity doctrine."* In the case of *current accounts* and *deposits* in banking institutions, for these purposes each branch must be considered as an *autonomous entity* (i.e. as if it were a distinct debtor), in accordance with the special structure of these institutions; consequently, the claim will be considered situated in the State where the office serving the customer's account is located.

313. The Insolvency Regulation does not contain specific rules for other "assets" such as *negotiable instruments* or *company shares*. This silence should not be understood as a referral to national laws. The location of these assets requires a uniform solution on the basis of the same "logic of enforcement" which inspires the rules of location of the Regulation. This means that, *prima facie, negotiable instruments* must be located, as documents, by their physical location (*situs cartae sitae*).

> *Rationale.* Negotiable instruments are documents which incorporate or represent a right. Whether or not this incorporation occurs is determined by the law governing the right. If the answer is affirmative, the right will circulate with the document. In this way, the rules on the transfer of tangible assets will be applied to the transfer of rights (and, therefore, benefit from the facilities for locating rights over tangible assets). For the purposes which now interest us, the consequence is that the territorial insolvency proceedings will "capture" all of the documents located inside the territory of the State of opening; the location of the debtor's centre of main interests is irrelevant.

Company shares must be considered, for the purposes of the Insolvency Regulation, as located wherever the company (i.e. the debtor) has its centre of main interests (in principle, the place of the registered office), just as with any other claim. In the case of shares incorporated in a document of title, the same rule applies as to other negotiable instruments; and in the case of shares represented through book entries, what matters is the location of the register or relevant account (see *supra* No. 311).

3. LAW APPLICABLE

3.1. Introduction: lex concursus and exceptions (Article 28)

314. According to Article 28, "*Save as otherwise provided in this Regulation, the law applicable to secondary proceedings shall be that of the Member State within the territory of which the secondary proceedings are opened*". This means that the

---

[317] The same solution had been adopted by the courts of several European States; it has also been included in Article 167 III of the Swiss Law on Private International Law.

law of the State opening the territorial proceedings will govern these proceedings and their effects, but also that the exceptions established in Articles 5 to 15 will be applicable. Consequently, the same conflict rules apply to both the main proceedings and the territorial proceedings. This solution is already given by the interplay of Articles 3 and 4 and is applicable in all cases of territorial insolvency proceedings opened in accordance with the Insolvency Regulation, i.e. in the cases of both Article 3.3 (secondary territorial proceedings) and Article 3.4 (independent territorial proceedings). Article 28 simply reiterates this solution for the sake of clarity.

The analysis of the conflict of laws rules which we carried out when studying the main proceedings is, *mutatis mutandis*, valid here. In the following sections we will address the special features of territorial proceedings as compared to the main proceedings.

3.2. Requirements for the opening of territorial proceedings

3.2.1. Requirements derived from national law

315. Pursuant to Article 4 in relation with Article 3.2, it falls to the law of the State where the debtor has an establishment to determine the conditions that must be satisfied for the opening of insolvency proceedings. This law decides the insolvency test to be applied. It will tell us, for example, if an external fact evidencing the insolvency ("act of bankruptcy test") is sufficient; if a failure to meet current payments has to be demonstrated ("cash-flow test"); or if proof is required that the debtor's assets are not adequate to meet its debts ("balance-sheet test").

Global perspective vs. national perspective: This same law will determine, in principle, if the point of reference for applying these criteria must be the situation of the establishment (national perspective) or the situation of the debtor as a whole (global perspective).[318] Without prejudice to what national laws may establish, the solution is to be deduced from the nature of the condition itself: (a) In the case of over-indebtedness, the inadequacy of the debtor's assets to cover its liabilities must be established by reference to all of the debtor's assets, not only to those located in the forum. (b) In the case of illiquidity, the point of reference should also be the global situation of the debtor. It makes little economic sense to consider a debtor illiquid (i.e. unable to meet his obligations at maturity) when he is duly paying in the State where his centre is located. However, illiquidity may be *presumed* if the debtor stops his payments in the State where the establishment is located. The main argument in favour of this latter solution is based on the excessive costs which would be borne by local creditors if they had to prove the behaviour of the debtor abroad (e.g. that he has failed to meet current payments in other countries). In this way, it may be sufficient for them to prove the behaviour of the establishment.[319] (c) In the case of "external acts of bankruptcy" (i.e. specific observable events which allow a creditor to apply for insolvency proceedings), the point of reference may well be the State where the establishment is situated.

---

[318] On this problem, see MANKOWSKY, pp. 1650 *et seq.*; WIMMER (1998), pp. 986–987; DUURSMA-KEPPLINGER/DUURSMA/CHALUPSKY, (2002), pp. 166–169.

[319] MANKOWSKY, *passim.*

3.2.2. *Requirements established by the Regulation*

316. The Regulation also establishes certain *uniform requirements* that must be satisfied before territorial proceedings can be opened. These requirements vary according to whether the territorial proceedings are independent or secondary. The differences between them obey the function which each of the proceedings fulfils within the normative model of the Regulation.

3.2.2.1. *Independent territorial proceedings (Article 3.4)*

317. The Insolvency Regulation allows territorial insolvency proceedings to be opened as independent proceedings, prior to the commencement of main proceedings. These insolvency proceedings are governed by the applicable national law (*lex fori concursus*). However, the Regulation establishes some uniform requirements. In effect, according to Article 3.4, *independent territorial proceedings* can only be opened under *either* of the two following conditions: (a) that main insolvency proceedings cannot be opened in accordance with the conditions laid down by the law of the Member State in whose territory the debtor's centre of main interests is located; (b) that the opening of territorial proceedings is requested by a creditor whose domicile, habitual residence or registered office is in the Member State in which the debtor's establishment is located, or whose claim arises from the operations of that establishment. These conditions are additional to the ones required by the law of the State where the establishment is located.

Rationale. One of the fundamental reasons for permitting the opening of territorial proceedings separate from the main insolvency proceedings is to protect local creditors (see Recital 11). The existence of an establishment expresses a difference in the nature of the presence of a foreign debtor in the market. In principle, it is not the same when the debtor from one State operates in a market of another State (F2) *from his own country* (F1), as when he operates *from the territory of that other State* (F2). In this second case, the environment in which the transaction is carried out may justify the protection of those creditors who were connected with the debtor through that establishment (local creditors), above all when they enjoy certain privileges or preferences which they will not enjoy according to the law of the State where the debtor has his centre of main interests. The Member States which participated in the drawing up of the 1995 Convention on insolvency proceedings agreed with this principle, but were divided as to how to express it in a concrete rule. Some States thought that the requirement that the debtor had an establishment (together with the territorial nature of the proceedings) was sufficient; beyond that, the normal play of the national rules concerning the opening of proceedings should be followed. Other States believed the normal play of the national rules concerning the opening of proceedings should be followed with certain additional conditions for opening (e.g. that it was requested by "local" creditors).[320] Article 3.4 of the Convention (which was adopted unchanged by the Insolvency Regulation) is the result of a compromise between the different approaches.[321] The final result does not allow for an unconditional referral to national law, but neither does it impose the restriction that the person requesting the opening of proceedings be a local

---

[320] See VIRGOS/SCHMIT Report, Margin No. 84.
[321] *Ibid.*

creditor, in the sense that the creditor's residence, domicile or office has to be situated in the same State as the debtor's establishment.

318. The *first* circumstance which permits territorial proceedings to be opened is the *impossibility* of opening main insolvency proceedings *"because of the conditions laid down by the law of the Member State within the territory of which the centre of the debtor's main interests is situated"* (Article 3.4.a). Here, the territorial proceedings perform a supplementary function.[322] Interested parties can participate in territorial proceedings when they demonstrate that, given the conditions for opening established by the law of the State where the debtor has his centre of main interests, they cannot obtain the opening of main insolvency proceedings. In this case, territorial insolvency proceedings may be opened at the request of any creditor, whether or not a local creditor, or even of the debtor himself; the latter possibility is implied in the Insolvency Regulation, because it expressly permits the opening of restructuring proceedings as independent proceedings.

Rationale. The typical situation contemplated by this precept is where the debtor cannot be subject to insolvency proceedings in the State where he has his centre of main interests because the law of that State requires, e.g. that the debtor be a merchant or trader and the debtor does not satisfy that condition, or because the debtor is a public company which the said law is not authorised to declare bankrupt. The function of Article 3.4(a) is to prevent the first circumstance from impeding the opening of insolvency proceedings in the State where the debtor has the establishment, which can be in the interests of the body of creditors, but also of the debtor himself for the purposes of preventing individual enforcements.[323]

319. The *second* possibility which permits the opening of independent territorial insolvency proceedings is that this be requested by a *"local creditor"*. Article 3.4(b) is founded upon a wide conception of who constitutes a local creditor. Any creditor is considered as local when: (*i*) he has *"his domicile, habitual residence or registered office in the Member State within the territory of which the establishment is situated"*; or (*ii*) his claim *"arises from the operation of that establishment"*. The reason for permitting these creditors to initiate territorial proceedings directly is that the opposite rule would simply entail a greater access cost for these creditors, but would not impede the opening of territorial proceedings: it would simply oblige them to first request the opening of main proceedings abroad and then secondary proceedings in the State of the establishment (i.e. to make two applications instead of one).

Explanation. It is worth clarifying certain points of this rule: (a) With regard to the first group of creditors, the rule functions as a presumption *iuris et de iure* of the local character of these creditors. The most common situation is that these creditors (with residence, domicile or registered office in the State where the debtor has the establishment) are connected with the debtor through that establishment. There will be very few situations where this is not the

---

[322] VIRGOS, p. 12; LÜKE (1998), p. 298.
[323] MANKOWSKY, p. 1658.

case and, therefore, the rule has not imposed any other requirement. (b) With regard to the second group of creditors (i.e. those "whose claim arises from the operations of that establishment"), the concept "operation" has to be interpreted in a broad sense.[324] Therefore, the notion encompasses claims arising from the management of the establishment (e.g. the renting of the buildings or the hiring of personnel) and those arising from the activities which that establishment carries out in the market (e.g. contracts with third parties), including claims which have a non-contractual basis. In these examples, the relevant issue is that the claim has arisen on the basis of the activities of the establishment, but it is not a requirement that the place of payment be located in the same State in which the establishment is located or, in the case of a claim in tort, that the damages have been produced in the territory of that State.

3.2.2.2. *Secondary territorial proceedings (Articles 27, 29 and 30)*

320. As in the previous case, secondary insolvency proceedings are also governed by the national law of the State of opening (*lex fori concursus*). The Insolvency Regulation, however, modifies in *two aspects* the conditions of opening laid down by the applicable national law. *In the first place*, the requirement for the insolvency of the debtor established by national law does not need to be satisfied; the recognition of the decision opening the main proceedings makes any further examination of the debtor's insolvency in other Member States unnecessary. Article 27: *"The opening of the proceedings referred to in Article 3(1) by a court of a Member State and which is recognised in another Member State (main proceedings) shall permit the opening in that other Member State, a court of which has jurisdiction pursuant to Article 3(2), of secondary insolvency proceedings without the debtor 's insolvency being examined in that other State"*.

In *the second place*, the Insolvency Regulation confers the right to request the opening of secondary proceedings directly upon the liquidator of the main proceedings. Article 29.a: *"The opening of secondary proceedings may be requested by: (a) the liquidator in the main proceedings"*. National law continues to apply to all other questions (see Articles 28 and 29.b); national law decides, for example, whether or not it is possible to open insolvency proceedings on the basis of the personal status of the debtor or which other persons may request the opening.[325] The restrictions established in Article 3.4 do not apply in this case.

Rationale. The Insolvency Regulation distinguishes clearly between *independent* and *secondary* territorial proceedings. While it tends to be restrictive with the former, it is more permissive toward the latter; and, thus, it widens the circle of persons authorised to request the opening or removes the need to prove that the debtor is insolvent. The difference in treatment has already been explained in more detail (*supra* No. 290). In the first case, the main proceedings have not yet been opened and, consequently, the risks associated with the opening of territorial proceedings (estate partitioning, opportunistic behaviour on the part of the creditors, etc.) become much more evident. In the second case, the main proceedings have already been opened and the Regulation establishes rules of coordination between the two sets of proceedings; this allows the benefits associated with the territorial proceedings to be optimised without detriment to the efficacy of the universal model (see Recital 19).

---

[324] See VIRGOS/SCHMIT Report, Margin No. 85.
[325] VIRGOS/SCHMIT Report, Margin No. 211.

321. The *first* of the modifications referred to is embodied in a rule aimed at facilitating the commencement of territorial proceedings when the *main proceedings* have already been *opened*: the examination of the debtor's insolvency is automatically dispensed with in other Member States (Article 27). This precept is a uniform rule by which the Regulation confers a *special effect* upon the decision to open main proceedings in a Member State: such a decision permits the opening of territorial proceedings, *without the courts of the second State being required to examine the insolvency of the debtor*. The debtor's insolvency must be taken for granted. The courts of the second State must, however, ensure that the decision to open main proceedings is covered by Article 16. In particular: (a) that the decision opens insolvency proceedings which are listed in Annex A; (b) that it has been handed down by a court which has declared that it bases its jurisdiction on Article 3.1; and (c) that it is effective in its State of origin (i.e. it produces effects in the sense of Article 2.f).

Explanation. Article 27 does not establish a presumption, but rather a rule of substitution of any condition required for insolvency proceedings to be opened against the debtor, which is replaced by the condition that main proceedings are already pending in another Member State and are recognised.[326] This rule applies regardless of the reason why the main proceedings were opened, even when that reason does not exist in the law of the State where the territorial proceedings are going to be opened.

322. The *second* modification directly empowers the *liquidator of the main proceedings* to request the opening of secondary proceedings (Article 29.a, which is not applicable to the *temporary* liquidator). This rule also expresses the relationship of dependence of the secondary proceedings with regard to the main proceedings: the liquidator of the main proceedings can make the most of the possible advantages which the opening of territorial proceedings may present. For example, and as already explained, a secondary proceedings may make sense in cases where the estate of the debtor is too complex and the number of creditors too large to be administered as a unit, and/or when the differences between national laws are so acute that difficulties may arise as a result of extending the effects of the *lex concursus principalis* to other States.[327] The liquidator of the main proceedings may also use secondary proceedings to palliate the effects of Articles 5 and 7 IR concerning rights *in rem* and reservation of title.[328]

The role of national law. (a) Article 29.b confirms that national law continues to apply to determine those persons who, in addition to the liquidator of the main proceedings, may request the opening of secondary proceedings. The Insolvency Regulation does not restrict the right to initiate insolvency proceedings either to local creditors or to those who can prove a specific interest. During the negotiations leading up to the 1995 Convention the decision was taken to suppress the provision contained in the initial versions by which only those creditors who might benefit from a more favourable legal regime in the secondary proceedings than in the main proceedings (e.g. creditors who were only privileged according to the

---

[326] See MANKOWSKY, p. 1652; WIMMER (1998), p. 986.
[327] See VIRGOS/SCHMIT Report, Margin No. 33.
[328] See WIMMER (1998), p. 987.

local law) could request the opening of the former.[329] Article 29.b does not exclude the debtor from requesting the opening of secondary proceedings; nevertheless, it is difficult to imagine this happening if we bear in mind that the most probable thing is that, in accordance with the *lex concursus principais*, the powers of the debtor will have been restricted and it will fall to the liquidator to represent the interests of the estate.[330] (b) In any case, the referral to national law must be understood as dependent upon whether or not it is compatible with the sense and purpose of the Insolvency Regulation. In contrast to independent territorial proceedings, the Regulation has not sought to restrict the power to open secondary proceedings to "local creditors." Consequently, a national rule restricting the possibility of requesting the opening to local creditors would be incompatible with the Regulation.

323. The Insolvency Regulation also contains a specific rule regarding the advancement of *costs and expenses* (Article 30). In effect, a number of Member States exclude the possibility of opening insolvency proceedings when the debtor's assets are insufficient to cover, wholly or in part, the costs and expenses of the proceedings. The Regulation respects these requirements and therefore permits the court to demand from the applicant, including the liquidator of the main proceedings, an advance payment of costs or to provide appropriate security. The wording "may require" employed by the precept does not empower the court to that effect but simply means that national legislation continues to apply.[331]

3.3. Aim of the proceedings: winding-up or restructuring

324. With regard to the aim of the insolvency proceedings, the Regulation also distinguishes between independent territorial proceedings and secondary territorial proceedings: while the former may be winding-up or restructuring proceedings, the latter may only aim at winding-up.

325. *Independent* territorial proceedings can be *winding-up* proceedings *or restructuring* proceedings, provided that they are included in Annexes A and B of the Regulation.[332] In the case of restructuring proceedings, the subsequent opening of main proceedings may trigger their *conversion* into winding-up proceedings if the liquidator of the main proceedings so requests (see Article 37).

Rationale. The fact that independent territorial *restructuring* proceedings are permitted requires an explanation. Territorial proceedings only affect assets located in the State of opening and only concern the establishment situated there; territorial proceedings do not extend either to establishments in other States or to the centre of administration. However,

---

[329] See VIRGOS/SCHMIT Report, Margin No. 227; BALZ (1996a), p. 953, where the solution is explained as the result of a compromise between the delegations: any creditor who is authorised to initiate insolvency proceedings is permitted to request the opening of secondary proceedings, but the possibility is limited to cases where the debtor has an establishment in the State in question; see also THIME, pp. 229–233; WIMMER (1998), p. 986.

[330] On the position of the debtor, BALZ, *Ibid.*; LÜKE (1998), p. 302; THIME, p. 230; DUURSMA-KEPPLINGER/DUURSMA/CHALUPSKY, (2002), pp. 504–505.

[331] VIRGOS/SCHMIT Report, Margin No. 228; on this requirement, see also THIME, p. 226.

[332] VIRGOS/SCHMIT Report, Margin No. 31.

business restructuring measures, if they wish to be effective, require decisions which are centralised and which encompass the whole company. That is why it is difficult to conceive the idea that an establishment can, on an isolated basis, be subject to a restructuring process. The natural *situs* of any company restructuring measures is the main proceedings. In spite of this fact, during the negotiations leading up to the 1995 Convention some Member States expressed an interest in leaving open the possibility of territorial restructuring proceedings to cover specific business situations; for example, those in which the company's centre of administration is located in one Member State but the greater part of its production activities take place in a different State, where its factories or other facilities are situated. In these cases, a majority of the company's creditors (private or public, workers or suppliers) may be located in this latter State, and this could justify the opening of independent territorial proceedings aimed at restructuring the company.

326. *Secondary proceedings*, in contrast, can only be winding-up proceedings from among those listed in Annex B (Article 3.3 *in fine* and 27 IR). Secondary restructuring proceedings are not allowed, except where the territorial proceedings were opened before the main proceedings and that once these have been opened, the conversion of the former, as envisaged by Article 37, has not been requested.

Any secondary territorial proceedings opened after the main proceedings must necessarily be *winding-up proceedings*. This term is expressly defined by the Regulation in quite broad terms: it shall mean insolvency proceedings involving the realisation of the debtor's assets, including those cases in which the proceedings are closed either as the result of a composition or other measures which bring the insolvency of the debtor to an end, or due to the insufficiency of his assets (Article 2.c).[333] Member States must indicate expressly which national proceedings belong to this category. This list has been included in Annex B of the Regulation.

The reason why secondary proceedings may only be winding-up proceedings and not restructuring proceedings is simple to explain.[334] Proceedings aimed at restructuring a company require global decisions which affect all of the debtor's assets. A complete restructuring of the debtor is only possible from a forum whose decisions also have a global scope. It is difficult to imagine a situation where an establishment which depends on an insolvent debtor can be restructured in isolation (except by selling it), because that establishment continues, as part of the debtor's organisation, to be responsible for all of the debtor's liabilities. Furthermore, coordination between the main proceedings and a territorial restructuring process would present significant technical difficulties. Both of these reasons made it advisable to exclude the possibility of opening secondary proceedings aimed at restructuring. The decision to limit secondary proceedings to winding-up proceedings expresses the primacy of the main

---

[333] This definition includes "one track" insolvency proceedings which may end by either realising the assets or restructuring the debtor, such as the German *Insolvenzverfahren* (see Annex B), provided that they are not pre-established as restructuring proceedings and that, in the event no agreement is reached, they are automatically converted into winding-up proceedings. BALZ (1996b), p. 523.

[334] VIRGOS/SCHMIT Report, Margin No. 221. BALZ (1996b), p. 523, emphasises the defensive function of secondary proceedings. "By opening a local liquidation proceeding, Member states can pull an emergency brake if they feel that unlimited recognition of foreign restructuring proceedings is unfair to their (or to their local creditors') interests."

proceedings. This primacy is maintained later by Article 33 *vis-à-vis* winding-up operations (by permitting them to be suspended) and Article 34 *vis-à-vis* negotiated compositions (which require the consent of the main liquidator unless the financial interests of the creditors in the main proceedings are not affected).

> *Explanation.* In this case, main proceedings have already been opened in the State of the debtor's centre of main interests, from where the restructuring of the company can be better organised. Furthermore, as indicated in the VIRGOS/ SCHMIT Report, it was considered that coordination between several sets of reorganisation proceedings concerning the same debtor would be too technically complex to be feasible (the debtor's assets may be divided among States, but not the debts).[335] In any case, if the national laws in question are sufficiently similar and the territorial proceedings were opened earlier, the liquidator of the main proceedings may allow them to continue as restructuring proceedings by not exercising the power conferred upon him by Article 37 whereby he can convert the territorial proceedings into winding-up proceedings.

327. The fact that the proceedings are winding-up proceedings does not mean that they must necessarily result in a winding-up, because the parties involved may agree otherwise: a *rescue plan*, a *composition* or a *comparable measure* is possible. Article 34 expresses this very clearly, although it makes the possibility conditional upon this being permitted by the law applicable to the territorial proceedings. If such is the case, negotiations will take place in the shadow of a single "exit" (in the absence of an agreement, the debtor will be wound up), which clarifies things. Any restriction of the rights of the creditors which are agreed upon in these proceedings only affects, in line with the merely territorial scope of the proceedings, the assets located in that State, except where all the creditors "having an interest" agree to an extension to assets located in another State (Article 34.2). For this reason, consent by creditors to a territorial composition cannot be interpreted as a waiver of the realisation of their claims upon the debtor's assets located in other States.

To facilitate these negotiations, the Insolvency Regulation confers upon the liquidator in the main proceedings the power to stay the winding-up process in secondary proceedings (see Articles 33, 34.1 II and 34.3).

3.4. Creditors' right to participate (Articles 32 and 39)

328. In contrast to what happens with the assets, with regard to the creditors who can participate, territorial proceedings are, at least in the Community sphere, *universal*: all creditors who have their registered office, domicile or habitual residence in a Member State, regardless of their nationality, are entitled to participate in territorial proceedings. This rule of participation applies both to *independent* territorial proceedings and to *secondary* proceedings (see Articles 39 and 32.1).[336] This rule is a uniform substantive rule which cannot be modified or altered by the Member

---

[335] VIRGOS/SCHMIT Report, Margin No. 221.

[336] A summary of the reasons which justify this solution can be seen in LÜKE (1998), pp. 300–301.

States. National law cannot, for example, restrict participation to local creditors or to those who enjoy a particular legal position (e.g. a privilege or preference) or whose claims arise from activities in the State where the secondary proceedings are opened.[337] With regard to creditors whose registered office, domicile or habitual residence is located in a non-Member State, national law applies.

3.5. *Other special features of territorial proceedings*

329. With regard to the application of the law of the State of the opening (*lex fori concursus*), we have already referred to the requirements for the opening, the right to request the opening, the creditors who can participate, the type of proceedings which may be opened, the possibility of a rescue plan or a composition in a territorial proceedings and the effects thereof, and the effects when the debtor is a company (see *i.a.* Nos 124, 128, 314 *et seq.*).

330. The exceptions to the application of the law of the State of opening (*lex fori concursus*) are the same as in the case of the main proceedings (see Articles 5–15). Nevertheless, due to the limited scope of this type of proceedings, their role will also be limited. Thus:

(a) Articles 5 (*rights in rem*) and 7 (*reservation of title*), insofar as they presuppose that the asset is located outside the State of opening and the effects of the proceedings are, *ex lege*, limited to the territory of the State of opening, will never apply. The same is true of Article 8 (*contracts relating to immoveable assets*), and, albeit in reference to registers, of Article 11 (with regard to Article 2.g II), because both are also based upon the location of the immovable asset or register, respectively, in a State other than the State of opening; and, *ex hypothesis*, the territorial proceedings cannot produce effects over assets located in other States.

(b) Article 6 (*set-off*) will only apply when the primary claim (i.e. the insolvent debtor's claim) is subject to a law other than the law of the State of opening of territorial proceedings *but* the centre of main interests of the *creditor* who invokes a right to set-off (and who is the debtor in the primary claim), is located in that State. This derives from Article 2.g III, as territorial proceedings only encompass assets situated there.

Example. The creditor has his centre of main interests in State F1, where territorial proceedings are opened because the debtor has an establishment there. In turn, the insolvent debtor has a claim in his favour *vis-à-vis* that creditor; the law which governs this latter claim is that of a different State F2. In these circumstances, the creditor may use his right to set-off pursuant to the law of F2, ex Article 6.

(c) The regime of voidness, voidability or unenforceability of the *lex concursus* governing the territorial proceedings only applies when the asset which the liquidator

---

[337] Virgos/Schmit Report, Margin No. 235; Lüke (1998), pp. 301–302. However, it must be borne in mind that the power to initiate the opening of independent territorial proceedings is restricted to "local creditors" (Article 3.4.b IR).

is seeking to restore to the estate was located in the territory of the State in question at the time of the opening; this circumstance will also determine the operation of Article 13 on detrimental acts.

> *Example.* The insolvent debtor assigns a claim to a third party prior to the declaration of opening. The debtor of the assigned claim (*debitor debitoris*) has his centre of main interests in the State where the territorial proceedings are opened (F1) and the claim is therefore considered to be located there (see Article 2.g). In accordance with the ordinary conflict of laws rules, the assignment is governed by the law of a different Member State (F2). If the liquidator of the territorial insolvency seeks to challenge that assignment pursuant to the *lex fori concursus* (F1), the third-party assignee may rely on the law of F2, in the terms laid down in Article 13.

(d) Article 14 (*protection of third parties*) may apply when the asset has left the State where the territorial proceedings are opened *after* the opening of the proceedings (in this case, the asset was situated in the secondary forum *at the time of* the opening and belongs to its estate).

(e) Article 15 (*effects on lawsuits pending*) will apply when the object of the proceedings is an asset located in the territory of the State of opening.

> *Example.* A third party claims in the debtor's domicile ownership of a movable good (ex Article 2 Regulation 44/2001); the asset is, however, located in the State where the territorial proceedings have been opened. In this case, the asset is subject to the territorial insolvency proceedings, but the effects of the declaration of opening on the lawsuit pending in the State where the debtor has his domicile are subject to the law of that State.

331. Furthermore, the *uniform rules* provided for in the Insolvency Regulation (*supra* Chapter VII) may also apply to the territorial proceedings, although with certain adjustments. Thus, (a) the rules provided for in Articles 21.1, 23, 39, 40 and 41 apply to the territorial proceedings just as they stand. (b) The application of Article 24 in territorial insolvencies is not excluded. However, this is unlikely to happen as it will only apply if the obligation honoured was subject to the territorial insolvency pursuant to the rule regarding location contained in Article 2.g III (i.e. when the *debitor debitoris* has his centre of main interests in the same State where the territorial proceedings are opened) but performance thereof, in contrast, is owed in another different State. (c) The rules provided by Articles 21.2 and 22, on the other hand, do not apply in the case of territorial proceedings.

3.6. Restrictions of creditors' rights (Articles 17.2 and 34.2)

332. Territorial insolvency proceedings are governed by the *lex fori concursus*. This law will tell us if and under what conditions the consent of the creditors is required, and also the degree of "sacrifice" which will be expected of them.

333. In principle, all creditors will be affected by the territorial proceedings, not only local creditors or creditors who lodged their claims in the territorial proceedings. The reason is that, as all creditors can participate in the territorial

proceedings and benefit from them (see Article 32.1), they must also assume the corresponding risk.

334. Nevertheless, this restriction is limited in effect. As the proceedings are territorial, any "sacrifice" on the part of the creditors only encompasses the assets of the debtor situated in the State of the opening of the territorial proceedings. Creditors will still have an outstanding claim in other States against the debtor for the unsatisfied part of their claim. The two provisions of the Insolvency Regulation which deal with this question state this principle very clearly:

(a) Article 17.2 establishes that *"any restriction of the creditors' rights, in particular a stay or discharge, shall produce effects* vis-à-vis *assets situated within the territory of another Member State only in the case of those creditors who have given their consent"*. Here, consent means individual consent; in other words, this supplementary restriction can be relied on only against creditors who have accepted it individually and not by a majority vote.[338] Creditors' consent cannot be replaced by a decision of the court.

(b) Article 34.2 reiterates the same limit in connection with a possible composition or rescue plan approved in secondary proceedings: *"any restriction of creditors' rights arising from a measure referred to in paragraph 1 which is proposed in secondary proceedings, such as a stay of payment or discharge of debt, may not have effect in respect of the debtor's assets not covered by those proceedings without the consent of all the creditors having an interest"*. A composition may be reached or a rescue plan approved in the secondary forum with effects on assets located in other States, provided that it is agreed to by "all the creditors having an interest". This last sentence means that the majority rule does not apply, but rather that the unanimous consent of the creditors affected by that extension is required.[339] As in the case of Article 17, the creditors' consent is a requirement of the Insolvency Regulation which cannot be replaced by a decision of the court or be modified by national law.

Differences. Article 17.2 refers both to *independent* and *secondary* proceedings and regulates the effects of territorial proceedings in other *Member States* as a mirror image of Article 3.2. Article 34.2 only deals with *secondary* proceedings and imposes a uniform requirement (which prevails over national law) for compositions or rescue plans. Furthermore, Article 34.2 presupposes that main insolvency proceedings with universal world-wide scope have been opened in the Community; for this reason it does operate (in contrast with Article17.2) *vis-à-vis* assets situated both in Member *and* non-Member States.[340]

335. Although the liquidation of assets can easily be organised on a territorial basis, this is not true of the discharge of liabilities; liabilities are assignable to the capital as a whole, not to specific assets. This idea is reflected in the Insolvency

---

[338] VIRGOS/SCHMIDT Report, Margin No. 157.
[339] VIRGOS/SCHMIDT Report, Margin No. 250.
[340] WIMMER (2002), p. 2525.

Regulation when: (a) it allows all creditors to participate in all proceedings; (b) it does not accept any restriction based upon the location of the creditor or the origin of his claim; (c) a discharge of debt in a territorial proceedings has no effect in respect of assets located in other States. In theory, it may be possible to divide the liabilities among several proceedings in proportion to the value of the assets belonging to each of the estates, but this is not the solution adopted. Under the Insolvency Regulation, a discharge in the secondary forum cannot reduce the liability of the debtor in the rest of the world.[341]

336. The laws of the Member States vary significantly with respect to the question of *discharge*. A distinction is necessary here between a discharge that results from a composition or insolvency plan and the availability of a "fresh start" for natural debtors by means of a discharge of the residual claims; the latter represents a distinct insolvency policy which is unrelated to the collective action problem that gives insolvency law its general shape.

337. Under a composition or an insolvency plan, all affected claims, whether or not they were lodged by their holders and whether or not they accepted the plan, may be discharged and replaced by the obligation provided by the plan. The problem here resides in the coordination between the main and the secondary proceedings.

338. A more difficult question arises in the case of natural debtors, with regard to the discharge of residual claims which allows a "fresh start". The Regulation does not establish any express restriction on this possibility in territorial proceedings. This allows for an element of flexibility, which may be necessary. For example, independent territorial proceedings are possible under the Insolvency Regulation; or claims may only be filed in the territorial proceedings and can be treated as "local debts" which may be fully extinguished by the territorial proceedings. However, it also causes problems when main and secondary proceedings are opened: if a discharge is granted in the secondary forum but not in the main forum (or is given under different conditions in each) a number of inconsistencies may arise, the most obvious being that it is unrealistic to think of a "fresh start" for a part (the establishment) when the whole (the debtor) is still liable for the unsatisfied claims. Under these circumstances, it seems logical that any new assets in the secondary forum should serve to cover the remaining liabilities, not to create "safe harbours" for a debtor's future earnings within the Community, thereby segmenting the market. Therefore,

(a) The decision on the question of the discharge should correspond to the main proceedings. This is in line with economic rationale. A "fresh start" policy may make good sense, but this decision should correspond to a single voice, that of the law of the State of the main proceedings, and not be the object of inconsistent policies and requirements; unity of the debtor and unity of the economic space of the Community are arguments which justify an interpretative reduction of the possibility of a discharge of residual claims taking place in the secondary proceedings. This

---

[341] WIMMER (2002), pp. 2588–2589, characterising, for this reason, a territorial discharge as procedural in nature.

solution is in harmony with the normative model adopted by the Insolvency Regulation: universal but for the protection of certain local interests of creditors and other possible interested parties; and also with the principles embodied in Articles 35 and 34.1 II.

(b) For the same reasons, a discharge granted in the main proceedings should also have universal effect. The limitation of Article 17.1 *in fine* to the recognition of the effects of the main proceedings only operates "*as long as*" the secondary proceedings are opened; once the assets belonging to the secondary estate have been distributed or the proceedings closed, the secondary proceedings will have exhausted their original function and the main proceedings regain their universal scope. This interpretation, combined with the applicable national law, guarantees a "fresh start" decision with full effects throughout the Community.

Part IV

Recognition of Insolvency Proceedings

Chapter 9

Recognition of Foreign Insolvency Proceedings

1. THE INSOLVENCY REGULATION'S SYSTEM OF RECOGNITION: GENERAL CHARACTERISTICS

339. The principle of universality of the main proceedings opened under Article 3.1 embracing all of the debtor's assets, wherever they are located, and affecting all his creditors, implies recognition of the proceedings and their effects in other States. The Insolvency Regulation guarantees this universality by means of a system of mandatory recognition in all Member States. However, recognition of the main insolvency proceedings does not prevent the opening of territorial proceedings. The possibility of commencing territorial proceedings under Article 3.2 offers a shield against recognition and implies that the debtor's insolvency will have different effects in a given territory; a result which, in turn, must be respected by the main proceeding.

The Insolvency Regulation devotes Articles 16–26 to regulating these questions. On the sphere of application of these rules, see No. 27. The system of recognition contained in the Regulation applies also to insolvency decisions taken by the court of opening *vis-à-vis* non-Member States, i.e. regardless of the fact that the conflict of laws rules applied in that case may not have been those provided for in the Regulation but national ones.

340. In order to understand the system of recognition set up by the Insolvency Regulation, we must bear in mind the *premises* upon which it was drafted: (a) the conception of insolvency proceedings as complex proceedings, in which a plurality of decisions are adopted, each one with a certain degree of autonomy; (b) the distinction between recognition and enforcement; (c) the policy of simplifying the requirements for recognition. Let us look at what these premises mean.

341. The *first premise* is the relative *autonomy* of the successive decisions which are taken within the framework of insolvency proceedings from commencement to closure. Insolvency proceedings are complex proceedings. For this reason, in the matter of recognition, the Regulation does not contemplate insolvency proceedings as a whole, but rather as a series of successive decisions, each of them with different effects. The structure of the Regulation follows this idea. Article 16 deals with the decision opening the insolvency proceedings, which is obviously the key decision, and its effects (see Articles 17, 18, 20 and 24), while Article 25 deals with the successive decisions taken in the course of the proceedings (e.g. a decision confirming a composition or granting a discharge) or within its framework (e.g. a decision on the avoidance of a detrimental act).[342]

---

[342] VIRGÓS, p. 26.

NB. This also explains why we may find that the declaration of opening of insolvency proceedings is recognised in another State while, in contrast, a judgement handed down in the framework of those proceedings may not be recognised.[343]

342. In accordance with the *second premise*, the Insolvency Regulation reiterates the traditional distinction between *recognition* and *enforcement* of foreign decisions. While recognition is immediate and automatic, enforcement is dependent upon prior court intervention, through a procedure of *exequatur* or *registration* for enforcement.

343. In a technical sense, recognition involves giving direct effect to foreign insolvency proceedings. The Insolvency Regulation provides for the recognition in other Member States of decisions relating to the opening, conduct and closure of insolvency proceedings which come within its scope (i.e. listed in its Annexes) and of decisions handed down in direct connection with such insolvency proceedings (Recital 22).

Through recognition, judicial decisions can carry their authority beyond their State of origin. The regime of recognition which the Regulation establishes is based on the principle of Community trust and the *favor recognitionis*. Its aim is to prevent national frontiers from acting as an obstacle to the efficient administration, throughout the Member States, of cross-border insolvency proceedings.[344]

344. This explains why the basic principle of the Insolvency Regulation is the principle of *automatic recognition*. Automatic recognition means recognition as of right, without the need for an intermediary measure, such as *exequatur*, registration or comparable procedure, in the requested State. Under the Insolvency Regulation, the decisions handed down by the court of opening of insolvency proceedings are recognised *ipso iure*.[345] It is sufficient for the foreign decision to satisfy the conditions laid down by the Regulation for that decision to immediately produce full effect in the rest of the Member States. This ensures the effectiveness of the insolvency proceedings as it saves costs and prevents the delays associated with a procedure of prior formal recognition.[346] For example, by showing the decision opening insolvency proceedings, the liquidator can gain access to the debtor's assets (e.g. bank accounts) in other States.

Automatic recognition does not mean *absence of control*. Only those decisions which originate in a Member State and satisfy the conditions laid down by the Regulation benefit from automatic recognition. It is obvious that doubts may arise or objections may be raised as to whether or not these conditions are satisfied. Given that recognition is not subject to any prior procedure of control, the authorities of the

---

[343] *Ibid.*

[344] VIRGÓS/SCHMIT Report, Margin No. 147; VIRGÓS, p. 26; see also LÜKE (1998), p. 286; VALLENS (1995), p. 309.

[345] VIRGÓS/SCHMIT Report, Margin No. 143; BALZ (1996a), p. 951; GOTTWALD (1997), p. 25; VIRGÓS, p. 26; LÜKE (1998), p. 285; LEIBLE/STAUDINGER (2000), p. 561; HOMANN, p. 370; DORDI, p. 356; BELTRAN SANCHEZ, p. 39; VALLENS (1995), p. 309; FLETCHER, p. 283; KEMPER, p. 1613; HUBER, p. 146; DUURSMA-KEPPLINGER/DUURSMA/CHALUPSKY, (2002), p. 354.

[346] LÜKE (1998), p. 286.

requested State which are called upon to perform an act or take a decision on the basis of the said foreign decision may verify *incidentally* whether or not the foreign decision satisfies the conditions of the Regulation.[347] The Regulation does not establish any procedure for control of this type, so the national law of the requested State must be referred to: (a) If the decision is invoked before the courts of a Member State within the framework of a judicial process which has a different object, but the outcome of which depends on that decision, the said court will have jurisdiction over the question of recognition as an incidental question. (b) If the decision is invoked before other authorities (e.g. in order to carry out a registration in a public register), the control procedure will be the same one provided for the prior verification of the legal requirements which those authorities must effect, if any, to carry out their duties, albeit incorporating verification that the decision conforms with the Insolvency Regulation.

> *Problem: recognition as a principal issue.* The system of automatic recognition with incidental control has the advantage of preventing the costs associated with the specific procedures for recognition of the *exequatur* type. But it also has certain drawbacks. Insofar as each judge or authority of the requested State confronted with the foreign decision confirms fulfilment of the conditions for recognition independently and without a *res iudicata* effect: (a) it is necessary to carry out this incidental control in each of the proceedings in which the foreign decision is alleged and (b) there is no guarantee that the outcome of the said incidental control is going to be the same in all of these proceedings (as each authority decides independently, we may find that one accepts recognition of the foreign decision and another rejects it).[348] A procedure of recognition as a principal issue would eliminate this uncertainty, as it would be binding on all later proceedings in the requested State. That is why it seems logical to allow, even though the Insolvency Regulation does not expressly provide for this, the possibility of requesting a declaration of recognition as a principal issue, by applying analogically (we are at the Community law level) the same procedure provided for by Regulation 44/2001 (see Article 33.2 thereof).[349]

345. To *enforce* is to put into execution. Enforcement implies the exercise of the State's coercive power. The principle of exclusive territorial sovereignty prevails here: *direct* application of coercive powers within the territory is limited to the authorities of the State where the assets or persons to which this action relates are situated. The Insolvency Regulation does not alter this state of affairs. Two of its provisions reflect this principle. The first is Article 18.3, which governs the exercise of the liquidator's powers in other States. These powers will normally entail the realisation of assets situated in other Member States. However, if coercion is needed (e.g. he does not hold possession of the assets), the liquidator must request the intervention of the local authorities (see *infra* Nos 365 *et seq.*). The second is Article 25, according to which *enforcement* of a foreign insolvency decision is not automatic,

---

[347] VIRGÓS/SCHMIT Report, Margin No. 152; VIRGÓS p. 26; TRUNK (1997), p. 243; LÜKE (1998), p. 285; HOMANN, p. 370.

[348] FLESSNER (1991) p. 119; TRUNK (1997), p. 243; LÜKE (1998), p. 286; EIDENMÜLLER (2001a), p. 9; HOMANN, p. 270; KOLMANN, p. 294.

[349] TRUNK (1997), pp. 243–245; against this, HERCHEN, p. 159; KOLMANN, p. 296.

but requires a prior process of authorisation by which the foreign decision is declared "enforceable" in the forum. With regard to this *"declaration of enforceability"*, Article 25 I of the Insolvency Regulation refers to General Regulation 44/2001, which establishes a process of *exequatur* or, in the United Kingdom and Ireland, of *registration for enforcement*.

346. The *third premise* is the *simplification* of the conditions that a foreign insolvency decision must fulfil to benefit from the system of recognition and enforcement of the Insolvency Regulation. To be recognised and, when appropriate, enforceable under this Regulation a decision must: (a) emanate from a Member State and from an authority, in the sense of Article 2.d, which has declared itself competent in accordance with Article 3; (b) relate to a matter within the subject-matter scope of the Insolvency Regulation; (c) not be vulnerable to the public policy objection specified by Article 26; and (d) be effective and, in the case of enforcement, enforceable in the State of origin; but it is not necessary that the decision be final. Whether or not an insolvency decision is enforceable is always a matter for the law of the State of origin (e.g. if it loses this character in the State of origin, it cannot be enforced in the forum).

Neither publication nor registration of the decision opening insolvency proceedings are a pre-requisite for recognition; publication and registration may, however, be relevant for other purposes.

2. DECLARATION OF OPENING: RECOGNITION AND EFFECTS

2.1. Automatic and immediate recognition (Article 16)

347. Article 16 of the Regulation establishes the principle of immediate recognition: "A*ny judgment opening insolvency proceedings handed down by a court of a Member State which has jurisdiction pursuant to Article 3 shall be recognised in all the other Member States from the time it becomes effective in the State of the opening of proceedings"*. This rule is complemented by Article 17, which states that recognition operates "with no further formalities"; i.e. simply by force of law, without the need of intermediary measures such as *exequatur* or registration. The meaning of this "automatic" recognition has already been explained (*supra* No. 344), so we shall now deal with other issues.

348. The Insolvency Regulation defines the concept of *"judgment"* with regard to the opening of insolvency proceedings or the appointment of a liquidator, and it defines this concept in very broad terms, by equating it to *"decision"*. According to Article 2.e the term "judgment" shall include the *decision of any court empowered to open such proceedings or to appoint a liquidator.* In turn, the term *"court"* is to be construed also very broadly (see Article 2.d and Recital 10) and may include *any judicial body or other competent body of a Member State empowered to open insolvency proceedings or to take decisions in the course of such proceedings*. *"Other competent body"* includes any competent authority other than judicial bodies, including an administrative authority, and may include, in the case of voluntary

liquidations, the corporate body empowered to pass a resolution to wind itself up (e.g. the body of members in the United Kingdom) and appoint a liquidator (e.g. the body of creditors in the United Kingdom); in this case a confirmation by the courts is necessary.

It is for this reason that we will speak of "decision" rather than of "judgment", which may transmit the impression that the Regulation only applies to judiciary proceedings, which is not the case. Article 16 applies, therefore, to any decision opening insolvency proceedings taken by any court, authority or body of persons empowered to do so according to their national law.

Rationale. The Insolvency Regulation uses the concept of court in a very broad sense with the aim of encompassing different national solutions. As we know, the Regulation does not establish which authorities have jurisdiction to open and conduct insolvency proceedings. This is a matter for the law of each Member State. This is why Article 2.d gives a definition which entails a referral to national law: *judicial body or any other competent body of a Member State empowered to open insolvency proceedings or to take decisions in the course of such proceedings.* The expression *"of a Member State"* should not be understood as a requirement that the body in question be a *state* body, which would go against the *ratio legis*, but rather that the national law governing that body gives it authority to open insolvency proceedings. Recital 10 of the Preamble to the Regulation tries to make this clear. Naturally, as the system of recognition established by the Regulation only applies to proceedings included in its sphere of application and listed in the Annexes, the national courts or authorities referred to by the Regulation shall only be those who, according to the law of each Member State are empowered to deal with the proceedings listed therein, which makes things simpler in practice. This referral to national law permits the concept of "competent body" to include the competent corporate body of a legal person which decides to wind itself up for reasons of insolvency and the creditors' meeting which organises the said winding-up, as in the case of a creditors' voluntary winding-up proceedings in the United Kingdom and Ireland.[350] Both States have included these proceedings in Annex A of the Regulation with a minor adjustment, because they add the need for *confirmation by the court*. The origin of this minor adjustment is explained in Margin No. 52 of the VIRGÓS/SCHMIT Report. The Regulation is worded with a view to insolvency proceedings dealt with by courts of justice. In order to facilitate the insertion of these non-judicial proceedings into the scheme of the Regulation and eliminate doubts in other Member States which do contemplate this type of proceedings, the Regulation requires those States with proceedings of this type (the United Kingdom and Ireland) to introduce into their respective national legislation a procedure of confirmation, by the courts of justice, of the nature of the proceedings and the appointment of the liquidator. The purpose of this confirmation is not to modify the nature of the proceedings, but simply to certify, for the benefit of other States, the decision of the competent bodies (the members' meeting and the creditors' meeting) to wind up the company for reasons of insolvency and to appoint a liquidator. This confirmation has merely evidential meaning. The Regulation does not make the recognition of the resolution to wind the insolvent company up dependent upon the judicial confirmation.[351] This means that the relevant time for establishing the effects of the insolvency is the time at which the decision opening proceedings becomes effective in the State of origin (see Article 2.f), not the time of the confirmation. If the liquidator wants to assert these effects in other States (for example, if the resolution has to be entered in the Registers of another Member State or if the

---

[350] See VIRGÓS/SCHMIT Report, Margin No. 66.
[351] See VIRGÓS/SCHMIT Report, Margin No. 52 IV.1.

liquidator wishes to exercise his powers there) he must necessarily have received this confirmation.[352]

349. The principle of immediate and automatic recognition established by the Insolvency Regulation operates as an obligation for Member States which applies even when this same debtor could not, on account of his capacity, be subject to insolvency proceedings in the recognising State, as is the case in some States with non-traders (see Article 16.1 II). This fact cannot constitute grounds for refusing recognition, either directly or via the clause on public policy. The explanatory report expressed it very clearly: the State requested "cannot invoke public policy to oppose recognition on those grounds".[353]

> *Rationale*. The reason for this is that only the courts of the debtor's "centre of main interests" are empowered to open main proceedings. It is presupposed that this is the State with which the debtor has the closest connection. It is therefore reasonable that it is this State which decides who may be declared insolvent and that the other States, whose relationship with the debtor is limited to the presence of an establishment or assets, do not frustrate this decision. The opposite premise does not present any problems: territorial insolvency proceedings may be opened in accordance with the law of the State where the debtor has an establishment, even when the law of the State of the centre of main interests does not provide for the opening of main proceedings (Article 3.4).

350. The general regime of automatic recognition is valid for *all* insolvency proceedings opened in the Member States pursuant to the Regulation, whether they are *main* proceedings or *territorial* proceedings. In the latter case recognition is naturally limited to the territorial effects of the proceedings.[354]

351. Recognition does not prevent the possibility of opening secondary territorial proceedings. Article 16.2 confirms something which is inherent to the system of the Insolvency Regulation. As we already know, the normative model which inspires the Regulation is a model which permits main proceedings to be combined with secondary territorial proceedings. In line with this solution, Article 16.2 expressly confirms that "*Recognition of the proceedings referred to in Article 3(1) shall not preclude the opening of the proceedings referred to in Article 3(2) by a court in another Member State. The latter proceedings shall be secondary insolvency proceedings*".

2.2. *Effects of recognition (Article 17)*

352. Whereas Article 16 establishes the basic principle of recognition of decisions opening insolvency proceedings, Article 17 distinguishes between the recognition of

---

[352] See VIRGÓS/SCHMIT Report, Margin No. 52 IV.2.
[353] VIRGÓS/SCHMIT Report, Margin No. 148; KEMPER, p. 1613; KOLMANN, p. 289.
[354] VIRGÓS/SCHMIT Report, Margin No. 146; BALZ (1996a), p. 951.

the main proceedings and the recognition of territorial proceedings. The reason lies in the different consequences which recognition entails in each case.

2.2.1. Main proceedings

353. In the case of the *main proceedings*, recognition means that the insolvency proceedings will produce in all other Member States the same effects as they have in the original *forum* (i.e. in the State of opening). The model of recognition which inspires the Regulation is, therefore, the *"extension model"*:[355] *the judgment opening the proceedings referred to in Article 3(1) shall, with no further formalities, produce the same effects in any other Member State as under the law of the State of the opening of proceedings* (Article 17.1). This rule ensures that the effects of the main proceedings are universal in character (*at least* as far as the Community is concerned) and will not be subject to variations according to the national laws of the individual States.

> *Extension vs. assimilation of effects.*[356] In order to determine exactly the effects that a foreign insolvency decision may have in other States, the national systems revolve around two opposing models: the assimilation model and the extension model. The *assimilation model* responds to the idea of "equating" foreign decisions with national ones; i.e. it entails granting a foreign decision the same effects as an equivalent national decision. This model has two drawbacks: (a) in the first place, a bankruptcy decree may produce different effects in the requested State and in the State of origin, with the risk of the contradictory results that this may lead to. (b) In the second place, the same decision may produce different effects in different States, in such a way that the rights of the parties may vary according to the country they are in; and if the decision has to produce effects *vis-à-vis* various people then the consequences for each of them may be different, also depending upon which country they are in. The *extension model* is based on the idea of accepting the foreign decision as it is, on its own terms and with its own effects. From a formal point of view, this model respects the foreign decision and acknowledges it as it stands: a decision can only be understood in the sense and with the scope with which it was rendered in the State of origin. The extension model ensures that all of the parties affected by the same foreign decision have equal rights and obligations, regardless of where recognition of that decision is requested. The Court of Justice has already decided that this model is applicable in the sphere of Regulation 44/2001.[357]

354. Pursuant to the *extension model*, the effects of the insolvency proceedings depend on the national applicable law. It is the *lex fori concursus* which determines the effects of the opening of insolvency proceedings in all Member States. The same principle applies, as a general rule, to subsequent decisions handed down in the insolvency proceedings.

---

[355] VIRGÓS/SCHMIT Report, Margin Nos 151 and 153; VIRGÓS, p. 28; FLESSNER (1997), pp. 5–7; LÜKE (1998), p. 296; VALLENS (1995), p. 309; HUBER, p. 147; KOLMANN, p. 278.

[356] For a more detailed treatment, VIRGÓS/GARCIMARTÍN, pp. 406–411; and in the sphere of insolvency, HOMMAN, pp. 351–358.

[357] STJCE Case 145/86; Although this ruling dealt with the 1968 Brussels Convention, it is equally applicable to Regulation 44/2001.

355. This statement applies to both the *procedural* and *substantive* effects of the opening. The decision opening insolvency proceedings has a broad range of effects in all systems: typically, the debtor loses, totally or partially, control over assets; an administrator or supervisor is appointed with rights and obligations in respect of those assets; creditor's claims are established; and individual methods of enforcement are stayed or suspended.[358] All of these are effects which, if provided for by the law of the State of opening, are simultaneously applicable in all of the Member States.[359]

Explanation. Some national systems of Private International Law distinguish between the *procedural* effects and the *substantive* law effects of foreign decisions.[360] The application of this difference in the sphere of insolvency poses severe problems of characterisation and is not well suited to a universal normative model. That is why the Insolvency Regulation bases itself upon an idea of unity of effects: unless the Regulation provides otherwise, both the procedural effects and the substantive law effects of foreign insolvency proceedings are determined by the law of the State of opening.[361]

356. Article 17.1 is the reflection, in the area of recognition of foreign insolvencies, of the conflict of laws rule contained in Article 4 and is subject to the same exceptions established in Articles 5–15.[362] Article 17.1 explains this idea when it states that the decision opening the proceedings shall produce the same effects as under the law of the State of opening, *"unless this Regulation provides otherwise"*. In the system of the Insolvency Regulation, the effects of the insolvency proceedings are not monopolised by the *lex fori concursus* (although this the primary rule), and this conflict of laws diversity is also present in the area of recognition. Article 17.1 refers implicitly to Articles 5–15, so that similar exceptions to the *lex fori concursus* operate in the case of insolvency proceedings opened in the forum and in the case of recognition of foreign insolvency proceedings. This means, for example, that a foreign decision opening insolvency proceedings will not prejudice the right of a secured creditor to individual enforcement when the collateral was situated, at the time of the opening, in the forum (pursuant to Article 5); that the same decision will produce over a contract regarding the use of an immovable asset only those effects provided for by the law of the location (Article 8); or that a general mortgage over the assets which make up the estate will not be given effect over registered assets in the forum if to do so infringes the system of *numerus clausus* of rights *in rem* (Article 11).

"Double function" of the Insolvency Regulation's conflict rules. In fact, what Article 17.1 tells us is that the effects of the recognition of foreign insolvency proceedings on those rights and

---

[358] It must be remembered that in the face of this intervention by the foreign *lex concursus*, local creditors always have the possibility of opening territorial proceedings or of participating in the main proceedings.

[359] VIRGÓS/SCHMIT Report, Margin No. 154; VIRGÓS, p. 27; LEIBLE/STAUDINGER (2000), p. 561; KEMPER, p. 1614.

[360] See HOMANN, *passim*.

[361] See LÜKE (1998), pp. 281–282; GEIMER, Margin No. 3501; HERCHEN, pp. 99–100; KOLMANN, p. 278.

[362] VIRGÓS/SCHMIT Report, Margin No. 153.

acts that are protected by special conflict rules are also to be determined by the law designated by those special rules. In this sense, conflict rules apply both in the sphere of applicable law and in the sphere of recognition, but with one difference. Once an insolvency problem has been decided and the court of opening (or any other court with jurisdicton) has established (applying the said conflict rules) by judgement the effects of the insolvency proceedings on a given right or act, there is no longer any open question as to the effect of the insolvency proceedings on that right or act. The judgement is conclusive as to those effects. The model of extension applies to its binding and *res judicata* effect, and the insolvency effects to be recognised are the effects as established by that judgment. There is no control regarding the law applied by the court of origin.

357. To benefit from the system of recognition it is necessary that the decision be effective in the State of origin, but not that the decision be final. The law of the State of opening determines whether the decision produces effects, and the *date* from which it begins to produce those effects in all Member States. The elimination of any lapse of time between effectiveness in the State of origin and recognition in other States is very important, as it eliminates any incentive which might otherwise exist for creditors to engage in opportunistic behaviour in those other States.

358. Recognition of the effects of the main proceedings is limited by the opening of *territorial proceedings* pursuant to Article 3.2. The main proceedings cannot have effect with regard to the assets and legal relationships which come under the jurisdiction of the territorial proceedings: *the judgment opening the proceedings referred to in Article 3(1) shall ... produce the same effects in any other state ... as long as no proceedings referred to in Article 3(2) are opened in that other Member State* (Article 17.1). This rule applies both to territorial proceedings opened before (independent proceedings) or after (secondary proceedings) the main proceedings. In this case, the main insolvency procedure cannot have direct effects but they can exert great influence in the territorial proceedings via the rules of participation and coordination provided for by the Insolvency Regulation;[363] and, in any case, they will benefit from any surplus assets from the secondary proceedings in the terms laid down in Article 35.

2.2.2. Territorial proceedings

359. Territorial insolvency proceedings opened according to Article 3.2 cannot encompass assets located in other Member States, as the effects of those proceedings are expressly restricted to assets of the debtor situated in the territory of the opening State (Article 3.2, *in fine*). In the case of territorial proceedings recognition means, as the Explanatory Reports expresses it, recognising the validity of the opening of the territorial proceedings and of the effects which they produce over the assets situated in the State of opening.[364] Article 17.2 states the consequence of this recognition: that the territorial effects of these proceedings cannot be challenged in other

---

[363] Virgós/Schmit Report, Margin Nos 153 *in fine* and 155; Virgós, p. 30; Balz (1996a), p. 952; Lüke (1998), p. 296; Leible/Staudinger (2000), p. 562.
[364] Virgós/Schmit Report, Margin No. 156.

Member States. This rule can be important, for example, when the liquidator in these proceedings seeks to recover assets which belong to the estate of the secondary proceedings but which have been transferred abroad without his permission *after* the proceedings were opened;[365] or when the liquidator in the territorial proceedings seeks to stay an individual execution of a claim which is located in the State where the territorial insolvency is opened but payable abroad.[366]

360. Article 17.2 of the Insolvency Regulation adds a special rule for cases where territorial proceedings are concluded by any formula of debt-rescheduling or debt-reduction: *any restriction of the creditor's rights, in particular a stay or discharge, shall produce effects* vis-à-vis *assets situated in the territory of another Member state only in the case of those creditors who have given their consent.* Article 3.2 establishes that the effects of territorial proceedings shall be limited to the debtor's assets which are located in the Member State which opened those proceedings. Article 17.2, in turn, applies this same limitation to the effects of any stay, discharge or other restriction of creditor's rights approved in territorial proceedings. It makes it clear that any such restriction will only produce effects with respect to the assets that are part of the secondary estate.

361. This rule applies whether the restriction is the result of a decision by the creditors adopted by a vote of the required majority or has been imposed by the court, according to the powers conferred upon it by the *lex fori concursus*:

(a) In the first case, the restriction applies and the agreement is only binding on the creditors with the same scope as the proceedings in which the agreement is reached, i.e. it only affects assets located in the opening forum. That is why, when the provision refers to creditors who have expressed their consent to the fact that the restriction also affects their rights with regard to assets located in another States, this consent is necessarily given on an individual basis. For the same reason, a decision by the majority of creditors in the territorial proceedings will not be enforceable outside those proceedings against anyone who did not give their individual consent. In short, if a composition, rescue plan or comparable measure aims to apply to assets which are not part of the secondary estate, it will be recognised in other Member States only if the impaired creditors have consented thereto on an individual basis[367].

(b) In the second case, the effects of the court's decision are also limited to the assets in the territorial estate; the court cannot replace the individual creditor's consent required by Article 17.2.

---

[365] Virgós/Schmit Report, Margin No. 156; Fletcher (1999), p. 284; Leible/Staudinger (2000), pp. 562–563; Homann, pp. 368–369; Geimer, Margin No. 3503; Huber, p. 148.

[366] In this case, payment of the claim can be sought abroad, specifically in the State where the performance is due, but the claim would remain subject to the territorial insolvency insofar as, pursuant to Article 2.g III of the Regulation, it was located in this latter State (due to the fact that it is in this State that the debtor of the claim – *debitor debitoris* – has his centre of main interests).

[367] Balz (1996b), p. 515.

3. THE LIQUIDATOR

3.1. Definition

362. The figure of the insolvency administrator plays a fundamental role in the scheme of the Insolvency Regulation. The Regulation uses the term *"liquidator"* and, as is the case with other concepts of the Insolvency Regulation, the concept of liquidator is defined in very broad terms, as *"any person or body whose function is to administer or liquidate assets of which the debtor has been divested or to supervise the administration of his affairs"* (Article 2.b).

The aim of this definition is to provide a wide concept of liquidator which encompasses any person or body upon which the functions of administration, supervision of the administration, or liquidation are conferred. Therefore, the key to the definition lies in the functional element.[368] This allows any body which carries out the said functions to be included within this concept, regardless of their title or nature. Nevertheless, in order to facilitate the application of the Regulation, it is also necessary for Member States to expressly designate those who, according to their national law, may fulfil this condition. *Annex C* of the Regulation contains this list. When, according to national law, it is the court itself which carries out these functions, it is necessary for the States to record this expressly in the said Annex.[369]

3.2. Powers: supervision, administration, disposal and realisation of assets (Article 18)

363. One of the central issues in any cross-border insolvency system is the recognition of the *appointment of the liquidator* and his *powers*. This is what Article 18 seeks to guarantee. The Article makes a distinction between main proceedings and territorial proceedings:

(a) In the case of *main proceedings*, the liquidator *"may exercise all of the powers conferred on him by the law of the State of the opening of proceedings in another Member State"* (Article 18.1). The universal scope of the main proceedings explains why the powers of the liquidator should be effective in all Member States. Article 18.1 reflects this idea and establishes a "model of extension" of the powers conferred on the liquidator by the State of opening: the liquidator may exercise all these powers in all other Member States.

(b) In contrast, in the case of *territorial proceedings* the fact that the liquidator may exercise his powers outside the State of opening is something of an exception. The proceedings opened on the basis of Article 3.2 are strictly territorial and therefore do not encompass those assets of the debtor which are located outside the State of opening. It is nevertheless true that there may be situations in which the

---

[368] POTTHAST, p. 107.
[369] VIRGÓS/SCHMIT Report, Margin No. 62.

liquidator finds himself obliged to exercise his powers in another State, for example, when an asset has been transferred outside the State of opening after the declaration of opening. In such a situation, the Regulation provides a special rule. Article 18.2 establishes that the liquidator *may in any other Member State claim through the courts or out of court that moveable property was removed from the territory of the State of the opening of proceedings to the territory of that other Member State after the opening of the insolvency proceedings. He may also bring any action to set aside which is in the interests of the creditors.*[370]

364. The legal status of the liquidator is subject to the *lex fori concursus*. This law determines, *inter alia*, the procedure for appointing the liquidator, the qualifications and qualities required to perform the function, including whether or not a legal person can perform this task, the regime of incompatibilities or prohibitions, the possibility of employing professionals to assist the liquidator, and the system of remuneration. It also specifies the functions and duties of the liquidator, his powers and the grounds and procedure for his removal.

> *NB.* The rules which determine the qualifications and qualities required in order to exercise the functions of liquidator vary from one Member State to another. Nevertheless, it must be remembered that these rules must respect the principle of non-discrimination on the grounds of nationality established in the EC Treaty (Article 12).[371]

365. The *lex fori concursus* will also determine the liability attached to the liquidator's failure to perform, or perform properly, his duties and functions, including the standard of care to be employed by the liquidator and his agents.

366. Article 18.1 governs the recognition in other Member States of the *powers* of the liquidator appointed in the main insolvency proceedings. As explained above, this provision is based on a "model of extension" of powers. The law governing the insolvency proceedings defines the extent of the liquidator's powers in all Member States: *"The liquidator appointed by a court which has jurisdiction pursuant to Article 3(1) may exercise all the powers conferred on him by the law of the State of the opening of proceedings in another Member State"*. The foreign liquidator is not equated with a domestic liquidator, but recognised as having the same functions and powers as in the State of opening.[372]

Depending on the applicable law, the liquidator's powers in other Member States may include: taking immediate control of the assets and of the business of the insolvent debtor; requesting provisional and protective measures; managing the business; administering and selling assets of the insolvency estate; registering rights; obtaining information concerning the debtor; intervening in lawsuits pending in which the debtor is a party, representing the insolvency estate in new lawsuits; exercising

---

[370] VIRGÓS/SCHMIT Report, Margin No. 224; BALZ (1996a), p. 951; LEIBLE/STAUDINGER (2000), pp. 562–563.

[371] POTTHAST, pp. 110–112.

[372] VIRGÓS/SCHMIT Report, Margin No. 159; VIRGÓS, p. 29; BALZ (1996a), p. 951; GOTTWALD (1997), p. 26; LÜKE (1998), p. 311; FLETCHER (1999), p. 285; HERCHEN, p. 139; LEIBLE/STAUDINGER (2000), p. 561; KEMPER, p. 1614; GEIMER, Margin No. 3506–3508; HUBER, p. 147; DUURSMA-KEPPLINGER/DUURSMA/CHALUPSKY, (2002), p. 376.

avoidance powers; deciding whether to continue performance or reject executory contracts; in liquidation proceedings, realising the assets of the insolvency estate. The liquidator may also transfer assets from the Member State where they are located to the Member State of opening (Article 18.1), with the restriction imposed by Articles 5 and 7.

367. The powers which correspond to the liquidator according to the law of the State of opening are subject to two types of *restrictions*. Some are established directly by the Insolvency Regulation (Article 18.1, and 3 *in fine*) and affect the *content* of the powers of the liquidator; others derive from the law of the State where the liquidator seeks to use those powers and affect their *exercise* (Article 18.3, first sentence).

368. The restrictions established by the Insolvency Regulation itself and which affect the *content* of the powers of the liquidator, can be divided into four categories:

(a) The general grounds of *public policy* (Article 26), which we shall analyse further on.

(b) The opening of *territorial proceedings* or the adoption of *preservation* measures ancillary to a request for the opening of such proceedings. According to Article 18.1, the liquidator appointed in the main insolvency procedure may exercise his powers in another Member State, *"as long as no other insolvency proceedings have been opened there nor any preservation measure to the contrary has been taken there further to a request for the opening of insolvency proceedings in that State"*. This restriction is logical, since the assets cannot be subject to the powers of the liquidators in two different proceedings at the same time. In principle, the liquidator appointed in the main proceedings may exercise his powers in any other Member States. However, if territorial insolvency proceedings are opened, the administration and liquidation of the debtor's assets located in the latter State corresponds exclusively to the local liquidator. In other words, once territorial proceedings have been opened in another Member State, the direct powers of the liquidator in the main proceedings no longer apply to assets situated in that State. In order to guarantee the future effectiveness of the territorial proceedings, this restriction also encompasses any preservation measure implemented there, further to a request for the opening of such secondary proceedings. In this way creditors can, *inter alia*, prevent the removal of assets by the main liquidator contemplated in Article 18.1.

NB. As already explained, this does not imply that the liquidator in the main proceedings loses all influence over the secondary estate, but that this influence must be exercised through the powers to intervene in the secondary proceedings which are conferred on him by the Regulation itself (see Articles 31–37).

(c) Rights protected by Articles 5 and 7. As we know, these provisions establish that the declaration of opening will not affect certain rights (rights *in rem* and reservations of title) constituted on assets located, at the time of opening, in another Member State. The aim of Article 18.1 *in fine* is to confirm this rule *vis-à-vis* the powers of the liquidator: the liquidator *"may in particular remove the debtor's assets from the territory of the Member State in which they are situated, subject to Articles 5 and 7"*. That is to say, the powers of the liquidator to remove or to carry out any other act of disposal with regard to those assets are restricted when the said action affects a right *in rem* or a retention of title. To the extent that it is required by the right *in rem*, the removal of those assets will be subject to the consent of the holder of the right *in rem*.[373]

(d) The powers of the liquidator "*may not include coercive measures or the right to rule on legal proceedings or disputes*" (Article 18.3).[374] The first restriction derives from the exclusive jurisdiction of the authorities of the forum over coercive enforcement measures to be carried out in their territory. If persons affected by the liquidator's acts do not voluntarily agree to those acts being carried out and coercive measures are required with regard to assets or persons, the liquidator, whose powers are recognised by virtue of Article 18.1, must apply to the local authorities to have them adopted and implemented.[375] The second safeguard has a different foundation and makes sense, above all, when it is the court itself which is performing administration functions or, in addition, when the law of the opening entitles the liquidator to resolve specific disputes.[376]

369. The *exercise* of the liquidator's powers is also subject to certain restrictions. As we have just seen, the nature, contents and scope of the liquidator's powers are determined by the law of the State of opening *(lex fori concursus)*. But according to Article 18.3, "*In exercising his powers, the liquidator shall comply with the law of the Member State within the territory of which he intends to take action, in particular with regard to procedures for the realisation of assets*".

370. The English text of Article 18.3 seems stronger than other linguistic versions and must be construed in accordance with them: compare "*shall comply with*" with "*doit respecter*" in the French text, "*zu beachten*" in the German version, or "*deberá respetar*" in the Spanish Text. The taking into account of these linguistic versions provides us with the key for understanding the meaning of Article 18.3. The idea underlying this provision is that the liquidator must take the constraints of the outside world as given. He must manage and operate the property under his control according to the requirements of the laws of the Member State in which the property is situated or in which he intends to take action, as any other person would be bound to do. For example, factories under his control cannot pollute in insolvency any more than they can outside of insolvency; the liquidator cannot remove cultural goods from the territory of a State if the rules concerning the protection of the historical and cultural heritage of this State prohibit the export of such a good;[377] the duty to inform the national authorities on matters related to employment must also becomplied with by the foreign liquidator with respect of the local establishment.[378]

---

[373] Virgós/Schmit Report, Margin No. 161.

[374] Virgós/Schmit Report, Margin No. 164; Virgós, pp. 29–30; Trunk (1997), p. 247; Balz (1996a), p. 952; Lüke (1998), p. 296; Leible/Staudinger (2000), p. 562.

[375] Virgós/Schmit Report, Margin No. 164.a.

[376] See Virgós/Schmit Report, No. 63 *in fine*.

[377] Virgós/Schmit Report, Margin No. 164; Balz (1996a), p. 952; Virgós, p. 29; Leible/Staudinger (2000), p. 562; see also Geimer, Margin No. 3507 and Potthast, pp. 112–113 (presenting the different models).

[378] Herchen, p. 145; Geimer, Margin No. 3507.

371. The same idea applies with regard to the *procedures for the realisation of* assets. Both the possibility of realising assets and the form in which this is done (e.g. a public auction, a private sale, etc.) are determined by the law of the State of opening (*lex fori concursus*). Where this law requires a particular form of realisation (i.e. a public auction), the procedural means to be followed (i.e. the way in which the public auction is to be effected) shall be determined by the law of the Member State in which the measure is to take place (e.g. where the property is situated). Conversely, even if the State where the property is situated requires a specific form of realisation (e.g. public auction), the liquidator may dispose it of by private sale if the law of the State of opening so allows.

> *NB.* This Article does not seek to distinguish between the content and the manner of exercise of a liquidator's powers, whereby the content (i.e. the substantive powers) become subject to the law of the State of opening (*lex fori concursus*) but the procedures and manners in which those powers are to be exercised are determined by the local law (*lex loci actus*).[379] Its aim is more attenuated: to ensure compliance with the general rules of the State where the liquidator exercises his powers. Article 18.3 does not subject the exercise of the powers of the liquidator to the relevant local law (it does not say that the exercise of those powers is governed by the *lex loci actus*), but rather is content to impose a duty to respect the local laws when exercising the powers conferred on the liquidator by the law of the State of opening.

The forms of realisation of assets in the different Member States may vary from a disposal through private sale to a judicial conveyance to which the normal rules regarding sale do not apply; from a sale of the estate, in all or in part, as a whole, to a piecemeal realisation. Furthermore, the role of the liquidator in deciding the form in which the realisation is to take place is also different in the various Member States. According to the Insolvency Regulation, both the freedom given to the liquidator and the forms of realisation are determined by the law of the State of opening. For example, it corresponds to this law to decide if the sale of immovable property located in another Member State can be effected in the market on an private basis or only by public auction conducted or supervised by an authority (judicial or otherwise). But if, pursuant to the law of the State of opening, an immovable asset has to be sold by public auction, then the liquidator can sell the assets only in accordance with the procedures laid down for public auctions by the relevant local law: that of the State in which the asset is located.[380]

3.3. Proof of the liquidator's appointment (Article 19)

372. As stated above, the appointment of the liquidator and the exercise of his powers benefit from the principle of automatic recognition provided for by the Regulation and consequently no preliminary procedure, registration or publication is

---

[379] Which would furthermore pose serious problems of characterisation POTTHAST, p. 117; HERCHEN, p. 144.

[380] VIRGÓS/SCHMIT Report, Margin No. 164; BALZ (1996b), p. 515; HERCHEN, pp. 143–146; LEIBLE/STAUDINGER (2000), p. 562.

required.[381] Nevertheless, in the exercise of his powers in other Member states, the liquidator may need to *prove* his *appointment* or the *scope of his powers*:

(a) For the first of these purposes, Article 19 provides that *proof of* the liquidator's *appointment* may be established by presenting " ... *a certified copy of the original decision appointing him or by any other certificate issued by the court which has jurisdiction*". The aim of this certificate is to establish evidence that the person designated in the certificate of appointment is the liquidator in a particular set of insolvency proceedings opened in another Member State. The original decision or the certificate is exempt from legalisation or any other similar formality, such as the "apostille" provided for by the 1965 Hague Convention.[382] The second section of Article 19 adds that a translation into the official language or one of the official *languages* of the Member State in whose territory the liquidator intends to act may be required. This translation must comply with the requirements established in that State for the translation of official documents.[383]

(b) The Insolvency Regulation, however, does not regulate *proof* of *the powers* of the liquidator. In the event of doubt or dispute, proof may be provided by means of a certificate issued by the court which has appointed him, specifying the said powers (under the same conditions as those established in Article 19), or by any other means of proof recognised by the law of the State where the liquidator intends to exercise those powers.[384]

> *Objections to the liquidator's powers.* The Insolvency Regulation does not contain specific rules on the procedures to be followed in the event of a dispute or challenge to the exercise of the liquidator's powers. The general rules will therefore apply, as explained in the VIRGÓS/SCHMIT Report (No. 166). The key to applying these rules lies in the grounds for opposition: (a) When opposition concerns *non-recognition*, in accordance with the Regulation, of the insolvency proceedings or of the liquidator's appointment, jurisdiction will lie with the authorities of the Member State where the liquidator intends to exercise his powers; this solution will also apply when the grounds for opposition are a *breach* by the liquidator of the provisions of the Regulation which govern the exercise of his powers in other Member States, such as Article 18.1 or Article 18.3. (b) When opposition concerns the *substance* of the exercise of those powers, and not only proof thereof (i.e. an objection that the liquidator is misusing his powers or that a given action requires the prior consent of the insolvency court), jurisdiction on the merits will lie with the authorities of the State of opening.

3.4. The temporary administrator (Article 38)

373. The Insolvency Regulation does not establish specific provisions regarding *temporary administrators*. This means that the general rules apply. The figure of the temporary administrator is contained in the legislation of some Member States and

---

[381] VIRGÓS/SCHMIT Report, Margin No. 160; on the rules regarding opposition to the powers of the liquidator, see Margin No. 166; see also, VIRGÓS, p. 29; LEIBLE/STAUDINGER (2000), p. 561.

[382] VIRGÓS/SCHMIT Report, Margin No. 169; BALZ (1996a), p. 952; LEIBLE/STAUDINGER (2000), p. 562.

[383] VIRGÓS/SCHMIT Report, Margin No. 169; see Article 55.2 Regulation 44/2001 ("Brussels I").

[384] VIRGÓS/SCHMIT Report, Margin No. 170; FLETCHER, p. 286.

his function is to protect the integrity of the debtor's assets during the period between the request for the opening of the insolvency proceedings and the decision appointing a definitive liquidator.[385] The fact that it is the general rules which apply to this figure means that the appointment and the powers of the temporary administrator are subject to the *lex fori concursus* and, in principle, also benefit from the rules regarding recognition contained in the Insolvency Regulation. The temporary administrator may exercise the powers conferred on him by the *lex fori concursus principalis* in the rest of the Member States.

374. Article 38 contains, however, a special rule. When the court with jurisdiction for the main proceedings has appointed a temporary administrator with the aim of ensuring the preservation of the debtor's assets, Article 38 establishes that the said administrator *"shall be empowered to request any measures to secure and preserve any of the debtor's assets situated in another Member State"*. According to the same provision, the measures which he may request are those *"provided for under the law of that State, for the period between the request for the opening of insolvency proceedings and the judgment opening the proceedings"*.

375. In order to understand Article 38 correctly it is necessary to bear in mind its relationship with Article 29 of the Regulation. This latter provision empowers the liquidator in the main proceedings to request the opening of secondary proceedings in another Member State where the debtor has an establishment. The problem is that this power is only conferred on the main liquidator, *and not* on the temporary administrator.[386] The temporary administrator cannot request the opening of secondary territorial proceedings in another Member State. This fact can be exploited by the debtor or by certain creditors to engage in opportunistic behaviour to the detriment of the rest of the creditors.

> *Example*. The declaration opening the main proceedings is not enforceable against creditors with a right *in rem* over assets located in another Member State (Article 5). As we have already seen, one of the advantages of secondary proceedings is that they circumvent the possible drawback of this rule. The liquidator in the main proceedings may request the opening of secondary proceedings with the aim, for example, of staying individual enforcements. Nevertheless, Article 29 makes the power to request these proceedings dependent upon the definitive appointment of the liquidator in the main proceedings. The consequence of this restriction is easy to see. In the time between the request for the opening of the main proceedings and the request for the opening of secondary proceedings by the definitive liquidator in another Member State, those creditors with a right *in rem* may, for example, have enforced their security rights over the debtor's assets which are located in the latter State.

In order to prevent these risks, Article 38 empowers the temporary administrator to request those preservation measures specifically aimed at ensuring the effectiveness of the future opening of insolvency proceedings in the forum in question. Article 38 is conceived fundamentally as a way to anticipate the possible opening of *secondary* insolvency proceedings, by protecting the secondary estate from

---

[385] Virgós/Schmit Report, Margin No. 262; Herchen, p. 158.
[386] Virgós/Schmit Report, Margin No. 262.

a pre-opening stage. This is also why Article 38 presupposes the existence of an establishment of the debtor in the Member State where the preservation measures are requested (see Article 3.2) and encompasses those measures which, under the national insolvency law of that State, correspond to *winding-up proceedings* (remember that according to Article 3.3, secondary proceedings can only be winding-up proceedings).[387] This *ratio* does not mean that a request to open secondary proceedings must necessarily follow on from the adoption of such preservation measures. Once appointed, the definitive liquidator in the main proceedings is free to decide whether or not to request the opening of secondary proceedings.[388]

> *Prima facie evidence.* In many systems, the adoption of provisional orders or preservation measures requires the submission of prima facie evidence (*fumus boni iuris*). However, by arguing an analogy with Article 27 (which establishes that, once the main proceedings have been opened, it is not necessary to prove the insolvency of the debtor in order to open secondary proceedings), it seems reasonable to understand that the temporary administrator may request the adoption of these measures without the need to prove the insolvency of the debtor. It will be sufficient to present the decision of the State which has jurisdiction pursuant to Article 3.1 of the Regulation, whereby it was considered necessary to appoint a temporary administrator.

376. Having said that, this provision must not be interpreted *a sensu contrario*. The main aim of Article 38 is solely to prevent an erroneous interpretation of Article 29. Article 29 could be interpreted in the sense that as the temporary administrator cannot request the opening of secondary proceedings, neither can he request preservation measures aimed at provisionally ensuring the effectiveness of those proceedings. Article 38 prevents this interpretation by stating he *can* request measures aimed at provisionally ensuring the effectiveness of those proceedings. But this does not mean the only thing that the temporary administrator can do is that which is permitted him by Article 38. The appointment and powers of the temporary administrator are recognised in the other Member States pursuant to the Regulation (see Article 25 1 III). Therefore, with the limit derived from Article 29, the temporary administrator may exercise in the other Member States the powers conferred upon him by the *lex fori concursus*. With regard to provisional orders or preservation measures, nothing in the Regulation prevents the temporary administrator from requesting the Courts of the State of the main proceedings to impose preservation measures upon assets located in other States, and requesting their enforcement afterwards in accordance with Article 25.1 III,[389] or from requesting such measures directly of the courts of the State where assets of the debtor are located.[390] In this case, the aim of the measures is the protection of the estate against dissipation by the debtor and individual attachment by creditors, and not (as in Article 38) to protect the future opening of local insolvency proceedings. To this end, the temporary administrator may act in any Member State; naturally, with the same restrictions which apply to any liquidator.

---

[387] VIRGÓS/SCHMIT Report, Margin No. 262.

[388] VIRGÓS/SCHMIT Report, Margin No. 262 III.

[389] LÜKE (1998), p. 295; KOLMANN, p. 298.

[390] VIRGÓS/SCHMIT Report, Margin Nos 263 *in fine* and 78.

3.5. Table of liquidators' powers and duties

377. Even if the specific provisions are analysed elsewhere in this book, it may be of interest, given the central role that liquidators will play in the smooth operating of the Regulation, to offer a quick view of the liquidator's powers and duties which are established in the Insolvency Regulation itself:

Powers	Duties
Common to main and secondary liquidators: 1. Request publication in other Member State of the opening decision and the appointment of the liquidator (Article 21) 2. Participate in other insolvency proceedings on the same basis as a creditor (Article 32.3)	*Common to main and secondary liquidators:* 1. Communicate relevant information to each other (Article 31.1) 2. Cooperate with each other (Article 31.2) 3. Inform all known creditors in Member States of the opening of insolvency proceedings (Article 40.1) 4. Lodge in insolvency proceedings opened in other Member States claims which have been lodged in their own proceedings, provided it is in the interest of their holders (Article 32.2)
Specific to main liquidator: 1. Remove assets of the debtor from the territory of another Member State, subject to Articles 5 and 7 and secondary proceedings (Article 18.1) 2. Exercise right ex Article 20 (creditor shall return what he has obtained in another Member State) 3. Request registration in another Member State (Article 22) 4. Request opening of secondary proceedings in other Member State (Article 29) 5. Request stay of the process of liquidation of secondary proceedings (Article 33.1) 6. Propose a rescue plan or a composition in secondary proceedings (Articles 34.1 and 3) 7. Consent or bar any rescue plan or composition reached in secondary proceedings (Article 34.1 II) 8. Claim surplus assets (Article 35) 9. Request conversion of previous territorial proceedings in winding-up proceedings (Article 37)	*Specific to main liquidator:* 1. Publish notice of the decision opening insolvency proceedings in any Member State where the debtor has an establishment, if the law of this State so requires (Article 21.2) 2. Take all necessary measures to ensure registration of the decision opening insolvency proceedings in any member State which requires mandatory registration (Article 22.2) *Specific to secondary liquidators:* 1. Give the main liquidator the opportunity to submit proposals on the liquidation or use of the assets in the secondary proceedings (Article 31.3) or, when the applicable law allows to close the secondary proceedings without liquidation, on a rescue plan or a composition in the secondary proceedings (Articles 34.1 and 3)
Specific to temporary administrator: 1. Request pre-opening preservation measures in other Member States (Article 38)	

(Contd.)

Powers	Duties
Specific to secondary liquidators:	
1. Claim in another Member States that assets belonging to the secondary estate were removed after the opening of proceedings (Article 18.2)	2. Place surplus assets under the power of the main liquidator (Article 35)
2. Bring any action to set aside detrimental acts (Article 18.2, *in fine*)	

4. RETURN AND IMPUTATION: ARTICLE 20 (REMISSION)

378. Article 20.1 establishes a rule regarding *return* in the event that main pro-ceedings are opened. The creditor who, after the opening of these proceedings, obtains individual satisfaction of his claim breaches the principle of collective action on *which* the insolvency proceedings are based. That is why Article 20.1 establishes that, in such a case, the creditor shall return what he has obtained to the liquidator, subject to Articles 5 and 7 (see further Nos 462 *et seq.*).

Article 20.2 adds a rule regarding *imputation*. As we know, the Regulation per-mits the opening of parallel insolvency proceedings against the same debtor; one set of main proceedings and the rest as secondary. For this reason, when a creditor obtains partial or total payment in one of those proceedings, he is exercising a right conferred upon him by the Regulation itself and does not have to return anything. In the event that he has only obtained partial satisfaction, he may participate in the rest of the proceedings which have been opened in other States. Having said that, in an attempt to ensure the equal treatment of all of the creditors on a European Community scale, Article 20.2 IR establishes that after receiving this payment he may not participate in the distribution resulting from the other proceedings until the claims of the other creditors of the same ranking have been satisfied in the same percentage. For a more detailed analysis, see Nos 465 *et seq.*

5. PUBLICATION, REGISTRATION AND ASSOCIATED COSTS: ARTICLES 21–23 (REMISSION)

379. The publication of the declaration of insolvency is not a condition for recog-nition, but it *can* be relevant for assessing the behaviour of the persons affected, both within the framework of the Insolvency Regulation (see, e.g. Article 24) and within that of the applicable national law. For this reason, the Regulation contains certain rules of publication aimed at announcing, in those States where the insolvent debtor has assets or carries out economic activities, the new legal situation which affects the said debtor. The Regulation also contains specific rules concerning registration in a public register. The general aim of all of these rules is to enhance legal certainty in

other States and markets.[391] For a more detailed analysis of these rules, see *supra* Nos 264 *et seq.*

6. Honouring of an Obligation to the Insolvent Debtor: Article 24 (Remission)

380. The level of information on the debtor's solvency and the corresponding monitoring which can be expected from a creditor cannot be counted on from a debtor. Insofar as the Regulation does not impose an obligatory system of publication, situations may arise in which affected third parties, being unaware of the opening of the proceedings, honour their obligations in good faith *with the debtor* instead of with the liquidator. For this reason, it may seem unjustified to consider this payment as not having discharged the debt (see Recital 30). Article 24 aims to prevent this from occurring. To this end, it establishes that any person honouring an obligation for the benefit of a debtor who is subject to insolvency proceedings will be considered to have discharged that obligation if he was unaware that the said proceedings had been opened; the second paragraph adds a presumption *iuris tantum* aimed at shifting the burden of proof: if the obligation is honoured prior to the publication provided for in Article 21, unawareness is presumed. If it is honoured after publication, the opposite is presumed (see also No. 273).

7. Recognition and Enforcement of "Other" Insolvency Decisions (Article 25)

7.1. Decisions included

7.1.1. In general

381. As we have already seen, the Insolvency Regulation contemplates insolvency proceedings as a complex procedure in which the successive decisions which are adopted enjoy relative autonomy. For this reason, Article 16 deals with the recognition of the declaration of the opening of the insolvency proceedings and the effects thereof (see Articles 17, 18, 20 and 24), while Article 25 deals with the recognition of *"other judgments"* (denoting, in broad terms, any *insolvency decision*): *"Judgments handed down by a court whose judgment concerning the opening of proceedings is recognised in accordance with Article 16 and which concern the course and closure of insolvency proceedings, and compositions approved by that court shall also be recognised with no further formalities"*. Therefore, with regard to *recognition*, the same rules apply as for the recognition of the declaration of opening. Recognition of the decision opening insolvency proceedings is obviously a precondition for the recognition of any other further decision handed down in those proceedings.

---

[391] Virgós, p. 23; Leible/Staudinger (2000), p. 564.a.

NB. On the concept of *"judgement"* and of *"court"* see No.348. Any judgment on *criminal matters* which may be handed down in connection with the insolvency of the debtor remains outside the sphere of application of the Insolvency Regulation.

382. Article 25 applies to the following insolvency decisions: (a) decisions handed down by a court whose decision concerning the opening of insolvency proceedings is recognised in accordance with Article 16 and which concern the *conduct and closure* of insolvency proceedings; (b) *compositions* approved or confirmed by that court; (c) *decisions* deriving directly from the insolvency proceedings and which are *closely linked* with them, even if they were handed down by another court; and (d) *preservation measures* adopted in connection with the opening or conduct of those proceedings.

The concept of decisions relating to the conduct and closure of the proceedings handed down by the court which declared the opening does not give rise to difficulties. Therefore, we shall concentrate on the rest of the decisions encompassed by Article 25.

7.1.2. *Insolvency plans, compositions and comparable measures*

383. According to Article 25, *"compositions approved by that court* (the court whose judgment concerning the opening of proceedings is recognised in accordance with Article 16) *shall also be recognised with no further formalities"* (parenthesis added). Thus, compositions approved by the court of opening are subject to the same rules of recognition and enforcement which we have already looked at. Naturally, recognition of the decision opening the insolvency proceedings is a pre-condition for recognition of the composition. Whether the composition has a contractual or judicial nature according to the law of the State of origin, it will be recognised in other Member States through Articles 16 and following of the Insolvency Regulation. However, a composition may not produce more effects in the forum than in the State of origin, nor can it be recognised with a different nature. The principle of *the extension of effects*, both of procedural and substantive nature, also applies here. Recognition includes effects such as the deferment of payment, the discharge of debt and the value of the composition as an enforceable instrument. Enforcement, in turn, requires the composition to be an enforceable instrument according to the law of the State of origin *and* to obtain a prior *declaration of enforceability* in the forum State by means of an exequatur or registration.

Explanation. Pursuant to Article 25.1, recognition of the composition seems to be conditional upon it having been *approved* by the court which opened the insolvency proceedings. Under the law of most Member States, compositions and comparable measures are produced in a two-step procedure. First the parties affected will adopt, by the legally required majority, the measure and then the insolvency court will decide whether to confirm or to reject it. Article 25 was drafted in the light of this solution. However, the national law in question might provide for only one decision maker, either the parties affected or the court (as is the case in France). Article 25.1 covers all of these alternatives. This can be easily understood in the light of the concept of *"court"* employed by the Regulation (the person or body empowered by national law to open one of the proceedings listed in the Annexes of the Regulation) and the implications thereof.

384. In principle, the composition has the same scope as the proceedings within whose framework it is adopted: (a) if the composition is adopted in the main proceedings *ex* Article 3.1, it will have universal scope, both with regard to the assets and with regard to the creditors affected, albeit naturally with the same exceptions as the proceedings themselves (i.e. Articles 5 and 7) and as long as no territorial proceedings have been opened. (b) If the composition is adopted within the context of territorial proceedings, its effects are limited to the assets which are located in that territory. For this reason, consent by creditors to a territorial composition cannot be interpreted as a waiver of the realisation of their claims upon the debtor's assets located in other States. This is clear in Article 17.2 for all territorial proceedings and in Article 34.2 for secondary proceedings (see Nos 332 *et seq.*).

385. Recognition of the composition in the other Member States is automatic; it does not require any intermediary measure in the forum, such as *exequatur* or registration. This means that the liquidator or the debtor himself may resort to the composition to oppose any claim put forward by a creditor bound by that composition.[392] The consequences of a breach of the composition on the part of the debtor are also determined by the law of the State of opening (*lex fori concursus*).

386. All of the above is, *mutatis mutandis*, valid for comparable measures such as *concordats*, *agreements*, *settlements* or *arrangements concerned with reorganising or restructuring* the debtor, and *insolvency plans*.

387. With regard to public policy as a restriction upon the recognition, see *infra* No. 406.

7.1.3. Insolvency-derived decisions

388. According to Article 25.1 II, the system of recognition of the Insolvency Regulation also applies to "*judgments deriving directly from the insolvency proceedings and which are closely linked with them, even if they were handed down by another court*" (i.e. any court other than the court of opening of the insolvency proceedings).

In order to understand this provision the following fact must be taken into account. The 1968 Brussels Convention and Regulation 44/2001 which followed it exclude insolvency matters from their sphere of application; in the ECJ ruling of 22 February 1979 (Case 133/78),[393] the European Court looked to the nature of the action exercised and not to the character of the judicial body as the determinative criterion. In the negotiating process leading up to the Insolvency Regulation it was considered that this criterion should not be modified (for more details see Nos 86 *et seq.*).

In this respect, Article 25.1 II fulfils a double function: (a) on the one hand, it ensures that the Insolvency Regulation will apply to those decisions which, in accordance with Article 1.2.b of Regulation 44/2001 are not included in the scope of application of the latter; and (b) on the other hand, it confirms that this delimitation is valid irrespectively of the character of the judicial body entertaining the action.

---

[392] See REINHART (1995), pp. 241–245.
[393] See also ECJ ruling of 29 April 1999, Case C-267/97.

This provision was needed to make it clear to the Member States that the Insolvency Regulation continues to apply to recognition of those decisions, even though the decision originates in a court other than the court which opened the insolvency proceedings.[394] Article 25.1 II does not restrict its scope of application to decisions handed down by the courts of the Member State which has jurisdiction according to Article 3, but refers indiscriminately to "another court". In Chapter 2, we have seen that there are good reasons to defend an interpretation of this provision which includes decisions taken by the courts of a Member State other than the State of the opening of insolvency proceedings (see Nos 95 *et seq.*).

389. For its part, Article 25.2 is solely aimed at preventing gaps between the two Regulations (Regulation 44/2001 and the Insolvency Regulation) and to this end it indicates that the recognition and enforcement of decisions other than those contemplated in section 1 of Article 25 shall be governed by Regulation 44/2001 (which replaces the 1968 Brussels Convention referred to in the text of Article 25), provided that that Regulation is applicable.

7.1.4. *Preservation measures*

390. Article 25.1 III also applies to *preservation measures*. In principle, the court with jurisdiction for the main insolvency may, given the universal nature of the proceedings, adopt preservation measures with extraterritorial scope, i.e. over assets or activities of the debtor which are located in another Member State. These measures will be recognised and enforced in the other States according to the regime of the Insolvency Regulation.[395]

391. The Regulation establishes a special rule (Article 25.1 III) to clarify that preservation measures adopted *after* the *request* for a declaration of opening, but *before* the *declaration* itself, also benefit from its system of recognition. Those measures adopted *after* the declaration of opening pose no problem as they are already covered by Article 25.1. However, measures which are adopted between the request and the declaration of opening are not covered by the literal terms of Article 25.1 I. The purpose of the third paragraph of Article 25.1 is to establish that this Article also applies to any measures adopted in this phase which are aimed at ensuring the successful outcome of the insolvency proceedings by preserving, *inter alia*, the integrity of the estate.[396]

> *Problem: measures prior to the request.* There is a gap in the Insolvency Regulation. In the first place, it establishes the general rule regarding recognition of the preservation measures adopted after the declaration of insolvency. Article 25.1 III extends this rule to the previous phase, i.e. the phase between the request for a declaration and the declaration itself. But the Regulation does not contain any rule whatsoever regarding measures adopted *before* presenting the request (*ante causam* preservation measures). If we bear in mind the fact that the aim of Article 25.2 is to prevent the existence of gaps between the Insolvency

---

[394] HERCHEN, pp. 229–230; HAUBOLD, p. 160.
[395] HERCHEN, pp. 158–161; KOLMANN, pp. 297–298; also HUBER, p. 150.
[396] See POTTHAST, pp. 117–118.

Regulation and Regulation 44/2001 ("Brussels I" Regulation), it does not seem possible to infer that this gap must be filled by referral to national law. The most reasonable thing is to think that the Insolvency Regulation will apply when the grounds for those measures are related to insolvency, and Regulation 44/2001 will apply when the grounds are general civil or commercial law.

392. Preservation measures adopted in the main proceedings will benefit from the regime of recognition and enforcement contained in the Insolvency Regulation even though they have been adopted *ex parte* (i.e. *unilaterally*). The only restriction on these measures is that imposed by the public policy of the requested State.[397]

7.2. Enforcement of decisions

393. As already explained, the Insolvency Regulation maintains a distinction between recognition and enforcement which is similar to that adopted by Council Regulation 44/2001 on Jurisdiction and the Recognition and Enforcement of Judgments in Civil and Commercial Matters. In fact, a number of questions in the Insolvency Regulation are treated through remittance to the text of Council Regulation 44/2001.

394. As far as *enforcement* is concerned, Article 25.1 *in fine* establishes that the "judgments" handed down by the judge in the main proceedings "*shall be enforced in accordance with Articles 31–51, with the exception of Article 34(2), of the Brussels Convention on Jurisdiction and the Enforcement of Judgments in Civil and Commercial Matters, as amended by the Conventions of Accession to this Convention*". This reference to the Brussels Convention must be replaced by the corresponding provisions of the Regulation which substituted it; in particular by Articles 38–58, with the exception of Article 45.1, of *Regulation 44/2001* on Jurisdiction and the Recognition and Enforcement of Judgments in Civil and Commercial Matters (see No. 396).

Relationship between Articles 16 and 25. The need for a procedure of *exequatur* or *registration* for the purposes of enforcement is determined by the nature of the effects which the foreign decision is desired to have in the forum (enforcement or not), and not by where this decision is contained (in the decision opening proceedings itself or in a different decision). Consequently, if the decision opening the insolvency proceedings contains rulings which are enforceable, their enforceability in other States is governed by Article 25, and not by Article 16, which only deals with recognition.[398]

395. Traditionally, enforcement has required the prior verification of the foreign decision by the authorities of the State where the enforcement is sought, through a

---

[397] Virgós/Schmit Report, Margin No. 207, justifying this solution in the sphere of the Insolvency Regulation in contrast to the jurisprudence of the Court of Justice established in Case 125/79 for the Brussels Convention.
[398] Thus, Virgós/Schmit, Margin No. 189; Balz (1996A), p. 953; Kemper, p. 1314, note 33; Eidenmüller (1996a), p. 7; Huber, p. 150; against, Trunk (1997), p. 246.

system of *exequatur*, registration or an equivalent procedure. The Insolvency Regulation does not change this regime. Therefore, foreign decisions cannot have direct access to enforcement in the forum, but must first obtain a "declaration of enforceability" from a domestic court, through a procedure of *exequatur* or registration.

396. The Insolvency Regulation does not regulate this procedure, but imports instead the enforcement mechanism established by the 1968 Brussels Convention, which has been now replaced by Regulation 44/2001 on civil jurisdiction and enforcement.

*Regulation 44/2001 displaces the 1968 Brussels Convention.*The Insolvency Regulation does not refer directly to Regulation 44/2001, but rather to the 1968 Brussels Convention on Jurisdiction and the Enforcement of Judgements in Civil and Commercial Matters, as amended by the successive Conventions on the accession of new Member States to this Convention; this Convention is the immediate predecessor to Council Regulation 44/2001 and was the text which was in force when the Insolvency Regulation was adopted, and this explains the referral. There is no doubt that all the referrals made by the Insolvency Regulation to the 1968 Brussels Convention are "dynamic" and they must now be understood as being made to Regulation 44/2001 ("Brussels I" Regulation). Article 68.2 of Regulation 44/2001 confirms this interpretation: "in so far as this Regulation replaces the provisions of the Brussels Convention between the Member States, *any reference to the convention shall be understood as a reference to this Regulation*".

397. The most important features of the regime of *exequatur* or *registration* for enforcement established by Regulation 44/2001 on jurisdiction and the recognition and enforcement of judgments in civil and commercial matters ("Brussels I" Regulation) are the following: (a) the request must be filed before the court or the competent authorities indicated in Annex II of the Regulation; territorial jurisdiction will be determined by the domicile of the party against whom the enforcement is requested or by the place of enforcement (Article 39); (b) the procedure is in the first instance unilateral and the judge must restrict himself to verifying *ex officio* the presentation of the documents indicated in Articles 53–54 (Article 41); (c) the decision handed down by that court is open to appeal, by any of the parties, before the courts indicated in Annex III of the Regulation; in such a case, the procedure is contradictory. The period for filing the appeal against the granting of the enforcement is one month if the party against which the said enforcement is requested has his domicile in the requested State; in all other cases, the period is two months (Article 43); (d) finally, a further appeal from among those provided for in Annex IV is possible against this decision. The "Brussels I" Regulation also contains specific rules with regard to the possibility of taking preservation measures during the *exequatur* procedure (Article 47) or the possibility of suspending the procedure if the decision was still not final in the State of origin (Article 46).

NB. Where the decision on recognition has *erga omnes* effect, the usual procedure of *exequatur* or registration should be adapted to the collective nature of the insolvency proceedings through the provision of adequate publicity.

398. This referral to Regulation 44/2001 on civil jurisdiction and enforcement contains an important exception: the grounds for rejecting the *exequatur* or

registration (Article 25.1 *in fine*). These grounds are not taken from Regulation 44/2001 but are established by the Insolvency Regulation itself (Article 26 *infra*). From the genesis of the Insolvency Regulation, it is clear that the desire was to exclude the regime of grounds for non-recognition of the Brussels Convention and subject rejection solely to the regime of the Insolvency Regulation itself.[399] That is why Article 25.1 refers to Articles 31–51 of the Brussels Convention, but excludes Article 34.2, which contained the grounds for rejection provided for in Articles 27 and 28 of the Convention itself. In Regulation 44/2001, which replaces the Convention between the Member States, the parallel Article to Article 34.2 of the Convention is Article 45.1. In short, the new Article 25.1 *in fine* of the Insolvency Regulation should be read as if it stated the following: *such judgments shall be enforced in accordance with Articles 38–58, with the exception of Article 45.1 of Council Regulation 44/2001 on Jurisdiction and the Recognition and Enforcement of Judgements in civil and Commercial Matters.*

399. The Insolvency Regulation, complemented by the Regulation 44/2001, only regulates *authorisation* for the enforcement (i.e. the *declaration of enforceability*). The *enforcement* itself is governed by the law of the State where enforcement is sought. If the conditions provided for by the Insolvency Regulation are fulfilled, the authorities of the requested State shall be obliged to grant this authorisation pursuant to the Regulation. National law thereafter determines the methods by which the decision of another Member State is enforced by the national authorities. The usual methods of coercive enforcement provided for by the national law will be used, albeit adapted, where necessary, to guarantee the "useful effect" (*effet utile*) of the Insolvency Regulation; i.e. to render effective in other States the specific decisions taken by the court of opening.[400]

8. GROUNDS FOR NON-RECOGNITION: ARTICLES 25.3 AND 26

8.1. General aspects

400. Article 26 of the Insolvency Regulation establishes public policy as the only *grounds for non-recognition* of an insolvency decision originating in another Member State and falling within the scope of application of the Insolvency regulation: *"Any Member State may refuse to recognise insolvency proceedings opened in another Member State or to enforce a judgment handed down in the context of such proceedings where the effects of such recognition or enforcement would be manifestly contrary to that State's public policy, in particular its fundamental principles or the constitutional rights and liberties of the individual".*

The Insolvency Regulation is based on mutual trust and on the equivalence of the courts of the Member States (i.e. on *Community trust*) and, therefore, on a general

---

[399] VIRGÓS/SCHMIT Report, Margin No. 192 *in fine*; HAUBOLD, p. 159. The purpose of this remission to the Brussels Convention was to share the procedures already established for civil and commercial matters.

[400] VIRGÓS/SCHMIT Report, Margin No. 190; VIRGÓS, p. 27.

presumption that the other Member State's decision is valid. This is why the only general cause it establishes for opposing recognition is where the effects of recognition would be contrary to public policy (Article 26).

401. This Article is complemented by a further two provisions: (a) Article 25.3, which excludes certain decisions that may enchroach on fundamental rights and are not central to the insolvency proceedings, from the obligation to recognise and enforce: *"Member States shall not be obliged to recognise or enforce a judgment referred to in paragraph 1 which might result in a limitation of personal freedom or postal secrecy"*. Here each Member State will decide according to its own standards. (b) Article 16.1 II, which imposes a restriction upon the application of the public policy clause: the declaration of opening shall be recognised even when *"... on account of his capacity, insolvency proceedings cannot be brought against the debtor in other Member States"* (*i.e.* in the recognising Member State). This provision clearly prevents Member States from resorting to public policy as grounds for non-recognition.

402. As already stated, the grounds for non-recognition have been reduced to a minimum. This restriction has major consequences:

(a) In the first place, it means that the foreign decision cannot be subject to review as regards its *substance*, not even with regard to the (mis)application of the rules contained in the Insolvency Regulation. All questions regarding the merits of the decision must be discussed before the courts of the State of origin of the decision. The Regulation excludes any general inquiry into the merits of a foreign decision. In the State where recognition is sought, the courts may only review the foreign decision in order to determine whether or not its recognition or enforcement in the forum would have effects contrary to the public policy of that State.[401]

(b) In the second place, the *international jurisdiction* of the court of origin cannot be reviewed in other Member States. These may only verify that the decision emanates from a court of a Member State which claims jurisdiction under Article 3 of the Insolvency Regulation. Opposition to the jurisdiction of the court of origin is also only admissible in that State.[402] Therefore, any interested party seeking to challenge the international jurisdiction of the court of opening of insolvency proceedings must go to that State to appeal against the decision asserting jurisdiction. Within the framework of those proceedings, it is possible to request a preliminary ruling to the European Court of Justice (see No. 4). Article 16 IR cannot be invoked to claim that the requested State may review the jurisdiction of the State of origin.[403] Although its wording could give rise to some doubt, Recital 22 is very clear on this point when it states, in the case of two States claiming jurisdiction, that *"The decision of the first court to open proceedings should be recognised in the other Member States without those Member States having the power to scrutinise the court's decision"*. The rule

---

[401] VIRGÓS/SCHMIT Report, Margin No. 202.1.

[402] VIRGÓS/SCHMIT Report, Margin No. 202.2; VIRGÓS, pp. 30–31; LÜKE (1998), p. 287; LEIBLE/STAUDINGER (2000), p. 568; GEIMER, Margin No. 3514; DUURSMA-KEPPLINGER/DUURSMA/CHALUPSKY, (2002), p. 358.

[403] HUBER, p. 146.

on international jurisdiction is common to both the court of opening and the court of the recognising State and may be interpreted and applied with the same authority by each of them. Once a decision has been handed down by the court of opening with regard to its interpretation and application, this decision benefits from the principle of mutual trust in other Member States. A review of the international jurisdiction of that court is not possible in other Member States. For this reason, the public policy test referred to in Article 26 of the Insolvency Regulation may not be applied to the rules relating to jurisdiction.[404]

> *Difficulty.* The scheme of recognition provided by the Insolvency Regulation presupposes that we are concerned with proceedings which fall within its *sphere of application*; i.e. that we are dealing with insolvency proceedings opened in another Member State and which benefit from the regime of the Regulation. This is true for both its substantive sphere, and for its territorial or spatial sphere: (a) with regard to its *substantive* sphere, the establishment of a system of a list of proceedings which are encompassed prevents problems of characterisation: in the case of proceedings included in those lists, the judge in the requested State must simply apply the rules regarding recognition and enforcement contained in the Regulation. Furthermore, the decision or "judgment" must be an insolvency decision; the Regulation does not apply to decisions on other matters even if handed down by the insolvency court (Article 25.2 IR reiterates this principle). (b) With regard to the spatial sphere, the debtor's centre of main interests fulfils a double function. If the insolvent debtor is not located in a Member State, the Insolvency Regulation is not applicable, but if it is located in a Member State, that state will have international jurisdiction to open main proceedings. If the courts of the recognising State were to control the spatial applicability of the Regulation, this would be tantamount to a judicial review of the international jurisdiction of the foreign court; and it is clear from the genetic argument that this was consciously excluded. Therefore, the courts of the recognising State must respect the decision on this question taken by the courts of the State of origin. That is why (i) if the latter considered that the debtor had his centre of main interests outside the EC and, consequently, did not apply the Insolvency Regulation, the judge of the requested State must respect this opinion and apply his national law (not the Insolvency Regulation) to the recognition of the decision originating in that State; (ii) if, on the other hand, the judge of the State of origin considered that the debtor had his centre of main interests inside the territory of that State and, consequently, applied the Insolvency Regulation, the judge of the requested State must likewise respect this opinion and apply the Insolvency Regulation to the recognition of the foreign decision.

8.2. Public policy

8.2.1. Elements of the test

403. The only grounds for non-recognition admitted by the Insolvency Regulation is *public policy*: Any Member State may refuse to recognise insolvency proceedings opened in another Member State or insolvency decisions handed down in the context of such proceedings when the effects of such recognition or enforcement

---

[404] LÜKE (1998), p. 287; HUBER, p. 146.

are manifestly contrary to its public policy. Public policy is what is known in continental legal theory as a "general clause" which operates to exclude certain results from a given legal system. Its function is to preserve the value-coherence of any legal system: typically, human rights and other constitutionally protected rights, idiosyncratic values of the community, and the States' ordopolitical policies have been protected by means of the public policy clause in the Member States.

404. Three important features should be taken into account with regard to the way the public policy test operates in the Insolvency Regulation:

(a) Public policy is based on the fundamental principles of the law of the requested State and therefore the concept does not necessarily have a uniform content throughout the Community. Each State determines the content of its own public policy and can define the criteria of which it is made up. However, Article 26 does not entail a "blank cheque" referral to national law:[405] the limits of the concept of public policy are a matter for the interpretation of the Insolvency Regulation as a part of Community law. Therefore, the European Court of Justice may review the limits within which the courts of a Member State may have recourse to the concept of public policy for the purpose of denying recognition. In other words, Article 26 does not permit broad interpretations by the national courts which go beyond what can be reasonably considered as necessary to protect the fundamental principles of the law of a given Member State.

Evolution. In spite of the fact that each State defines its fundamental principles and its constitutional rights and guarantees, we must bear in mind that all of the Member States to a large extent share the same fundamental principles (e.g. the 1950 European Convention for the protection of Human Rights and Fundamental Liberties or, more recently, albeit lacking any direct legal force, the European Union's Charter of fundamental rights). This fact not only helps to significantly reduce the play of this exception, but also provides an objective criterion for review by the ECJ.[406] Obviously, the new European Constitution, once in force, will represent a major step forward in this sense.

(b) "Manifestly" means that the provision should only operate in exceptional cases, where this contrary nature is obvious or unequivocal.[407]

(c) Furthermore, the public policy review required by this provision is not an abstract control, but a *results-based control*. The question is not about compatibility *in the abstract* (e.g. due to the differences between the laws involved) with the public policy of the requested State, but *in concrete terms*, in view of the result achieved. The question is whether, in the light of the specific circumstances of the case, recognition or enforcement of that decision would bring into the forum a result or an effect which is incompatible with that public policy.[408] Because the verification of

---

[405] See also, with regard to the "Brussels I" Regulation, ECJ C-7/98, dated 22 March 2000, Margin No. 23.

[406] See ECJ ruling C-7/98, Margin No. 25.

[407] VIRGÓS/SCHMIT Report, Margin No. 205; VIRGÓS, p. 31; LEIBLE/STAUDINGER (2000), p. 567; DUURSMA-KEPPLINGER/DUURSMA/CHALUPSKY, (2002), p. 361.

[408] See SPELLENBERG, p. 186.

conformity with public policy is geared towards the *result* of recognition or enforcement, *all* of the specific circumstances of the case must be taken into account,[409] including the connections of the case with the requested State at the relevant time (i.e. the *Inlandsbeziehung* or domestic contacts).[410] The formula used by Article 26 whereby any Member State "*may* refuse to recognise" also reflects this idea of a case-specific test of compatibility.

8.2.2. Content

405. The public policy clause of Article 26 protects fundamental principles of the law of the forum, of both a *procedural* and *substantive* nature; the first refers to the procedure followed in the foreign State, the second to the material outcome thereof.[411]

406. From the *procedural* point of view, public policy protects debtor and creditors from any failure to observe due process. Due process requirements become especially important when, as occurs in the Insolvency Regulation, a review of the substance of the foreign decision is not permitted. The assessment in question must be carried out from the perspective of the requested State, with the restriction indicated in the previous paragraph: public policy does not entail a general review of the correctness of the foreign proceedings, but rather of essential procedural guarantees, such as the adequate opportunity to be heard and the right to participate in the proceedings.

Due process and insolvency proceedings. In very general terms, the right to due process consists of three specific guarantees: being notified of the proceedings, being given the opportunity to put allegations before the court, and being given the opportunity to provide proof to substantiate such allegations. The latter two guarantees involve the right to participate in the proceedings. It is the first of these guarantees, concerning service and notification abroad, which has presented most problems in non-insolvency related practice within Europe. That is why the 1968 Brussels Convention regulated the issue as autonomous grounds for non-recognition (Article 27.2) apart from the general public policy clause (Article 27.1). Regulation 44/2001 has retained this same solution, although it has substantially modified the contents of the said provision. According to its Article 34.2 recognition of a foreign decision will be denied *where it was given in default of appearance, if the defendant was not served with the document which instituted the proceedings or with an equivalent document in sufficient time and in such a way as to enable him to arrange for his defence, unless the defendant failed to commence proceedings to challenge the judgment when it was possible for him to do so.* This new formula provided by Article 34.2 is more in line with what the public policy clause would require.

The Virgós/Schmit Report explains how this procedural guarantee works in the sphere of the Insolvency Regulation.[412] In principle, the inclusion in the Insolvency Regulation of a provision similar to Article 34.2 of Regulation 44/2001 did not make much sense, either vis-à-vis the debtor or the creditors. *Vis-à-vis the debtor,* because in many cases the application for commencement is made by the debtor himself (typically in the case of

---

[409] Virgós/Schmit Report, Margin No. 204.

[410] See Spellenberg, p. 191.

[411] Virgós/Schmit Report, Margin No. 206; Virgós, p. 31; Lüke (1998), pp. 287 and 291; Herchen, p. 104.

[412] Margin No. 206.

reorganisation procedures). And in those cases in which the application for commencement is made by a creditor (in which case service to the debtor will be necessary), because the main jurisdiction corresponds to the courts where the debtor has his centre of main interests (Article 3.1). In such circumstances, it is difficult to imagine that the courts of another Member State are better placed to review service than those of the debtor's centre. *Vis-à-vis the creditors*, because Article 34.2 of Regulation 44/2001 contemplates a situation in which the service of the document instituting the proceedings is served upon the defendant; this does not apply to creditors because they are not "defendants". However, insolvency proceedings concern and directly affect creditors' rights and the principle of due process requires notice to be given of the proceedings to those whose rights are going to be affected. What happens is that the form in which this notice has to be given needs to be adapted to the collective nature of this type of proceedings and to the need to inform unknown creditors. The relevant issue, from the public policy perspective, is not so much that individual notice has been given, but that *the appropriate means have been used, according to the circumstances of the case*, to inform all affected parties of the commencement of the proceedings. Effective notification may be achieved through different means: publication in an official gazette or a commercial newspaper, use of public registries and individual notice are the most common options. What means are appropriate depends on the circumstances of the case, such as the geographical scope of the debtor's activities. The Insolvency Regulation establishes a set of rules specifically aimed at guaranteeing that creditors and other interested parties receive prompt notice of the proceedings, so that they have an opportunity to participate and to dispute the assertion of jurisdiction or the commencement itself: individual notice to known creditors (Article 40), publication and registration in other Member States (Articles 21 and 22). These rules complement the requirements on notice of the law of the State of opening (*lex fori concursus*). If the appropriate means have not been used, any diligent creditor who has not been informed about the proceedings, and whose right has been negatively affected by this, may invoke the public policy clause to oppose recognition. As is the case with Article 34.2, *in fine*, of Regulation 44/2001, this may be done only if the remedies available in the State of opening have been exhausted. As we shall see later, a negative response does not apply to the entire insolvency proceedings, but only to those decisions which negatively affect the rights of the creditor in question. Indirect proof of this is Article 24 IR. In any case, if, in the course of the proceedings, *individual decisions* are adopted *vis-à-vis* a specific creditor (for example, regarding the set-aside of a given transaction), it seems reasonable to demand guarantees which are, *mutatis mutandis*, equivalent to those contained in Article 34.2 of Regulation 44/2001.

The other aspect of the due process guarantee which may be of relevance is the right to participate in the proceedings. This right will be particularly important with regard to compositions and reorganisation plans.[413] As in the previous case, collective proceedings present certain special features that make it unsuitable to apply the standards of an ordinary lawsuit. Recognition can be opposed if the interested parties (typically, the creditors) were not given an effective opportunity to participate in the proceedings. However, because insolvency proceedings are collective proceedings (i.e. proceedings in which the creditors are forced into a collective group with a resulting loss of power to act individually), this right to participation can be satisfied through adequate "class" representation. In the laws of Member States, the creditor's collective interests may be represented by a meeting of creditors, a creditor's committee or a creditors' representative (even appointed by a neutral

---

[413] SPELLENBERG, pp. 194–197; FLESSNER (1992), pp. 203–204; LÜKE (1998), p. 291; HERCHEN, pp. 104–105.

authority), or a combination of these.[414] In the case of a rescue plan or a comparable measure, it is not a public policy requirement that the creditors consent to the plan. The *lex fori concursus* may empower the insolvency court to impose a plan upon the parties. Here it is not due process which it is at stake but the economic model of insolvency law: whether courts or market players decide. This is a risk assumed by the creditors when dealing with a debtor established in a given jurisdiction, as the *lex fori concursus* will determine the insolvency model and the respective role of debtor, creditors, courts and other authorities. The basic means of protection given to the creditors by the Insolvency Regulation against that specific risk is the possibility of opening secondary proceedings. Articles 5, 6 and 7 IR also play a protective role.

407. In the area of insolvency law, the *substantive* contents of public policy are *essentially* expressed by two elements: the principle of non-discrimination and the protection of private property. The principle of *non-discrimination* on the grounds of nationality is one of the basic principles of Community legislation (see Article 12 of the EC Treaty). The Insolvency Regulation itself confirms this with regard to the creditors and extends it to other criteria such the residence or domicile (Article 39). This means, for example, that recognition of a foreign decision can be opposed if that decision has entailed a greater economic sacrifice for certain creditors based solely on the fact that they are foreign or have their domicile in another Member State.[415]

Property rights, as guaranteed by a number of national constitutions, can also form part of the public policy clause.[416] From the point of view of the debtor, the public policy clause could be invoked when, for example, a declaration of insolvency is, in reality, a pretext for a confiscation contrary to the fundamental principles of the requested State;[417] from the point of view of the creditors, when a sacrifice of their rights is imposed upon them which is manifestly disproportionate or arbitrary. In the Community context such situations are not to be expected.

Inlandsbeziehung. When it comes to specifying the public policy clause one of the relevant facts to be taken into account is the greater or lesser connection with the recognising Member State. This can be important. In principle, the property rights guaranteed by each Constitution are not universal, but are restricted to the assets located within the territory of the State in question.[418]

408. The public policy clause cannot be used to prevent results implicitly contemplated by the Insolvency Regulation itself. Furthermore, national courts cannot use the public policy clause to introduce this requirement unilaterally into the system of the Regulation.[419]

---

[414] See European Principles, § 2.6.

[415] See STAEHLIN, pp. 58–59; also SPELLENBERG, p. 196.

[416] See HERCHEN, pp. 104–111; GEIMER, Margin No. 3516.

[417] See, with examples, HANISCH (1985), p. 1236.

[418] REINHART (1997), p. 1739.

[419] BALZ (1996a), p. 953; HUBER, p. 146; see also, FLESSNER (1992), pp. 205; *cfr.* HERCHEN, pp. 105–106.

For example, public policy cannot be invoked: (a) To reject the recognition of foreign rehabilitation proceedings simply due to the fact that the creditors have been dealt with worse than they would have been in a winding-up process. The Regulation renounced the imposition of any guarantee of the liquidation-value as a condition for the recognition of rescue plans and comparable measures, such as the "best interests of creditors" test or similar, according to which a plan is not recognised unless the creditors affected receive at least what they would have received in a liquidation. (b) To reject recognition by alleging that it would not have been possible to subject the debtor to an insolvency process in the forum (Article 16.1 II).[420]

NB. On this point, and with regard to the play of the public policy clause, the declaration of the Republic of Portugal (OJ, C 183, of 30 June 2000) must be taken into account; see *infra* No. 457.

409. Article 25.3 anticipates the possible recourse to public policy in a matter of high sensitivity and, consequently, excludes from the obligation to recognise or enforce any insolvency decision which has the effect of restricting the *personal freedom* or the *postal secrecy* of the insolvent debtor or of any other person. Insofar as these decisions directly affect fundamental liberties, the Member States decided to retain the freedom to decide upon recognition and enforcement, even when the said decisions originate in another Member State.[421]

410. The Insolvency Regulation does not contemplate the existence of a decision which is *irreconcilable* in the requested State as grounds for non-recognition or enforcement (compare this with Regulation 44/2001, Articles 34.3 and 34.4). The reason is that it would be difficult for such a situation to arise as the jurisdiction established by the Insolvency Regulation is exclusive. Nevertheless, such situations may arise in practice: e.g. with regard to decisions originating in a non-Member State with which a Member State has a convention on Recognition (it must be remembered that the Insolvency Regulation respects international Conventions entered into by Member States with non-Member States before the Insolvency Regulation itself entered into force).

Example. Let us imagine a corporate debtor whose centre of main interests is in a Member State (F1), but which has been incorporated in a non-Member State (F2) where its registered office is also situated. It might occur that insolvency proceedings have been opened against that debtor in non-Member State F2 on the basis of the location of his registered office, and that this declaration has been recognised in a Member State other than the first (let us say, State F3);[422] the powers of the liquidator appointed in F2 have likewise been recognised in F3. If insolvency proceedings are opened afterwards against the same debtor

---

[420] HUBER, p. 146.

[421] VIRGÓS/SCHMIT Report, Margin No. 187; see also BALZ (1996a), p. 952; LEIPOLD, p. 195.

[422] Recognition of the decision of non-Member State F2 will be governed by the national system of Private international Law of Member State F3, including any international convention in force.

in Member State F1 on the basis of the location of the centre of its main interests (Article 3.1) and the corresponding liquidator is appointed, any recognition of this decision in Member State F3 would be irreconcilable with the decision, already recognised and operative in that State, which had been handed down by non-Member State F2.

In such situations, the question of whether an insolvency decision is irreconcilable with a domestic decision or with an earlier decision given in a non-Member State and which fulfils the conditions for recognition in the forum State, has, therefore, to be resolved on the basis of Article 26 and the public policy clause.

411. In this context, it has to be remembered that national insolvency proceedings opened in a Member State but *not included in the Annexes* of the Insolvency Regulation are not eligible for recognition in the forum under the Regulation. Neither can the opening of unlisted insolvency proceedings be used to prevent the recognition of "listed" insolvency proceedings, or of insolvency decisions handed down in the framework of these proceedings, even where these unlisted proceedings were opened earlier.[423] Once main proceedings have been opened in a Member State in accordance with the Regulation, any previously opened territorial proceedings not listed in the Annexes of the Regulation may not continue and cannot shield local assets from the effects of the main proceedings. The national law must provide for a solution which accords with the prevalence of the Regulation, e.g. the closing of the unlisted territorial proceedings.[424]

8.2.3. Partial recognition and non-recognition

412. The Insolvency Regulation admits *partial recognition*. Where the foreign decision contains declarations which can be recognised on a separate basis and some prove contrary to public policy and others do not, that decision may be recognised partially, by accepting only the former.[425]

We are also dealing with a partial recognition when recognition is sought for a composition but only *vis-à-vis* certain creditors (for example, those who have presented a claim for payment outside the composition).[426] This does not present any problems.

413. The *consequences of non-recognition* vary according to the type of decision in question and, furthermore, depending on whether the defects in the decision can or cannot be remedied by a new decision in the State of origin. Thus, for example, non-recognition of the declaration of opening means that the debtor will not be divested, and may continue administering his assets, and creditors may continue pursuing their individual actions, including enforcement.

---

[423] Virgós/Schmit Report, Margin No. 145.
[424] Virgós/Schmit Report, Margin No. 261.
[425] Spellenberg, p. 193; Aderholt, p. 203; Geimer, Margin No. 3521.
[426] Reinhart (1995), pp. 245–246.

If, in spite of the declaration of opening having been recognised, an individual decision is not recognised, for example, the exclusion of a specific creditor in conditions which are manifestly contrary to the public policy of the recognising State, that creditor may pursue his individual claim in the forum, including enforcement;[427] the stay of individual enforcement actions ordered by the foreign insolvency proceedings will not be given effect against him in the forum.

9. DIRECTIVES ON REORGANISATION AND WINDING-UP OF CREDIT INSTITUTIONS AND INSURANCE UNDERTAKINGS

414. The Directives on credit institutions and insurance companies are also based on the principle of *automatic recognition*: the reorganisation measures and winding-up proceedings adopted by the competent authorities of the home Member State (i.e. the State of origin) shall produce full effects, including against third parties, throughout the Community in accordance with the legislation of that Member State, without the need for any further formalities (see Articles 3.2 II and 9.1 II of the Directive on credit institutions and Articles 4.3 and 8.2 of the Directive on insurance companies). This principle applies even when the legislation of the recognising State does not provide for reorganisation measures such as the ones applied in the home Member State or makes the implementation of those measures subject to conditions that are not fulfilled.[428]

The Directives do not address the problem of *enforcement*; Regulation 44/2001, as the general rule on this matter in the Community law system, will apply.

415. The law of the State of origin also determines the time from which the measures begin to produce effects (Article 3.2 III of the Directive on credit institutions and Article 4.4 of the Directive on insurance companies).

416. As in the case of the Insolvency Regulation, the publication required by the Directives is not a precondition for the effectiveness of decisions (Article 6.5 of the Directive on credit institutions and Article 6.3 of the Directive on insurance companies). In the case of administrators or liquidators, their appointment will be accredited by the presentation of a duly certified copy of the decision regarding the appointment or by any other certificate issued by the administrative or judicial authorities of the home Member State. A translation into the official language or languages of the Member State in whose territory he wishes to act may be required, but no legalisation or similar formality may be required (Article 28.1 of the Directive on credit institutions; Article 27.1 of the Directive on insurance companies).

417. The administrators and liquidators are entitled to exercise in the territory of all of the Member States all of the powers which they can exercise in the territory of the home Member State (Article 28.2 of the Directive on credit institutions; Article 27.2 of the Directive on insurance companies). In exercising his powers, the administrator or liquidator must respect the legislation of the Member States within

---

[427] SPELLENBERG, p. 196.
[428] DEGUÉE, p. 273.

the territory of which he wishes to take action, in particular with regard to the realisation of assets and the provision of information to employees (Article 28.3 of the Directive on credit institutions and Article 27.3 of the Directive on insurance companies). In order to adopt coercive enforcement measures the administrator or liquidator must request the intervention of the authorities of the requested State (see Article 28.3 of the Directive on credit institutions and Article 27.3 of the Directive on insurance companies).

Part V

Coordination between Insolvency Proceedings

Chapter 10

Coordination between Insolvency Proceedings
Opened in Different Member States

1. THE MODEL OF INTERNATIONAL COORDINATION

418. The Insolvency Regulation permits insolvency proceedings to be opened against the *same debtor* in two or more Member States. So far we have seen that the proceedings opened in the State where the debtor has his centre of main interests have universal scope and that any other proceedings which may be opened in a Member State where the debtor possesses an establishment (Article 3.2) have merely territorial scope. The Regulation does not establish any limit to the number of territorial proceedings which may be opened. If the debtor has establishments in several States, then insolvency proceedings may potentially be opened in all of those States. Whether or not they are opened will depend upon whether those empowered to request the opening of proceedings choose to do so. For a creditor, this will only make sense when the expected value of his claim in the territorial proceedings is greater than in the main proceedings or in situations in which it is not possible to open main proceedings. Naturally, nothing in the Regulation prevents only one set of main proceedings from being opened in the Community against the same debtor, even though he has establishments operating in different Member States; the plurality of proceedings is simply a possibility which the Regulation offers to those involved.

In this section, we will look at how the various proceedings are related in the event that several proceedings *are* opened against the same debtor.

419. A basic function of insolvency law is to impose on the parties involved, both debtor and creditors, a framework of collective cooperation which permits the value of the insolvent debtor's estate to be maximised (*ceteris paribus* more is preferred to less) by taking the most suitable decisions regarding reorganisation or winding-up on the basis of economic rationale. Naturally, once it becomes possible to open different insolvency proceedings against the same debtor, it becomes essential to provide mechanisms of coordination between the different proceedings which re-establish this principle of collective action. That is why Recital 20 of the Insolvency Regulation emphasises the fact that an efficient use of the assets of the estate will only be possible if the concurrent proceedings pending are coordinated.

420. The majority of the Insolvency Regulation's rules regarding coordination are found in Chapter 3, the chapter dealing with secondary proceedings. This is not a matter of chance. It is a clear indication that the Regulation considers the relationship between proceedings to be based on a *"main/secondary"* scheme in which

the dominant role falls to the main proceedings. This scheme is made up of five fundamental ideas:

(a) Only a single insolvency procedure can have universal scope under the Regulation and this ("the *main proceedings*") can only be opened by the courts of the State where the debtor's centre of main interests is located (Article 3.1 IR).

(b) When *main proceedings* are opened, any other insolvency proceedings already opened (Article 36) or subsequently opened (Article 27) in a Member State are considered secondary proceedings and are subject to mandatory rules on coordination with the main proceedings. These rules ensure that the secondary proceedings, without waiving the fulfilment of their own functions, pay due attention to the interests of the main procedure.

(c) Under the Insolvency Regulation, the driving role of coordination corresponds to the liquidators (i.e. the insolvency representatives), not to the judges. These may carry out the functions of supervision and, where appropriate, initiative, which correspond to them in accordance with the applicable national law; but the Regulation situates the liquidators in the forefront of the coordination. Furthermore, the main/secondary scheme is reproduced in the relationship between the liquidators. The Regulation confers the dominant role upon the liquidator in the main proceedings, who will enjoy special powers to intervene in and influence secondary proceedings.

(d) All creditors may participate in both the main proceedings and any secondary proceedings (Article 32.1); unless a creditor is opposed to this, the liquidators shall present in all other proceedings the claims which creditors have presented in their proceedings.

(e) Dividends are consolidated in such a way that dividends obtained in one set of insolvency proceedings are deducted from the dividends to be obtained in other proceedings.

421. The orientation towards the universal model which underlies the Regulation explains to a large extent the rules on coordination which it establishes between proceedings. In this respect, the Insolvency Regulation treats national insolvency proceedings opened against the same debtor not as isolated elements, but rather as interdependent proceedings which form an integral part of a system for solving the problems arising from cross-border insolvencies.

Development. This concept explains provisions such as the rule regarding the unrestricted participation of local creditors (Article 32.1), the rule which places any surplus from secondary proceedings at the disposal of the main proceedings (Article 35), the rule which converts all insolvency proceedings into secondary proceedings once main proceedings have been opened (Article 36), the rule regarding the consolidation of dividends (Article 20.2); and even the fact that the main liquidator may himself request the opening of secondary proceedings (Article 29.a). It also explains the powers conferred upon the liquidator in the main proceedings, whereby he may propose uses for the estate in the secondary proceedings (Article 31.3), obtain a stay of the process of liquidation in the secondary proceedings (Article 33), prevent the approval in secondary proceedings of any composition or restructuring plan which has not received his consent, except where the financial interests of the creditors in the main proceedings are not affected (Article 34.1); he may also request that local restructuring proceedings opened prior to the main proceedings be converted into winding-up proceedings (Article 37 in connection with Article 3.4). The application of local law to the secondary proceedings *ex* Article 4 guarantees that, in spite of the primacy of the main proceedings, local interests will always be protected.

422. In order to facilitate an understanding of the model of cooperation established by the Insolvency Regulation, this might be a good point in which to modify its systematic structure and regroup the rules in four blocks: (1) rules regarding participation; (2) rules regarding cooperation between the liquidators; (3) rules regarding the alignment of proceedings; and (4) rules regarding distribution. In this way it will easier to "visualise" the overall system of coordination provided by the Regulation. Some of the rules which comprise this system have already been studied when explaining secondary proceedings and here we shall simply look at them from the point of view of the role they play in coordination.

2. HYPOTHESIS OF COORDINATION

423. The main/secondary scheme adopted by the Insolvency Regulation presupposes that the insolvency proceedings are against the *same debtor* and that main insolvency proceedings *have been opened*. However, two situations may easily arise in which these conditions are not fulfilled:

(a) The concurrence of two or more *independent territorial proceedings* against the *same debtor* located in a Member State. Given that the opening of main proceedings is not a prerequisite for the opening of territorial proceedings (see Articles 3.3 and 3.4), this hypothesis is plausible, though probably not very likely.

(b) The concurrence of two or more *main* insolvency proceedings against *different* but *linked debtors*. This might be the case of the insolvency of companies which, while legally independent, are a component of a larger economic unit (a policorporate enterprise or a company system) or, more generally, in the case of companies which form part of the same group.

424. Coordination is also necessary in those two cases. The main/secondary scheme followed by the Regulation must not become an obstacle to any application by analogy of its rules on coordination to these situations. Naturally, those rules on coordination which presuppose the existence of main proceedings and follow an idea of *subordination* (even if in a weak form) cannot be applied here. In the first case, because all of the proceedings opened are territorial; and in the second case, because all of the proceedings opened are, legally, main proceedings. But, in contrast, all of those other rules on coordination which respond to an idea of *unity can* be applied. It is worthwhile distinguishing between the two cases.

(a) The VIRGOS/SCHMIT Report gives the example of two territorial proceedings opened against the same debtor without main proceedings having been opened in the Member State where the debtor has his centre of main interests. In this case, *"it should be possible to apply, by analogy, the same ... rules which serve to coordinate secondary insolvency proceedings inter se"*[429] specifically, the application of the provisions relating to the duty of the liquidators to cooperate (Articles 31.1 and 2); to the presentation of their claims (Article 32.2); to their participation on the same basis as a creditor in other proceedings (Article 32.3); and to the imputation of payments (Article 20.2).

(b) In the case of debtors who are linked owing to their being a component of a larger economic unit (a poli-corporate enterprise or company system) or forming part of a group of companies, the idea of *economic* unity (the common enterprise or the belonging to a same group) may justify the application by analogy, in the appropriate cases (because the application by analogy requires this justification to be assessed in the light of each specific case), of the rules on coordination to the insolvency proceedings opened *according to the Insolvency Regulation* against each of the debtors who are related to each other. The fact that the insolvency proceedings over each of the legally existing debtors are governed by the Insolvency Regulation together with this idea of unity justifies the application of the general rules on coordination. Specifically, the rules regarding the duty to cooperate and communicate information which may be relevant to the parents' or subsidiaries' insolvency proceedings (Article 31) and participation of the liquidator in other proceedings on the same basis as a creditor (Article 32.3). The *ratio* of Article 31.3 justifies granting the liquidator of the parent company the possibility of proposing a global plan covering the parent company and one or more of the subsidiaries (see No. 452, which is applicable *mutatis mutandis*). Protocols regarding the coordination of the proceedings could also be entered into (see No. 441). On the other hand, there does not appear to be sufficient likeness or identity of reason to justify the application by analogy of the provisions referring to distribution (Article 20), surplus assets (Article 35) and the extraordinary powers of the main liquidator (Articles 33, 34 and 37), the use of which would require an additional justification.[430]

3. RULES REGARDING PARTICIPATION (ARTICLE 32)

425. The Insolvency Regulation is based on the principle that *"any creditor may lodge his claims in the main proceedings and in any secondary proceedings"* (Article 32.1). It is a creditor's right to lodge his claims in only one or in several

---

[429] On the application of these rules to the relationships between different territorial proceedings see, in favour, VIRGOS/SCHMIT, Margin No. 39; BALZ (1996a), p. 953 and (1996b), 525; VIRGOS, p. 36.

[430] See an articulated proposal to modify the Insolvency Regulation to establish rules of coordination for groups of companies, in VAN GALEN, point III.

proceedings, although as we shall now see, unless a creditor expressly opposes such action, the rule followed is that of the multiple filing or "cross-filing" of claims by the liquidators in the different proceedings opened.

This principle of participation is very important from the point of view of coordinating proceedings, because it permits the creditors' majority reached in the main proceedings to be reproduced in all of the other proceedings; and if the liquidator files those claims, this permits the main liquidator to "impose" this majority in the secondary proceedings, thereby clearly strengthening his power to influence the latter.[431] In the event that a reorganisation plan or a global composition is envisaged, this principle can be decisive.

426. In line with this principle, the Regulation establishes that the liquidators in the main proceedings and the secondary proceedings *shall file* in other proceedings the claims which creditors have filed in their respective proceedings: *"The liquidators in the main and any secondary proceedings shall lodge in other proceedings claims which have already been lodged in the proceedings for which they were appointed, provided that the interests of creditors in the latter proceedings are served thereby, subject to the right of creditors to oppose that or to withdraw the lodgement of their claims where the law applicable so provides"* (Article 32.2).

427. *All* of the creditors benefit from this provision and not only those who have their habitual residence, domicile or registered office in a Member State; the literal sense of Article 32 does not leave any room for doubt in this respect.

428. The purpose of this provision on cross-filing is to facilitate the exercise of the rights of the creditors by permitting the liquidator to substitute them in the filing of their claims, and to strengthen the influence of the liquidators in the other proceedings. This provision also represents the *general rule*: in principle, *unless* the creditors are opposed thereto or no benefit is derived therefrom, the liquidators *shall* file their claims in all other proceedings. These two qualifications are easily explained:

(a) To impose *"in all cases"* an obligation to file claims does not make sense when filing them does not lead to any benefits for the claims thus filed; in such a case the rule would impose a net cost without any return. This is why the Regulation only imposes upon the liquidators an obligation to file *"provided that the interests of creditors in the latter proceedings are served thereby"*. This interest or utility is measured in *collective terms*: whether it is of interest for the body of creditors in the proceedings for which the liquidator was appointed or for a specific group of them. This empowers the liquidator to file only those claims which may benefit from direct participation in other proceedings; for example, if the assets to be distributed in the territorial proceedings are only sufficient to satisfy creditors with a type of preference or privilege, and not ordinary creditors, the liquidator is justified in only filing

---

[431] Of course, the reverse situation can also be possible, when the majority of creditors originate from the secondary proceedings, although this is less likely.

the claims of the former. On the other hand, the liquidator is not obliged to evaluate this interest in specific terms for each individual creditor.[432]

> *Rationale*. The liquidator is not obliged to evaluate the individual interest of each creditor. The specific assessment of each claim would be an impossible task. It is a personal matter for each creditor to make this assessment, as each individual is better placed to assess his own interests. The liquidator is therefore only obliged to deal with the interests of the creditor as part of the body of creditors as a whole or as a member of an insolvency "class". The VIRGOS/SCHMIT Report adds that the liquidator will also file a claim when the creditor has informed him of his interest in the said claim being filed.

(b) The aim of Article 32.2 explains why the rule is not mandatory for the creditor or creditors. The latter may oppose the filing of their claims by the liquidator in other proceedings and may withdraw claims which have already been filed.[433] In this latter case, the right of the creditors to withdraw claims depends upon the law applicable to the insolvency proceedings in which the claim or claims in question have been filed by the liquidator, because the Regulation delegates the possibility of withdrawal to the provisions of the applicable national law (Article 32.2, *in fine*: "*where the law applicable so provides*"). The costs incurred by the filing and who bears them are questions governed by the applicable national law (Article 4). Avoidance of these costs for the creditor may be a reason to oppose the filing.[434]

429. The filing of a claim by the liquidator has the same effects as the filing of a claim by the creditor; the liquidator acts in the name and on behalf of the creditor.[435] However, the question of whether or not the liquidator may, beyond the filing of the claims, represent those creditors in other proceedings (e.g. by voting in the creditors' meeting or approving a composition or insolvency plan), has not been resolved. The Insolvency Regulation leaves this question to the *lex concursus* which governs the proceedings for which the liquidator was appointed; this law determines all his functions and powers. The reason for this referral to national law lies in the diversity of conceptions of the national laws of the Member States with regard to the role and functions of a liquidator.[436] The Insolvency Regulation does not interfere in the different formulas provided for by national law, whether representative (with the result, for example, that the liquidator may exercise the voting rights of the absent creditor) or not. Naturally, representation based on express *powers of attorney* may also be a possibility.

> *Problems associated with cross-filing*. What happens if the liquidator and the creditor file the same claim in the same proceedings? The claim continues to be the creditor's claim,

---

[432] VIRGOS/SCHMIT Report, Margin No. 239.

[433] VIRGOS/SCHMIT Report, Margin No. 239, indicating the reasons why the creditor may not be interested in the liquidator presenting his claim; see also BALZ (1996a), p. 954; LEIBLE/STAUDINGER (2000), p. 570.

[434] VIRGOS/SCHMIT Report, Margin No. 239 III.

[435] VIRGOS/SCHMIT Report, Margin No. 238.

[436] BALZ (1996b), p. 525.

regardless of who files it; the claim is considered to have been filed by the creditor and only he will be able to vote and receive dividends. Another problem arises when the claim is filed by two liquidators when both are authorised according to their national law to exercise the voting rights of their creditors when the latter do not attend the creditors' meeting. In this case the claim is considered to have been filed, but the Regulation does not contain rules regarding who is empowered to exercise this right (whether both by mutual agreement or only one of them, for example the one in whose proceedings the creditor, and not another liquidator, has filed his claim). Several provisions aimed at regulating questions of representation were abandoned in the course of the negotiations on the wording of the provision, so the solution now lies in the hands of national law.[437]

430. Article 32 only regulates the filing of claims by the liquidators on behalf of the creditors, but does not modify the other rules regarding the filing of claims. The uniform rules of the Regulation (Articles 39, 41 and 42) continue to apply and, in matters not provided for by these rules, the law of the proceedings in which the claims are filed applies (Article 4.2.h); this law will determine the deadlines for filing claims, the admissibility and manner of the filing (although the Regulation imposes some specific solutions in these areas; see Chapter VII), the consequences of the late filing of a claim, and the costs incurred by the verification of the claims.[438]

Admission in different proceedings. Apart from the uniform rules already studied, verification and admission of claims will take place separately in each of the proceedings under the conditions established by the respective *lex fori concursus*. For this reason, admission in one set of proceedings does not entail, *by itself*, admission in other proceedings: the conditions and the persons who may oppose such admission are different in each of the proceedings. However, the decision admitting the claim may be used as a means of proof of the claim in other proceedings.

431. Finally, and without prejudice to the above, Article 32.3 confers on the liquidators a direct right to *participate* on their own behalf in other proceedings on the same basis as any other creditor, in particular by forming part of the creditors' meeting. The specific content of this right to participate and the exercise thereof are subject to the national law of the proceedings in which a liquidator seeks to act: if he has been appointed liquidator in proceedings opened in State F1 and he seeks to exercise this right in proceedings opened in State F2, the law of this latter State F2 will be applied.[439] The aim of this provision is to better guarantee the expression, in other insolvency proceedings, of the interests which each liquidator is responsible for safeguarding, by offering him a channel of direct participation in the proceeding opened in other Member States, above all in the deliberations of the creditors.

---

[437] VIRGOS/SCHMIT Report, Margin No. 240.
[438] VIRGOS/SCHMIT Report, Margin No. 236.
[439] VIRGOS/SCHMIT Report, Margin No. 240.

4. RULES REGARDING COOPERATION (ARTICLE 31)

432. Article 31 of the Insolvency Regulation is based on the principle of cooperation between the liquidator in the main proceedings and the liquidator(s) in secondary proceedings. This principle translates into a *general duty* to "cooperate with each other", and *two specific obligations*: an obligation to exchange information and a further obligation to allow the main liquidator to present proposals regarding the use of the assets in the secondary proceedings.

At the vertex of this system of cooperation is the main liquidator. According to the literal wording of Article 31, no explicit duty is imposed upon the liquidators in different secondary proceedings to cooperate *inter se*.[440] This does not prevent such cooperation from taken place, but makes it clear, according to the model provided by the Regulation, cooperation occurs with the intermediation and under the direction of the main liquidator.

433. The Insolvency Regulation does not contain rules regarding the liability of the liquidators in the event of a breach of the duty to cooperate. It falls to the national law applicable to the proceedings for which he has been appointed liquidator to establish the consequences of a breach of those duties which the Regulation imposes upon him in his role as liquidator.[441]

4.1. Obligation to exchange information

434. In the first place, the Insolvency Regulation establishes a reciprocal *duty to communicate information* between the liquidators in the main and secondary proceedings (Article 31.1): *"Subject to the rules restricting the communication of information, the liquidator in the main proceedings and the liquidators in the secondary proceedings shall be duty bound to communicate information to each other. They shall immediately communicate any information which may be relevant to the other proceedings, in particular the progress made in lodging and verifying claims and all measures aimed at terminating the proceedings"*.

It must not be forgotten that all of these proceedings affect the same debtor, who possesses centres of activity in several States. Insofar as all the creditors of that debtor participate or may participate in several proceedings (Article 32.1), the exchange of information and cooperation between the liquidators is essential in order to ensure that the various sets of proceedings are conducted efficiently.[442] This information is an indispensable prerequisite for any form of subsequent coordination between the various sets of insolvency proceedings.

---

[440] BALZ (1996b), p. 525.

[441] VIRGOS/SCHMIT Report, Margin No. 234.

[442] VIRGOS/SCHMIT Report, Margin No. 229; VIRGOS, p. 34; BALZ (1996a), p. 954; LEIBLE/STAUDINGER (2000), p. 569; BELTRAN SANCHEZ, pp. 41–42; EIDENMÜLLER (2000b), p. 26.

435. The courts of the centre of main interests will normally have the debtor under its direct control. For this reason, the main liquidator will be in a better position to obtain information from the debtor (e.g. on the existence and the whereabouts of assets abroad). Also, as vertex of the system of cooperation, the main liquidator will operate as a sort of "clearing house" which receives information from and passes it on to the various liquidators.[443]

436. The duty established in Article 31.1 encompasses any information which may be relevant for the other proceedings. In particular, the provisions mention information regarding the progress being made regarding the filing and verification of claims and all measures aimed at terminating the proceedings. Furthermore, Article 31.3 establishes that it is a specific duty of the secondary liquidator to inform the main liquidator of any *use* or *realization* of relevant assets in the secondary proceedings which may affect the main proceedings.[444] In more general terms the VIRGOS/SCHMIT Report gives an open list of information which may be relevant, including information regarding:[445]

(a) the debtor's assets;
(b) actions planned or under way in order to recover assets, actions to obtain payment and actions to set-aside;
(c) possibilities for liquidating the assets;
(d) claims filed;
(e) the verification of those claims and any disputes arising from them;
(f) the ranking of creditors;
(g) planned reorganization measures;
(h) proposed compositions;
(i) plans for the allocation of dividends; and
(j) the progress of operations in the proceedings.

437. For this information to be useful, it must be communicated in due time; for this reason, Article 31.1 requires this information to be transmitted "*immediately*".

438. This obligation to inform may be *limited* by national rules which restrict the communication of information for the purposes of protecting secrets or protecting computerised personal data, and Article 31.1 states expressly that these rules must be respected.

4.2. *General duty to cooperate*

439. The *generic duty* of mutual cooperation is established in Article 31.2: "*Subject to the rules applicable to each of the proceedings, the liquidator in the main*

---

[443] BALZ (1996b), p. 525.
[444] VIRGOS/SCHMIT Report, Margin No. 233.
[445] VIRGOS/SCHMIT Report, Margin No. 230.

proceedings and the liquidators in the secondary proceedings shall be duty bound to cooperate with each other". It only refers to the liquidators, because it is on them that the model of coordination provided for in the Regulation rests. Through this duty to cooperate the Regulation aims to ensure the greatest possible efficiency in the administration and, where appropriate, winding-up of the debtor's estate.

NB. The duty to cooperate on a reciprocal basis refers to the liquidators, because it is on them that the model of coordination provided for in the Regulation rests. However, it also appears reasonable for this principle to apply, *mutatis mutandis*, to the competent legal authorities, even though they act on a secondary level.

440. This duty to cooperate must be carried out without entering into conflict with the functions and duties imposed on the liquidators by the national law applicable to each of the insolvency proceedings. This is why Article 31.2 imposes upon the main liquidator and the liquidators in the secondary proceedings the duty to cooperate with each other *"subject to the rules applicable to each of the proceedings"*. In turn, we also know that national laws have to respect the *"effet utile"* of the Regulation and cannot take advantage of this provision to evade the objective of Article 31.

441. The Insolvency Regulation restricts itself to imposing the duty to cooperate, but does not provide any indication of the ways in which this cooperation should function in practice; this will therefore be dependent upon national legislation. This rule permits the liquidators to coordinate the administration and supervision of the debtor's assets and activities in any way permitted by the national laws of the proceedings which have to be coordinated.[446] Obviously, there is no list of the measures which may be subject to coordination. In practice, however, they tend to be the following:

(a) the disposal of relevant assets;
(b) the exercise of the right to vote;
(c) the application of the power to continue or not any contracts pending execution;
(d) the use of actions to set aside detrimental acts;
(e) the raising of new finance; and
(f) the drawing up of a restructuring or reorganisation plan.[447]

Protocols and other formulas regarding coordination. Although not expressly provided for, Article 31 is not opposed to the possibility of entering into agreements or protocols regarding coordination of the proceedings, provided that this is permitted by the national law of each of the proceedings and that the rules of the Insolvency Regulation are respected. The way these agreements or protocols work in practice varies greatly. In many cases non-binding agreements or protocols are drawn up, which have the advantage of avoiding the

---

[446] See EIDENMÜLLER (2001b), p. 26, on the problem of "agreements or protocols" between liquidators.
[447] EIDENMÜLLER (2001b), p. 11.

complications related with the legal nature of these agreements between liquidators and with the role of the courts, but where, once they are adopted as a code of conduct, the concrete measures listed in them can be seen as a specific expression of the generic duty to cooperate which is imposed by the Insolvency Regulation and thus create a basis, in the event that they are not respected without providing either justification or an alternative, for a legal action for a breach of the duty to cooperate established in Article 31.2.

There is room within the framework of the generic duty to cooperate established by Article 31.2 for other formulas of coordination to be developed by national laws. Some are as simple as appointing the same person as liquidator in the different proceedings.

4.3. *Proposals regarding the use of assets in the secondary proceedings*

442. Third, Article 31.3 establishes a *specific obligation*: "*The liquidator in the secondary proceedings shall give the liquidator in the main proceedings an early opportunity of submitting proposals on the liquidation or any other use of the assets in the secondary proceedings*". This provision reflects the primacy of the main proceedings; its systematic connection with Articles 33, 34 and 37, which we shall analyse later, must be taken into account. The obligation established by Article 31.1 gives the main liquidator the opportunity, for example, to prevent the disposal of assets in the secondary proceedings when it appears advisable to conserve them for the purposes of restructuring the company.[448] As we have already seen, it corresponds to the national law which governs the secondary proceedings to determine any possible liability on the part of the liquidator appointed in those proceedings which arises from a breach of this duty.[449]

5. RULES REGARDING THE ALIGNMENT OF PROCEEDINGS

443. As we know, the Insolvency Regulation permits the opening of territorial insolvency proceedings wherever the debtor possesses an establishment. All territorial proceedings opened after the main proceedings must necessarily be *winding-up* proceedings, whereas if they are opened beforehand, they can be *restructuring or winding-up* proceedings. The reasons for this difference have already been explained. We shall now look at the problems which may arise when the main proceedings and one or more territorial proceedings pursue conflicting ends, whether due to the type of proceedings opened or to the particular measures envisaged. In theory, the main proceedings and secondary proceedings can be combined in four possible ways, depending upon whether they are aimed mainly at restructuring or winding-up.

---

[448] VIRGOS/SCHMIT Report, Margin No. 233; BALZ (1996a), p. 954; VIRGOS, p. 36; LEIBLE/STAUDINGER (2000), p. 569. The liquidator in the secondary proceedings must support such measures, except when they come into conflict with his own obligations, as they are a specific expression of the generic duty to cooperate.

[449] VIRGOS/SCHMIT Report, Margin No. 234; VIRGOS, p. 36.

The relationships between parallel insolvency proceedings can be outlined as follows:

Main proceedings	Secondary proceedings	Remedy
Winding-up	Winding-up	Articles 33+34
Restructuring	Winding-up	Articles 33+34
Restructuring	Restructuring (*ex* Article 3.4)	Articles 34+37
Winding-up	Restructuring (*ex* Article 3.4)	Articles 34+37

444. The normal situation is where there are main proceedings in progress and secondary proceedings are opened at a later moment. In this case the main proceedings may be aimed at winding-up or restructuring, while the territorial proceedings may only be aimed at winding-up. If both are winding-up proceedings, general coordination should not present any special problems, and Articles 33 and 34 can always be resorted to with regard to specific measures. However, if the main proceedings are aimed at restructuring and the territorial proceedings at winding-up, the latter may jeopardise the measures taken in the former. In such cases, the specific remedy which the Regulation places at the disposal of the main liquidator is Article 33, which permits a stay of liquidation in the secondary proceedings in order to permit a solution which is more in line with the measures being taken in the main proceedings. This provision is supplemented by Article 34 which confers upon the liquidator control over a closing without liquidation of the secondary proceedings, either by giving him the right to initiate proposals (which, for the duration of the stay provided for in Article 33, corresponds solely to him; see Article 34.3), or because any composition or restructuring plan negotiated in the secondary proceedings requires his consent if it is to be effective (see Article 34.1.II).

445. Territorial proceedings opened before the main proceedings may be aimed at winding-up or restructuring. This second possibility gives rise to greater problems of compatibility with the main proceedings. In the first place, save for exceptional circumstances, it is difficult to understand a situation in which, while the debtors estate is being wound up with global scope in the main proceedings, partial restructuring proceedings are under way regarding this same debtor in another Member State. In such a case, the Regulation places another specific remedy at the disposal of the liquidator in the main proceedings: the conversion of the secondary proceedings from restructuring to winding-up proceedings, if the said liquidator so requires (Article 37).[450] In the event that the two (or more) proceedings opened are restructuring proceedings, the main liquidator may choose to follow the general rules regarding coordination; but, faced with the clear difficulty of coordinating two sets of restructuring proceedings *vis-à-vis* the same debtor, he may also choose to

---

[450] Bearing in mind the declaration made by Portugal, see No. 457.

take advantage of Article 37 to convert the secondary proceedings into winding-up proceedings, knowing that he may, at a later stage, use Article 33 (stay of liquidation) and Article 34 (closure of the secondary proceedings without liquidation) if necessary.

> *Costs of the proceedings.* Opening two or more insolvency proceedings increases the *direct* costs of administering the insolvency. Opening two or more restructuring proceedings against the same debtor may significantly increase the *indirect* costs: the operating costs will necessarily be greater and the general competitivity of the company will suffer (e.g. part of the work of management will have to be devoted to coordinating efforts) and the increased slowness of the proceedings may lead to an increase in the risk of the company's assets depreciating in value.

5.1. Stay of liquidation (Article 33)

446. Article 33 seeks to respect the primacy of the main proceedings without ceasing to take into account the interests of the secondary proceedings. On the one hand, a *stay of the process of liquidation* in the secondary proceedings may, for various reasons, be in the interests of the creditors in the main proceedings, for example, to allow a global plan for the orderly liquidation of the assets on a world-wide scale to be approved (e.g. the preservation of the assets of the secondary estate may prove useful for the global sale of the company) or in order to achieve a composition or carry out a global restructuring.[451] In order to safeguard these interests, Article 33 permits the liquidator in the main proceedings to request a total or partial stay of the process of liquidation in the secondary proceedings: "*The court, which opened the secondary proceedings, shall stay the process of liquidation in whole or in part on receipt of a request from the liquidator in the main proceedings, provided that in that event it may require the liquidator in the main proceedings to take any suitable measure to guarantee the interests of the creditors in the secondary proceedings and of individual classes of creditors. Such a request from the liquidator may be rejected only if it is manifestly of no interest to the creditors in the main proceedings. Such a stay of the process of liquidation may be ordered for up to three months. It may be continued or renewed for similar periods*".

When the liquidator in the main proceedings requests it, the court dealing with the secondary proceedings must decree the stay, except where this is *manifestly* not in the interests of the creditors in the main proceedings. The condition that the stay be manifestly *not* in the interests of the creditors, and the fact that it can *only* be refused on those grounds, highlights the exceptional nature of the refusal. The only interests which are assessed for these purposes are those of the creditors in the main

---

[451] VIRGOS/SCHMIT Report, Margin No. 243; VIRGOS, p. 36; BALZ (1996a), p. 954.

proceedings.[452] This rule provides the liquidator in the main proceedings with a substantial degree of control over the secondary proceedings.

447. Nevertheless, this power is subject to certain *restrictions*. In the first place, the court which is dealing with the secondary proceedings may require the liquidator in the main proceedings to provide an adequate guarantee to protect the interests of the creditors in the secondary proceedings as a whole or, where appropriate, of certain groups of those creditors. This guarantee may refer, for instance, to the preservation of the value of the estate (or of specific assets), if there is a risk of devaluation, or to the payment of interest to those creditors who have a legal right to continue receiving it during the proceedings.[453] Furthermore, the stay is limited to maximum of three months; at the end of this period the stay may be extended for another three months with no restriction whatsoever on the number of successive extensions (Article 33.1). The VIRGOS/SCHMIT Report (Margin No. 245) expressly states that a new stay may be requested after the renewal of proceedings which have been previously stayed.

448. The stay does not put an end to the proceedings; all it does is *paralyse* the winding-up operations.[454] For this reason, the effects conferred upon the opening of the secondary proceedings by their applicable law continue to operate.

449. In any case, the court will end the stay: (a) at the request of the liquidator in the main proceedings; (b) on its own initiative, at the request of a creditor or at the request of the liquidator in the secondary proceedings when such a measure no longer appears justified, particularly by the interests of the creditors in the main proceedings or the secondary proceedings (Article 33.2). In this latter case, consideration of the interests of the secondary proceedings may, by itself, be sufficient to put an end to the stay.

NB. Insofar as the interests of the creditors in the secondary proceedings are not sufficient to initially refuse the stay (at the most, it would justify the requirement of an adequate guarantee), this latter rule was conceived implicitly for those situations in which the stay is extended.

450. See next paragraph on the possibility of proposing a rescue plan or composition during the phase when the proceedings are stayed.

5.2. *Ending of secondary proceedings without liquidation, through a composition or reorganisation plan (Article 34)*

451. The Insolvency Regulation refers to national law to decide if secondary proceedings can end without winding-up by means of a *rescue plan*, a *composition*

---

[452] VIRGOS/SCHMIT Report, Margin No. 242.

[453] BALZ (1996b), 526.

[454] VIRGOS/SCHMIT Report, Margin No. 245.

or a *similar measure*. The national law applicable to the secondary proceedings in question will determine whether or not this solution is possible, under what conditions (e.g. the votes necessary) and who is empowered to request it. The Regulation establishes the power of the liquidator in the main proceedings to propose, on his own initiative, a negotiated solution by means of one of these measures in Article 34.1: *"Where the law applicable to secondary proceedings allows for such proceedings to be closed without liquidation by a rescue plan, a composition or a comparable measure, the liquidator in the main proceedings shall be empowered to propose such a measure himself"*.

452. If secondary proceedings are opened, a reorganisation can be accomplished either through a combination of different plans (e.g. a main plan and a secondary plan) or by means of a single global plan covering all the proceedings, both main and secondary. However, in the latter case, the plan will have to be approved in both the main and the secondary proceedings, according to their own rules and majorities, with regard to their respective estate.

453. When the composition or rescue plan is not requested by the main liquidator, the Insolvency Regulation establishes certain restrictions to ensure the "supremacy" of the main proceedings. It must be taken into account that a measure of this type is normally associated with a restructuring of the debt. All of this may affect the interests of the main proceedings or simply obstruct the global solution designed in them. For this reason, Article 34.1 II establishes that, in order for this measure to be final, the agreement of the liquidator in the main proceedings must be obtained: *"Closure of the secondary proceedings by a measure referred to in the first subparagraph shall not become final without the consent of the liquidator in the main proceedings; failing his agreement, however, it may become final if the financial interests of the creditors in the main proceedings are not affected by the measure proposed"*.

When taking his decision, the main liquidator must take into account the interests of the creditors in the main proceedings, including an interest in the company being restructured and continuing in business.[455] In the absence of the consent of the main liquidator, the Regulation only permits the secondary proceedings to be closed by means of a composition if the measures approved in the secondary proceedings do not affect the financial interests of the creditors in the main proceedings. The financial interests refer to the dividends which correspond to the creditors in the main proceedings. If, in the absence of a measure approved in the secondary proceedings, the creditors in the main proceedings could not reasonably have expected a greater dividend, the financial interests of the latter will not be affected. If the plan or composition is subject, in accordance with the applicable law of the local proceedings, to confirmation or authorisation by the courts, the judge must verify that such is the case.

Financial interests. This concept is narrower than the concept of the "interests" of the creditors of the main proceedings which is used in other provisions. The financial interests are estimated by evaluating the effects of the rescue plan or composition on the dividend to be

---

[455] VIRGOS/SCHMIT Report, Margin No. 249 II.

paid to the creditors in the main proceedings. If, in the absence of the rescue plan or composition, and after the transfer of any surplus assets from the secondary proceedings (ex
Article 25), the said creditors could not reasonably have expected a larger dividend, their
financial interests shall not be considered to be affected by the said measure.[456] The dividends that the creditors in the main proceedings would receive if the composition or plan
is approved must be compared with the hypothetical dividends they would receive in the
absence of such measure.

454. When the process of liquidation has been *stayed* in the secondary proceedings pursuant to the provisions of Article 33, only the liquidator in the main
proceedings or the debtor with the liquidator's consent may propose a rescue plan,
a composition or a similar measure (Article 34.3): *"During a stay of the process of
liquidation ordered pursuant to Article 33, only the liquidator in the main proceedings or the debtor, with the former's consent, may propose measures laid down in
paragraph 1 of this Article in the secondary proceedings; no other proposal for such
a measure shall be put to the vote or approved"*.

The reasons for this restriction are easy to understand if we remember that the
stay is adopted at the request of the liquidator in the main proceedings and in the
interests of the creditors in those proceedings. The natural forum for presenting a
global restructuring (or winding-up) plan with regard to the debtor is the main proceedings and the Regulation recognises this fact. This is why the Regulation avoids
the possibility of partial measures which might disrupt the plan: firstly, by staying
any winding-up operations which may have been initiated in the secondary proceedings; and secondly, by conferring the monopoly for presenting proposals regarding restructuring or composition upon the main liquidator or the debtor with that
liquidator's consent. The most reasonable thing, therefore, is that, for the duration of
the stay, any measure which may affect the objective of the proceedings can only
be adopted with the agreement of the liquidator.[457] For this reason the Regulation
prevents any measure aimed at closing the proceedings by means of recovery plan,
concordat or similar measure from being put to a vote or approved unless it has been
proposed by the liquidator in the main proceedings or by the debtor with the former's
consent (Article 34.3).

NB. The Insolvency Regulation does not pronounce itself on the question of what happens
if the creditors in the secondary proceedings reject the global plan (necessary for debtor's
rehabilitation), proposed by the liquidator in the main proceedings, notwithstanding the fact
that the benefits they receive under this plan are greater than those they would receive in
liquidation. A rejection under these conditions is not consistent with the aims of secondary
proceedings, which are to protect the interests of the local creditors or to facilitate the
administration of the insolvency estate (see No. 287). In fact, this could become a possible
means of extorsion exercised by creditors in secondary proceedings. Therefore, it may be
characterised as an action against the requirements of good faith.

---

[456] VIRGOS/SCHMIT Report, Margin No. 249 III.
[457] VIRGOS/SCHMIT Report, Margin No. 251.

5.3. Subsequent opening of the main proceedings (Articles 36–37)

455. As already said, the Insolvency Regulation is based upon the idea that the natural place for an insolvency restructuring is the State where the debtor's centre of main interests is located. A winding-up is easy to organise on a territorial basis by dividing the assets according to where they are located (whether or not this is the best way of realising them is another matter). In contrast, a business reorganisation presupposes the continuity of the business and involves measures which affect or may affect all aspects of the debtors' operations (financial, business and company structure). This is difficult to conceive without unified management and decision-taking.

456. The Regulation permits the opening of independent territorial proceedings (see Article 3.4) without any main proceedings having been opened in the State where that debtor has his centre of main interests. However, it is to be expected that main insolvency proceedings will normally follow. In this case, the *independent* territorial proceedings become *secondary* proceedings. To this end, Article 36 IR establishes that once the main proceedings have been opened, the provisions of the Regulation devoted to secondary proceedings will also apply to the territorial proceedings opened previously, *"insofar as the progress of those proceedings so permits"*. The principle is application of the rules regarding secondary proceedings; the latter sentence simply allows the courts to adapt the application of Articles 31 to 35 of the Regulation to the circumstances of the case and to avoid a retrospective review of the earlier stages of the territorial proceedings.

457. In this same situation, and bearing in mind that any secondary proceedings opened subsequent to the main proceedings must of necessity be winding-up proceedings (Article 3.3 and 27), the question arises as to whether the territorial proceedings opened prior to the main proceedings, and aimed at restructuring the company, should automatically become *winding-up* proceedings once the main proceedings are opened or whether they can continue to be restructuring proceedings. The Insolvency Regulation does not impose a solution, but rather chooses to leave the decision in the hands of the liquidator in the main proceedings. As established in Article 37, the liquidator in the main proceedings may request that *territorial restructuring proceedings* be converted into *winding-up* proceedings if this is in the interests of the creditors in main proceedings: *"The liquidator in the main proceedings may request that proceedings listed in Annex. A previously opened in another Member State be converted into winding-up proceedings if this proves to be in the interests of the creditors in the main proceedings. The court with jurisdiction under Article 3(2) shall order conversion into one of the proceedings listed in Annex B"*.

This provision reflects the primacy of the main proceedings. The court is not obliged to order the conversion simply because the liquidator in the main proceedings requests it; the conversion must be shown to be in the interest of the creditors in the main proceedings. The mandatory wording of section 2 of the provision ("the court with jurisdiction ... *shall order* conversion") presupposes that the conditions laid down in section 1 are satisfied; i.e. that such conversion is justified in the light of the interests of the creditors in the main proceedings. The national court will therefore verify that the liquidator's request is effectively in the interests of the creditors in the main proceedings.[458] If the liquidator does not request the conversion or the court does not order it, the territorial proceedings can continue to be restructuring proceedings. The Insolvency Regulation does not prevent national law from being going further and conferring upon the liquidator the power to request the closure of territorial restructuring proceedings.[459]

> *Declaration of the Republic of Portugal.* On this point, Portugal made the following declaration (OJ C 183, of 30 June 2000): *"Article 37 of Council Regulation (EC) No 1346/2000 of 29 May 2000 on insolvency proceedings, which mentions the possibility of converting territorial proceedings opened prior to the main proceedings into winding-up proceedings, should be interpreted as meaning that such conversion does not exclude judicial appreciation of the state of the local proceedings (as is the case in Article 36) or of the application of the interests of public policy as provided for in Article 26".*[460]

6. Rules Regarding Distribution

6.1. *Assets remaining in the secondary proceedings (Article 35)*

458. As we know, the Insolvency Regulation is based on the model of universalism. The main proceedings encompass all of the debtor's assets and secondary proceedings are seen as exceptions to this rule. This relationship between the two kinds of proceedings explains Article 35 of the Insolvency Regulation, according to which *"If by the liquidation of assets in the secondary proceedings it is possible to meet all claims allowed under those proceedings, the liquidator appointed in those proceedings shall immediately transfer any assets remaining to the liquidator in the main proceedings"*. The expression *"shall transfer"* ("remitirá" in the Spanish version, "transfère" in the French version) is somewhat ambiguous. Rather than a transfer in the sense of a change of position, it must be understood in the legal sense; the liquidator must perform all of those acts which are necessary in order to place the assets which comprise the said surplus under the power of the liquidator in the main proceedings. Article 35 of the Regulation is inspired by Article 22 of the 1990 Istanbul Convention where the expression *"transfer* of the remaining assets" means precisely that:[461] "by transfer the committee of experts means a purely administrative transaction in connection with the management of the bankruptcy".

459. Article 35 as it is worded appears to presuppose that the secondary proceedings will end after the total or partial liquidation of the assets in those proceedings. However, the Regulation also allows for the ending of secondary proceedings without liquidation, pursuant to a composition, a restructuring plan or an equivalent

---

[458] Virgos/Schmit Report, Margin No. 258.

[459] Virgos/Schmit Report, Margin No. 257.

[460] Virgos/Schmit Report, Margin No. 210.

[461] Thus, *Explanatory Report, European Convention on certain international aspects of bankruptcy*, No. 115.

measure (Article 34). If this is the case, two points have to be taken into account: The first is that, in order for Article 35 to come into effect, it is necessary for the secondary proceedings to produce a surplus after satisfying the creditors who have filed claims in those proceedings. The second is that, where the proceedings have ended without liquidation, this satisfaction depends upon the composition or restructuring plan, i.e. upon the specific content in each case: a surplus may be produced, for example, as a result of the waiver by the creditors of the satisfaction of part of their claims over those assets. A composition may even be specifically aimed at permitting a transfer of assets from the secondary to the main proceedings.[462]

460. Article 35 is important for various reasons, regardless of how often it is applied in practice. The first reason is that it is one of the rules which reflect the primacy of the main proceedings within the model of mitigated universalism provided by the Regulation. The second reason is that, although indirectly, it indicates an order for liquidating and distributing dividends. The provision presupposes that distribution will occur firstly in the secondary proceedings and afterwards in the main proceedings; these latter proceedings, as we shall see, also act as a kind of "clearing house" for the dividends received in the different proceedings.

6.2. Return and imputation

461. Article 20 establishes two rules concerning return of payments received by individual creditors after the opening of the main insolvency proceedings and imputation of dividends obtained in different insolvency proceedings concerning the same debtor. The common objective of these rules is to maintain the collective system of distribution as a whole.

6.2.1. Rule regarding return (Article 20.1)

462. In the first place, Article 20.1 establishes a rule regarding return in the event that main proceedings are opened. This rule is a necessary consequence of the universal scope of the main proceedings. The creditor who, after the opening of these proceedings, obtains total or partial satisfaction of his claim breaches the principle of collective satisfaction on which the insolvency proceedings are based. That is why Article 20.1 establishes that "*A creditor who, after the opening of the proceedings referred to in Article 3(1) obtains by any means, in particular through enforcement, total or partial satisfaction of his claim on the assets belonging to the debtor situated within the territory of another member State, shall return what he has obtained to the liquidator, subject to Articles 5 and 7*".

Article 20.1 imposes upon the creditor the duty to return "what he has obtained". The liquidator may demand either the return of the asset obtained or the equivalent in monetary terms.[463]

---

[462] BALZ, Note of the President of the Committee of Experts, EC Council, Doc No. 7161/91 DRS 28 (CFC).

[463] VIRGOS/SCHMIT Report, Margin No. 172; LEIBLE/STAUDINGER (2000), p. 563.

Development. The provision leaves some points unresolved and these will need to be clarified through *autonomous interpretation*.[464] Article 20.1 does not resolve, for example, the problem of determining if, insofar as the rule regarding return means that the benefit obtained ends up being collective, the creditor can deduct the expenses which he has incurred in obtaining payment of the claim. In principle, this question should be resolved by examining whether or not the creditor has acted in good faith; if he was unaware of the declaration opening the insolvency proceedings, he may deduct the said expenses; if he was aware of the opening and in spite of this he continued his actions until personally receiving satisfaction of his claim, he will not be able to deduct them. This solution acts as a disincentive to this type of individual behaviour, which is contrary to the basic principle of collectivisation that inspires the insolvency proceedings.

463. In the case of Articles 5 (third parties' rights *in rem*) and 7 (reservation of title), the creditor is not obliged to return what he has obtained in the payment of his claim, insofar as this payment is covered by the value of the guarantee. The reference to Articles 5 and 7 is easy to explain. According to these provisions, the rights *in rem* of the creditors and third parties over the debtor's assets which are located outside the State of opening are excluded from the scope of insolvency proceedings. Therefore, as long as these provisions apply, the creditor who satisfies his secured claim through the realisation of the collateral does not enrich himself at the expense of the estate, nor does he breach the principle of collective satisfaction.[465]

464. The effects of Article 20.1 are restricted to Member States. In the event that the creditor has received satisfaction over assets located in a non-Member State, it falls to national law to decide what happens. In these cases it may be logical to establish a different rule, thereby permitting, for example, an imputation similar to the one established in Article 20.2 in order to reward the efforts made to obtain satisfaction over assets situated in non-Member States; in particular when individual enforcement by creditors is the only available alternative, because the non-Member State does not recognise the insolvency proceedings opened in the forum and, consequently, the only possible way for the creditors to enforce their rights is by means of individual enforcement outside any insolvency proceedings.

Rationale. In a world context, it may be more convenient for national law to establish a different solution and provide for the possibility that the liquidator or the court authorise creditors to attempt to enforce their claims abroad on an individual basis, and instead of obliging them to hand over what they have obtained, apply to this case a similar rule to that regarding imputation established in Article 20.2 IR. For example, when it becomes known that the State where the assets are located is not going to recognise the insolvency proceedings which have been opened in the forum or when the difficulties associated with locating and realising those assets so justifies. In these cases the individual act on the part of the creditor indirectly benefits the rest of the creditors.

6.2.2. *Rule regarding imputation (Article 20.2)*

465. The Insolvency Regulation permits various sets of insolvency proceedings to be opened against the same debtor. For this reason, when a creditor manages to

---

[464] See further examples in REINHART (2003), p. 895.
[465] VIRGOS/SCHMIT Report, Margin No. 173.

obtain payment, whether in part or in full, in one of these sets of proceedings he is merely exercising a right. He does not have to return anything and, if he has only obtained partial satisfaction, he may participate in the rest of the proceedings which have been opened in other States. With this in mind, the Insolvency Regulation takes the European Community (except Denmark, see *supra* No. 3) as a reference for the distribution of dividends. For this reason, it makes it compulsory to take into account the amount obtained in each set of proceedings by means of a sort of consolidated account on a European scale:[466] *"In order to ensure equal treatment of creditors a creditor who has, in the course of insolvency proceedings, obtained a dividen on his claim shall share in distributions made in other proceedings only where creditors of the same ranking or category have, in those other proceedings, obtained an equiva-lent dividend"* (Article 20.2).

For the same reason, Article 20.2 does not require in order to be applicable that second proceedings be opened before the creditor receives the dividends of the first proceedings. Therefore, it is also applicable with regard to dividends obtained in prior proceedings of the type contemplated in Article 3.4.

466. The fundamental objective of Article 20.2 is to attempt to ensure a principle of equal treatment for all creditors. This is why Article 20.2 begins by stating this objective: *"in order to ensure the equal treatment of creditors ... "*. Naturally, given that the law applicable in each of the insolvency proceedings is different and the ranking of claims may also be different, full equality is impossible. The aim of Article 20 is therefore of necessity more modest and centres in the implementation of the principle of equality as far as this is compatible with this basic diversity.

This objective, *equality*, must serve as a guide to interpretation. In the first place, in order to establish an appropriate order of calculation for the purposes of max-imising overall value. In this respect, Article 20.2 contains the implicit idea that the main insolvency proceedings must function as the *vertex of the system* and therefore any *final* distribution arising from those proceedings must, in normal conditions, take place last. Article 33 regarding the stay of liquidation in secondary proceedings, Article 34 regarding measures ending secondary proceedings and Article 35 regard-ing assets remaining in secondary proceedings presuppose that the main proceedings will close at a later point in time or, at least, that the possibility of a later comple-mentary distribution in these proceedings is reserved.

Fast-track proceedings. Seen from this perspective, it would make sense for national legis-lators to simplify their insolvency proceedings by establishing abbreviated or fast-track pro-cedures for territorial proceedings. Until now the national proceedings listed in the Annexes of the Regulation are the ones initially conceived by national legislators as main proceedings, which seems logical because those proceedings were essentially drawn up with a domestic perspective.

467. Furthermore, equality requires a common term of comparison and this interpretation offers a logical one. As there is no unified scheme of asset distribution

---

[466] Virgos/Schmit Report, Margin No. 171.

in Europe (because each national law has its system for ranking claims and distributing the result of liquidating assets), it is justifiable to take the scheme of distribution of the main proceedings as the parameter for calculating this equal treatment. This is consistent with the characterisation of the insolvency proceedings based on Article 3.1 IR as the main proceedings. In this way, the calculation of the final dividend is not dependent upon circumstances otherwise exposed to chance and manipulation, such as which of the different insolvency proceedings opened finishes last.[467]

468. The method of calculation itself is relatively simple.[468] The method applies both to winding-up and to restructuring proceedings, although in the latter case it seems appropriate for the composition or plan itself to deal with this question. The method is made up of four rules:

(a) Nobody may obtain more than 100% of their claim.

(b) The claim is always filed for the total original amount (100% of its initial value), and not for the remaining amount; i.e. the satisfaction obtained in other insolvency proceedings is not deducted from the original amount. Should the claims not be filed in each set of proceedings for 100% of their amount (without deducting the part satisfied in other proceedings), it will not be possible to ensure equal treatment for those creditors who participate in several proceedings.

The only exception to this second rule concerns claims which are secured by a right *in rem* or through set-off. This exception derives from Article 4.2.i, which establishes that the national law of the State of opening (i.e. the law applicable to the proceedings of the distribution in question) will determine "the rights of creditors who have obtained partial satisfaction after the opening of insolvency proceedings by virtue of a right *in rem* or through a set-off" and from Articles 5, 6 and 7 which exempt these rights from the effects of the insolvency proceedings. The Regulation does not establish any rule whatsoever as to whether those claims secured by a right *in rem* or through a set-off may be filed, when the guarantee or set-off does not cover the whole of value, for the original amount of the claim or for only the remaining part of the claim once the secured part has been deducted. This question is left to the rules of the State whose law governs the proceedings in the distribution of which those creditors seek to participate.[469]

NB. If the first solution is chosen and the claim is lodged for its original amount in proceedings opened in two Member States (F1 and F2), then the rule on imputation of Article 20.2 IR should be applied; otherwise the secured creditor would be paid "twice" with regard to the secured part of his claim. If the second solution is chosen, the original claim will be divided in two parts, the secured and the unsecured, which will be treated as if they were two different claims. Therefore, satisfaction in F1 of the *secured* part of the claim will not be discounted in thedistribution to be effected in F2 in connection with the *unsecured* part of the claim.

---

[467] *Cfr.* RAMMESKOW BANG-PEDERSEN, pp. 408–409.
[468] VIRGOS/SCHMIT Report, Margin No. 175; LEIBLE/STAUDINGER (2000), p. 564.
[469] VIRGOS/SCHMIT Report; Margin No. 175.2.

(c) The claim does not participate in the distribution until such time as the creditors with the same ranking have obtained an equal percentage of satisfaction in these proceedings to that obtained by the holder of the right in the first proceedings.

For example, if a creditor obtains 20% of an ordinary unsecured claim in proceedings opened in State F1 from a total amount of 1000, he may only participate in the distribution from proceedings opened in State F2 (where he has also filed his claim) once the ordinary creditors have obtained, in this second set of proceedings, 20% of their claims. If the percentage of satisfaction for ordinary creditors in State F2 reaches 30%, that creditor may only participate for the difference, i.e. for 10%; and this 10% will, as we have said, apply to the total of his claim (to the 100% of the initial amount of 1000).

Conversely, if the first proceedings are in F2, where the creditors obtain a percentage of satisfaction of 30%, then, in spite of having also filed their claims in the proceedings opened in F1, they will not be able to participate in the distribution in State F1, given that the ordinary creditors in F1 are only obtaining 20%, while they have obtained 30% in F2.

Practice. The Explanatory Report illustrates this. If a number of claims have been filed in both the insolvency proceedings opened in F1 and those opened in F2, the liquidator in F2 may calculate the distribution in F2 by stages, for each rank. In our example, until 20% (which is the dividend obtained in F1) he will not take into account the claims already satisfied in F1. Once the claims which were only filed in F2 have obtained 20%, and if there are remaining assets to be distributed, a new calculation will be made in order to determine the new dividend and this new calculation will also include the claims filed and partially satisfied in F1 together with the claims only filed in F2, and so on.[470]

(d) The ranking of each claim is determined by the *lex fori concursus* of each set of proceedings. As different national laws correspond to different insolvency proceedings, it may occur that the ranking of the same claim filed in two different sets of proceedings is different in each one. When it comes to applying Article 20.2, the only ranking which should be taken into account is the one conferred upon the claim by the law governing the proceedings in which distribution is to be effected. Therefore, in order to calculate the dividend which corresponds to that claim it is only necessary to take into account the percentage of satisfaction which has been obtained in other proceedings, but not the ranking assigned to that claim in those other proceedings. To continue with the same example, if the creditor's claim is an ordinary claim in F1 but enjoys a preference in F2, the basis for calculation is that he has already obtained 30% in F1, no matter what the ranking was; for the purposes of calculation, this percentage is compared with the dividend corresponding to preferential claims in F2. If these claims obtain a dividend of 70% in F2, the creditor will be entitled to a dividend of 40% in F2 (70% minus 30% obtained in F1 = 40%).

Distorsions. The different ranking of the claims in the different proceedings means that the order of liquidation (i.e. the fact that one set of proceedings ends before the other) may

---

[470] VIRGOS/SCHMIT Report, Margin No. 176.

affect the dividends finally received.[471] That is why it is important for the main proceedings to always act as the vertex for calculation (i.e. in the last instance), in such a way that the differences arising from the different order of closure of the territorial proceedings can, up to a point, be "compensated for" in the final distribution resulting from the main proceedings.

469. Article 20.2 does not expressly limit its action to the Member States. In principle, it would not seem necessary to do so, because the Insolvency Regulation, save for exceptions, only governs relationships *vis-à-vis* Member States. Thus, when the Regulation talks about insolvency proceedings it is referring (see Article 2.a) to one of the proceedings listed in Annex A, which are proceedings necessarily belonging to Member States. Having said that, it is also true that, in the distribution to be carried out in proceedings opened in a Member State, it would be paradoxical to deduct that which has been obtained in proceedings opened in another Member State and, in contrast, not deduct that which has been obtained in proceedings opened in a non-Member State: this would mean that creditors who obtain satisfaction in a non-Member State would receive better treatment than those obtaining satisfaction in a Member State. This would entail a kind of inverse discrimination. The only way to avoid this result is either to oblige creditors to return what they have obtained in non-Member States through insolvency proceedings opened there over the same debtor (e.g. where such proceedings are not recognised in the forum); or, and this appears more logical, to apply Article 20.2 to insolvency proceedings opened in non-Member States. The fact that the wording of the provision is not limited to Member States combined with the absurd consequence which the opposite solution may bring about justifies the application of this Article in its literal terms.[472]

7. Credit Institutions and Insurance Undertakings

470. Directives 2001/24/EC and 2001/17/EC on the reorganisation and winding up, respectively, of credit institutions and insurance undertakings do not contain rules on coordination of parallel insolvency proceedings. Both Directives adopt a model of unity of proceedings; no secondary proceedings are allowed for institutions and undertakings which have their head office in the Community. However, where a credit institution or an insurance undertaking which has its head office outside the Community possesses branches in more than one Member State, then each branch will receive individual treatment in regard of the application of the Directives (see Recital 22 Directive 2001/24/EC and Recital 29 Directive 2001/17/EC). In such cases, the only provision the Directives contain is a generic mandate to the administrative or judicial authorities who "shall endeavour to coordinate their actions" (see Articles 8.2 and 19.9 of the Directive on credit institutions, and Article 30.2 of the Directive on insurance undertakings).

---

[471] Rammeskow Bang-Pedersen, *passim*, with multiple examples.
[472] Reinhart (2003), p. 895.

Bibliography

ADERHOLD, *Auslandskonkurs im Inland. Entwicklung und System des deutschen Rechts mit praktischen Beispielen unter besonderer Berücksichtigung des Konkursrechts der Vereinigten Staaten von Amerika, England, Frankreichts sowie der Schweiz*, 1992.

BALZ, "Das neue Europäische Insolvenzübereinkommen", *ZIP*, 1996, p. 948 *et seq.* (cit. 1996a).

BALZ, "The European Union Convention on Insolvency Proceedings", *A.B.L.J.*, 1996, p. 485 *et seq.* (cit. 1996b).

BASEDOW, "The Communitarization of the Conflict of Laws under the Treaty of Amsterdam", *CML Rev.*, 2000, p. 687 *et seq.*

BELTRAN SÁNCHEZ, "El Reglamento de la Unión Europea sobre procedimientos de insolvencia", *Tribunales de Justicia*, April 2001, p. 31 *et seq.*

BORRAS, "Derecho internacional privado y Tratado de Ámsterdam", *R.E.D.I.*, 1999–2, p. 383 *et seq.*

BUREAU, "La fin d'un îlot de résistance Le Règlament du Conseil relatif aux procédures d'insolvabilité", *Rev. crti. dr. internat. privé*, 2002, p. 613 *et seq.*

CALVO/CARRASCOSA, "Insolvencia de la empresa y Derecho internacional privado", *Justicia* 98, p. 419 *et seq.*

CANDELARIO MACIAS, "Aproximación a la iniciativa de Reglamento del Consejo europeo sobre procedimientos de insolvencia", *Dir. Fall*, 6/1999, p. 1226 *et seq.*

DEGUÉE, "La directive 2001/24/CE sur l'assainissement et la liquidation des établissements de crédit: une solution aux défaillances bancaires internationales?", *Euredia*, 2001–2002, p. 242 *et seq.*

DORDI, "La Convenzione dell'Union Europea sulle procedura di insolvenza, *Riv. Dir. Internat. Pr. e Proc.*, 1997, p. 333 *et seq.*

DROBNIG, "Bemerkungen zur Behandlung der Rechte Dritter, inbesondere von Sicherungsrechten", in STOLL (ed.), *Stellungnahmen und Gutachten zur Reform des deutschen Internationalen Insolvenzrecht*, 1992, p. 177 *et seq.*

DROBNIG, "The Recognition on Non-possesory security interests created abroad in private international law", *General Report to the 10th Congress of Comparative Law*, 1981, p. 269 *et seq.*

DUURSMA-KEPPLINGER/DUURSMA, "Der Anwendungsbereich der Insolvenzverordnung", *IPRax*, 2003, pp. 505 *et seq.*

DUURSMA-KEPPLINGER/DUURSMA/CHALUPSKY, Europäische Insolvenzverordnung, 2002 (cit. 2002).

EHRICKE, "Die neue Europäische Insolvenzordnung und grenzüberschreitende Konzerninsolvenz", *EWS*, 2002, p. 101 *et seq.*

EIDENMÜLLER, *Unternehmenssanierung zwischen Markt und Gesetz*, 1999.

EIDENMÜLLER, "Europäische Verordnung über Insolvenzverfahren und Zukünftiges deutsches internationales Insolvenzrecht", *IPRax*, 2001, p. 2 *et seq.* (*cit.* 2001a).

EIDENMÜLLER, "Der nationale und der internationale Insolvenzverwaltungsvertrag", *ZIP*, 2001, p. 3 *et seq.* (*cit.* 2001b).

ESPLUGUES, *La quiebra internacional*, 1993.

FAVOCCIA, *Vertragliche Mobiliarsicherheiten im internationalen Insolvenzrecht*, 1991.

FLESSNER, "Internationales Insolvenzrecht in Europa", *FS Heinsius*, 1991, p. 111 *et seq.*

FLESSNER, "Insolvenzplan und Restschuldbefreiung im Internationalen Konkursrecht", in STOLL (ed.), *Stellungnahmen und Gutachten zur Reform des deutschen Internationalen Insolvenzrecht*, 1992, p. 201 *et seq.*

FLESSNER, "Dingliche Sicherungsrechte nach dem Europäischen Insolvenzübereinkommen", *FS Drobnig*, 1998, p. 277 *et seq.*

FLETCHER, *Insolvency in Private International Law*, 1999.

FLETCHER, "A Culling of Sacred Cows – The Impact of the EC Insolvency Regulation on English Conflict of Laws", *Essays in Honour of Sir Peter North*, 2003, p. 167 *et seq.*

FUMAGALLI, "II Regolamento comunitario sulle procedure di insolvenza", *Riv. Dir. Proc.*, 2001, p. 677 *et seq.*

GEIMER, *Internacionales Zivilprozessrecht*, 4th edn., 2001.

GARCIA GUTIERREZ, *La compensación de créditos en Derecho internacional privado*, 2003.

GARRIDO, "Some Reflections on the EU Bankruptcy Convention and its Implications for Secured and Preferential Creditors", *Int. Insolv. Rev.*, 1998, p. 79 *et seq.*

GOODE, *Commercial Law*, 1995.

GOODE, *Principles of Corporate Insolvency Law*, 1997.

GOTTWALD, *Grenzüberschreitende Insolvenzen*, 1997.

GOTTWALD, "Le insolvenze trans-frontalier: tendeze e soluzioni europee e mondiali", *Riv.trim.dr.pr. e proc.*, 1999, p. 149 *et seq.*

GRASMANN, "Effets nationaux d'une procédure d'execution collective étrangère", *Rev.crit.dr.internat.privé*, 1990, p. 421 *et seq.*

GUZMAN, "International Bankruptcy: In Defense of Universalism", *Mich. L. Rev.*, 2000, p. 2177 *et seq.*

HANISCH, "Die Wende im deutschen internationalen Insolvenzrecht", *ZIP*, 1985, p. 1233 *et seq.*

HANISCH, "Die Wirkung dinglicher Mobiliarsicherungsrechte im grenzüberschreitenden Insolvenzverfahren", *Études de Droit International en l'Honneur de P.* Lalive, 1993, p. 61 *et seq.*

HANSMANN/KRAAKMAN, "The Essential Role of Organizational Law", *Yale L.J.*, 2000, p. 387 *et seq.*

HAUBOLD, "Europäisches Zivilverfahrensrecht und Ansprüche im Zusammenhang mit Insolvenzverfahren", *IPRax*, 2002, p. 157 *et seq.*

HAUBOLD, "Mitgliedstaatenbezug, Zuständigkeitserschleichung und Vermögensgerichtsstand im Internationalen Insolvenzrecht", *IPRax*, 2003, p. 34 *et seq.*

HENCKEL, "Die internationalprivatrechtliche Anknüpfung der Konkursanfechtung", *FS Nagel*, 1987, p. 93 *et seq.*

HERCHEN, *Das Übereinkommen über Insolvenzverfahren der Mitgliedstaaten der Europäischen Union vom 23.11.1995*, 2000.

HEß, "Die Europäisierung des internationalen Zivilprozeßrecht durch den Amsterdamen vertrag- Chancen und Gefahren", *NJW*, 2000, p. 23 *et seq.*

HOMANN, "System der Anerkennung eines ausländischen Insolvenzverfahrens", *KTS*, 2000, p. 343 *et seq.*

HUBER, "Internationales Insolvenzrecht in Europa", *ZZP*, 2001, p. 133 *et seq.*

JACKSON, *The Logic and Limits of Bankruptcy Law*, 1986.

JAHR, "Vis attractiva concursus", en KEGEL/THIME, *Vorschläge und Gutachten zum Entwurf eines EG-Konkursübereinkommens*, 1988, p. 305 *et seq.*

JAYME/KOHLER, "Europäisches Kollisionsrecht 2000: Interlocales Privatrecht oder universelles Gemeinschaftsrecht?", *IPRax*, 2000, p. 454 *et seq.*

KEMPER, "Die Verordnung (EG) Nr. 1346/2000 über Insolvenzverfahren", *ZIP*, 2001, p. 1609 *et seq.*

KOLMAN, "Europäisches internationales Insolvenzrecht – die Verordnung (EG) Nr. 1346/2000 über Insolvenzverfahren", *E.L.F.*, 2002, p. 167 *et seq.*

KRAMER, *Juristische Methodenlehre*, 1998.

KRINGS, "Unification législative internationale récente en matière d'insolvabilité et de la faillite", *Uniform L. Rev.*, 1997, p. 657 *et seq.*

LEIBLE/STAUDINGER, "Die europäische Verordnung über Insolvenzverfahren", *KTS*, 4/2000, p. 533 *et seq.*

LEIBLE/STAUDINGER "El artículo 65 TCE: ¿Carta blanca de la Comunidad Europea para la unificación del Derecho internacional privado y procesal", *A.E.D.I.P.*, 2001, p. 89 *et seq.*

LEIPOLD, "Zum künftigen Weg des deutschen internationalen Insolvenzrechts", en STOLL (ed.) *Vorschlage und Gutachten zur Umsetzung des EU-Übereinkommens über Insolvenzverfahren im deutschen Recht*, 1997, p. 185 *et seq.*

LOPUCKI, "Cooperation in International Bankruptcy: A Post-Universalist Approach", *Cornell L. Rev.*, 1999, p. 696 *et seq.*

LOPUCKI, "The Case for Cooperative Territoriality in International Bankruptcy", *Mich. L. Rev.*, 2000, p. 2216 *et seq.*

LÜER, "Zur Neuordnung des deutschen Internationalen Insolvenzrechts", in STOLL (ed.), *Stellungnahmen und Gutachten zur Reform des deutschen Internationalen Insolvenzrecht*, 1992, p. 96 *et. seq.*

LÜKE, "Das europäische internationale Insolvenzrecht", *ZZP*, 1998, p. 275 *et seq.*

LÜKE, "Europäisches Zivilverfahrensrecht – das Problem der Abstimmung zwischen EuInsÜ und EuGVÜ", *FS Schütze*, 1999, p. 467 *et seq.*

MANKOWSKY, "Konkursgründe beim inländischen Partikularkonkurs", *ZIP*, 1995, p. 1650 *et seq.*

MCBRYDE/FLESSNER/KORTMANN, *Principles of European Insolvency law*, 2003.

MICKLITZ/ROTT, "Vergemeinschaftung des EuGVÜ in der Verordnung (EG) Nr 44/2001", *EuZW*, 1/2002, p. 15 *et seq.*

MOSS/FLETCHER/ISSAC (eds.), *The EC Regulation on Insolvency Proceedings: A Commentary and Annotated Guide*, 2002.

PANTHEN, *Der Sitz Begriff im Internationalen Gesellschaftsrecht*, 1988.

PAULUS, "Das inländische Parallelverfahren nach der Europäischen Insolvenzverordnung", *EWS*, 2002, p. 497 *et seq.*

PAZ-ARES/GARCIMARTÍN, "Conflictos de leyes y garantías sobre valores anotados en intermediarios financieros", *R.D.M.*, 2000, p. 1479 *et seq.*

PIELORZ, "Inlandsvermögen im Auslandskonkurs. Zur Handlungsbegugnis ausländischer Konkursorgane in Deutschaland", *ZIP*, 1980, p. 239 *et seq.*

POTOK (ed.), *Cross Border Collateral: Legal Risk and the Conflict of Laws*, 2002.

POTTHAST, *Problem eines Europäischen Konkursübereinkommens*, 1995.

Principles of European Insolvency Law, 2003.

RAMMESKOW BANG-PEDERSEN, "Asset Distribution in Transnacional Insolvencias: Combining Predictability and Protection of Local Interests", *A.B.L.J.*, 1999, p. 385 *et seq.*

REINHART, *Sanierungsverfahren im internationalen Insolvenzrecht*, 1995.

REINHART, "Zur Anerkennung ausländischer Insolvenzverfahren, Eine Besprechung des Works-Data-Urteils des Bundesgerichtshofes", *ZIP*, 1997, p. 1734 *et seq.*

REINHART, in *Münchener Kommentar zur Insolvenzordnung*, 2003, p. 677 *et seq.*

SANCHEZ LORENZO, *Garantías reales en el comercio internacional*, 1993.

SCHOLLMEYER, *Gegenseitige Verträge im internationalen Insolvenzrecht*, 1997.

SIEHR, "International Aspects of Bankruptcy", en *Transnational aspects of procedural law*, 1998, p. 873 *et seq.*

SPELLENBERG, "Des ordre public im Internationalen Insolvenzrecht", in STOLL (ed.), *Stellungnahmen und Gutachten zur Reform des deutschen Internationalen Insolvenzrecht*, 1992, p. 183 *et seq.*

STAEHLIN, *Die Anerkenung ausländischer Konkurse und Nachlassverträge in der Schweiz (Artt. 166 ff. IPRG)*, 1989.

SWARTING/LIVIJN, "European Council Regulation of 29 May 200 on Insolvency Proceedings – the First Year from a Swedish Perspective", published in www.iiiglobal.org.

TAUPITZ, "Das zukünftige europäische Internationale Insolvenzrecht – insbesondere aus international – privatrechtlicher Sicht", *ZZP*, 1998, p. 315 *et seq.*

THIME, "Partikularkonkurs", in STOLL (ed.), *Stellungnahmen und Gutachten zur Reform des deutchen Internationalen Insolvenzrechts*, 1992, p. 212 *et seq.*

TORREMANS, *Cross-Border Insolvencies in EU, English, and Belgial Law*, 2002.

TROCHU, *Conflits de lois et conflits de jurisdictions en matière de faillité*, 1967.

TRUNK, "Regelungsschwerpunkte eines Ausführungsgesetzes zum Europäischen Insolvenzübereinkommen", in STOLL (ed.), *Vorschlage und Gutachten zur Umsetzung des EU-Übereinkommens über Insolvenzverfahren im deutschen Recht*, 1997, p. 232 *et seq.*

TRUNK, *Internationales Insolvenzrecht*, 1998.

VALLENS, "Le droit européen de la faillite : premiers commentaires de la convention relative aux procédures d'insolvabilité", *Recueil Dalloz*, 1995, p. 307 *et seq.*

VAN GALEN, "The European Insolvency Regulation and Groups of Companies", INSOL Europe Annual Congress, 2003.

VIRGÓS, "The 1995 European Community Convention on Insolvency Proceedings: an Insider's View", *Forum Internationale*, No. 25, March 1998

VIRGÓS/GARCIMARTÍN, *Derecho procesal civil europeo*, 1996.

VIRGÓS/GARCIMARTÍN, *Derecho procesal civil internacional. Litigación internacional*, 2000.

VON WILMOWSKY, *Europäisches Kreditsicherungsrecht*, 1996.

VON WILMOWSKY, "Aufrechnung in internationalen Insolvenzfällen – kollisionsrecht der Insolvenaufrechnung", *KTS*, 1998, p. 343 *et seq.*

VON WILMOWSKY, "Choice of Law in International Insolvencies – A Proposal for Reform", in BASEDOW/TOSHIYUKI (ed.), *Legal Aspects of Globalization*, 2000, p. 197 *et seq.*

WESSELS, *Internationaal insolventierecht*, 2003.

WESSELS, "International Jurisdiction to Open Insolvency Proceedings in Europe, in particular against groups of companies", *forthcoming in Working Papers, Institute for Law and Finance*, Frankfurt, www.ilf-frankfurt.de

WESTERBROOK, "A Global Solution to Multinational Default", *Mich. L. Rev.*, 2000, p. 2276 *et seq.*

WIMMER, "Die Besonderheiten von Sekundärininsolvezverfahren unter besonderer Berücksichtigung des Europäischen Insolvenzübereinkommens", *ZIP*, 1998, p. 982 *et seq.*

WIMMER (ed.), *Franckfurter Kommentar zur Insolvenzordnung*, 3rd edn., 2002.

Index

Note: By paragraph number

Actio pauliana 234

Actions to set aside 90, 121, 175, 190, 194, 205, 217, 230, 231–244

Acts of disposal by the debtor 245–251

Aircrafts 222–227, 246, 311

Applicable Law 21, 27, 32, 39, 109–133, 135–283, 313, 328–330, 356

Arbitration 121, 261

Assets (*see* Rights *in rem*; Location of assets)

Assignment of claims 146

Automatic cancellation clauses (*see* Contractual set-off)

Automatic recognition 343–344, 349

Autonomous concept 45

Body of creditors 121

Centre of main interests 27, 44–70, 297

Claims
  filing, verification, and admission 121, 280–282, 425–431, 436
  ranking 121
  (*see also* Lodgement of claims; Location of assets)

Compositions 121, 126–133, 326

Community Patent 228–229

Community trademark 228–229

Conflict of jurisdictions 70

Conflict-of-laws rules (*see* Applicable Law)

Conflict mobile 146

Contracts (*see* Current contracts)

Contractual set-off 191–195

Convention on Insolvency Proceedings of 23rd November 1995 3–4

Coordination between insolvency proceedings
  main/main scheme 423–424
  main/secondary scheme 27, 127, 289, 420–423
  rules of cooperation 432–442
  rules of distribution 458–469
  rules of participation 425–431
  rules regarding the alignment of proceedings 443–457
  territorial/territorial scheme 423–424

Corporations (insolvency of corporations) 57–60, 122–133 (*see also* Debtor)

Costs of the proceedings 121, 323

Court 348

Credit institutions (*see* Directive 2001/24/EC regarding the reorganization and winding-up of credit institutions)

Creditors' right 12, 27, 110, 121, 276–283, 327, 406–407, 425–431

Creditor's voluntary winding-up 348

Current contracts
  in general 92, 121, 196–198, 329
  consumer contracts 201
  contract of employment 207–209, 329
  contract relating to immovable property 199–205, 329
  (*see also* Reservation of title; Contractual set-off; Payment systems)

Debtor 31, 44, 121, 297

Debtor in possession 35

Debtor's estate 72, 121

Decisions (judgment) 340, 348

Decision opening insolvency proceedings 344

Denmark 2

Detrimental acts (*see* Actions to set aside)

Directive 2002/47/EC on financial collateral arrangement 7, 311

Directive 2001/24/EC regarding the reorganization and winding up of credit institutions 7, 24, 29, 32, 38, 40, 106–107, 134, 193–194, 198, 206, 210, 220, 227, 230, 244, 251, 262, 272, 275, 283, 311, 414–417

Directive 2001/17/EC regarding the reorganization and winding up of insurance undertakings 7, 24, 29, 32, 38, 40, 106, 108, 134, 194, 198, 206, 210, 221, 227, 230, 244, 251, 262, 272, 275, 283, 414–417.

Directive 98/26/EC regarding settlement finality and payments and securities settlement systems 7, 212, 214, 311

Directors disqualifications 125

Discharge of debts 121, 304, 326, 331–337, 360–361

Distribution of proceeds 121

Divestment of debtor 34, 121

Due process 406